THE DANFORTH STUDY OF CAMPUS MINISTRIES

# THE CHURCH, THE UNIVERSITY, AND SOCIAL POLICY

*The Danforth Study of Campus Ministries*

VOLUME II:

WORKING AND TECHNICAL PAPERS

# THE CHURCH, THE UNIVERSITY,

# AND SOCIAL POLICY

*The Danforth Study of Campus Ministries*

✍ VOLUME II ✎

WORKING AND TECHNICAL PAPERS

*Edited and with Introductions by*

KENNETH UNDERWOOD

WESLEYAN UNIVERSITY PRESS

*Middletown, Connecticut*

ISBN: 0–8195–6009–X

*Library of Congress Catalog Card Number: 69-17794*

*Manufactured in the United States of America*

*First printing, November 1969; second printing, April 1970*

# CONTENTS

# PUBLISHER'S NOTE

THIS book is the second of two volumes containing the basic reports and papers of the Danforth Study of Campus Ministries, appearing under the general title *The Church, the University, and Social Policy*. Volume I consists of the report of the director of the Danforth Study, on the process of inquiry, the data, and the resulting implications for policy. The present work. Volume II, contains working and technical papers by scholars, ministers, university and church administrators, students, and others who participated in the study.

A number of collateral books and monographs have also arisen from this enterprise. These are published by a variety of presses and represent a variety of relationships to the Danforth Study. They include, for example, *The Campus Clergyman*, by Phillip E. Hammond (New York: Basic Books, 1966), begun before the Danforth inquiry was commissioned but completed during a leave supported by the Danforth Study; and *The Gathering Storm in the Churches*, by Jeffrey K. Hadden (New York: Doubleday, 1969), based on data from the ministers' survey prepared and conducted by the Danforth Study.

# PREFACE

THIS volume of working and technical papers is a mixture of all the kinds of materials we have found necessary to make judgments about the situation of the campus ministries. It contains chiefly the papers produced by scholars from a variety of disciplines and shows how and what they found to be the condition of the religious leadership in higher education in the United States generally in the period from 1963 to 1968. Sociologists pore over their survey date; historians discern larger trends in the culture and church; psychologists probe the meaning of interactions of persons in religious groups; social ethicists speculate about future possibilities for the church and university; and theologians discern God's judgment and redemption at work in unlikely places—even formidable movements in the ecclesiology of Christendom.

But persons other than scholars are represented here. We have included reflections by campus ministers on their own attempts at reform (Paul Schrading); interviews with a cross section of Episcopal pastors facing the racial panic of urban America; a transcript of a consultation with doctors, hospital administrators, researchers, campus ministers to medical centers, about the ethical and theological issues in medical education—all in an attempt to show the unorganized materials we worked with in this study. We wanted to give you your own chance to provide order and meaning to them.

There are also long reflective papers and snatches of thought from men's minds: Thomas Green on inquiry and action, David Duncombe on what scientific experimentation in religious education would be like, Robert Lynn on the advantages to the church of living on the margins of American society. They reveal the kind of papers that came to us in the progress of this study and what kind of inquiry started us off on new lines of speculation.

There is little doubt that the churches, like the universities, will in the future, be expected to teach from materials such as the study provides. The student wants an informed point of view and a chance to review at least some of the instruments of research, the views of other scholars, the raw, human materials which were formed into policy conclusion. A few church educators now do this; but most teaching emerges out of a confessional stance that seldom compares its method with other disciplines, but proceeds to follow an established line of interpretation and allows few students to check from other perspectives the story they tell.

The other perspectives and disciplines that participated in the Danforth Study were never asked to be other than themselves. They were asked to write their reports to satisfy their own standards of accuracy and credibility. So the material is as it came to us, out of the professional competencies, inchoate struggles for meaning of crises, shocked ministers, controlled instruments of forced choice, and all the rest that makes up the materials of contemporary policy research. The introductions by the editor attempt simply to indicate the significance of the material for policies of the churches and universities and to place the work in the context of other inquiries now being conducted.

# PART I

*The Valued People and the Evaluators*

# ⅸ 1 ⅾ

## THE RADICAL MINISTRY[1]

### Phillip E. Hammond

## *Introduction*

Phillip Hammond, a member of the social science faculty at the University of Wisconsin, specializes in the sociology of occupations. He has spent several years in study of the campus ministry as an emerging profession in American society. He sees this ministry as a radical group which threatens the organizational integrity of the church, but necessary if the church is to adapt to a changing environment. He perceives the church as generally concerned to segment this radical element in its midst, so that it can control it and still get ideas from it. He is equally concerned that the campus ministry keep its cutting intellectual edge, its power to innovate, its wider concerns in the world by voluntarily accepting its separation from the main stream of the church. He hopes campus clergy will develop and enforce their own independent, professional standards.

The director of the study sees ʾthe situation of the campus ministry somewhat differently and, therefore, was anxious to have Hammond's essay available so that an important issue could be raised. It is this: how can campus ministries maintain themselves as precursors in the church, not separating themselves from its major issues and problems, but using the resources of the university to help achieve a new cultural and religious leadership that suggests models for the ministry at large?

The survey data developed by the Danforth study staff reveal widespread movements in the church toward greater attention to critical inquiry in religious education and less reliance on apologetic, proclamatory preaching in the formation of belief. The parish ministry, almost as strongly as the campus clergy, support the exploration of the meaning of religion for vocation and the opening up of opportunities for more disciplined study of their cultural and theological environment.

---

1. This chapter is based on data from two studies: one of campus ministers by Hammond, with the support of the National Institutes of Health and the Danforth Study of Campus Ministries, the other of parish ministers by Robert E. Mitchell, with the support of the Russell Sage Foundation.

Back of such data is recognition of a shift in basic concepts of how belief is formed and a greater openness to the use of a variety of learning procedures in the church. Is the occasion which the campus ministry confronts one requiring mainly a defensive response of keeping a radical posture intact, or is it an occasion for a free and disciplined movement to bring the leadership of the church into a wider and deeper experience of its own processes of learning, worship, and action?

KU

IN pursuit of their goals, all organizations face a dilemma: how to adapt to changing environments without sacrificing organizational integrity. The dilemma may be thought of as a problem in balancing the commitments of members to the purposes of the organization, on the one hand, and to (their roles in) the organization's structure, on the other. Too inflexible a commitment to the organizational structure by some members can result in the defection of other members who claim that the goals have been forsaken. Too inflexible a goal commitment, however, can produce insensitivity to changing pressures, with a resultant lowered ability to achieve the organization's goals.

Organizations grow, die, barely struggle along, or change into other entities; and each response reflects some degree of viability. Viability, as an attribute of any organization, refers, therefore, to its degree of stability in the face of change.

Church organizations do not escape the dilemma. They have goals to achieve and personnel variously committed to those goals. They have environments to adapt to and an identity to maintain. In general, it seems there have been two responses, neither of which yields optimum viability: the sect response, which maximizes goal commitment at the expense of adaptation, and the church response, which adapts at the expense of goals.

Forces toward breakdown can come in the form of environmental pressures or from the inside in the form of redefined goals, changes in role commitment, or efforts to alter the organization's boundaries. Inside pressures for change might be called "radicalism," and agents for such change "radicals." They are potential threats to organizational integrity, but they may also anticipate needed adaptation. The viable organization, therefore, finds room for its radicals, but typically does so by segmenting them, thereby minimizing disruption that radicals might create without sacrificing their potential insights by excluding them altogether. A common feature of organizations is thus the differentiation of radicals—a social structure serving two functions: a "safety valve" function of draining off dissidence and a "leavening" function of providing a source of new ideas.

Many organizations have social structures that function in these two ways. They may be called "research and development groups" in industrial corporations, "institutes" at universities, or "war colleges" in the military. In churches, the safety-valve and leavening functions are typically served by such structures as monasteries, seminaries, and special orders. We shall argue here that for Protestant churches the campus ministry serves as an organizational device for segmenting radicals. Although that is not its manifest purpose, it siphons off potentially disruptive personnel, thus serving the safety-valve function; and especially it contributes to organizational change, thus serving the leavening function.

## The Churches' Dilemma

At least since Troeltsch's monumental work on the impact of religious ideology on church structure, the organizational importance of many mansions in the religious house has been recognized. It is now generally acknowledged that church organizations atrophy unless regularly renewed, but that the forces for renewal may also destroy. An *organizational* problem for religion, no less than for other organizations, is therefore one of segmenting the radical element, thereby containing and using it. The medieval church, in Troeltsch's words, "controlled this (radical) tendency by allowing it to express itself in the formation of new Religious Orders and confraternities."[2] At the same time, "from this ascetic class the primitive Christian energy once more radiates fresh vitality into all merely relative approximations to the Christian standard."[3]

MacMurray, who goes so far as to claim that the two forces of modernity—the Renaissance and the Reformation—stem from the medieval pattern of monasteries, says of them:

> It is here that the creative forces of the spiritual life are to be found; and here that the ferment of Christianity is most powerful and most difficult to deal with. If the will to power in the church is to maintain itself, it must suppress the spiritual creativeness within its own bosom. . . . The function of the monastic system (therefore) is to segregate the creative forces which would seek to realize Christianity and in so doing destroy the dualist structure of society.[4]

The medieval church, in other words, is cited as an example of a viable religious organization. "The church of the thirteenth century was relatively successful in finding a place ... for the expression of the radical-individualizing tendencies of Christianity."[5] But as Yinger and other observers of church and sect are quick to point out, the *degree* to which religious organizations "contain and use" their radicals is variable. They differ in their provisions for meeting the safety-valve and leavening functions.

> It is commonly observed, for example, that the proliferation of religious divisions is far more extensive under Protestantism than under Catholicism. . . . Protestantism, with its greater emphasis on individual experience . . . encouraged the development of *different* religious structures. Catholicism reflects the variations in religious needs *within* its pattern.[6]

## The Campus Ministry as a Radical Segment in Protestantism

Dating from the turn of the century, the churches' work on college campuses has grown steadily. Currently it contains about 1,300 full-time workers, or 1 per cent of the ministerial force of the ten denominations supporting almost all the full-time campus clergy. The great majority are employed by a denomination and, as directors of "foundations" ringing the campuses, administer programs that include study groups, social events, theological discussions, social action, and so on.

Evidence that the campus ministry contains "radicals" is seen in the comparison of results from two studies, one of parish clergy, the other of their campus counterparts. The data on campus ministers were collected in spring, 1963, by mail questionnaire sent to all known full-time Protestant campus clergy. The return from this population universe was 79 per cent for an N of 997. The parish minister data were collected three years earlier by mail questionnaire sent to a 10 per cent random sample of eight denominations which are members of the National Council of Churches. Smaller samples were taken of two nonmember denominations. The return rate in this study was 68 per cent for an N of 4,077.

Table 1-1 contains evidence of radicalism. There it can be seen that, relative to parish ministers, campus clergy are more liberal in their attitudes toward labor unions and the United Nations, are more critical of their denominations, are more favorable toward ecumenical affairs, are better educated, and have wider interests. These data are convincing. The differences are maintained across ten denominations, and within denominations they persist in all age groups.

TABLE 1-1

*Percentage of Campus Ministers and of Parish Ministers*
*Who Agree with Various Statements*

| Statement | Campus Ministers (N=997) | Parish Ministers (N=4,077) |
|---|---|---|
| **Political attitudes:** | | |
| 1. Strongly approve of the purposes of the United Nations | 73% | 57% |
| 2. Strongly approve of the purposes of the AFL-CIO | 21 | 11 |
| **Breadth of interest:** | | |
| 3. Regularly read *Christian Century* | 67 | 33 |
| 4. Regularly read *Christianity and Crisis* | 44 | 6 |
| 5. Very interested in news of national and international affairs | 75 | 62 |
| 6. Very interested in news of own denomination | 35 | 68 |
| 7. Very or quite interested in news of other denominations | 57 | 68 |
| **The church and social action:** | | |
| 8. Would very much like to see church-sponsored examination of major ethical issues | 66 | 57 |
| 9. Agree own denomination is too conservative in the field of social action | 53 | 17 |
| **Ecumenical attitudes:** | | |
| 10. Agree own denomination is not sufficiently ecumenical-minded | 42 | 10 |
| 11. Strongly approve of the National Council of Churches | 51 | 42 |
| 12. Strongly approve of the World Council of Churches | 59 | 44 |
| **Miscellaneous:** | | |
| 13. Agree own denomination does not have clearly defined policies | 27 | 15 |
| 14. Have B.D. degree | 84 | 65 |
| 15. Have Ph.D. Degree | 13 | 2 |
| 16. Choose, as closest to own belief regarding the Bible, "An infallible revelation of God's will" | 8 | 24 |

## *Organizational Consequences of the Campus Ministry*

From these data some important consequences of the existence of a campus ministry can be inferred.

1. MORE PERSONS ARE RECRUITED AND KEPT IN THE MINISTRY THAN OTHERWISE WOULD BE.

Probably any increase in the diversity of jobs offered by an organization will attract and hold more diverse persons, but careers in education and religion have a special affinity. The job anticipated by the second largest number of seminarians, for example (the largest number expect to be parish ministers), is teaching.[7] An investigation of 111 former ministers discovered that no fewer than 72 were "teachers or administrators in universities, colleges, or public schools".[8] Campus ministers report that, were they to leave the campus ministry, they would prefer (by a two-to-one ratio) teaching over the parish ministry. The campus ministry represents, therefore, not only a different career possibility for clergymen but an especially important one. An educational occupation that is contained *within* the church stands to attract and hold persons who might otherwise be in education *outside* of the church.

2. RADICALS ARE REMOVED FROM THE PARISH STRUCTURE.

Campus posts also serve as locations for ministers who might otherwise leave the parish. More than seven in ten campus clergy have experience in a parish setting. Leaving, of course, is not always a result of conflict, but Table 1-1 makes it clear that those who leave are more radical than those who stay, and radicalism does explain some of the moves. One campus minister, for example, had been a parish minister in a border state and intended to remain so. But he was "eased out" by his superior over the question of civil rights and urged to take his denomination's ministry at the state university. Another told of his inability to communicate liberal theology to primarily noncollege-educated congregations. He then asked to be assigned to a campus post.[9]

Insofar as these ministers' experience is common, it suggests that liberal agents are removed from parish settings. Thus the campus ministry not only provides a "retreat" for dissident clergymen but also supplies some insulation for the larger segment of the church. If the foregoing is essentially true—that an outlet is created for ministers frustrated by the constraints of the parish—the *extent* to which this is true should differ by denomination according to their degree of constraint. Churches in which "radical" sentiment is relatively rare have greater need for an outlet. To test this hypothesis, we have classified denominations by the proportions of parish ministers expressing certain liberal-conservative attitudes. This classification serves as a measure of the constraint a liberal may feel. A comparison of the answers by campus and by parish clergy to various items indicating criticism of the church reveals that in more restrictive denominations the difference is greater between the two groups. For example, in the United Church of Christ (a denomination in which liberal sentiment is common), campus ministers, compared with parish ministers, are more critical, by 15 per cent, of their denomination for being too conservative in social action. In contrast, Missouri Synod Lutheran campus ministers are 53 per cent more critical than are *their* parish counterparts. Table-2 supplies the evidence on three such issues for all ten denominations.

The table does not indicate, however, that radicalism is less of a factor in liberal denominations. It merely means that, for them, radicalism regarding *political-theological* issues is less of a factor in creating conflicts. Were the data available, they would probably indicate that campus ministers in politically and theologically liberal denominations are radical in other ways. The point is that a campus ministry segments "radicals," providing them with a legitimate base and insulating them from the parish.

3. THE CAMPUS MINISTRY SERVES TO SUSTAIN RADICALISM.

If the short-run consequence of removing some persons to the campus ministry is to leave the parish structure less radical, probably the long-run effect is quite the opposite. One reason for such a speculation stems from the known differences in radicalism between academic communities and the general public.[10] The campus minister is in a location that nurtures and sustains intellectualism in general and perhaps radicalism (as defined here) in particular. Certainly it provides a context in which questioning traditional procedures is less frowned upon. Insofar as this radicalism is linked to the "intellectualist-anti-intellectualist" conflict in Protestantism, the campus ministry may represent a strategic realignment of forces in the church. Seminaries no doubt remain the commonest battleground for this issue, but the creation of still more university-based positions might well have a radical effect on how the issue is fought.

4. RADICALISM IS RETURNED TO THE CHURCH THROUGH MINISTERS WHO THEMSELVES RETURN TO THE PARISH.

The turnover of campus ministers is quite high, estimated at 14 per cent annually. The majority of those who leave go back into a local parish. Granted, the more conservative are more likely to return to the parish, but even these persons' answers to the items of Table 1-1 are far more radical than

TABLE 1-2

Relationship between Denominational Constraint and Differences between
Campus (C) and Parish (P) Clergy in Three Issues Indicating
Criticism of Their Denominations

| Denominations Ranked by Degree of Constraint[a] | Percentage Who Criticize Their Denominations for | | | | | | | | | No. Cases | | Percentage of Parish Ministers Who Strongly Approve of the | |
| | Being Too Conservative In Social Action | | | Not Being Ecumenical Enough | | | Not Having Clearly Defined Policies[b] | | | | | | |
| | C | P | Difference | C | P | Difference | C | P | Difference | C | P | UN[a] | WCC[a] |
|---|---|---|---|---|---|---|---|---|---|---|---|---|---|
| Least: | | | | | | | | | | | | | |
| United Church | 22 | 7 | 15 | 12 | 6 | 6 | 27 | 30 | 3 | 71 | 288 | 61 | 54 |
| Disciples | 70 | 17 | 53 | 46 | 13 | 33 | 45 | 39 | 6 | 32 | 291 | 60 | 50 |
| Episcopal | 50 | 28 | 22 | 29 | 17 | 12 | 26 | 19 | 7 | 125 | 467 | 65 | 38 |
| Presbyterian, USA | 28 | 9 | 19 | 10 | 5 | 5 | 7 | 4 | 3 | 113 | 585 | 54 | 48 |
| Methodist | 37 | 9 | 28 | 49 | 10 | 39 | 27 | 15 | 12 | 272 | 1,566 | 57 | 44 |
| Lutheran | 66 | 16 | 50 | 54 | 7 | 47 | 26 | 8 | 18 | 79 | 273 | 57 | 43 |
| American Baptist | 77 | 19 | 58 | 70 | 16 | 54 | 63 | 25 | 38 | 68 | 330 | 49 | 33 |
| Presbyterian, US | 69 | 20 | 49 | 68 | 16 | 52 | 37 | 6 | 31 | 43 | 188 | 40 | 33 |
| Southern Baptist | 77 | 20 | 57 | 48 | 17 | 31 | 29 | 9 | 20 | 133 | 62 | 36 | 5 |
| Most: | | | | | | | | | | | | | |
| Mo. Synod Lutheran | 71 | 18 | 53 | 65 | 14 | 51 | 3 | 1 | 2 | 31 | 87 | 19 | 2 |

[a] Denominations are ranked on the basis of parish ministers' combined strong approval of the UN and the WCC. Greatest approval = least constraint. Had different items from Table 1-1 been used, the ordering of denominations would change but little.
[b] Percentages are nonweighted averages of the three age groups (20-29, 30-39, 40+) in each denomination.

those of parish ministers. Furthermore, not only conservatives return to the parish. It is reasonable to speculate, therefore, that those resuming parish duties are more likely to serve as agents of change in the church because (a) they are more radical to begin with than ministers who never were campus ministers and (b) they come from their campus ministerial years having had that radicalism supported.

5. RADICALISM IS RETURNED TO THE CHURCH THROUGH CAMPUS MINISTERS' CLIENTS WHO BECOME CHURCH MEMBERS.

Probably the campus ministers' influence on the church via their clients is a radical one. It is true that little is known of the effects on the clients of campus ministers. But most, if not all, of the persons *who become church members* following campus ministerial contact are of two kinds: First, there are students from active church backgrounds whose attitudes more nearly reflect a parish ministerial viewpoint. Insofar as their attitudes are altered, they will probably change in the radical direction. Second, there are persons who, because of their radical attitudes, would not affiliate with the church were it not for campus ministerial contact. Both cases represent additions to the radical sector of church membership.[11]

6. RADICALISM IS RETURNED TO THE CHURCH BY CAMPUS MINISTERS' GREATER LEADERSHIP POTENTIAL IN RADICAL CAUSES.

Two major forces impinging on the church are the civil rights movement and the move toward ecumenism. Either issue stands to force organizational change. The campus ministry has been disproportionately involved in both movements.

In the case of civil rights, the reason is that they are more radical to begin with and more strategically located, having immediate access to a major source of manpower for many demonstrations: students.

Whereas the civil rights movement challenges the church's goals, ecumenism not only challenges goals but also is a direct threat to denominational integrity. That it may prove to be an organizational necessity if such goal challenges as civil rights persist only accents the leavening function of persons in the church who are at the ecumenical forefront. In disproportionate numbers here, too, campus ministers have been active. Willem A. Visser 't Hooft, as the first general secretary of the World Council of Churches, had his ecclesiastical experience in European student work.[12] His is no isolated case.

It is . . . to the student Christian movements . . . that tribute must be paid for aggressive and radical ecumenical pioneering. Existing in the different countries of Europe, Britain, the United States, and the Far

> East . . . (they) met together on a world basis, and kept in contact with
> each other through their speakers and their literature. Not a part of the
> churches officially, the student Christian movements . . . have regarded
> themselves in both a spiritual and a functional sense as close to the
> churches, indeed as the representatives of the church on the university
> campuses of the world. Free from ecclesiastical control, with the imagina-
> tion stimulated by the intellectual climate of the great universities and the
> small colleges as well, they have been able to point the way. . . . It is from
> the student movements that some of the greatest of ecumenical leadership
> has come and continues to come.[13]

This account suggests the importance of communication networks and availability for leadership through which motivation can be channeled. And this, it seems, is where campus ministers have entered. They have been in a position to assume leadership and have had ecumenical experience and prior access to communication networks across denominations.

Some reasons for this availability and experience are clear. First, many campus ministers are chaplains to entire student bodies and therefore cannot appropriately restrict their ministry to persons of their own denominations. Second, the campus ministry's situation has spawned change in an ecumenical direction when, for example, it has felt the need to relax rules for giving and receiving communion. Third, many of the concerns of parish administration are minimized because they are assumed by college administrators or the denomination. Fourth, the very lack of structure for many campus ministers encourages interdenominational co-operation; for example, in negotiations with college administrators over matters such as visitation privileges in dormitories, obtaining church preference lists at registration time, and so forth.[14]

In brief, campus ministers, as seen in Table 1-1, are less interested than are parish ministers in news of their own denominations, but more interested in the National and the World Council of Churches. As in the case of civil rights, however, not only do campus ministers *favor* the changes implied but their segmentation puts them in a better position to *act* on those changes.

## Structural Mechanism Involved in the Segmentation of Radicalism

Control over channels of communication in an organization is of crucial significance if that organization is to contain and use its radicalism. In the case of the safety-valve function, expression of radicalism is restricted to places and times where it is thought to be least disruptive; in other words, where communication can be allowed to go unpunished. Provision for selective target audiences along with selectively decreasing visibility to other audiences would seem to be the structural mechanisms through which the safety-valve function operates; for example, a campus minister permitted his radicalism in the particular company of academics and young adults.

If the structural devices for providing an outlet for radicals (so their commitment is maintained and their communication is selectively directed) are readily understood and practiced by many organizations, the structural means whereby the segment leavens the whole are not. The case of the campus ministry suggests several leavening mechanisms.[15]

1. RECRUITMENT.

Called "co-optation" in some contexts, or quota hiring in others, the practice of attracting more heterogeneous personnel, if only by offering a wider range of positions, is one device for seeing that innovation is more likely *brought into* the organization.

2. RADICALS ARE CLUSTERED FOR MUTUAL REINFORCEMENT.

Among ministers on campuses with more than one minister, for example, fully 86 per cent report at least weekly contact with one another. A series of separate questions relating to formal and informal relations with clergy of their own and other denominations was asked of the *parish* ministers, although here the time period was not a week but a month. Sixty-five per cent reported that they met informally with clergy of their own denomination at least once a month, whereas the second highest percentage, 57 per cent, was reported for informal contact with clergy of other denominations. It would seem clear that parish clergy have less contact with one another than do campus clergy.

3. THE ROUTINE LOCATION OF THE RADICAL SEGMENT IN OR ALONG-SIDE POPULATIONS WITH PARTICULAR CHARACTERISTICS.

The alignment of radical clergymen with the university community serves to maintain the former's propensity to change. The practice of locating professional schools in universities would seem to be another example of the importance of this mechanism, as would its antithesis: the practice of isolating novitiates from any contact other than with planned echelons of the parent organization.

4. FREEDOM FROM ROUTINE DUTIES.

Which is to say freedom from the *usual* constraints impinging on other sectors of the organization. Campus ministers' duties are *different* and may include the tasks of leading civil rights protests or assuming ecumenical leadership. The fact, for example, that most campus ministers need not assume major responsibility for their salaries, but may rely on the denomination's support, quite clearly allows them certain extraordinary freedoms that the great majority of parish ministers do not have.

5. "CIRCULATION OF RADICALS."

Granted, in the case of campus ministers, the habit of returning to the parish after a term of serving higher education is not typically anticipated by either the church administration or the campus clergyman, yet this is the path usually followed. As such, it is structurally analogous to a corporation's practice of electing board members regularly from all its divisions, or of a university's "handing around" its administrative offices to persons from various disciplines. The chance of infusing new ideas increases with the circulation of different types of individuals.

6. THE CIRCULATION OF THE CLIENTS OF RADICALS.

The argument was presented above that the impact of the campus minister on would-be church members in most cases would have to be radical, given the differences between campus clergymen and their parish counterparts. The content of those differences is irrelevant to the operation of the mechanism, provided only that differences systematically exist. In similar fashion, the mechanism operates in the case of executives-in-training who circulate from department to department. The result is an increased probability that use will be made of a radical segment.

## Conclusion

Every organization has its potential "radicals": persons whose commitment to the organizational structure and/or its goals is unusual. If there exist structures for their segmentation, radicalism is more likely to be contained and also more likely to be used. Such segmentation not only serves as an escape valve for disruptive forces, therefore, but also may serve as a source of organizational change.

The campus ministry illustrates both these functions—the safety-valve and the leavening—and it illustrates also a number of the mechanisms by which they operate. These include devices such as heterogeneous recruitment, mutual reinforcement, location of the radical segment alongside populations with known characteristics, freedom from usual duties, circulation of radicals, and circulation of the clients of radicals.

NOTES

2. Ernst Troeltsch, *The Social Teachings of the Christian Churches*, trans. Olive Wyon (2 vols.; New York: Macmillan, 1931), p. 701. See also pp. 237-245, 700-703.

3. *Ibid.*, p. 272.

4. John MacMurray, *The Clue to History* (London: SCM Press, 1938), pp. 155-56.

5. J. Milton Yinger, *Religion in the Struggle for Power* (Durham, N.C.: Duke University Press, 1946), p. 21.

6. J. Milton Yinger, *Religion, Society and the Individual* (New York: Macmillan, 1957), p. 134. (First emphasis added.)

7. See the study of 17, 565 seminarians by K. R. Bridston and D. W. Culver, reported in *Seminary Quarterly*, V (Spring, 1964), p. 2.

8. H. G. Duncan, "Reactions of Ex-Ministers toward the Ministry," *Journal of Religion*, XII (1932), pp 101-115.

9. Examples are from case interviews with campus ministers. A similar problem is discussed by Marshall Sklare in *Conservative Judaism* (Glencoe, Ill.: Free Press, 1955). He speaks of the difficulty faced by seminarians who are trained by the churches' best intellects only to be sent into parishes with no provision for fulfilling their intellectual aspirations.

10. For example, compare the civil libertarianism of social scientists, community leaders, and the general public as reported in P. F. Lazarsfeld and W. Thielens, *The Academic Mind* (Glencoe, Ill.: Free Press, 1958), pp. 391-392, and S. A. Stouffer, *Communism, Conformity and Civil Liberties* (Garden City: Doubleday, 1955), pp. 40-43.

11. The disconfirming cases—persons made so radical by campus ministerial contact that they leave the church and others who react to campus ministers by becoming less radical—we assume are rare. This is only assumption, however.

12. "Certainly his experience in the World's Student Christian Federation stood him in good stead, giving him personal contacts and the knowledge of how to take initiative." (Mackie, in R. C. Mackie and C. C. West, eds., *The sufficienty of God* [London: SCM Press, 1963], p. 8). On the history of ecumenism see also R. S. Bilheimer, *The Quest for Christian Unity* (New York: Association Press, 1952); R. Rouse and S. Neill, eds., *A History of the Ecumenical Movement* (Philadelphia: Westminster, 1954); Robert Lee, *The Social Sources of Church Unity* (New York: Abingdon, 1960).

13. Bilheimer, *op. cit.*, pp. 81-82. "By 1895 the Student Christian Movements ... had already coalesced in the World's Student Christian Federation. This was the movement which was destined to produce the great bulk of leadership of the modern ecumenical movement." (Rouse, in Rouse and Neill, *op. cit.*, p. 341).

14. Thus, fully 70 per cent of campus ministers would like to see "the merger of various denominational campus ministers on the same campus whenever possible." The propensity for the campus ministry, from its beginnings, to be interdenominational is discussed in Clarence P. Shedd, *The Church Follows Its Students* (New Haven: Yale University Press, 1938), Chap. V, p.67.

15. A similar discussion, although in different terms, is found in Eugene Litwak, "Models of Bureaucracy Which Permit Conflict," *American Journal of Sociology, LXVII (1961), 177-184.* Litwak identifies several "mechanisms of segregation," procedures "by which potentially contradictory social relations are co-ordinated in some common organizational goals."

# PART II

*The Historic Shape of the Future Church*

# ≥ 2 ≤

## A MINISTRY ON THE MARGIN

### Robert W. Lynn

## *Introduction*

This chapter first appeared as a speech delivered to a conference of leaders of Councils of Churches. We have claimed it for this volume because Robert W. Lynn has been a close associate from the beginning of this study, and his "A Ministry on the Margin" was first formulated in a New York colloquium of the study.

The chapter is not so much a look backward toward the Protestant educational patterns of the past as it is a look to the future possibilities he sees in a Protestantism that understands at last how operative but irrelevant are interpretations of evangelical faith, American destiny, and Christian character out of our nineteenth-century past. We are freed today from the past century's ambition to try to represent and direct a whole culture. We can stand a bit on the edge of society and pick the places where educational indifference needs our criticism, where discernment of new patterns of learning can be placed in historic context by those who have studied the movements of primary, secondary, higher, and extension education.

Robert Lynn provides us with a model of this kind of vision on the margin of society. What is needed now is some similar vision by those who still operate at the centers of power in church and public education, so that the courageous, rigorous acts of a Bishop Sheen on the policies advocated by Robert Lynn need not be turned back because of the pressure of parochial parish interests. This happens in part because the leaders of these movements of change have not yet produced the innovations in parish adult education that are necessary to prepare for change. Hopefully, the campus ministers provide a few clues as to how this can be done.

KU

As W. H. Auden once said that the difference between the tragic hero of the Greek drama and the tragic hero of dramas written in the Christian era was as follows: the Greek hero was a man of necessity, whereas the hero of Shakespeare's tragedies, for instance, was always a man of possibility. It strikes me that this not only is suggestive about the difference between two eras and two forms of drama but likewise indicates the sense of the Christian life. In this secular age, grace can be interpreted as a sense of possibility, a relief from the imperative of necessity, and an awareness of the gift of possibility. I want to discuss a gift that can be described as a ministry on the margin.

Many have observed the growing centrality of the university, now more crucial to our society than ever before. There is a converse trend; that is, the way in which Protestant efforts in education are becoming increasingly marginal in the enterprise of American education. The Sunday school of one hundred years ago compared rather favorably with the public school of its time; in adult education the church was the leader until about twenty-five or thirty years ago. There has been a decline in the church-related colleges, and resources and money in personnel, once reasonably sufficient for campus ministry, have now grown inadequate to meet the total demand. Thus I would reiterate the truth of John Gardner's statement that a society which once hinged around the church is now more and more pivoting around the university, and the church is marginal to that university.

Thus far, the response of the church to this situation has been one of passivity compounded of timidity and cultural complacency left over from another day. At times, resentment over this cultural displacement brings forth one of those awful seasons of ill-tempered talk we have recently witnessed after the Supreme Court decisions on religion in public education. What is significant is the tendency of American Protestants to see in these decisions not only the completion of the process of cultural disestablishment but also an undesirable displacement of the church as it is moved more and more to the margin.

Yet the movement toward the margin is not simply a displacement from former privilege. The thrust toward the margin offers a new call of the people of God to be a critic on the margin of American society, to be the one who stands on the edge of that society and is able to discern patterns in a new way and to perceive the places of educational neglect.

One creative response to the problems of center-city education was done on a shoestring with much imagination and little fanfare. The Northern Student Movement was among the first to discover the importance of tutoring, remedial reading instruction, and reaching youngsters in a one-to-one relation. Their work is a parable for the church. The aim and intent of a marginal ministry is not institutional survival, but rather to sustain that which is at the center of society: in this case, higher education. Why? Not because of any desire to protect our own constituency or keep it safe for Protestantism, not because of any desire to infiltrate this world and so coerce and try to dominate it, but rather because the destiny of human beings is involved in the university, and very much depends on the quality and the variety of the education which goes on in the university. The ministry would seek to sustain because it affirms that God cares for the health and the vitality of higher education.

The mention of God is not decorative embroidery. The call to sustaining action means to affirm this university because in God's creative and governing activity it is an entity to be respected. One way of fulfilling this affirmation is to study. I mean the study that takes place when, for instance, a council secretary takes seriously the fact that there are resources that will help him understand his situation in higher education.

In our study and action I hope we can demonstrate a new kind of freedom. First of all, freedom from the past, from too much dependence on institutions of evangelical Protestantism such as the Sunday school, the voluntary associations, such as the YMCA and YWCA, and the church-related college. These evangelical Protestants wanted to be represented in every nook and cranny of society by visible church organizations. To be visible everywhere, to cover the culture, to impregnate, to saturate: this was the imperious, benevolent vision of our forefathers.

This orientation still governs, however inchoately, our thinking and action. For example, we still feel driven to support and maintain vast superstructures of organization. In the wake of those evangelical Protestants, we have become the somewhat weary caretakers of the debris left over from the past.

Or take the campus ministry. The church has tended to think of the Christian ministry on campus as a reflection of the parish structure. So we have had the campus ministry, misunderstood by Protestants as "a church home away from home." Though present leadership is far too sophisticated ever to think in this vein, some of its constituency are still haunted by this misunderstanding; hence the drive in many quarters to place a campus minister in every institution of higher education. Even in the most prosperous times of the 1940's and 1950's, that constituted a difficult feat. Now, it is patently impossible. We face not only limited resources in the light of increasing possibilities but also the irrelevance of the drive to create visible organizations to cover each aspect of life in this culture.

For a group that has been moved to the margin, such a drive toward cultural presence is not only foolish; it is faithless. I am arguing not just for modesty, but rather for the freedom that comes from being on the margin—the freedom now to be selective, the freedom to be partial. At last we can forgo cultural imperialism and begin to take and select that which most needs to be done at this moment.

For instance, the day of the denominational seminaries is over. Likewise the interdenominational seminaries, even those located along the Atlantic seaboard, must realize that their day is over unless they integrate their work much more systematically and carefully into the life of the university. Ten to fifteen years from now some of the main-line denominations in this country will be sending their students directly to a state or private university, where they will receive just as adequate training (in combination with an internship) as they now do in most seminaries. Now, that opens up a lot of potential resources. And I would like to see those former seminaries used as centers of adult education across this country or turned into schools for the urban poor. Perhaps those church-related colleges, which long ago should have faded off the scene, could convert themselves into education centers that would concentrate on the most crucial educational problems facing the American people.

The same freedom in being on the margin obtains elsewhere. One of the important opportunities that are coming in the immediate future is the supplementary educational center envisioned by the federal Education Act of 1965. The supplementary centers are to be a means of bringing together various educational agencies scattered throughout a community so as to anticipate new ways by which people may be educated. They will not take the place of the public schools; but they could be arenas for experimentation, supplementation, and remedial work. American Protestants could throw themselves, their resources, and their imagination into the delicate and intricate task of the formation of these centers.

What concerns me is that we participate fully and freely in attempts at innovation. In short, I am arguing that we are now free from excess dependence on patterns of the past. No longer need we do everything. In this freedom we have the gift to be selective and partial, and not feel guilty. That is a part of the gift of being on the margin.

Inherent in this moment also is the freedom for the future. Here I want to use as an example the possibility of joining with the Roman Catholics in new forms of Christian education. The history which once divided Protestants and Roman Catholics in this country is no longer determinative, at least in the field of education. Here at least we have the liberty to recognize one another and to join forces.

Like the Protestant, the Roman Catholic educator today is threatened by a crisis, the meaning of which is marginality. He is faced with the spiral of educational costs, the lack of teaching nuns, the necessity of paying lay teachers competitive salaries, the large classes, as well as much self-criticism by the younger priests. When the new generation begins to take over, there will be even more criticism in the Catholic community concerning parochial schools.

Now, what is our responsibility in this situation? Part of the freedom of being on the margin is the liberty now to support these schools as public ventures in education; that is, public in the sense that they take care of the education of 15 per cent of the American younger generation. We are free now to look at those who once were our competitors and to suggest that we lend our Sunday school buildings to crowded Catholic schools. That is part of our freedom in this new day.

Another way we can help is in the politics of shared time. It is one thing for the National Council of Churches to make pronouncements about shared time as the way out of the current impasse over federal aid to parochial schools. It is quite another thing to participate in the local politics of education where Protestants are immediately apprehensive and anxious lest this be a way of subsidizing the Catholics. For shared time to become a reality in many communities, there will have to be the sustained support of non-Catholics, both Jews and Protestants. Here, too, is a place where we can help.

But beyond that, I see something new in the days ahead. Gradually over the next forty years Protestants and Roman Catholics will move together in their common work of education. By the year 2000 we shall see the normative pattern of educational institutions in this country to be Christian centers of instruction, funded and built jointly by Protestants and Roman Catholics, staffed by Protestants and Roman Catholics alike, drawing upon common curricular resources. These centers will be necessary not only because of the euphoria engendered by the ecumenical movement but also because of economic necessity (the high cost of educational hardware). One can see in the future the development of education that goes beyond the congregation. Just as the neighborhood public school is obsolete, so the neighborhood congregation as a basis for organizing education is obsolete. One of these days, we shall see the pattern whereby people will worship in one congregation, but receive their education in an ecumenical center.

God has moved His people. He has moved us out of the center of American life and over to the margin. But this marginality is a gift. May God give us the grace to see that we have been thrust to the margin so that we can do a new job. We can be free from the burden of the past and free for the future which He is giving us.

# PART III

*The Pastoral Structures of Faith and Ministry*

# ❧ 3 ❧

## A TYPOLOGY OF WORLD VIEWS

### Parker J. Palmer

## *Introduction*

The reader may not like the premises from which Parker Palmer mounts his study of religious commitment, but at least they have been put squarely on the line. This kind of conceptual and analytical precision is necessary if we are to distinguish the different kinds of religious commitment operative in society and to achieve some consensus in the scientific community as to the phenomena under study. For example, the studies by Will Herberg and many other scholars fail to argue the possible positive, integrative functions of religion in their attacks on "culture religion." Neat dichotomies between supernaturalism and "naturalism," "science," and "technology" are assumed in many scientific inquiries without the kind of rigorous conceptual analysis Parker Palmer brings to his own attempt to formulate a typology of religion and its functional alternatives as world views.

This chapter, as the only representative of the papers Parker Palmer did for the study, may lead readers to miss the actual range of his intellectual insight and curiosity. He is as anxious to contribute to a model for the study of the self (an "organic entity constituted by its social and subsocial environments and by its own creative, decision-making faculties") as he is to take on the past conceptual apparatus of sociologists in defining religion. He wishes also to make sure we see the church and university not simply in official and operational terms but as institutions with different "missions" and "embodiments of purpose."

Thus, throughout the study he helped the staff to live in constant awareness of abstractions which are facile in conversation and of the ultimate necessity of locating them in the world of phenomena. He is convinced of the centrality of the study of religious phenomena as a key to all sorts of human behavior, for beliefs have to do with assumptions from which men proceed to live, face death, give meaning to work and leisure. Therefore, the issue which his chapter poses from the start is a basic one for the university: does the study of religion begin with the assumption that the phenomenon studied can be or will be studied as a "unified complex," a reality to be grasped at its own level, or will it be examined only as it interacts or intersects with sociology, psychology, philosophy, literature? If religion is not perceived in the former terms by a considerable body of scholars in a particular university, there is little likelihood that that institution will develop a department of religious studies or will explore the relations of these studies to practice of religion in organizations led by campus or parish ministers.

KU

Sociologists of religion have grown increasingly uneasy with the ways in which they have conceptualized their subject matter.[1] Their malaise comes in part from the critical attacks of theologians and philosophers who often criticize the adequacy of behavioral measures of religiousness and sometimes deny the possibility of studying the phenomenon by scientific means. But the uneasiness stems in even greater measure from scientific problems faced by the sociologists themselves, particularly the failure to develop a conceptual apparatus which has any significant degree of descriptive and/or explanatory power.

In this chapter I have attempted to develop a set of concepts, and some attendant theoretical leads, which may speak to this problem in the sociology of religion.[2] Beginning with the problem of conceptualizing "religion," the discussion extends to include an entire class of "world views," of which the religious orientation is but one member. By using the term "world views" I hope to suggest the fundamental nature of the concepts analyzed here: my hope is to conceptualize the basic ways in which men orient toward the world and organize their experience—ways which form the foundations of social action. (I should, however, make clear at the outset that I intend to deal with these concepts on the cultural, and not the social, level of analysis. I shall not attempt to relate these cultural elements to social systems except parenthetically as it becomes necessary for clarity. My primary task is to explore a much-neglected area of cultural systems: my primary aim is to provide a typology by which the basic ways in which men perceive and organize their worlds may be conceptually distinguished.)

Since this chapter will deal with the "logic" of concept formation as well as apply that logic to a set of substantive problems, it might be well to offer a word of orientation on this matter: Science has come a long way from the naive realist view that there are "things out there" which the observer's mind may grasp in some definitive way. The philosophical revolution behind this development has been carried forward largely by physical scientists, although social scientists are beginning to speak their language. In essence, the new view of science suggests that "out there" and "in here" are analytical, not metaphysical, categories; that perceptual phenomena and conceptual organization are interwoven to become something we can call "fact." When one philosopher (quoted approvingly by a major sociologist) defines "fact" as "an empirically verifiable statement about phenomena in terms of a conceptual scheme," he is illustrating this larger intellectual movement.[3] It is within this movement that the sort of conceptual analysis conducted here may have significance for social science. It cuts across every phase of the scientific enterprise, being both methodological in its concern with the logic of science and theoretical in its attempt meaningfully to order the phenomena of scientific investigation. It would seem to be the philosophical position most likely to open existing conceptual structures to the critique and revision they so badly need.

The chapter begins with a critical review of some of the major conceptualizations of religion which have been offered to date. Out of that review comes a set of criteria for the conceptualization of world views which are suggested by the strengths and weaknesses of previous work. In the next section the typology of world views is spelled out in detail. In the final section I attempt to defend its scientific utility in the areas of historical and survey research.

## Some Typical Conceptualizations of Religion: A Critique

1. The "institutional" conceptualization of religion purports to measure religiousness through various indices of involvement in religious institutions; for instance, church membership, frequency of attendance at services of worship, activities in church subgroups, and the like.[4] Measures of this sort seem to be popular primarily because of the ease with which they may be quantified and, therefore, checked for "reliability."

But beneath these surface niceties the institutional conceptualization of religion raises a host of serious questions which go surprisingly unasked (let alone answered) in the workaday studies of the sociology of religion. First, it begs the question of what constitutes religiousness by answering it in terms of a commitment to a "religious" institution, thereby pushing the question back from the individual to the institution. Second, even if the first problem could be solved, the proponents of this concept are left with the implicit assumption that involvement in the religious institution means the same thing to all men, or at least all men with a similar level of involvement.[5] We already know enough about the smorgasboard of motives behind church attendance to reject this out of hand.

The proponents of the institutional measure might well reject these criticisms on the grounds that they are not interested in plumbing religiousness, but simply in tracing the causes and consequences of church membership. Such a defense is weak for at least three reasons. First, it fails to specify what is special about a "religious" group as compared to any other group—if not its assumed religiousness. Second, it assumes that group membership means something to the individual apart from his definition of that membership. Third, this qualification on the meaning of institutional involvement is very seldom made in the literature; it is too easily assumed that a correlation between church attendance and some other behavior or attitude is a correlation with religiousness.

2. A second sort of definition sees the religious phenomenon as "multidimensional." Glock, for example, has specified five dimensions of religiousness within which "all of the many and diverse manifestations of religiosity prescribed by the different religions of the world may be ordered."[6] These dimensions are "the experiential, the ritualistic, the ideological, the intellectual and the consequential."[7] Thus, for example, the experiential dimension measures religiousness in terms of "direct knowledge of ultimate reality."

Clearly, this conceptualization is a vast improvement over the institutional, but problems remain. At bottom, it seems again to beg the question of what constitutes religiousness. If we are, for example, to study religiousness in terms of the individual's religious *experience*, how are we to specify the nature of that particular kind of experience; that is, how are we to say that such and such is *religious* experience? Again, how are we to distinguish conceptually between the *ritual* of the magician and that of the religious believer?

The proponents of this approach could reply that they will define religious ritual, for example, in terms of the historical, taken-for-granted definitions of the world's religions. But this counterargument raises other difficult questions. First, it fails to take account of the meaning attached by the actor to the ritual in which he is engaged; observing sheer ritual (of which there are many obvious varieties) gives no assurance that it is religious ritual from the point of view of the participants. Again, an instrument which simply gauges the individual's knowledge of his "religious" tradition tells us nothing of what that knowledge means to him, and it is most likely that it is the meaning of the knowledge and not the knowledge itself that will motivate him. Second, these measures (as do those involving institutional affiliation) limit us to studying religion only in terms of historical religious systems; no room is left for the analysis of emergent "religions." Third, by depending so heavily on the self-definitions of historical religions, this conceptualization tends to substitute ordinary language, with its lack of determinacy and uniformity, for the scientific language toward which sociology ought to be striving.[8]

3. A third class of definitions centers on what Glock calls the "experiential" dimension. Here religion is seen in terms of man's relation to some transcendent, nonempirical ultimate reality. Representatives of this view are Bellah, for whom religion is that belief system which invokes a "transcendent authority" as opposed to belief systems which have "empirical referents":[9] Wach, for whom religion is "a response to what is experienced as ultimate reality";[10] and, on the theological side, Tillich, for whom religion is the state of being ultimately concerned.[11]

In many respects these definitions have great virtue. Certainly they get closer to the inner state of the actor than many other types. But they also raise some crucial issues. From an analytical point of view it is difficult to see how *any* belief system (religious or nonreligious) does not rest on some perception of nonempirical truth or, if you will, ultimate reality. Kolb has pointed out that the Nazi ideological slogan of "blood, soil and race" did not refer to "hemoglobin, dirt and genes";[12] that is, the slogan did not have hard and fast empirical referents, and the question remains for the investigator as to whether Naziism may be fruitfully classified as a religion. Similarly it can be argued that the physical scientist (and, at the extreme, the world view of scientism) rests his enterprise on some nonempirical assumptions concerning the nature of physical "reality": for example, that the world is real, regular, and worth studying.

If this criticism is correct, definitions of religion which center exclusively on man's orientation to some nonempirical ultimate fail to meet the most elementary test of a scientific conceptualization; they fail to discriminate among phenomena. If the definiendum of "religion" can be shown to be present in belief systems we might justly classify as "ideological" (such as Naziism) or "scientistic" (like, the making of a total faith out of science), an adequate conceptualization has not been achieved.

4. A fourth class of definitions comes from the functionalist camp. Here religion is conceptualized in terms of what it does in and to the social system. Thus Hoult writes, "From the sociological point of view religion (conceived functionally) is simply a necessary element for enduring social organization."[13]

Primary among the problems posed by such a definition is the failure to account for the "functional alternatives" to religion.[14] Thus, for example, the Nazis made traditional religion functionally irrelevant to the Third Reich while organizing that social system around a set of beliefs many observers would want to call an ideology; that is, there would seem to be conceptually distinct kinds of belief systems around which societies organize themselves.

If the proponents of this definition wish to argue that whatever organizes a society (at the level of belief systems and values) is a religion, we have again failed to arrive at a conceptual discrimination between religion and other kinds of beliefs. This argument would make all societies "religious," which is scientifically indefensible since it leaves the analyst without a true scientific variable (that is, societies, by definition, do not vary on this quality).

Another problem with the functional definition of religion is semantic, and more than "merely" so. The functional syntax (as in "Religion exists in order to . . .") lends itself too easily to the interpretation that truth, as perceived by the actor, is instrumental, a means to an end. But as H. Richard Niebuhr has pointed out, "Objectivism rather than pragmatism is the first law of knowledge."[15] Even the magician, who attempts to manipulate ultimate reality, must be convinced of its objective reality lest his whole operation founder on the rock of cynicism.

Finally, it should be noted that the functional "definition" tends to be more of a theory than a definition, if a definition deals with what something *is* and a theory with what something *does*. The task of conceptualization is that of isolating the elements which make up a phenomenon rather than specifying the relations of that phenomenon to others—as the functional definitions does. To specify what something does before clarifying what it is, is to beg the conceptual question.

## Some Criteria for the Conceptualization of Religion

If the preceding has been a helpful analyis of some of the flaws in current conceptualizations of religion, it should point some directions for the future. In this section I shall attempt to draw out some of those directions by developing a number of criteria for the conceptualization of religion.

1. The first criterion concerns the level of generalization on which a concept should be located, and in the case of religion the individual level seems more appropriate than the social. This is not to suggest that religion is not embedded in the social matrix or that the individual is not a social animal. But it is to say that the first point at which to seek the nature of religiousness is in the individual's orientation toward the world and not in characteristics of the collectivity. Certainly religious belief has social causes and social consequences; but the nature of the belief itself is paramount, and beliefs are held by individuals, not reified groups.

Another way of phrasing this argument is to suggest that "methodological individualism" seem preferable to a quest for Durkheimian "social facts," at least at this stage of our investigation.[16] That is, it seems potentially more fruitful to begin by collecting psychological data to reach sociological conclusions rather than assuming the existence of some underlying stratum of social reality. Only by understanding the actor's definition of the situation and then by classifying these definitions into common types (thereby avoiding atomism) can we determine precisely what perceived social reality underlies the individual's attitudes and actions.

2. A conceptualization of religion should be phenomenological, insofar as that is possible.[17] This criterion is put forth with a healthy skepticism over the feasibility of radical phenomenology. There is good reason, as in the work of Michael Polanyi,[18] to doubt whether one can divorce perception from all that constitutes personhood to seek the bare bones of phenomena as "given" in experience.

But with that reservation, phenomenology still serves as a critical norm for the conceptualization of religion. The norm simply exhorts us to look for the elements of psychological experience which might best be arranged in a conceptual configuration termed "religious" and to do so without any presuppositions about the causes or consequences of these elements. The search for causes and consequences must be reserved for the point at which we wish to test the adequacy of the concept; that is, the point at which we wish to move beyond conceptualization into the formation of theory.

3. The preceding discussion raises the critical issue of nominal vs. real definitions. Bierstedt offers the following clarification:

> A nominal definition (sometimes called a verbal definition) "is a declaration of intention to use a certain word or phrase for another word or phrase." . . . the definition has no truth claims; that is, it can neither be true nor false. . . A real definition is a proposition announcing the conventional intension of a concept . . . it has truth claims.[19]

Bierstedt argues that the ultimate test of the nominal definition is its utility; its adequacy is judged by its ability to order empirical data into meaningful patterns. Thus, the primary use of the nominal definition is methodological. The real definition, however, is subjected to the ultimate test of "truth." Its use is in substantive theory, and "its concepts have referents in the real world."[20]

Bierstedt's discussion has at least two implications for this analysis. First, the use of nominal definitions seems most appropriate in fields which are not yet in a position to make adequate substantive generalizations about their subjects; that is, in fields which do not yet possess the standard of "truth" to which real definitions must be subjected. The sociology of religion is certainly such a field. It might, therefore, be advisable to establish and compare nominal definitions of religion on the basis of their utility in organizing diverse observations whose *gestalt* is not yet clear.

Second, there is some question as to whether there exists such a radical distinction between nominal and real definitions as Bierstedt suggests. Might they be more accurately described as two poles of scientific procedure between which the scientific enterprise must live in tension? If we believe that "objective truth" is harder to come by than older philosophies of science indicated and that truth standards (against which real definitions are tested) are formed in part by a manipulation of nominal definitions, we live in a continual dialectic between the nominal and the real with the hope of reaching some synthesis between "subjective" conceptualization and "objective" reality. The later, substantive portions of this chapter exist in precisely such a tension.

4. A major criterion of any scientific concept is that it be capable of operationalization, if by that term is meant not only laboratory manipulation (often impossible in social science) but also empirical observation of natural or statistical variation.[21]

Unfortunately, this criterion has often made theologically sensitive definitions of religion appear useless to the social scientist. Tillich's notion of religion as the state of being ultimately concerned is, to put it mildly, difficult to translate into empirical indices. Despite these difficulties, I do not wish to endorse an unfortunate tendency in the sociology of religion; namely, the premature foreclosure of efforts to join theological insight to scientific method. Any science is in deep difficulty when it permits transient methodological commitments to dictate substantive theory. Furthermore, even though theology and science do not share the same criterion of truth, they at least share the criterion of communicability, and on this basis alone some significant dialogue should be possible. It is the intent of the next section of this chapter to open some of the possibilities for such a dialogue.

5. A fifth criterion for a conceptualization of religion is that it be capable of measuring religiousness in terms other than those associated with the historical world religions. The substantive argument for doing so is simply the possibility that new religions are constantly in the process of emerging and that tradition-bound categories will prevent the sociologist from being aware of their presence, let alone discerning their contours.

There are also two powerful methodological arguments for this approach. First, any measure of religiousness is obviously biased to the extent that it yields referents which are either socially accepted or socially rejected to any great degree. On a measure of religiousness couched in the terminology of Christian orthodoxy, say, it would be easy for the suburban homeowner to score high and the college student to score low simply because orthodoxy is given lip service in one reference group and not in the other, and not because one were actually more or less religious than the other. A good scientific precedent for this argument is found in the F-scale, which was constructed as "a scale that would measure prejudice without appearing to have this aim and without mentioning the name of any minority group."[22]

Second, there is always the possibility of a nonverbalized, "inarticulate" religious faith.[23] This becomes a pressing problem in the study both of lower-class persons who live in subcultures where verbal skills are not highly prized and in the study of sophisticated populations whose members may have religious self-understandings, but reject traditional religious categories.

6. A conceptualization of religion—and other world views—should be typological rather than continuous in format. Traditionally, scales in this area have forced respondents into either "high religiousness" or "low religiousness" or something between. This procedure overlooks the fact that there are world views or faiths which are not at all religious (as seen by either actor or observer), but have a content of their own and cannot be defined simply in terms of a vacuum of traditional religious belief. Without a typology of various faith orientations, the door is closed on systematic investigation into the form, the frequencies, and the social locations of world views other than the religious.

Just as the typological approach avoids the "more-or-less" limitation, so it avoids the problems of defining alternative world views as antireligious. It is fairly common, for example, to see antireligiousness used as the decisive criterion of the scientistic orientation, even though few scientists would be willing to see this occasional feature of their faith as its *raison d'etre*. The typological approach regards religion as one among several world views, rather than taking religion as the base against which other orientations may be accurately defined and measured.

7. A scientific concept must be capable of discriminating among phenomena. Unless a concept can specify "A" and "not-A", it is useless, just as propositions which are so general they have no exceptions are impotent as tools of advanced inquiry. The failure to discriminate was found earlier in the functional, institutional, and ultimate reality conceptions of religion; all of these tend to force any and all respondents into the religious sphere. To be sure, they are capable of making distinctions of degree within that sphere—although they are infrequently used to do so—but the sphere is implicitly assumed to encompass the whole of human "religious" orientations.

It is impossible to determine the causal efficacy of religious commitment unless one can compare the variation it produces with the variation produced by some nonreligious commitment. Operational definitions which fail to make such discriminations will not, then, produce comparative data.

### Toward a Conceptualization of Religion and Other World Views

In the work of Joachim Wach, religion is defined as "a response to what is experienced as Ultimate Reality" by the actor.[24] Among other things, this response is held to involve "an encounter" and "a dynamic relationship between the experiencer and the experienced."[25] The encounter and the relationship are characterized by an attitude of "awe, as distinguished from fear" on the part of the experiencer.[26] On the "objective" side, the ultimate reality is thought by the actor to be full of mysteriousness, energy, majesty, and power.[27]

Many of these themes are elaborations of Otto's classic work in *The Idea of the Holy*.[28] Otto's major category for the analysis of ultimate reality is, of course, "the numinous."[29] He sees the Holy as possessing elements of "awefulness," "overpoweringness," "energy or urgency," and as being "wholly other."[30] These characteristics elicit certain basic responses in the actor, primary among which are "fascination" and "awe," which Otto is also careful to distinguish from "fear."[31]

The emphasis which Otto and Wach place on the relation to ultimate reality as a basic dimension of religion is taken up again in Tillich.[32] However, the former seem to have been more successful than Tillich in isolating the special qualities of the ultimate which distinguish the response of the "religious" individual. Tillich's analysis, as argued earlier, leaves the door open for a wide variety of world views to be characterized as "religious," since every world view rests on some vision of ultimate reality, something possessing onthological status beyond which the actor is unwilling or unable to move in terms of awe, reverence, and respect.

In Wach and Otto we have at least an implicit recognition that religion is defined not only by a *relation to* ultimate reality but also by a special *perception of* that ultimate; that is, we have a critical analytical distinction. The religious individual perceives an ultimate which is characterized by power, mystery, and wholly-otherness; such a perception does not hold true for a scientistic or philosophical orientation, although these orientations, too, have their ultimates.

Further steps toward the definiton of religion have come by contrasting it with other world views; that is, by attempting to make further critical distinctions. Perhaps the most common discrimination made in the literature is that between religion and magic. Wach states,

> Upon initial encounter with Ultimate Reality, two ways are revealed: that of magic and that of religion. . . . We term as "magic" the techniques which develop out of the desire to conquer, control, and manipulate the apprehended power. . . . Religion differs from magic in that it is not concerned with the control or manipulation of the powers confronted. Rather, it means submission to, trust in, and adoration of what is apprehended as the divine nature of Ultimate Reality.[33]

Malinowski strikes a similar note when he distinguishes magic from religion by defining it as a "body of purely practical acts, performed as a means to an end."[34] And Weber follows the same line of thought in *The Sociology of Religion*.[35]

These distinctions between religion and magic are so well known as to make further emphasis unnecessary. For my purposes, however, it is important to note the primary basis for the distinction: religion is seen as an attitude of trust and submissiveness on the part of the believer, while magic consists in the believer's attempts to manipulate ultimate reality. All the writers cited regard the *perception* of the ultimate as essentially the same in both magic and religion; it is seen as "Holy," to use Otto's term. What differs is the response or *relation* to the ultimate; in religion the actor relates in terms of subordination, while in magic the relation is one of attempted domination.

Another critical distinction between religion and other world views is that between religion and science. Wach makes the point that science and magic have a common dimension. In noting that magic consists in "the techniques which develop out of the desire to conquer, control, and manipulate the apprehended power," he goes on to state that "the same motivation is at work in science, as the brilliant German physicist, von Weizsacker, has shown in *The History of Nature.* He contrasts instrumental knowledge," the search for, and application of, means for a desired end, and "insight," "that knowledge which considers the coherence of the whole."[36]

Wach does not intend totally to equate science with magic, but simply to point out a trait they hold in common. In the terms of our discussion, that trait is a characteristic *relation* to what is apprehended as ultimate reality. Regardless of what specific relation science may bear to magic, Wach makes it clear that science, like magic, is to be distinguished from religion along this "instrumental" dimension.

A similar theme is pursued by Leuba in his classic *Psychological Study of Religion:*

> That which magic shares with science . . . is the desire to gain the mastery over the powers of nature, and, perhaps, the practice of the experimental method. The experimentation of magic is, however, so limited and so unconscious that it can hardly be assimilated to the modern scientific method.[37]

Leuba further argues that

> the essential presupposition of science—that which differentiates it alike from magic and from religion—is the acknowledgement of definite and constant *quantitative* relations between causes and effects, relations which completely exclude the personal element. . . . Magic does not, any more than religion, encourage the *exact* observation of external facts, but rather promotes self-deception with regard to them.[38]

Thus Leuba sees science differing from religion not only by virtue of the domineering stance which the scientist takes toward the reality he responds to but also by virtue of the nature of that reality itself; for example, unlike religious reality, scientific reality is "quantifiable." Without agreeing with all the nuances of the Wach and Leuba analyses, I only wish to point toward certain classic distinctions between religion, magic, and science as members of a class of world views—distinctions which, I am attempting to show, revolve around differences in *perceptions of* and *relations to* ultimate reality.

Another important distinction between religion and other world views is made by Otto when he contrasts religion and philosophy. Otto emphasizes the element of "energy" or "urgency" as primary in the ultimate reality which dominates the religious consciousness. He goes on to note that in this element "We have . . . the factor that has everywhere more than any other prompted the fiercest opposition to the 'philosophical' God of mere rational speculation, who can be put into a definition. And for their part, the philosophers have condemned these expressions of the energy of the numen, whenever they are brought on the scene, as sheer anthropomorphism."[39]

Disregarding the apologetic overtones of Otto's statement, we can see another basic distinction emerging. Religion is differentiated from philosophy by its *perception* of ultimate reality. Where the religious ultimate is characterized by energy and urgency, the philosopher's ultimate tends toward passivity.

Parsons, in *The Social System,* also makes a marked distinction between religion and philosophy.[40] He argues that for both world views (or, in his terms, "belief systems") the orientation toward nonempirical problems is central. The religious view, however, sees these problems as problems of *meaning;* they have strong existential themes. The philosophical view treats the nonempirical problems as "essential," not existential. For religion, as opposed to philosophy, "The primary question is no longer that of interest in whether a proposition is 'true,' but, in addition to that, is a commitment to its implications for the orientation of action as such."[41] In the transition from philosophy to religion, according to Parsons, there is a "transition from *acceptance to commitment.*"[42]

Parsons' distinction between religion and philosophy, then, hinges directly on how the actor *perceives* ultimate reality. The religious vision sees a nonempirical realm full of highly personal problems and meanings; what issues from it is crucial for the course of the actor's life. The philosophical view sees the nonempirical realm in "colder," more detached terms; the ultimate here is subject primarily to intellectual speculation. In this sense Parsons' distinction bears many resemblances to that of Otto.

Another important distinction has been made in the literature between religion and ideology. This is especially significant in connection with the tendency to universalize religion as discussed above; for instance, the effort to identify Communism and Christianity by comparing ultimate commitments, nonempirical propositions, eschatologies, and so forth. Tillich, who has written much which fostered these efforts, has also contributed to the task of conceptual discrimination. In *Christianity and the Encounter of the World Religions* he draws a line between "religion" and "quasi religion," with the latter being the class of which "ideology" is a member.[43] Religion, in Tillich's terms, is the orientation toward an object of ultimate concern, but quasi religion consists in the elevation of that which is finite and contingent (such as the state) to the status of the infinite and the unconditioned. A similar distinction is made by Wach when he notes, "The intense and possibly sacrificial devotion with which somebody may 'worship' a loved person, his race, his social group, or his state are instances of semi-religious loyalties. Because they are directed toward finite values, they are idolatrous rather than religious."[44]

These distinctions bear heavy evaluative, theological burdens which will make them distasteful to many of a scientific bent, but they still may have heuristic utility. The fact that the distinctions made by Tillich and Wach may be made on scientifically indefensible bases does not mean that they are bereft of scientific utility. One demonstration of this fact is found in a sociological study by Bellah in which he suggests that religion is *expressive* of ultimate values, while ideology consists of social *prescriptions* on how to put those values into effect.[45] This distinction revolves around the fact that ideology is more fully articulated with social structures and processes, at least in the mind of the actor. These structures, in the language of Tillich and Wach, are seen as embodying ultimate reality.

Parsons makes a similar distinction between religion and ideology when he describes the latter as

> a system of beliefs, held in common by the members of a collec-
> tivity . . . which is oriented to the evaluative integration of the collec-
> tivity, by interpretation of the empirical nature of the collectivity and of
> the situation in which it is placed, the processes by which it has developed
> to its given state, the goals to which its members are collectively oriented,
> and their relation to the future course of events.[46]

In a further note on ideology Parsons states that the notion can refer not only to the "belief system shared by members of a collectivity" but also to an "aspect of the belief system of an individual actor." The latter form he terms "personal ideology."[47]

In all these analyses ideology is defined as an identification between a social (or psychological) system and an ultimate reality. In terms of the classical Marxian definition, ideology identifies a group with ultimate truth and in the process justifies the life of that group. Thus, it is not enough to note the similarities between a religious movement and an ideological movement: it is equally important, and critical for conceptual clarity, to note their salient differences. In the present framework that difference is one of *relation* to the ultimate; religion maintains a separate and submissive relation, while ideology maintains a relation of identification.

In this review and recasting of classical scholarship, five characteristic types of world views have been distinguished: religion, magic, science, philosophy, and ideology. The distinctions made between them rest on the premise that for every actor there is an ultimate reality, but that actors differ in the ways they *perceive* and *relate* to those ultimates. I shall now attempt to summarize and formalize this discussion by developing a typology of world views based on these distinctions.

Along the dimension of *perceptions of ultimate reality*, we may distinguish two major ideal-types: the Holy and the nonholy. These categories, of course, will be analytically fruitful only to the extent that we can separate out their major elements; and this is attempted below:

TABLE 3-1

*Perceptions of Ultimate Reality*

| *The Holy is perceived as . . .* | *The Nonholy is perceived as . . .* |
|---|---|
| 1. *A mystery,* in that it is not open to human comprehension. | 1. *A problem,* in that it poses difficult but solvable problems. |
| 2. *Extraordinary*, in that it differs in degree or kind from the structures of everyday life.[48] | 2. *Ordinary*, in that it is fully articulated or equatable with the structures of everyday life. |
| 3. *Manifestly powerful*, in that it constantly exhibits active power which is not conditioned by human intervention.[49] | 3. *Latently powerful*, in that it is an inactive reservoir of power which can be summoned and used by man. |

The second distinction between types of worldviews consists in different *relations* assumed by the actor to the perceived ultimate reality. Thinking again in terms of ideal-types, three major categories of relationship can be distinguished: submission, identification, and domination.

TABLE 3-2

*Relations to Ultimate Reality*

*Submission involves . . .*

1. *Being grasped* by the ultimate in the sense of being held by a superior power.

2. *Contemplating* the ultimate in the sense of viewing and meditating on something beyond one's reach.

3. *Faithfulness* on man's part in the sense that one submits willingly to a superior wisdom.

*Domination involves . . .*

1. *Grasping* the ultimate in the sense of being capable of apprehending a perceived power.

2. *Manipulating* the ultimate in the sense of directing a power toward one's own end.

3. *Pragmatic* attitudes on man's part in the sense that commitment depends on what the perceived power is able to produce.

*Identification involves . . .*

The amalgamation of empirical social structures and/or processes with nonempirical ultimate realtiy.

TABLE 3-3

*A Typology of World Views*

*Perceptions of Ultimate Reality*

| *Relations to Ultimate Reality* | Holy | Nonholy |
|---|---|---|
| Submission | 1. Religion | 4. Philosophy |
| Identification | 2. Religious Ideology | 5. Secular Ideology |
| Domination | 3. Magic | 6. Secularism |

The relationship of "identification" involves no array of theoretically analyzable elements (unlike the cases of "submission" and "domination"). It can be analyzed further only with regard to the *specific* identification that occurs; for instance, the Nazi identification of ultimate reality with the potential of the "Aryan race" or the Japanese identification of ultimate reality with the Meiji Emperor. Thus, analysis of the relation of identification is an empirical rather than a theoretical task; on the theoretical level we can only specify the category of identification as an important one for empirical analysis.

It is now possible to cross–tabulate the two dimensions of world views and form a six-cell typology:

Unless otherwise noted, the words "religion," "secularism," and so on will henceforth be used in this chapter as they are defined in the typology. That is, by "religion" I shall mean a world view in which the ultimate is perceived as holy and related to in terms of submission; by secularism, a world view in which the ultimate is percieved as nonholy and related to in terms of domination. There is, to be sure, a strong element of nominalism in this approach, and for this reason my use of these words may sometimes conflict with common usage. Thus, what others have called the "religion" of "the American way of life"[50] becomes in the present context a "religious ideology" because it tends to identify the structures of American life with holy ultimacy.

When such violations of ordinary usage do occur, the only line of defense is scientific. That is, is it more helpful in terms of description, explanation, and prediction to call the "American way of life" faith a religious ideology rather than a religion? The question is not as simple, or as futile, as it seems at the outset; for in science, a rose does not smell as sweet by any other name. On the contrary, science depends heavily on accurate classification, or conceptualization, to remain alert for clues to the similarities and differences between phenomena—clues which are indispensable at the critical points of explanation and prediction. Thus, it is vital to know whether the "American way of life" faith is best classed with "religious ideology" of Meiji Japan or the "religion" of many a traditional society, for on such classification depends the acuity of our reconstruction of its past and prediction of its future development.

## The Utility of the Typology in Historical and Survey Research

In broad terms, then, the utility of this or any other set of concepts hinges on the way it organizes the data: is it coherent, is it "meaningful," does it yield hypotheses, is it consonant with demonstrated theory? Limitations of space and knowledge prevent me from giving these questions their full due, but in this final section I shall try to be at least suggestive about them by outlining some applications of the typology in both historical and survey research.

One of the intriguing problems in the sociology of religion has to do with the role of religion in traditional societies that undergo rapid modernization. What follows is an effort to use the typology in suggesting an ideal typical line of religious development in such situations—a development in which religion is seen as both dependent and independent variable, sometimes being shaped by purely "secular" movements, sometimes being the necessary condition for such movements to occur.[51]

The traditional society may be fairly characterized as beginning in the *religious stage*. As suggested by the typology, this stage is defined by a world view in which ultimate reality is perceived as "holy" and related to in terms of "submission." Frequently, these attributes find expression in a religious law or detailed ethic which, deeply rooted in the "religious" ground of values, closely regulates a wide range of social behavior,[52] including that which modern society would regard as essentially "provate."

With respect to the demands of modernization, the primary point to be made about the religious stage is that it is extremely stable and, by the same token, unable to foment much social change. There is one *prima facie* reason for this: the religious law or ethic prohibits the sort of personal and social innovation necessary for modernization. But there is another, more subtle, reason for the immobility of societies in the religious stage; namely, the structure of the religious world view itself.

The religious world view frequently has a dualistic vision of reality (especially in the West), and if not dualistic, it posits at least a difference in degree between lower and higher orders of reality.[53] Whether the difference be one of kind or degree, the religious world view tends to be conservative precisely because the problems of this world may be sloughed off to "another world" or "a higher level of reality." These serve as ultimate reference points which, in a variety of ways, can function to take the individual's mind off his troubles in "this world." Thus, the religious world view provides an escape valve for the release of the pressures which might encourage social change.

If such a society is faced (as they have been, universally) with external pressures toward modernization, it is evident that severe system strains will result. The critical dilemma of modernizing societies in the religious stage is formed by their religious tradition: on the one hand, the tradition hampers movement toward modernity; on the other hand, the tradition cannot simply be ignored or overthrown. What does a society with traditional authority (in Weber's terms) do when modern forms of authority are needed?

The answer would appear to be that one *uses* tradition by appealing to it (or carefully selected elements of it) for the formation of a new authority which is, paradoxically, a product of tradition, yet capable of superseding tradition. Such an authority must (*a*) function to give the leverage on tradition which is necessary to overthrow it and (*b*) infuse the social system with the "energy" needed for change.[54]

(The "use" or "manipulation" of the religious—or any other—world view is one of the most interesting problems in this area of study, for manipulation is usually the act of the nonbeliever; one does not "use" religion if one is a true believer. And yet the man who is publicly known to be a nonbeliever cannot—especially in traditional society—wield the symbols of religious tradition with any effectiveness. So, what must be the relation of the manipulator, the social engineer, to the religious institution? One possibility is that traditional societies must produce "pseudo-religious elites"; that is, leaders who are publicly identified with religion, yet privately in tension with it.[55] Whatever the answer, it is important to note that the manipulation of the holy for societal ends may, on the cultural level, be the first and most significant step a society can take toward secularization and that its social-psychological consequences may be severe.)

The problems and processes discussed above result in the movement of society from the religious to the *religious ideological stage.*[56] Here, as suggested by the typology, one finds an identification of society and/or social leadership with the holy; typical examples are latter-day doctrines of "the chosen people" and "the divinity of kings." In the latter, especially, we see a shift from traditional authority to charismatic authority.

In these ways tradition is used to infuse the society with the energy for change;[57] for example, the leader who is made divine by tradition has excellent chances of altering that tradition. In these ways, contemporary leadership is able to live with tradition and at the same time supersede it.[58] Typically, in this stage the religious law or ethic is abandoned in favor of a much more "open" belief system: one of the key results of this move is the emergence of a "private" sphere in which the individual is free to make his own choices, unencumbered by traditional or governmental authority.[59]

Where the religious society sees reality as a dualism or a continuum, society in the stage of religious ideology is monistic, in that it sees reality (in both the descriptive and the normative senses) as one; in simple terms, god is in society and society is in god. Such a society has no "escape valve" in the sense discussed above: it must confront all its problems directly because there is no other realm to which to refer them. There are two ways, then, in which the religious-ideological society has the energy for change: not only is it identified with the sacred (a source of active power) but also it must stand squarely in front of those pressures resulting from societal dysfunctions since it has no place to divert them.

In the religious stage we saw a society with great stability, but very little energy for change. In the religious-ideological stage we have precisely the reverse: a society with great energy for change, but very little stability. The source of its instability is the same as the major source for its energy; namely, its self-deification. This society's monism means not only that it must confront its problems squarely but also that its problems may come to be understood as imperfections in the sacred. Because the society has identified itself with god, the shortcomings of the society are the shortcomings of god.

For a period of time this fact will work in favor of the religious-ideological society, for men are loath to believe that their gods are flawed. The problems of the society may, in fact, be ignored for a considerable duration. But eventually they will catch up with the empirical system, for in the stage of religious ideology society has made the impossible effort to deify the human, to make infinite the finite, to make unconditioned that which is supported by conditions. Sooner or later, then, we may expect that societies in the religious-ideological stage will face "the death of the gods" as the deified social system begins to show its weaknesses in handling internal or external threats.

The functional problem for societies in this stage is that of transferring the energies for change which they have developed into a more stable system, one which does not face the death of the gods. This may be done in a moment of desperation—when one of the gods has been mortally wounded—or at a time of rational, long-range planning. Whatever the circumstances or timing may be, the transfer must occur.

At this point another decisive move toward secularism occurs, because the key problem is one of moving from charismatic to legal-rational authority.

Just as the initial shift from traditional to charismatic authority had to appear continuous with tradition, so this shift from charismatic to legal-rational must appear continuous with charisma. This is often done by building on the sense of nationhood developed during the religious-ideological stage—a stage in which the "people" were understood as banded together in some divine mission. This makes it possible now to appeal not to the gods, but to the will of the populace.[60] Thus, the sanctity of "the people" may be seen as a residue of the religious-ideological identification of society with the divine—a residue which is stripped of its sacredness so as to give it the sort of secular stability which modernity demands.

All of this issues in a shift from religious ideology to *secular ideology*—a shift which may be the most difficult of all those involved in the transformation of world views. I say this because it involves an alteration in the basic *perception* of ultimate reality (from sacred to secular), while the other shifts involve the simpler matter of changing human *relations* to a constant ultimate reality.

The functional problem of the religious-ideological stage was that of dealing with the "death of the gods," since the social system itself had been identified with the sacred. This problem is solved in the secular-ideological stage by identifying the social system, not with a sacred ultimate, but with a secular ultimate. Thus, as the typology suggests, society comes to be seen in terms of problems rather than mysteries, potential power rather than manifest power, and the ordinary rather than the extraordinary. All of this suggests a "cooling off" of the social view of the ultimate, a process of secularization which makes the social system much less vulnerable to the vicissitudes of history, since one now expects occasional failure rather than constant perfection. For example, the problem of evil, which looms large during the religious-ideological stage, now virtually disappears, since the public realm is under human, not divine, control.

All of this may be put in more precise terms by utilizing a crucial distinction between ultimate and proximate values.[61] In the religious-ideological stage, society is organized around ultimate values; this situation, of course, presupposes a strong consensus about such values (a consensus which the traditional society, by definition, has readily available). In the secular-ideological stage, society is reorganized around proximate values, and the ultimate values which, laced through and through the social fabric, had caused the basic problem of the religious-ideological stage are now relegated to the *private* realm.

Note that here, as in the shift from religion to religious ideology, no futile effort is made to abandon or renounce tradition. The secular-ideological stage would not come about if its proponents insisted on the total abolition of ultimate values. Rather, those ultimate values are relegated to a position where they cannot influence the body politic of the secular public; that is, they are relegated to the realm of private choice.

The functional "shrewdness" of this move is readily seen when we note that the form this relegation most often takes is that of declaring "the freedom of religion."[62] Thus, the disposal of ultimate values into the private realm comes as one of the great blessings of liberal society, while its major (although tacit) function is ridding the social system of the dysfunctional potential of those values.

It is highly likely that society at this stage will witness a fantastic proliferation of religious sects,[63] for at least two reasons. First, the stage of secular ideology, by privatizing religion, releases many divergent religious energies which were suppressed during the religious-ideological period—a period which demands something approximating an "official religion." Second, the shift from religious ideology to secular ideology also creates a vacuum of meaning; the ultimate values around which society was previously organized are now relegated to the private sphere, and individuals need some form of public identification (as in sects and churches) to play their earlier role.

A social system at the stage of secular ideology is extremely energetic and stable. The energy of the religious-ideological stage has been harnessed and its instability eliminated. But the problem with such a system is that it tends to produce a high degree of alienation and anomie—precisely because the threads of ultimacy, which allowed a man to locate himself in the social fabric, have been ripped out. How may a man understand himself a member of this social system (in the sense of gaining identity from it) when the system does not permit him to articulate his own understanding of ultimacy within it?

The inability of society at the stage of secular ideology to answer that question is, on the cultural level, the root cause of its anomie and poses its basic functional problem: How can it elevate its proximate public values to the status of ultimates so as to bring the public and private spheres into greater accommodation?[64] That is, how can it provide free men with public identities—without, of course, returning to the ills of premodern society? Or is it the case that freedom and public identity are incompatible? It is in answering these questions that the fourth and final transformation of world views occurs.

In the *secular* stage, society has succeeded in making the old ultimates functionally irrelevant (perhaps even to the point of extinction through atrophy) by elevating the old proximate values to the status of new ultimates. For example, in earlier stages it was the great religious traditions with their assertion of a god or gods which supported ideas of interpersonal ethics. In the secular stage a new humanism emerges, in which belief in man, shorn of any superhuman support, is paramount. That is, belief in man, which previously was a proximate belief rooted in conceptions of superhuman ultimates, now becomes itself an ultimate. (Note that I have referred constantly to "superhuman" rather than "metaphysical" roots; the superhuman may die, but the metaphysical never does. Even the new humanism is metaphysical in that its trust in man goes beyond the empirical level of man's observable traits.)

On the surface it would appear that society at this stage has no functional problems. It has solved the problem of the religious stage by providing a source of societal energy; it has solved the problem of the religious-ideological stage by secularizing that energy so as to make it less vulnerable; and it has solved the problem of the secular-ideological stage by elevating public values to the status of ultimates, thereby reducing alienation and anomie. On the surface, this would appear to be an energetic, stable, and highly "successful" version of the social system.

The basic problem here is one of interpretation or, more precisely, modes of interpretation. If we employ a simple functional analysis, it is easy to claim that the religious values which previously integrated society have been replaced by secular values (that is, that a functional alternative to religion has been found) and that social cohesion is secure. But on a deeper level of analysis one must raise certain critical questions about the "quality" of the values around which secular society is organized.

As is evident in the typology, the main attribute of secular society is its presumption at domination—domination of everything from the physical to the cultural world. This stage represents the pinnacle of man's faith in his own power—the power to make the world the way he wishes, the power (quite literally, in terms of projections in biology) of life and death.

What we may have here, instead of a significant advance over earlier stages, is a curious mixture of both their strengths (see above) and weaknesses. Thus, we find here the self-deification of man in a way reminiscent of the religious-ideological stage; but this deification is rooted, not in any mystical assumptions about man's heritage or fate, but in the brute fact of his technological prowess. Again, we find here the problem of meaning in a way reminiscent of the secular-ideological stage, but this time the problem is rooted, not in a discrepancy between private and public values, but in the inability of the public faith (viz., in science) to meet and solve all the exigencies and crises of meaning in human life.

Seeing the secular epoch in this way sensitizes us to the possibility that it may set the stage for the return of society to an earlier stage or for a sort of cyclical process in which the transformation begins again. The secular stage is full of strains which seem likely to create widespread, if tacit, malaise over its value base, and under these conditions something like a "religious revival" does not seem unlikely.[65]

The chart on page 51, is an effort at summarizing this theoretical discussion:

In addition to these notes on the utility of the typology in the area of historical research, it is also possible to record some preliminary findings on its applications in the area of survey research.[66] These findings are not altogether satisfactory, for reasons that are not hard to discover. They have to do primarily with the fact that survey research demands precise operationalization of the concept; moreover this precision must be couched in the form of verbal propositions which fit the bounds of a precoded questionnaire and are capable of quantitative translation. These are probably premature demands to make in an area of research where the concepts themselves, let alone their indicators, are still under debate. Nevertheless, the effort seemed worth-while simply because of the kind of discipline survey research brings to concept analysis and the sounding board that survey data sometimes provide.

In selecting the propositions which would serve as indicators of the concepts,[67] an effort was made to use statements worded at a high level of generality, in order to get at the broad parameters of the individual's world view and to avoid the biases which result when one uses traditional religious language. While this approach seems to have been successful by and large, there is one point at which it failed almost completely: in the attempt to measure various kinds of "identification" of ultimate reality with various groups (that is, in the attempt to measure "ideology"). In retrospect, the reason for this failure seems clear. The individual's general attitude toward social structures is not as important as his attitudes toward the specific groups in which he participates. Further attempts at survey research must take this into account, but for now I can report on only four of the six world views: the religious, the magical, the philosophical, and the secular.

Limitations of space prevent me from detailing the full findings of our

TABLE 3-4

*The Transformation of World Views in Social Modernization*

| Stage* | Characteristics | Assets and Liabilities | Functional Problem | Agents of Change | Appeals for Change |
|---|---|---|---|---|---|
| I. RELIGION | Distinction between society and the holy with society being submissive to the holy. | Great stability (e.g., "escape-valve" function of religion) but little energy for change. | Manipulation of religious symbols to provide energy for change. | Pseudo-religious elite. | To tradition. |
| II. RELIGIOUS IDEOLOGY | Identification of society (or social leadership) with the holy. | Great energy for change but very unstable (due to "death of the gods" phenomenon). | Transferring energy for change into more stable system by moving from religious to secular base. | Demo-crats. | To consent of the governed. |
| III. SECULAR IDEOLOGY | Identification of society with nonholy (with holy being relegated to private sphere). | Stable and energetic, but organized around proximates, not ultimates. | Elevating proximates to ultimates in order to reduce alienation and marginality. | Techno-crats. | To expertise (scientific). |
| IV. SECULARISM | Domination by society of non-holy. | Stable and energetic, but organized around secular ultimates. | Problem of meaning (in Weberian sense). | | |

*See "Typology of World Views" for further definitions of these stages.

survey, which was based on a twenty-five-page questionnaire distributed to a probability sample of 329 undergraduates at a large western university. But even in a limited report it is surely important to indicate the extent to which the world-view measure of "religiousness" conforms to the more traditional measures of that phenomenon. Perhaps the best approach lies in correlating the frequency of church attendance with the students' positions in the typology of world views:

TABLE 3-5

*Church Attendance*

|  | High | Medium | Low | TOTAL |
|---|---|---|---|---|
| World Views: Rel. | 50% | 26% | 22% | 31% |
| Sec. | 21 | 33 | 41 | 34 |
| Mag. | 19 | 20 | 17 | 18 |
| Phi. | 9 | 20 | 20 | 17 |
| TOTAL | 100% | 100% | 100% | 100% |
|  | (89) | (73) | (167) | (329) |

The table clearly indicates that the more frequently one attends church, the greater his chance of having a religious world view: the less frequently he attends, the more likely he is to have a secular world view. As far as gross tendencies are concerned, the typology of world views does not do violence to measures based on church attendance.

But it is equally clear that simply classifying people on the basis of church attendance obscures a variety of world-view delineations; for example, one-fifth of the frequent attenders are classified as secular, and one-fifth of the infrequent attenders are classified as religious. This and several other tables give no reason for resting easy with church attendance as a measure of religiousness.

Another interesting commentary on traditional measures of religiousness emerges when we correlate world views with religious affiliation:

TABLE 3-6

*Religious Affiliation*

|  | Catholic | Protestant | Jewish | None | TOTAL |
|---|---|---|---|---|---|
| World Views: Rel. | 54% | 37% | 19% | 20% | 32% |
| Sec. | 21 | 28 | 39 | 44 | 34 |
| Mag. | 7 | 19 | 23 | 20 | 18 |
| Phi. | 17 | 15 | 19 | 15 | 16 |
| TOTAL | 100% | 100% | 100% | 100% | 100% |
|  | (42) | (118) | (31) | (112) | (303) |

It is predictable that the Roman Catholics would contain the largest proportion of individuals classified as religious, for calling one's self Roman Catholic still has more religious specificity than "Protestant" or even "Jew." And it is no surprise that the Jewish group and those who claim no religious affiliation look so much alike in terms of world views; particularly among college students, calling one's self a Jew may be more a cultural identification than a religious tag. In any event, it is clear that traditional religious labels, like frequency of church attendance, obscure world-view orientations.

Perhaps the most interesting data from the present survey emerged when we correlated the world views with the academic fields in which our respondents were majoring. For purposes of comparison with traditional measures of religiousness, we first inspected the frequency of church attendance among people in each of these majors:

TABLE 3-7

*Major Field*

| Church Attendance: | Engineering | Social Science | Business | Humanities | Physical Science |
|---|---|---|---|---|---|
| Frequently & Occasionally | 60% | 53% | 50% | 47% | 38% |
| Seldom & Never | 40 | 46 | 50 | 53 | 62 |
| TOTAL | 100% | 100% | 100% | 100% | 100% |
|  | (37) | (53) | (26) | (82) | (29) |
| Rank A: | 1 | 2 | 3 | 4 | 5 |

The rank order of these groups on church attendance will come as no surprise. The least attendance is found among majors in physical science, a fact which might well be attributed to the "scientistic" training of these students, which tends to make them distrust religion. Students in the humanities, whose studies involve philosophical and literary critiques of religion, also rank low in church attendance. At the other end of the curriculum one finds engineering students. Perhaps their relatively high rate of attendance can be attributed to their curriculum (which is probably not as corrosive of religious belief as is that of the liberal arts student) and the fact that they are very likely to come from, and go back to, the normal American community of taken-for-granted religiosity. The next most frequent church attenders are social science students who, at the undergraduate level, include many potential social workers and others whose main motivation is to "help people"; these, too, would seem to be likely candidates for church involvement.

Although the preceding paragraph is admittedly a caricature of theories on the relations between academic discipline and church attendance, it is not far removed from the spirit of much theorizing of this sort. These caricatures, and the theories they represent, are challenged by the data in the next table, in which the "religiousness" of students in various major fields is measured by the typology of world views rather than frequency of church attendance:

TABLE 3-8

*Major Field*

|  | Engineering | Social Science | Business | Humanities | Physical Science |
|---|---|---|---|---|---|
| World Views: Rel. | 24% | 19% | 19% | 32% | 45% |
| Sec. | 48 | 25 | 46 | 33 | 24 |
| Mag. | 10 | 29 | 15 | 18 | 10 |
| Phi. | 16 | 27 | 19 | 17 | 21 |
| TOTAL | 100% | 100% | 100% | 100% | 100% |
|  | (37) | (53) | (26) | (82) | (29) |
| Rank A: | 4 | 3 | 5 | 2 | 1 |

Here, the major fields have been ranked from high (1) to low (5) on a continuum which represents the relative preponderance of the religious over the secular world view in each group. When this ranking is compared with the ranking by church attendance (see table 3-7), it is discovered that the two rankings have a correlation coefficient of -.70. That is, if both church atten-dance and the typology of world views are taken as indicators of religiousness among these groups of students, the two indicators order the groups in nearly inverse ways (perfect inversion being represented by a correlation coefficient of -1.00).

What kind of explanation can be adduced for this inversion? In the first place, one suspects that the physical science students are likely to be less secularistic (a world view involving the overextension of science) precisely because they are schooled in the uses and misuses of scientific method. I have some evidence to support this assertion, in the form of a comparison between freshmen and senior physical science majors (at one point in time). While 33 percent of the freshmen in our sample had a secularistic world view, only 9 per cent of the seniors did. While it is not necessarily true that this group of seniors looked like this group of freshmen when they (the seniors) entered college, or that it is training in physical science that makes the difference, this finding at least points to a worth-while research route.

Among the business students an equally interesting difference was found between the classes. Here, 33 per cent of the freshmen had a religious world view, and only 15 per cent of the seniors did. And while 33 per cent of the freshmen had a secularistic world view, 50 per cent of the seniors did. What seems to have happened here (again, with appropriate reservations about the data) is an increase in the domineering stance characteristic of secularism and a decrease in the submissive stance characteristic of religion. If the physical science students come to learn the limitations of scientific method, the business (and engineering) students seem to be inculcated with a manipulative attitude which leads to secularism. Perhaps it is in this area, in the impact of training and experience on the formation of world views, that some of the most important survey work can be done with the typology.

## NOTES

1. Evidence for this claim is found in Thomas Luckmann, *The Invisible Religion* (New York: Macmillan, 1967), and in many issues of the *Journal for the Scientific Study of Religion*; e.g., Vol. VI, No. 2 (Fall, 1967).

2. Earlier versions of this chapter were written for the Danforth Foundation Study of Campus Ministries and as an M. A. thesis in the Department of Sociology, University of California, Berkeley. I wish to thank the Danforth Foundation; Dr. Kenneth Under-wood, Director of the Study of Campus Ministries; and Dr. Philip Selznick, Dr. Neil Smelser, and Dr. Charles McCoy, members of my Thesis Committee. Thanks are also due to the members of the San Francisco Bay Area Research Colloquim of the Danforth

Study of Campus Ministries: Dr. Charles McCoy (Chairman), Dr. Gertrude Selznick, Dr. W. H. Cowley, the Rev. Richard Gelwick, the Rev. William Laurie, the Rev. Robert Minto, and Dr. Herbert Reinelt.

3. Talcott Parsons, *The Structure of Social Action* (New York: The Free Press of Glencoe, 1964), p. 41.

4. Michael Argyle, *Religious Behavior* (Glencoe, Ill.: The Free Press, 1961), gives examples: Chapter I.

5. This criticism has roots in a larger body of sociological theory, running from W. I. Thomas' famous maxim "If men define situations as real, they are real in their consequences" to the more elaborate theory of "action" of Talcott Parsons and others.

6. Charles Y. Glock, "On the Study of Religious Commitment," in *Review of Recent Research Bearing on Religious and Character Formation*, published as a research supplement to the July-August, 1962, issue of *Religious Education*.

7. All quotes in this section, unless otherwise noted, are from *ibid*.

8. Carl G. Hempel, *Fundamentals of Concept Formation in Empirical Science* (Chicago: University of Chicago Press, 1962), p. 48.

9. Discussed in Charles Y. Glock, "The Sociology of Religion," in Robert K. Merton *et al.*, eds., *Sociology Today* (New York: Basic Books, 1962), pp. 156-157.

10. Joachim Wach, *The Comparative Study of Religions* (New York: Columbia University Press, 1961), p. 30.

11. Paul Tillich, *Systematic Theology*, (Chicago: University of Chicago Press, 1961), I, 11 ff.

12. Beyond this picturesque illustration, I am grateful to Dr. William L. Kolb, now Dean at Beloit College, Beloit, Wisconsin, for setting out many of the lines of inquiry pursued here.

13. Thomas F. Hoult, *The Sociology of Religion* (New York: Dryden, 1958), p. 31.

14. Robert K. Merton, *Social Theory and Social Structure* (New York: The Free Press of Glencoe, 1962), pp. 33-36, for a discussion of "functional alternatives."

15. H. Richard Niebuhr, *The Kingdom of God in America* (New York: Harper, 1959), p. 12.

16. "Methodological individualism" is discussed in Ernest Nagel, *The Structure of Science* (New York: Harcourt, Brace, and World, 1961), pp. 535-546. On "social facts" see Emile Durkheim, *The Rules of Sociological Method* (New York: The Free Press of Glencoe, 1962).

17. Cf. G. van der Leeuw, *Religion in Essence and Manifestation* (New York: Harper, 1963), II, 671 ff.

18. Michael Polanyi, *Personal Knowledge* (Chicago: University of Chicago Press, 1960).

19. Robert Bierstedt, "Nominal and Real Definitions in Sociological Theory," in Llewellyn Gross, ed., *Symposium on Sociological Theory* (New York: Harper, 1959), pp. 121-144.

20. *Ibid.*, pp. 126, 127, 128.

21. Hempel, *op. cit.*, p. 39.

22. T. W. Adorno *et al.*, *The Authoritarian Personality* (New York: Harper, 1950), p. 222.

23. H. Richard Niebuhr, *Radical Monotheism and Western Culture* (New York: Harper, 1960), p. 38.

24. Wach, *op. cit.*, p. 30.

25. *Ibid.*, p. 31.

26. *Ibid.*, p. 49.
27. *Ibid.*, pp. 46 ff.
28. Rudolf Otto, *The Idea of the Holy* (New York: Oxford University Press, 1958).
29. *Ibid.*, Chapter II.
30. *Ibid.*, Chapters IV, V.
31. *Ibid.*, Chapter VI.
32. Tillich, *loc. cit.*
33. Wach, *op. cit.*, p. 38.
34. Bronislaw Malinowski, *Magic, Science and Religion* (Garden City: Doubleday, 1948), p. 70.
35. Max Weber, *The Sociology of Religion* (Boston: Beacon, 1963), p. 28.
36. Wach, *op. cit.*, pp. 52-53.
37. James H. Leuba, *A Psychological Study of Religion* (New York: Macmillan, 1912), p. 189.
38. *Ibid.*, pp. 188-189.
39. Otto, *op. cit.*, p. 23.
40. Talcott Parsons, *The Social System* (New York: The Free Press of Glencoe, 1963), Chapter VII.
41. *Ibid.*, p. 332.
42. *Ibid.* (emphasis added).
43. Paul Tillich, *Christianity and the Encounter of the World Religions* (New York: Columbia University Press, 1963), Chapter I.
44. Joachim Wach, *Types of Religious Experience: Christian and Non-Christian* (London: Routledge and Kegan Paul, 1951), p. 33.
45. Robert N. Bellah, "Religious Aspects of Modernization in Turkey and Japan," in S. M. Lipset and Neil Smelser, eds., *Sociology: The Progress of a Decade* (Englewood Cliffs: Prentice-Hall, 1961), pp. 603-607.
46. Parsons, *The Social System, op. cit.*, p. 349.
47. *Ibid.*, p. 331.
48. It should be noted that in defining the "holy" as "extraordinary" I am deliberately trying to avoid some of the implications of the more traditional category of "wholly other" (cf. Otto). The latter category tends to exclude various non-Western religious systems, especially Shinto, which, as I shall note later, I am interested in trying to comprehend. While this minor alteration clearly does not solve the problem, it is at least a step in that direction.
49. The distinction between the "holy" as "manifestly powerful" and the "nonholy" as "latently powerful" is a deliberate effort at avoiding the implications of the traditional approach of limiting the sources of "power" to "the holy" (cf. van der Leeuw). The latter tack seems quite limiting when one is attempting to comprehend the world views of modern society.
50. Will Herberg, *Protestant, Catholic, Jew* (Garden City: Doubleday, 1960), Chapter V.
51. Two points should be made about the exposition that follows. First, while the presentation is largely theoretical in the sense that it derives in great measure from the "logic" of the typology itself, it also reflects data emerging from a study of Turkey and Japan in which I am currently engaged; because of space limitations, only passing reference will be made to these data in the footnotes. Second, the "line of religious development" traced out here is strictly ideal-typical; while I believe it does have empirical referents, its main purpose is to play a heuristic role by suggesting an

ideal-typical sequence of events from which the data can be meaningfully organized and the investigator alerted to significant deviations from theory.

52. Bellah, *op. cit.*; Hideo Kishimoto, ed., *Japanese Religion in the Meiji Era* (Tokyo: Obunsha, 1956), p. 9.

53. This qualification, with special reference to Shinto, is discussed above in note 48.

54. With reference to Japan, see Robert N. Bellah, *Tokugawa Religion* (New York: The Free Press of Glencoe, 1967), p. 165; S. N. Eisenstadt, "Transformation of Social, Political and Cultural Orders in Modernization," *American Sociological Review*, Vol. XXX, No. 5, (October, 1965), p. 665; and Robert Scalapino, "Ideology and Modernization: The Japanese Case," in David Apter, ed., *Ideology and Discontent* (New York: The Free Press of Glencoe, 1964), p. 103. Turkey seems to provide an interesting example of the "deviant case analysis" noted above in note 51. That is, Ataturk directly rejected traditional Islamic religion rather than attempting to "use" it in the way the theory suggests; but in the minds of many observers Turkey has paid a price for this fact. See, for example, Herbert J. Muller, *Freedom in the Modern World* (New York: Harper, 1966), pp. 464, 469. In the thought of Ziya Gokalp, Turkey may have had an effort at "using" Islam on behalf of modernization in order to correct some of Ataturk's excesses; see, for example, Bellah, "Religious Aspects" and Robert F. Spencer, "Cultural Process and Intellectual Current: Durkheim and Ataturk," *American Anthropologist*, Vol. LX (1958).

55. David Apter, *The Politics of Modernization* (Chicago: University of Chicago Press, 1965), p. 45; Theodore L. Stoddard, ed., *Religion and Politics in Haiti* (Washington: Institute for Cross-Cultural Research Studies, 1966), pp. 59-60; and Scalapino, *op. cit.*, p. 104.

56. The notion of "religious ideology" seems parallel to Apter's concept of "political religion" and Parsons' term "sacralized polity." See Apter, *Politics of Modernization, op. cit.*, especially Chapter 9, and his "Political Religion in the New States," in Clifford Geertz, ed., *Old Societies and New States* (New York: The Free Press of Glencoe, 1963); and Parsons' "Introduction" To Weber, *op cit.*

57. The notion of "energy" is discussed with reference to modernization in Eliezer B. Ayal, "Nationalist Ideology and Economic Development," *Human Organization*, Vol. XXV, No. 3 (Fall, 1966).

58. Apter, *The Politics of Modernization*, p. 64.

59. Bellah, "Religious Aspects."

60. *Ibid.*; and Scalapino, *op. cit.*

61. This distinction may be parallel to that between consummatory and instrumental values. See Apter, *The Politics of Modernization*, p. 85.

62. On Japan, see the appendix to *Religions in Japan* (Washington: Supreme Commander for the Allied Powers, undated, mimeo.); on Turkey, see W. C. Smith, *Islam in Modern History* (New York: New American Library, 1957), pp. 180, 188-189; and Niyazi Berkes, *The Development of Secularism in Turkey* (Montreal: McGill University Press, 1964), p. 90.

63. On Japan, see H. Neill McFarland, *The Rush Hour of the Gods* (New York: Macmillan, 1967).

64. On Turkey, see Manfred Halpern, *The Politics of Social Change in the Middle East and North Africa* (Princeton: Princeton University Press, 1963), p. 130.

65. For example, one writer has used the "theoretical framework" of Marshall McLuhan to suggest that "the development from *mythos* to *logos*, from traditional society to modernity is being reversed in significant respects." Thomas F. O'Dea, "The

Problem of Meaning for American Youth," in *The New Student* (Cambridge, Mass.: The Church Society for College Work, 1967), p. 12.

66. This survey was financed by the Danforth Foundation as part of its larger Study of Campus Ministries. Other findings from it are reported elsewhere in the reports from the Study; the survey was not limited to an assessment of the utility of the typology of world views.

67. The typology was operationalized for survey purposes by attempting to develop items which would form two scales, one for each of the major dimensions of the typology. The first dimension, along which we tried to measure "perceptions of ultimate reality," and which ranged from "holy" to "nonholy," consisted of the following items: (a) With his proven ability to control the forces of nature, man is potentially the greatest power in the universe. (b) There is nothing which science cannot eventually comprehend. (c) There is no power in the universe which man, theoretically, cannot someday control. (d) Science is capable of disproving religion even though many people may go on believing it it.

The second dimension, along which we tried to measure "relations to ultimate reality," and which ranged from "submission" to "domination," consisted of the following items: (a) The thought of being at the mercy of forces beyond my control is intolerable to me. (b) Faith is a poor substitute for assurance and knowledge. (c) It's who you know rather than what you know that's important in getting ahead. (d) You can't blame people for taking all they can get. In every case, and answer of "agree" was given zero points; "undecided," one point; and "disagree," two points. The individual's score on each scale was the total of his points on the four items.

# ⊰ 4 ⊱

## RELIGIOUS COMMITMENT AND THE REALMS OF ACTUALITY

### Charles McCoy

## *Introduction*

There is general agreement among sociologists of religion and theologians that religion is a multidimensional phenomenon, but little agreement as to what are its major components. Charles McCoy attempted in one of the first essays of the San Francisco Bay colloquium to delineate what his own theology sees as the realms of actuality which are influenced by a more basic and pervasive reality: the Supreme Being of Christian and other faiths.

The model of inquiry and learning which seems to emerge from this chapter is one in which students and teachers seek to discern religious phenomena in the larger transformations of culture. An example is the attempt of men to go beyond fragmented, technical roles in business, church, politics, and the university to a new mode of relating themselves to one another through their influence in these institutions for the service of larger human and public goods. What this means in the conscious organization of the student activities and how they relate curriculum to other associations and loyalties has scarcely been thought about in the universities. One cannot help but get the impression that the neglect of these basic ontological issues in education has gone on so long that universities are in for a long and difficult period of crises and convulsions.

The learning model implied by McCoy allows the student much greater freedom than in the past to "cut out" of courses and formal paraphernalia of the university which are now empty of function and represent exaggerated institutional claims on student time. The places of learning and inquiry, the opportunities for vocational experience, are too rich and varied today for students to confine their education to the formal classroom. The general effect of McCoy's theology is to make the enhancement of responsible action in the major realms of power a crucial educational concept. The university, if it takes this concept seriously, will want to help the student explore the moral demands of business, family, mass media, church, university, governments, and so on, and particularly the student's relations to work and career, for these are the realms of actuality to which one's response becomes the clue to faith.

B ASIC to research on the Christian campus ministry, and indeed to any investigation of religion, is an adequate conceptualization of religion. Unhappily, such an understanding is not easily available. Charles Glock, a sociologist of religion, suggests that one central problem is the variety of definitions of religion, in which persons equate religion with one or another dimension of a multidimensional phenomenon. "Investigators and commentators have not given adequate attention to conceptualizing religion or religiousness in a comprehensive way.... Their work, as a result, does not provide a satisfactory basis for assessing either the state or the meaning of religion in America."[1] Glock proposes four dimensions which must be included in the study of religiousness: the experiential, the ritualistic, the ideological, and the consequential. "A further requirement is that the criterion of indicators of religiousness within a dimension also be cited.... Two types of indicators may be distinguished: indicators of degree and indicators of kind."[2]

Gerhard Lenski, also troubled by the inadequate conceptualization of religion, distinguishes two basic types of religious commitment: the commitment of individuals to socioreligious groups and the commitment to a type of religious orientation.[3] In the first he includes both communal and associational kinds of relation in order to determine the degree of involvement; in the second he distinguishes between doctrinal orthodoxy as a measure of religious orientation and devotionalism or pietism.

Despite these more sophisticated proposals than one usually finds in actual use in the sociology of religion or the study of campus ministry, a fundamental problem remains. Both of these sociologists assume that whatever is conventionally called religion in our society is what is to be studied as religion.[4] The result is that they continue to operate in terms of a popular conceptualization, not a rigorous one, an essentially ethnocentric one rather than one broadly useful. Such an unexamined conceptualization will immediately label Naziism or "the American way of life" as ideologies. The problem is to formulate a careful conceptualization of religion so that one may decide to what extent, if any, we are justified in referring to these seeming ideologies as religions. A rigorous conceptualization must draw on sholarship in the history of religions and theology as well as sociology. While we must start with conventional views, these must be sifted and given precise expression. Only by this procedure can we arrive at the comprehensive conceptualization for which Glock calls.

## Distinguishing Religious Commitment

Though religion clearly is marked by commitment, not all commitment is religious. Our first task must be to distinguish religious commitment.

Commitment has various meanings. It is the act of entrusting, the acceptance of responsibility, an agreement to act in a specific way, or a promise made involving trust and loyalty. Commitment may be made by either individuals or groups and implies assent to purposes and acceptance of obligations to act in ways agreed upon.

Commitments may also be of varying kinds and degrees. Some are very limited in the obligation incurred. One may be committed to a luncheon engagement. While a person who had made such a commitment would be expected to keep it in ordinary circumstances, no one would question his integrity if he failed to keep a casual luncheon appointment because his wife had suddenly been taken seriously ill. We recognize ascending levels of commitment and acknowledge that people must act in terms of the greater ones.

Other commitments are of a more serious kind. It may be a financial agreement to contribute to a church or hospital; it may be a promise to take a particular stand over a period of time. One may usually withdraw from these kinds of commitments, should some change in circumstances occur. But responsible people are expected to arrange affairs so that they may adhere to commitments made.

On a more embracing level are marriage covenants, basic vocational choices, decisions about goals in life. In this range of commitment, fundamental loyalties and personal identity are at stake.

Commitments in these varying ranges are made by persons in their social interrelations and by collectives. A treaty between nations involves solemn covenant and commitment. Nations may not always keep their commitments, but the one which scorns its treaties as "scraps of paper" acquires a global name hard to live down.

Any level of commitment we have discussed has religious implications. That one keeps luncheon appointments, can be depended on to keep his promises to support a cause, cleaves to his wife for better or worse—all these are functions of religious commitment, but are not identical with it.

Religious commitment extends beyond other levels of commitment in importance and controlling function. It embraces subordinate commitments; it denotes that ultimate level of commitment which takes priority over other levels and orders the lesser commitments making up the fabric of human existence. Religious commitment forms the perimeter of life to the degree that we are decision-making beings; it encompasses thought because thinking is commitment to criteria of validity; it embraces allegiance, as our relations are permeated by loyalties of varying intensities. Discover the religious commitment of an individual or social group, and you discover what is considered most real and enduring, what is of highest worth, and what can be trusted most completely.

## Religion as Ultimate Commitment

In seeking for a more adequate way to formulate the term "religion," we must delineate carefully the relation of religious commitment to commitments not of this kind.

One way to do this is by distinguishing ultimate from proximate commitments. Proximate commitments are those which supersede all others. As suggested above, serious illness of a wife obviously overshadows most luncheon appointments. But some executives might call an ambulance if the luncheon date were a crucial one with company president or important client. A draft call from the nation takes one away from business and home. But commitments to a transcendent order supersede the commitments to a community and nation. Every person has commitments, but the ordering of them and that which forms the final, ultimate level of commitments for each is not the same. To delineate what is the ultimately controlling commitment for an individual or group is to disclose his religious commitment.

In calling this commitment *ultimate* we mean that it is the final encompassing commitment in the actual realm of the person holding the commitment. Anyone who takes seriously the loyalties to which he is called in the great world religions may regard a hedonistic or positivistic commitment as somewhat restricted. Nevertheless, if commitment to pleasure is the genuinely final loyalty of a person, that is *his* ultimate commitment. From the phenomenologists we must learn to bracket the question of final truth in the interest of describing accurately what persons *regard* as ultimate. Only in this way can we hope to study the actual realms of persons in their religious dimensions.

## The Relation of Commitments

Though I want to distinguish ultimate religious commitment from less inclusive commitments, we must note that there is a close relation among all our various commitments. Borrowing from Thomas Kuhn, a historian of the physical sciences, we may say that we become aware around us of "the existence of this strong network of commitments." [5] Kuhn is speaking of the commitments which inform the scientific practitioner as to what the world is like and the procedures to follow in exploring it. This structure of action by which a scientific community shapes its acts, Kuhn calls a paradigm. The commitments which make up the network comprising a paradigm are various—conceptual and theoretical, instrumental and methodological. First, "the most obvious and probably the most binding . . . are explicit statements of scientific law and about scientific concepts. . . . While they continue to be honored, such statements help to set puzzles and to limit acceptable solutions."[6]

At a lower level are commitments to certain kinds of instruments and the ways to employ them.[7] And then there are commitments which prove to be both metaphysical and methodological. Descartes' influence led most physical scientists to assume

> that the universe was composed of microscopic corpuscles and that all natural phenomena could be explained in terms of corpuscular shape, size, motion, and interaction. That nest of commitments proved to be both metaphysical and methodological. As metaphysical, it told scientists what sorts of entities the universe did and did not contain: there was only shaped matter in motion. As methodological, it told them what ultimate laws and fundamental explanations must be like: laws must specify corpuscular motion and interaction, and explanation must reduce any given natural phenomenon to corpuscular action under these laws.[8]

Most of all, however, there must be the commitment "to understand the world and extend precision and scope with which it has been ordered."[9]

Thus, levels of commitment are not separated, but interpenetrate one another. The over-all commitment, the paradigm, has a structure of derivative commitment; yet it is the ascending levels of commitment which define the paradigm.

As Kuhn points out, dealing with actuality in terms of the level appropriate to the physical sciences involves a "network of commitments" which derive from the controlling paradigm of the community to which one belongs. I would suggest that paradigms, with their interlocking commitments, control our handling of other levels of unity, whether that level be that of commonplace objects such as clothes and cars, shoes and ships, or the level of social unities and loyalties.

I would add one more level of unity, more encompassing than conceptual frameworks or world views. It is the level of religious commitment. Here we are dealing with that which has been "internalized," which defines the self and the reality confronting the self. It is actuality not as observed, but as lived. It is the horizon and perimeter of all possible conceptualization because it is the totality of that to which one is wholly committed as real and valuable. Therefore, religious commitment is not separable from other experiences. But it is distinguishable as the most encompassing level of commitment, just as the term "army" is distinguishable as the most encompassing term for military categories. Because being a self and having a history, dwelling within a realm of actuality, means having an ultimate commitment from which derive all other commitments—that is, having a "god"—the issue resolves itself into discovering in every action structure this religious commitment which defines an actual realm of human existence.

## *Religious Commitment and Conventional "Religion"*

Some question can arise as to whether this way of conceptualizing religious commitment does not extend the potential location of religion beyond the limits of the traditional historical religions. The answer obviously is yes, and appropriately so. Any conceptualization which applied to one particular religion only, or to several only, would have a priori blinders built in. Instead, religion must be conceptualized with the examples in mind where it is most clearly present; then this framework must be applied to the entire range of human experience and religion identified wherever it appears.

To formulate religious commitment exclusively in terms of participation in organizations or activities associated with traditional religion will, on the one hand, mean ignoring the diversity of motives leading persons to the participation and, on the other hand, overlook the force of conviction which has brought these organizations into existence and provides continuing power, both cohesive and divisive.

In the same way, to conceptualize religious commitment in terms of doctrinal beliefs will not take account of the variety of motives which lead one to espouse a particular creed and, further, may make it impossible to grasp the depth of faith which, more than credal articles, is the essence of religion.

Furthermore, in terms of doctrine, how does one state the convictions so as to represent commitments adequately? A unilinear scale running from liberalism to fundamentalism clearly does not do justice to the powerful currents of neo-Thomism in Roman Catholicism and neo-Reformation thought in Protestant Christianity. Even a unilinear notion of doctrinal commitments which represents adequately the Judaeo-Christian tradition will not do justice to the diversity of views which permeate Western culture. Whether we are willing to call all of this variety of commitments religious is another question, but it is clear that a conceptualization of the commitments of persons in American society must be multidirectional rather than in terms only of the biblical, Christian views of God, man, and the world.

This view is supported by an examination of the meaning of religion in our history. Though the word "religion" and its derivatives are scarcely used in the Jewish and Christian Scriptures, it is apparent that the biblical context of competing faiths in Palestinian and Greco-Roman cultures requires a multidirectional conceptualization of religious commitment, not a unidirectional one that requires "religiousness" to be measured by allegiance only to one faith orientation. In the Greco-Roman world it is especially apparent that there were multiple directions of faith, with gods for many forms and powers of human social existence. As the Judaeo-Christian tradition has come to dominate the official life of Western culture, our conventional terminology has tended to make us forget the multidirectional quality of human loyalty and trust. It is unfortunate that scholarly usage has frequently followed the popular language rather than the conceptualization which would be historically more adequate and contemporarily more useful in research.

Clearly in our own time a multidirectional conceptualization of religious commitment is necessary if conventional church participation is to be distinguished from Christian conviction and Christian conviction distinguished from the many other faith orientations present in contemporary society. Whether one calls this "religious commitment" or uses some other terminology is not the important issue. What is crucial is that the object of our study be conceptualized so as to take into account the multidirectional quality of the governing commitments by which persons in society and social groupings inform and guide their action. I am inclined to think that the best term to use is "religious commitment" understood in this more generalized sense, rather than as tied to the traditional organized religions.

## Investigating Religious Commitment

Even those who agree with the analysis given above may have doubts that reliable indicators of religious commitment can be found. On the one hand, we must avoid dealing with religious commitment from a naively self-centered religious perspective. This has often been done from the standpoint of some religiously dogmatic position; but it has also been done from a framework of social scientific dogma which reduces everything to social phenomena. In either case the depth of conviction which characterizes religiousness will be missed. We cannot rise "above" our human perspective and view religion from the standpoint of God. Van der Leeuw puts the matter with succinctness: "Experience is a phenomenon. Revelation is not; but man's reply to revelation, his assertion about what has been revealed, is also a phenomenon from which, indirectly, conclusions concerning revelation itself can be derived."[10] We must, then, discover our indicators in the field of common actuality, seeking to reconstruct from these indicators the realm of actuality of the subject group or individual with as much of its inclusive perimeter and internalized depth of conviction as possible.

The task is to reconstruct the formative ultimates of what I propose to call a *realm of actuality*. A realm of actuality is an ordered field of human commitments, valuation, and conceptions governing a context of action. As persons and communities do not act toward illusion, a realm of actuality also points toward what is regarded as actual or real. It may be explored as it is manifested in individuals or groups; personal existence, however, is never exclusively one or the other, but is always both individual and social. A realm of actuality has a structure of action present in it. We seek the pervasive elements in a realm of actuality which bind it into a whole, giving to it an over-all form or style and defining its perimeter or horizon.

Human action provides the data from which a realm of actuality may be reconstructed. In reconstruction we move from physical action to the total structure of action in terms of which observable action has meaning. We explore religious commitments through patterns observable in common actuality, but understood as the inclusive meanings shaping a field of human action.

The areas where indicators of religious commitment are to be found may be conveniently designated under four headings: the *teleological*, the *normative*, the *relational*, and the *federal*. Though distinguishable for purposes of analysis, these areas are too intimately interwoven to be disjoined. These indicators provide means for the investigation of religion as social phenomenon, but suggest means for discovering the ultimate shaping realms of actuality; that is, that to which human agents are responding.

The teleological area concerns purposes. As we discover the purposes and causes for which individuals and social groups live, we shall gain insight into the network of commitments which shapes their realm of actuality. To the extent that final goals can be distinguished from instrumental ones we shall be closer to the religiousness of the realm. The actual allocation of energies and resources is a better clue to goals than are stated purposes.

The normative area concerns what is regarded as valuable and the principles or rules regarded as guiding right action. As actions reflect valuing and norms, they provide clues from which a realm of actuality can be re-enacted in the observer and the controlling, most comprehensive level of commitments inferred. The remembered past and anticipated future as enshrined in repeated actions provide clues to the "sacred history" which is the basis of authoritative principles of action.

The third area, the relational, concerns ultimate commitment as indicated by the direction and intensity of involvement. If religion concerns the response to ultimate reality in its intensity, the character of human relations will aid us in distinguishing unimportant commitments from important ones and important ones from religious commitments. One measure of direction and intensity in relation is *identification.* To what extent do persons find their real identity in their relations to particular groups or individuals, as compared with other relations? To what extent do actions in particular relational contexts permit persons to be who they really conceive themselves to be? Or, on the group level, what actions seem to be vehicles of authentic selfhood? Another measure of this direction and intensity is *expressiveness.* To what degree are certain relations and actions expressive of a person and to what extent peripheral? When does an individual or group feel involved and deeply interested, rather than related, for motives not directly a part of the immediate action? A person may attend church for the business connections it provides. To discover this nonexpressive character of the "religious" organization for an individual is one avenue toward an understanding of his true religiousness. When we discover what social groupings he finds expressive, we move closer to a delineation of his ultimate commitments.

The federal area concerns how goals, valuing, norms, and quality of relations fit together into a network of commitments, the pattern forming a realm of actuality. As teleological, normative, and relational patterns are uncovered, we shall discover the total unity emerging which gives wholeness and holiness to self and social entities. The federal indicator thus directs attention to the comprehensive element of religious commitment. We must not presuppose a monotheistic pattern, but we shall seek for meaning in the selves under study. As we seek for the enveloping action in a novel, so we seek for the total pattern in life styles. The form of this network of commitments will be among the best guides as we seek out religious commitment. By developing instruments based on these indicators, religious commitment may become more accessible to investigation by the behavioral sciences than is possible with the conventional conceptualizations used previously.

## A Preliminary Framework

The visual image implied here is that of human vitalities which always have direction and force. The commitment of vitalities occurs in acts, and the network of acts is action, characterized by selves in interaction, but also by these selves conceiving their action as taking place in a larger frame of action and meaning. The pattern of meaning which informs and guides human action is the structure of action. The structure of action, including acts and meaning as a living whole, is a realm of actuality. The ultimate point (or points) of commitment governing a realm of actuality delineates its religiousness by indicating the god or gods to whom the action of every realm of actuality is both response and responsible.[11]

A basic and useful typology of religious commitment would divide religiousness into three classes: polytheism, henotheism, and radical monotheism. Henotheism centers religious commitment on some finite structure—the family, the nation, a class, a race—and shapes trust and loyalty around this cause. Polytheism has recourse to multiple centers of value and purpose. Loyalties are scattered among multiple causes, as the self moves from context to context. Radical monotheism, in Niebuhr's view, denotes loyalty given to being itself, and not to any single manifestation of being. God is regarded as the source of the whole, and not contained by any part. Monotheism of this kind is as much aspiration as actualization, and yet the actual commitment reaches toward the whole beyond the totality which one can conceptualize. It reaches for God beyond the gods.[12]

Whether one finds any of these types in pure form, the typology will aid the investigation of religious commitment so long as we heed Dilthey's warning that typology is to aid the understanding of historical variety, and not to foreclose its riches of individuality. Beyond this, typology must include the major world religious perspectives. It must include what appear as ideologies to nondevotees—Marxist communism, humanism, scientism—and

70 *Pastoral Structures of Faith and Ministry*

must seek to distinguish when these perspectives operate as ideologies, that is, as rational expressions (rationalizations) of other commitments, and when they operate as religions, that is, as expressions of ultimate commitments.

With this understanding of religious commitment we may perhaps sharpen our conceptual tools for research in campus ministry, or, indeed, for research, both sociological and theological, on that network of commitments which informs and guides all human action.

NOTES

1. Charles Y. Glock, "The Religious Revival in America," in Jane C. Zahn, ed., *Religion and the Face of America* (Berkeley: University of California Extension, 1959), p. 41.

2. *Ibid.*, p. 28.

3. Gerhard Lenski, *The Religious Factor: A Sociological Study of Religion's Impact on Politics, Economics and Family Life* (Garden City: Doubleday, 1961), p. 17.

4. Thomas Luckmann, *The Invisible Religion* (New York: Macmillan, 1967), aims a similar indictment at sociologists of religion, who, he says, have not been doing their conceptual homework and, as a result, have rendered all but church religion invisible to their research.

5. Thomas S. Kuhn, *The Structure of Scientific Revolutions* (Chicago: University of Chicago Press, 1962), p. 42. Kuhn refers us also to W. O. Hagstrom for a similar formulation in the sociology of science and to Michael Polanyi in the philosophy of science where the notion of "tacit knowledge," acquired from the social matrix and through practice but not articulated, is developed.

6. *Ibid.*, p. 40.

7. *Ibid.*, pp. 40-41

8. *Ibid.*, p. 41.

9. *Ibid.*, p. 42.

10. G. van der Leeuw, *Religion in Essence and Manifestation* (New York: Harper and Row, 1963), II, 679.

11. See H. Richard Niebuhr, *The Responsible Self* (New York: Harper, 1963), for an analysis of human action as response.

12. See H. Richard Niebuhr, *Radical Monotheism and Western Culture* (New York: Harper, 1960), Chapter II, for the source of this typology.

PART IV

*The Priestly and Preaching Structures of Faith and Ministry*

# ℘ 5 ℘

## LITURGY AND POLITICS

### Julian N. Hartt

## Introduction

Julian N. Hartt, a theologian at Yale University, was asked to write on two subjects in contemporary theology whose relationship has seldom been analyzed. We asked him to speculate about the content of concern for matters of social policy and politics in the priestly activities of the church: liturgy, ritual and preaching. If these activities are to hold up to the laity what the church considers transcendent and sacred, it seemed to us that we ought to know what public covenants—other than agreement to nurture a baby in Christian family love, or to ordain a priest to service—might look like. The examples in the campus ministry of artistic breakthroughs—such as jazz masses, dancing nude in the sanctuary, reading effectively plays of T.S. Eliot and novels by Camus, doing original student contributions to the theater of the absurd—have lost something of their earlier momentum, and the pews cry for insight into the body of the church and its analogues in politics and systems analyses in the university. Can Christians celebrate in congregations that a highway has been diverted, a stream depolluted, a slum-school reign of administrative terror ended, a suburban school released from middle-class expectations or teacher-school lock step?

Second, we wondered what the nature of a basic orientation toward social policy and politics that had felt the presence of such liturgy might be like. What would a parish or campus minister act and think like if he put at the center of his fundamental intentions the discovery of forces and powers controlling his society and how he should deal with these? If justice is that "most inclusive goal of man," whereby, as Hartt says, "every constituent member of that society is to get what is due him purely and simply as a member of that society," does the direction of the affairs of his church or whatever organization the minister is responsible for enhance this justice?

This piece is in typical Julian Hartt style: a bit more the proclamation of his own first principles than a theology of liturgy and social policy, but surely an important engagement with what is going on in the church and university. This kind of proclamation is hard to come by. A challenging theo-logos is laid on the line, and we are grateful for it.

KU

I

THE university chapel as a center for worship is exposed to a wide variety of criticism. Guns on the left bark objection to the persistence of any archaic ritual. From the right comes fire aimed at the presumption of the chapel in making any traditional sacramental gestures. The center attacks the substitution in liturgical matters of aesthetical whims, theological hunches, and prophetic passion for clear cogent principle.

So far as I can see, the chapel line is not dramatically crumbling under these attacks. Perhaps this is the case because they converge accidentally. But the friends and leaders of the chapel may also feel reinforced by the movement of denominational campus ministries into the chapel position. One ought to ask what accounts for this movement. Some answers are always at hand, such as the attraction of a fully licensed university operation, with all the rights and privileges thereto appertaining, for bretheren who have hitherto been condemned to peripheral status. A rather different answer, however, might be made out. I shall state it and then suggest what is required to make it stick.

The university chapel is a presiding genius in the liquidation of traditional liturgical forms. Yet at the moment the chapel is also a severely idealistic critic of the political order. I do not see many clear indications that the people of the chapel are thinking hard or well about the interconnections of these two things. But surely the resources for that are at least as available in the university chapel as in demoninational structures.

Thus the chapel is emerging as a Christian center close to the "action." That would seem to make it a choice strategic base for launching a reconstruction of the liturgical life of the faithful.

Now, what is required to make this answer really stick?

1. An exploration of the interconnections of the political and liturgical orders.

2. A fresh attack on the ambiguities of Christian ethical concern.

3. Renewal of worship; that is, creative reconstruction of the liturgical-political order.

II

The phrase "liturgical-political order" is used to suggest an interlocking of the realms of politics and religion, so that the function of liturgy is not so much to dramatize the intramural life of the church as it is to show God, piercing and claiming the powers of the world for His purpose.

Thus the corporate life of Israel is a liturgical order. In the faith of Israel the very sense of life is informed and suffused with the mysterious righteousness of the Lord. This does not mean God is seen in all things and heard in every voice. Rather, nothing escapes His knowing or threatens His purpose. This Lord has made known how the life of His people is to be ordered. Therefore going up to the Temple and observing seasons and days are important; but they are not salvific of themselves. Only the Lord is strong to save.

A very different kind of liturgical order is manifested in the tragic drama of Hellenism. There we see that the gods take an interest in human life. But they care variously, indeed. It is almost as though the vagaries of mortal life are reflected faithfully in the whimsies of immortal powers. Or is it the other way around? No doubt the issue is theologically momentous. The liturgical order does not wait upon the outcome. What appears to be raw contingency is the bewildering disguise of Necessity. The sportive gods themselves cannot break out of that order. The great liturgical question is whether even the sublime high gods can render the iron divine order humane and benign.

Given this vision of its cosmic context, what is the proper ordering of human life? One that respects the divine ordination of boundaries, limits, and natures. So even that benign god, Reason, seeks not to change things, but to comprehend what they are.

Hellas and Israel are, then, two realizations of political order responsive to an overriding, overarching moral order. Hellas reads that moral canopy, beneath which all momentous affairs of state pursue a prefigured course, pretty much as an eternal intelligible order. Israel hears it as the word of a living and jealous Lord.

For various reasons Hellas gave a value to political order Israel did not and indeed could not match. Even so the last and greatest word of Hellenic life on the subject of politics, Aristotle's, reveals an intimate connection with the liturgical order still intact. He did not expect that rulers would be godly men. If they are wise and just the state will prosper until its license expires. The acquisition of such virtues is not an accident. Theology plays an important role in the discipline requisite for leadership of public affairs.

American theocracy as a liturgical-political order is, of course, much nearer to us than Israel and Hellas. It is important that certain remarkable features of the Puritan liturgical-political order not be neglected.

One of these is a conviction that the new world is the scene in which a covenanted people will create on earth a faithful reflection of the Kingdom of God in heaven. Spiritually armed with this conviction, the Puritan clan faced the threats of the howling wilderness; but the righteous and Godly company endured and at last prevailed.

That was not just good luck. "Luck" was not in the Puritan theological vocabulary. God's gracious, sovereign hand had done it. And the self-government of the village was faithful political reflection of the self-discipline of the Christian.

Another element of note in the Puritan liturgical-political order is to be found in the quality of worship in which that order is celebrated. I refer here to the high importance the Puritans attached to doing things in good order. No more here than in anything else did they suffer chance or whim gladly. Their hymns, homilies, and prayers radiate unbrookable confidence in the great destiny on earth and in heaven to which God has called them.

A third feature of the Puritan liturgical-political order could be projected from what we have so far reviewed. It does not allow a separation of the political realm from the religious. Expressed positively, the governance of the state is as much within the direct providence of divine calling as, say, the preaching of the Gospel. As it worked out, this meant that moral excellence of character was an indispensble qualification for political leadership.

The plays of Shakespeare present a liturgical-political order different from any so far sketched. I discuss it here because it has long penetrated American theology of politics.

Shakespeare knew enough about the history of England and about human nature to reject any temptation to represent the ruler as a man of pre-eminent righteousness. The seventeenth century saw a remarkable theological-political innovation called the Divine Right of the monarch. Shakespeare is mercifully free of the taint of that heresy. Who challenges the king does not *eo ipso* challenge God. The bard depicts all too clearly how kings are made and undone.

Nonetheless the governance of the state calls for wisdom and compassion beyond attainment anywhere. When they are lacking, the body politic sickens. Shakespeare's princes do not petition heaven for these graces. But when the ruler falls, he may well recognize the magnitude of his failure: not merely that his own person is now in mortal jeopardy but that the nation is endangered.

If the one-time king is not capable of acknowledging the proper dimensions and cause of his failure, Shakespeare provides characters who can and do. They are likely to take the next step; namely, to shore up the sagging walls of the state. Thus when in *Lear* the cup of tragedy overflows and all are about to be inundated by boundless horror and pity, there is a sharp recalling to the affairs of state; and on that note the play ends.

At that point we have *not* been returned to a capping cliche, "life goes on." Shakespeare is saying that the political order has an authoritative claim on the affections and loyalty of its people. This claim is such that private emotion must give place to the grand public affections on the strength and purity of which the state is able to endure. The drama itself has an important liturgical function right here. Playing on either historical of fictive occasions, it focuses heart and mind on the present moment in the destiny-stressed history of this England; and to pungent fears as well as to lambent hopes it gives immortal expression. *That is liturgy, whatever names of God are intoned in it.*

The Shakespearean account of the liturgical-political order has taken up life far beyond the boundaries of Elizabethan art and English history. Notably for our purpose it has produced modulations in the Puritan order: America is an "almost chosen people" rather than a folk on which God has inscribed a clear and invincible election. Kings are clay and irresolute spirit; but the death of a king calls for display of public emotion, whatever the cost to private comfort; for the nation can claim its destiny only if it claims a place second only to God in the affections of its people.

### III

There may be something in modern experience that systematically rejects all the historic patterns in which the liturgical and the political have been woven together. I suppose that the theological call for a "desacralization of politics" is an affirmative response to such a factor in the modern mind. This seems to promise more than a thorough stripping away of pseudo mystery from the political order. Is perhaps the target the transcendent rather than the sacred? Does "the desacralization of politics" plead for a complete domestication of every value factor within the human commonwealth? Is this, moveover, the direction to which "normative sensibilities" incline?

Though we are uncertain about much of the business into which we ought to be put by "normative sensibility," we can be reasonably certain about some of it. The manageable part is an appeal to idealities. Furthermore, we can be sure that every such appeal will be shabbily treated by both unleavened masses and self-certified cultural elites. But happily for mankind, ideals are not thus invalidated.

*So if the liturgical-political invocation of a transcendent realm were consistently to be understood as an expression of an idealistic commitment, it might be acceptable to normative modernity. This assumes that the best of modern spirituality is itself oriented to an inclusive ethical commonwealth overarching all boundaries.* That order is not identifiable with any empirical state of affiars.

Responses of the university chapel to recent developments in national politics provide interesting clues to directions in which reconstruction of political-liturgical order is moving. *In the chapel, idealism has assumed cultic form.*

On the positive side, the idealistic reconstruction is producing its own heroes, saints, and prophets. A master hero valiantly attacks the entrenched forces of the political system; and he does this without thought of gain for himself, unarmed except for Truth.

The new order also has prophets. It is the calling of the prophet to proclaim the acceptable service of divine righteousness and to point the finger of divine wrath at every obstacle placed by self-serving politicians and their priestly apologists in the path of the innocent.

And the new order has its martyrs: men who perferred to let life be brutally snatched from them, rather than to betray the vision of the Great Future.

What we have here is more than a vigorous, high-minded political protest. It is liturgical; incipiently, perhaps, but really, nonetheless. It is a cultic celebration of a moral order that exacts requital for injustice and needless violence. It can be called cultic because the decisive gestures employed have twofold meaning: one for the outer world, the other for the dedicated participant. The latter dimension of meaning runs beyond the "literal" and sets the tone for the whole enterprise.

Another way of describing these cultic features is to say that they are incantational. They are designed to draw into the engagement with evil moral forces that otherwise would remain dormant.

Thus a significant part of the evil, against which the new liturgical-political order marshals the forces of righteousness, has a religious quality. *It is the idolatrous sanctity that makes our political institutions unresponsive to the demands of justice.* Defenders are prone to claim that the System is the creation and the guardian of pure religion. Thereby the best of traditional religion in America is irremediably compromised by a sense of a divine righteousness that cannot be drawn into bloody squabbles over human arrangements.

That lofty piety at its best was seriously defective. The God it worshiped was too inscrutable. How could any practical guidance be wrested from such a God? How could belief in such a God be distinguished from any absolute determinism? From such theological schemes one can extract an odd nectar for comfort in tribulation. But how can one even dream of using them—any of them—both to illuminate and to reform public policy?

Given these sentiments, it is not so very remarkable that the university chapel has become the context in which an anxious and avid search for an inclusive new piety goes on. A theology adequate to a transcendently idealistic involvement in transforming society, an ethics appropriate for a constituency liberated at last from ancient guilt and fear, worship enriched by the best comtemporary art—these are the chief elements of the new liturgical-political order sought by the leading spirits of the chapel.

There is much to commend in this quest. Yet the usages of traditional pieties may be both more durable and more perspicuous than their radical critics in the chapel suppose. Even so Tradition at its best is a point of departure, and not the pre-eminent criterion. But if Tradition is not the pre-eminent criterion, we should stop using it as an important negative criterion, as a definition of what we certainly do *not* want. For if the past is really dead, we should have simply forgotten it. There is little sense and no salvation in beginning each day with a solemn injunction to forget the past.

The quest for a new order can be faulted at another point. Its prophets do not apprehend that the old order tried religiously to cope with a powerful tension in human life created by the inescapable demands of finite order and the inordinate demands of divine righteousness. This tension is the heart of the religious problem.

## IV

Whatever the faults of the quest for a new order, we cannot overlook the manifest seriousness of the chapel in exposing the ambiguity of the church's ethical concerns. I believe that this ambiguity is generated in part by a persistent sense of that agelong tension referred to above. But but I think that this sense has lost much of its vividness. The Standard Package of contemporary (American) life seems, in fact, to be a denial of that tension. The man "who has it made" has met all the important expectations of both man and God. The righteousness of God offers no threat to the perfection of his self-esteem.

In the church the Gospel is often handed out as part of this Standard Package. It is something God himself has prescribed to be taken with one's favorite beverage whenever the world—or one's own very self—threatens to become too much for one. But the tougher interpretation of ethical ambiguity runs as follows. The ethical life of the church and the Christian is bound to be ambiguous because the contemporary world is demonically complex. Our madding world does not allow simple good or simple evil.

Given this sense of the world, we should expect to find reconciliation for it in a liturgical-political order. One of the grand functions of such an order to to do just that: to tame guilt, modulate anxiety, and proportion hope to descryable possibility. Guilt, anxiety, and hope all convey a sense of God's inordinate demands.

The ethical complexity of the world produces a superabundance of guilt. Liberal revisions of the received liturgical-political order are largely inspired to cope with that. They look for a way to reduce guilt for the immensity of needless suffering in the world. I am not flying the planes dropping hellish death-fire on innocent Vietnamese; but they are American planes; and I am an American. Therefore I have guilt transcending my power to cope with it.

Yet the emerging liturgical order goes beyond the best efforts of the liberal system to tame this infinity of guilt. Now we are summoned to acknowledge our *unconscious* corporate guilt. Once it was deemed sufficient to confess one's witting but unavoidable complicity in social evils. Now we are convicted of secret longings for the perpetuation of those evils.

But this must be seen in its close relations with a second liturgical innovation; that is, a gesture symbolically canceling the wall of alienation: I freely submit to being raped in one sense or another by the systematic victim of rape, and this liturgical gesture must be held in the closest possible relation to a third one. That is unreserved participation in the idealistic crusade against the whole damning and damnable System, but particularly against its political idols and overlords.

The second prime objective of liturgical order is the modulation of anxiety. Human societies generally have in their prehistory an active ingredient of anxiety. That is why every success in assuaging and subduing anxiety may well occasion new outbreaks of it. That is why one must think of modulating anxiety rather than of destroying it.

The liturgical order emerging in the chapel offers bright promises for fresh modulations of anxiety. In place of the nostrums of self-help blandly tucked into the Standard Package by an apostate church, the prophetic chapel offers the sublime alternative of helping others, and especially the alienated others. Wakeful and concerned Christians do not need to be immobilized by anxiety over the dark clouds obscuring truth, beauty, and goodness for so many people. Meaningful action is possible—action that may arrest the awful drift toward destruction. Providentially this kind of political engagement can also arrest or even excise the cancer of anxiety about one's personal significance. The System threatens to swamp the individual moral agent. Have at the System, not with pointless imprecation, but with converted and shrewd action: in order to become yourself, you must do for others.

The third prime objective of liturgical order is the proportioning of hope to descryable possibility. Here, again, we find a need as old as human society itself. Always there has been the problem of tying a significant part of imagination to the possible future, which is different from time-free fantasy. But hope itself becomes a snare and a delusion if it is not tied into descryable possibility. It is all very well to say that hope mocks at every rational calculation of probability. Hope nonetheless requires discipline. Exhausted by too many excursions into never-never on tickets issued by anxiety, boredom, or sheer playfulness, hope then has nothing left on which to rise and make great history out of mean occasions.

A liturgical-political order is viable only so far as it provides a normative envisagement of time-bound possibility. That is why so many of these systems appeal ultimately to Revelation, if by that we mean a self-manifested Reality that binds time and creaturely power to itself. For then the possibilities that matter ultimately are descryable only from the ground whereon Revelation sets the people. Given a tribal God, the future is great with the people's aggrandizement: We shall fill the canvas entire. Given a God whose concern ranges in creative solicitude across all of human life and the world, the future is great with the perfection of man: we do not yet know what together we shall become.

For all the liberal emendations of the traditional order, it is still woefully inadequate to the needs of contemporary life. On one side it unnaturally restricts the images of hope by setting around them an anthropology and a cosmology invalidated by science. And on the other side it offers a kind of freedom to hope for eternal happiness that makes men indifferent to the problems of this world.

Therefore the chapel of protest promises to become the chapel of reconstruction and in that latter capacity make a fresh bid for mastery of the normative envisagement of time-bound possibility. The ethical boundaries of the possible must be thrown far beyond even their liberal definitions, because these have been tutored too long and too thoroughly by agelong fears and stale pieties. Prudence and self-interest have been too long in the saddle of national policy. Even if the fabric of society were to be ripped from top to bottom by revolution and the nation should be stripped of its armed might, this would not be an unseemly price to pay for justice and peace; for the System is rotten to the core.

It is silly and perverse to pretend to discover in such rhetoric the signs of a treasonable commitment to international conspiracy. The informing principle here is ideality, a vision of the ideal state of affairs, the sublime commonwealth of free and loving persons. The items of traditional Christian belief that survive in this climate are the ones most suitable to carry idealistic freight; and of these, notably Jesus the Friend of man.

Perhaps this means that the needs of hope have become exorbitant in our world—have, in fact, acquired power to dictate to the past as well as to the present. Indeed, one may begin to wonder how else Jesus Christ could so swiftly and surely move back and forth from being a timeless avatar of moral value (Love) to being a lovable hippie-type Palestinian character.

In more tranquil times we might feel warranted in trying to straighten out such formal theological matters. But now a nation's soul may be lost and thereafter much of the world's body. It is not, then, wholly proper to permit the political to dictate all the important terms to the liturgical in the construction of a new order?

I think not. All men die, and nations too. About death the standing problem is not When, but How? A viable liturgical-political order offers a meaningful celebration of death, that of both Everyman and empire.

That sort of celebration is hardly possible unless the people for whom the order is created are disposed to see the whole of things comprehended by divine righteousness. I do not find the university chapel excessively eager to get on with this bedrock necessity. And as such, it cannot be taken for granted.

## V

The chapel is teaching the church not to settle for low-lying goals in criticizing the shape and direction of American life. The chapel is also a model of dedication in pursuing an imperatively needed reconstruction of liturgical-political order.

But church and chapel alike need a more generous platform for reconstruction than the bashfulness of the church and the stridency of the chapel have found. What is needed is a platform that will properly relate: (1) ideal aims, such as Justice and Harmony, to (2) the celebration of God's presence in a mode transcending inordinate demand. But also the relation of (1) to (3) the national Covenant must be revised, in order that (4) the worship of Christ as Prophet, Priest, and King may achieve its proper place in the church and in the Christian. Rightly to worship Christ as Prophet, the ethical aims of the state, Justice and Harmony, must be resolutely pursued. Rightly to worship Christ as Priest is to accept God's presence as transcending His own ordinate demands. Rightly to worship Christ as King is to allow that love of which he is paradigm and pioneer to become the ground motive in making the nation responsive to the demands of Justice and Harmony.

1. As a nation we are at the point where the demands of Justice and Harmony are at once exorbitant and inescapable. Thus God in His absolute righteousness governs the world.

The demands of justice are so heavy because even the richest nation in the world cannot do everything needful and good at once. A realistic and reasonable schedule of priorities for the correction of gross inequities is hard to come by. It is many times harder to enforce on the general will. Unusual gifts of information and imagination are indispensable for the former. Singular courage and great powers of persuasion are necessary for the latter.

Prophetic adumbrations of a new order make much of the imperative need for a new schedule of priorities. Idealistic critics of the national government advocate as part of that the liquidation of every national commitment in Asia except disinterested friendship and best wishes for a happy resolution of problems. No one knows whether such a resolution of the conflict in Vietnam would assure a massive attack on the domestic problems that threaten to make harmony a daydream rather than a descryable possibility. So the question is whether the risk ought not to be taken in full stride toward a just society at home. Singular courage and great powers of persuasion would be necessary to put this across. Prophetic accusation requires the courage part. The persuasion part comes into play in remolding the general will to accept measurable loss of security and comfort for the uplifting of the downtrodden and alienated. Here the question of ground motive becomes decisive.

Reconstruction of the political-liturgical order must therefore make much of the conviction that Justice and Harmony are the vital political content of God's righteousness revealed as inordinate demand. The demand is inordinate because no finite order can encapsulate or domesticate Justice and Harmony. In His righteousness, God uncovers the critical flaw in every human arrangement made with an eye to Justice and Harmony. He does not do this with an eye to shriveling every creaturely pretension. His interest is the free flow of life toward every richer variety. But, unlike us, He will not sacrifice harmony to variety nor variety to harmony.

Christ as Prophet brings this divine concern into the inner courts of human life. He proclaims a Kingdom of boundless richness on which hope can draw forever without the slightest hint of exhaustion. But it is a Kingdom whose inviolable Law shines in unbearable lambency wherever man's self-esteem throttles or corrupts the flow of mercy toward suffering.

2. The Gospel which Christianity accepts as Revelation celebrates God's presense in the world in a form transcending inordinate demand. God will not always chide, neither will He remember our iniquity forever. This does not point to some golden far-off time ahead when God will be overtaken by a fit of amiable forgetfulness. Rather, God comes into our affairs as a healing Presence. He created mankind to be one body. It *is* therefore one body. But it is a body suffering many lesions. Naturally, then, the simple demand of life itself, for the health of wholeness, is felt as inordinate; indeed, a veritable counsel of perfection.

Christ as Priest mediates the divine life for the restoration of health and the beauty of wholeness. He is our Justification. In Him we accept the Law of the Kingdom as a rule of life rather than a sentence of death and a seal of damnation.

The Priestly office of Christ has political content: the state cannot legislate mercy, but it can revise the canons of retributive justice with a view to overcoming ancient pseudometaphysical distinctions between criminal and sound citizen. Punitive law will stand in the record as long as history runs. But it can be modulated into something humane, restorative, reconstructive. That is mediatorial work. The Christian has excellent reason for accepting it as a proper service of God.

3. Reconstruction of the political-liturgical order must include as a vital and primary element the relationship of the ideal aims of the state to the national Covenant. Theologically understood, the foundation of this nation is a pledge to Almighty God. Before the law all men shall be equal; and no man

shall be forcibly bound to serve another; and every man shall be free to worship and serve God as he sees fit, provided that he does not use his liberty to destroy the rights of others guaranteed by this reign of law.

"Covenant" is a way of interpreting the history and destiny of this nation. The sense of being an "almost chosen people" is manifested at every important juncture, at least down to the recent past. One would hardly deny that Covenant has, nonetheless, served as excuse for such things as cruel presumption, the violent erasure of human rights, and bland indifference to dreadful exploitation. Of these horrid things it is legitimate and important to ask whether they have been properly confessed; and if not, why not.

At this point, too, the reconstruction of the liturgical order is a crying need, for the good confession of sin is no more than begun by public acknowledgement of guilt. What matters most is restitution to the injured, so far as that is possible, and thoughtfully proposed amendment of life, so that the same injury shall not befall the same victim again, or his descendants, either.

But can the requirements of a good confession be legitmately or helpfully transferred from private person to the state? How in the world can a *government* confess its sins?

The principal difficulties in grasping what is at stake here spring from the restriction of confession to feelings of remorse and to rhetorical displays. But on the decisive points, restitution and amendment, a government can indeed "bring forth fruits worthy of repentance."

Nevertheless, we may well wonder whether such action is not very much easier and thus more plausible in international affairs than in domestic ones. How, for example, can the government make amends for the brutal deprivations of basic rights which Negroes have long suffered? Here rhetorical gestures seem more plausible than anything else.

Perhaps we are confused about this by the elevation of an inadequate model. The model ought not to be that of a person giving back something many of our people have never had; that is what we seek. This calls for a redress of the soverign will of the people: the powers of the state shall be used to level the barriers, whatever they are, which have defeated fair access to the fundamental rights and goods of this society.

The worship of Christ as King is germane to the principle of the national Covenant. The kingship of God's Christ has a magisterial provenance in the commonwealth of man because he is the God-man. He is the Prince of the Kingdom of God. And he is Incarnate God, God domiciled of His free and soverign choice in this "tabernacle of flesh," in this human history. Thus the power, authority, and law of the Kingdom of God have been implanted in the commonwealth of man; and they will not withdraw, ever.

Second, the kingship of Christ instructs us in the art of governance. He does not tell us how to construct a state. But we can learn from him how to order every motive to the governance of love.

This does not mean that men are in Christ, obliged to make love the motive in the pursuit of political ambition or in the execution of political ambition or in the execution of political responsibilities. Rather, his revelation of love is the ultimate criterion by which motives and perfor- mances are to be appraised. Do they build up the common life? If they aim only at reducing damage to the corporate body (and there are times when that is the best that can be done), do they so serve that end, that amplification and purification of that life will be possible later? Thus Christ as King is worshiped when men, already predisposed to govern and be governed humanely, perceive what the model of humanity really is and bend every effort to emulate it.

Third, the governance of Christ in and over the national Covenant comes to light in the objective disposition resident in that pledge to make all who dwell in this land brothers in the love of that freedom which devotion to justice along can realize. Thus the wide inequalities of natural gifts are nothing to the point of an objective disposition to guarantee fundamental humanity to all. No law can do that. But that is not the point. The point is a public intention to do that, a promise built into institution and social process. God knows the Promise has been violated. But in a larger sense it has not been and will not be violated. God sees to that. Christ, Prince, Son, Saviour, enables us to live hopefully with the terrible bright consequences.

## VI

The University chapel has an unparalleled opportunity to forge and test reconstructions and the political-liturgical order. What is the university, if it is not the unique center of critical conflicts of value systems? Here the pressure of the ideal is keenly felt, not only by the restless young but by everyone who believes in the pursuit of wisdom.

Moreover, the university is swiftly and steadily becoming the laboratory as well as the training ground of public leadership. The art of government has here a paramount claim. It is not the monopoly of political science; it is a generic and constitutive concern of the whole university.

Finally, the chapel has a unique pastoral-priestly responsibility. It is derived in part from the vulnerabilities of its young people. Here an ancient model of Pastor must be questioned all the way into the ground, the picture of the Innocent about to step into a demonically seductive world. The actuality is shockingly different. The world is overflowing with forces dedicated, so to speak, to alienation. It is wrong to cast students as such into the category of the alienated. Alienation is their fate, if it be not averted or transformed. Nothing is so effective for that purpose as sound preparation to attack the causes of alienation in the world.

The Christian church, in the university and elsewhere, ought to have an answer for the question, "But what is that sound preparation?" At least the text is quoted often enough: "whoever would seek to save his life. . . " Christian liturgy is built around a ground conception of losing one's life for Christ and the world. Christian life is a political strategy for losing one's life where and when it can do the most for God, for country, and for the commonwealth of man.

# THE STUDENT PARISHIONER:

## RADICAL RHETORIC AND TRADITIONAL REALITY

### N. J. Demerath, III, and Kenneth J. Lutterman

## Introduction

The data from the Wisconsin student survey will be subjects of many articles and interpretations.[1] This chapter probes only one dimension of this rich lode: the nature of orthodoxy and dissidence in the student parishioner. The work has concentrated chiefly on the analysis of change from the freshman to the senior years and has come up with a general conclusion that no major patterns of change with respect to religion, politics, or educational values occur. This kind of data has been known for some time with respect to college careers, Jacob's book summarizing what was evident to the experts for some time.[2] There are sources of life commitment deeper than those fashioned in formal education.

But these data are fairly unique in their application to the campus ministry. They allow us to conclude, as Demerath notes, "that the differences which exist between campus religious groups and the campus at large are due more to differences in initial recruitment than to differential impact over time." The campus ministries are for the most part the captives of their captive audiences; their influence over campus religious life or any other aspect of education is slight, indeed.

These data can be looked upon as the death note to a valiant and well-intentioned profession, or it can, as we would prefer, be looked upon as

---

1. The authors made the following acknowledgments at the start of their chapter: "The Danforth Study of Campus Ministries funded the investigation from the beginning, but use of the University of Wisconsin Computing Center was made possible through support, in part, from the National Science Foundation, other United States government agencies, and the Wisconsin Alumni Research Foundation (WARF) through the University of Wisconsin Research Committee. Victor Thiessen was an enormous asset to the methodological and computer aspects of the study. We are also indebted to Patricia Blair for long hours of clerical and editorial assistance."
2. Paul Jacob, *Changing Values in College* (New York: Harper, 1957).

an opportunity to give up responsibilities for what had been merely a reinforcement of attitudes likely to persist anyway. There is a great opportunity now to make some major alterations in the work and mission of one of the best-educated and most energetic and adaptable segments of the whole ministry. The major alterations are not going to come as a great shock to the more perceptive and needed leaders. What they need now is massive, dedicated support from the church at large.

When an institution has come to a dead end, it should be recognized as such and a reassessment of the situation made. The campus ministers have not effected a major impact on the student parishioners with whom they have been spending most of their time, money, and energy. Therefore, alternative strategies of allocating ministerial personnel should be explored. This chapter does not go into such matters, but we are raising them here so that the survey data will not be read as so many dead facts.

The data are clear, for example, that many campus ministers will find a far more receptive audience for their true views on religion, ethics, and society among students formally unaffiliated with the churches than among their denominational legatees. Thus, why not place these people in surroundings where they meet students in daily terms outside usual church affairs and with programs that meet their deepest religious interests, and which no longer stigmatize them in their relation to other parts of the academic community?

There are and will be other agencies on campus which can conduct a religious witness on an intellectual and social community-action plane and which need more careful examination than that reflected in a revamping of denominational student centers: religious study departments that are more varied than the seminary images; ecumenical centers for involvement of a variety of private institutions in continuing education; the placement of former campus ministers with innovative dynamism in large suburban churches that are now needing high-level, university-oriented adult education programs.

A campus student body such as these men have been studying is no longer a liberal arts chaplain's parish; it has massive structures built into the whole professional, technical, reform life of the state, with extension education going on that touches every parish. Such a campus no longer belongs to the campus ministers; they are there principally to open up its life to the whole community in a religiously and socially meaningful way. So the sooner we begin to rotate conventional parish clergymen into supervised university settings and send campus ministers out to discover what is going on in the parishes, the sooner the realities of our survey data will come through to the religious leaders.

The people who have been studied—the students—move and act and believe in ways that the church is going to have to adopt if they are to become members in good standing in both the academic and religious communities. God did not put a whole generation on the earth to develop its resources as a cosmic joke. These students, as we tried to make clear in the

California studies, have some strong and valid convictions about what it takes to reach judgments on crucial religious and ethical issues. They are combining them with real expertise in economics, the humanities, the environmental sciences, and so on. It is now time that all clergy when on campus be freed to come into this student world, to participate on an open basis with students and faculty in the major work of the university, its inquiry and learning, and then take this to the church in a variety of ways. Such roles are much less frustrating, artificial, and lonely than the roles we have imposed from the past. This is the reason for the importance of Part V of Volumes I and II on prophetic learning.

A second major observation about the student survey has to do with its careful attention to the relations between orthodoxy and dissidence. Much past research has assumed a simple dichotomy and opposition between these elements of belief. But the Wisconsin study reveals a strong tendency for many respondents to give assent to seemingly contradictory tenets of belief without being greatly burdened by their inconceivability. What may seem contradictory to the researcher may in the Judaeo-Christian faith of the believer be not only uncontradictory but the very essence of the paradoxes, ironies, and mysteries of the faith they hold.

The respondents may be simply tending to agree indiscriminately to statements of orthodoxy as a religious act, confirming as true the old American "faith in faith." But the situation is complicated by the discovery that for a very substantial number of students, their orthodoxy is also accompanied by strong affirmations of dissidence. The beliefs at issue are not inconsequential, but for most students are of some importance in their lives. The items of greatest saliency are a combination of elements of Christian orthodoxy (Jesus was God's only Son; of statements of ethic dimensions of faith; of expectation of life after death). But added to them is a total configuration of salient religious items of belief, highly dissident in content (such as "Religion hampers man's development by making him dependent on a higher power," "Christianity has overemphasized the evil of man and has neglected the goodness of the world, including man," "Organized religion is irrelevant today when it tries to deal with political and economic problems in religious terms"). As the researchers note, "Orthodoxy and dissidence may not be mirror-images of each other, but rather complementary in some instances." A combination of the two may be a better single religious variable than either taken alone. A complex method of computer analysis bears this out. A master index of the dominant campus religion factor is considerably higher when these items are combined than when indices of orthodoxy and dissidence are treated alone; the higher the self-perception of religion as an influence in one's life, the more likelihood of the combination.[3]

---

3. A detailed discussion of the complex methodological issues raised in research attempting to measure religious beliefs is conducted by Jay Demerath, Kenneth Lutterman, and Judith Lyons in " 'So What' and 'That Too,' Twin Problems in the Measurement of Religious Beliefs," prepared for the Conference on the Study of Religious Beliefs, April, 1968, Southern Methodist University.

These data have profound policy implications for daily church practice. They indicate the need of much greater provision in all denominations for occasions to inquire into serious doubts and differences of belief, for ministerial roles and boards of control or review which invite confrontation of orthodoxy and dissidence, the mixing of questions and specialties in serious investigation of the impact that education, work, and peer group influences have on student lives.

The strength of the Demerath-Lutterman contribution is that it tests as far as is methodologically consistent the effectiveness of existing institutional structures, chiefly the priestly and preaching modes of ministry, in promoting a variety of goals much respected now among Christians, semi-Christians, educators, i.e., Christian freedom to think, to inquire, to participate in politics in a variety of ways, among others. The report of the director was unwilling to presuppose that the church needs no priestly, pattern-maintenance emphasis in Christian practice; but it was willing to question it as the only effective and viable mode of Christian learning and to question that this mode could survive without some restoration of balance in the institutionalized modes of ministry.

The director pleads an agnostic position as to predictions of how the conservative pattern-maintenance community will receive the innovative structures proposed. What has to be faced is that resistance will be tied to an illusion of a formal theological dichotomy between conservative religion and the technological-scientific community. The break will come when the leaders see that the realities of student academic majors, career ties, and faith solutions no longer fit these old assumptions.

                                                                    *KU*

# 6

## THE STUDENT PARISHONER: RADICAL RHETORIC AND TRADITIONAL REALITY

N. J. Demerath, III, and Kenneth J. Lutterman

### *Part* I

THE evangelizing missionary has always sought out souls in their natural habitats at the risk of "going native." And so it is not surprising that, in an age of campus radicalism,[1] the campus clergy should itself take on radical trappings. Certainly this form of religious radicalism has been widely heralded of late. Consider the results of a recent study, comparing national samples of campus clergy and parish ministers:

> Relative to parish ministers, campus clergy are more liberal in their attitudes toward labor unions and the UN, more critical of their denominations, more favorable toward ecumenical affairs, better educated, and have wider interests. These data are convincing. . . . The differences are maintained across ten denominations and, within denominations, across three age groups.[2]

Or, if one's taste runs to more qualitative evidence, here is the gut corroboration of one of the nation's most popular radicals, Paul Goodman:

> If one wants to talk for real, in terms of happiness and duty, about sexual morals or the drug laws, it is useless to go to the school psychologist . . . but one might have a meeting at the existentialist chaplain's. I never expected to see the day when the church would be the leader in "immorality"! . . . What happens to medicine in present urban conditions? What is the ethical and community responsibility of civil engineers? What is the responsibility of lawyers to change the laws under which they practice, so that justice may be done? . . . Does it make a difference to physics that the bulk of money for research and development is military? It is an amazing and melancholy fact of

American universities that such essentially *professional* questions are likely to be discussed, if at all, in the YMCA or Hillel, not in the departments or divisions. . . . It is not surprising to find a young campus chaplain providing a forum for political action, funds for social action in the neighborhood, and facilities for the student-initiated "free university." On the other hand, I doubt that the ministers are as useful as they used to be in providing conventional pastoral services like personal counseling, solace or spiritual guidance.[3]

All of this suggests a rare agreement between radical social philosophy and sociology, or between Paul Goodman and survey research in any form. This would seem to be a consensus that defies rupture; but, alas, no. Peculiarly enough, a dissenting voice comes from within the church itself and from a man whose popular following on the college campus rivals Goodman's own and for many of the same reasons. Here is what Harvey Cox has to say about campus religious groups in his religioliterary "happening," *The Secular City:*

As the enterprise grew, more and more hours had to be spent in coordinating the relationships between the various foundations and in clearing schedules. As with the churches in most home towns, the complex of foundations presented a picture of lively activities and full bulletin boards. But the activities were all going on inside a special world existing *next* to the world of the university. The whole purpose of the movement to the university had been lost by the fashioning of what amounted to a "home away from home" (it was even so-called on some campuses) where students with the same denominational brand-mark could establish a set of relationships with each other at the expense of the relationships offered within the university itself.

Naturally, for many the fellowship of the foundation house served as a compensation. Those who didn't make the campus newspaper staff could turn the mimeo handle for the Wesley Foundation News. Those who could not meet the financial or genealogical standards of fraternities could find solace on a Saturday night at a Baptist doggie-roast. But the whole notion of witness and service *within* the university was totally lost. Meanwhile harried foundation directors were kept busy attending . . . conferences, coordinating their work with that of the other foundations, counselling for hours on end, keeping a roof on a fifty-thousand dollar building, and explaining to denominational officials why only 9 per cent of the Presbyterian preference students ever participated in the program.[4]

How, then, to account for all these different conclusions? Is one "side" right and the other wrong? Are both sides talking about quite different aspects of the same general phenomena? The issues are clearly urgent, not only for the church but perhaps more so for the university and for the sociology of both religion and higher education. It was precisely in order to answer these questions and to confront the debate with data that the present study was launched.

THE RESEARCH DESIGN

Perhaps the most obvious possibility for reconciling the implicit dispute between Hammond, Mitchell, and Goodman, on the one hand, and Harvey Cox, on the other, is that both sets of generalizations are accurate, but refer to different groups in different settings. One may have primary reference to the large, "quality" university, while the other may have the smaller, denominational college in mind; one may refer largely to the traditional lairs of religious liberalism (such as Unitarians or Hillel) while the other may be aimed at the more traditional, yea even conservative groups, ranging from the Lutherans of various callings to the Inter-Varsity Christian Fellowship.

Our research design sought to take these possibilities into explicit account. For one thing, it involved administering the same questionnaire on several different campuses representing several different types of schools. The total sample includes places as diverse as the Universities of Wisconsin and Michigan, on the one hand, and Alma College, on the other, filling in the continuum with Wayne State and Kalamazoo. Thus, we have data on large, nationally reputed universities as well as a so-called streetcar university, and both denominational and nondenominational small colleges. It is true that all these schools are concentrated in Wisconsin and Michigan. But this was calculated, since funds prohibited a national sample of either schools or students, and we compromised by holding region constant. Note, however, that the foregoing is partly academic and partly misleading for purposes of the present paper. Here we shall focus solely on data from the University of Wisconsin. Because of lack of time and because of our greater knowledge of the Madison "scene," we decided to develop a model of analysis with the Wisconsin data and then apply it later to the other campuses for their similarities and differences.[5]

But in addition to representing different types of schools, we also sought to represent different types of religious groups in each. For example, fifteen widely diversified campus religious groups are represented in the Wisconsin sample, ranging from Quakers to the Evangelical United Brethren, from

Unitarians to the Inter-Varsity Christian Fellowship, and from the ALC-ULC Lutherans to the Lutherans of the Missouri and Wisconsin Synods. Yet it took a peculiar sample, indeed, to turn up sufficient numbers in any of the fifteen campus religious groups to sustain statistical analysis. Cox's suggestion that "only 9 per cent of the Presbyterian preference students ever participated in the program" is roughly accurate not only for Presbyterians but for most other denominations as well. This means that a purely random sample of the student body as a whole would be hard pressed to turn up an analyzable number of "religious-niks," even if the members of all religious groups were combined together. Clearly it was necessary to use a variation of "quota sampling" and to sample from within the campus religious groups themselves. In fact, in a given group the number of participants was so small that sampling was eschewed altogether in favor of taking the entire "population" of members, less the inevitable attrition in response rate.[6]

Table 6-1 shows the results of this procedure. The fifteen religious groups are ordered in terms of the number of respondents from each. Since we sought to stay as close as possible to their actual proportionate strength, their relative sizes in the sample are a good reflection of their relative sizes in reality, although the very smallest groups are somewhat overrepresented because of our attempt to get at least a minimally stable number for analysis.

TABLE 6-1

*Sample Distribution of 15 Campus Religious*
*Groups at the University of Wisconsin*

| | |
|---|---:|
| Catholics (Newman Club) | 207 |
| Methodists | 123 |
| Hillel | 114 |
| Wisconsin Synod Lutherans | 113 |
| Presbyterians | 102 |
| ALC-LCA Lutherans | 99 |
| Episcopalians | 96 |
| Missouri Synod Lutherans | 72 |
| Northern Baptists (ABC) | 43 |
| United Church of Christ | 41 |
| Southern Baptists | 29 |
| Quakers | 29 |
| Evangelical United Brethren | 28 |
| Inter-Varsity Christian Fellowship | 27 |
| Unitarians | 18 |

In general, it is no surprise to learn that, in a heavily Catholic and Lutheran state, the state university's largest religious group is the Catholic Newman Club with 207 sample members, unless one sums all three of the Lutheran groups for a total of 284 respondents. The Methodist, Hillel, Presbyterian, and Episcopalian groups are also large. On the other hand, the Unitarians, Quakers, and Southern Baptists are among the smaller groups.

Note, however, that this is not a final estimate of the sizes of these groups in our final over-all sample. Some groups were later augmented slighly through the second stage of our sampling—a sampling of the Wisconsin student body as a whole. Such a sample was clearly crucial if we were to do more than simply compare religious groups with each other, and we were at least as concerned with the question of who does not belong to any group.

Here, too, our sampling procedure was somewhat unorthodox. The conventional technique for such purposes is to draw an elegant sample in which every student has the same probability of being included and then to mail out questionnaires with several successive waves of follow-up notices, ranging from thinly veiled threats to the most gentle cajolings. And yet orthodoxy is expensive in research as elsewhere; moreover, even though the sample is elegant at the point of design, it may be haphazard, indeed, after a slim and possibly biased response rate plays hob with the original calculations. In our case, we were able to save money without sacrificing much ultimate precision by sampling classrooms instead of students. Using a number of classes scattered strategically throughout the curriculum, we gave out the questionnaires one day and collected them during the next few ensuing class meetings. Not only was this cheaper but it allowed us to ask for the students' co-operation more directly and personally than would be the case with post cards in a mass mailing. Nor is co-operation always quickly forthcoming for a questionnaire that asks for more than an hour's time directed to questions that are often more embarrassing than engaging. In any event, this procedure yielded a respectable response rate of some 67 per cent and a sample of 1,288 Wisconsin students whose distribution compares surprisingly well with the actual population on such things as age, sex, grade-point average, and major.

At this point it is tempting to report a series of comparisons between the two different samples in order to answer the question: How does the campus religious community differ from the student body as a whole on matters ranging from Christ to Vietnam, from conceptions of sin to views of the civil rights movement, and from views of the university itself to perspectives on moral relativism and ethical self-fulfillment? Such comparisons are perfectly feasible with the data at hand, but they are of doubtful utility. While it is certainly meaningful for various purposes to talk of a general sample of the students, it is just as certainly without meaning to talk about any "campus religious community" as a whole. Indeed, one objective of this research is to explode such stereotypes rather than pander to them. Before we begin to compare campus religious members with any other segment of the university community, we had best not overlook the enormous variation that exists among the religious groups themselves.

WHICH CAMPUS RELIGIOUS COMMUNITY?

Because it is not easy to analyze fifteen distinct religious groups in terms of a number of complex variables operating simultaneously, it is first necessary to reduce the fifteen to more manageable and more parsimonious clusters. This immediately raises the question of the basis on which the reduction should occur. One possibility is suggested in Table 6-2. There the fifteen groups are ranked in order of the percentage of their sample members who chose the most orthodox, most traditional conception of God from among eight possible statements they were asked to consider. Thus, 97 per cent of the Southern Baptists chose the statement: "I have faith in God as

TABLE 6-2

*Proportion of Various Wisconsin Campus Religious Groups Opting for the Most Traditional Conception of God*

| | |
|---|---|
| Southern Baptists | 97% |
| Inter-Varsity Christian Fellowship | 93 |
| Missouri Synod Lutherans | 86 |
| Evangelical United Brethren | 86 |
| Wisconsin Synod Lutherans | 81 |
| Catholics | 81 |
| ALC-LCA Lutherans | 57 |
| Episcopalians | 49 |
| Methodists | 45 |
| Northern Baptists (ABC) | 42 |
| Presbyterians | 40 |
| United Church of Christ | 26 |
| Hillel | 14 |
| Quakers | 7 |
| Unitarians | 0 |

a person who is concerned about me and all mankind and to whom I am accountable," but only 81 per cent of the Catholics, 57 per cent of the ALC-LCA Lutherans, 45 per cent of the Methodists, 26 per cent of the sample from the campus outlet of the United Church of Christ, and a flat 0 per cent of the campus Unitarians. If statistical variance makes the world go round, this should set it spinning.[7] Moreover, it may be worth noting that 34 per cent of the general student sample opted for this most traditional statement, a figure that is higher than four of the nominally "religious" groups represented in the table and not much different from several others.

But as captivating as Table 6-2 may be, it has its limitations as a basis for reducing the various religious groups into a smaller set. For one thing, the question itself has only limited validity and does not begin to tap the several dimensions of religious belief that we shall investigate later. For another, belief itself should be a *dependent* variable in the study and not built into the *independent* variable. In seeking an independent variable for categorizing groups, it makes much more sense to consider the kinds of dimensions that were implicit in the quotations with which we began this chapter. Neither Hammond and Mitchell, Goodman, nor Cox were talking primarily about beliefs per se. They all were focusing more on a kind of organizational style, and their expressed differences were over the extent to which the campus ministry was attempting to break new ground, cultivate new relationships, and serve an emancipating function for the church while nurturing the deviants within it. Clearly not all of our fifteen religious groups have been radical to the same extent in shaping and pursuing their programs. What are some of the differences between them?

Consider the following seven statements to which members of the groups were asked to respond on a six-point scale ranging from strongly agree to strongly disagree:

1. Many campus ministers are too radical in their political and social views.

2. A major purpose of campus religious groups ought to be to keep students from being swept off their feet by forces of secularization in the university.

3. My campus religious group is very receptive to change and experimentation.

4. It is important for the minister and students in a campus religious group to reach close agreement on religious issues.

5. My campus clergyman encourages students to use their intellectual training to criticize and reform the church.

6. There are strong inhibitions in my group about expressing religious doubt.

7. The campus minister should seek to bring his students a program as nearly as possible like that of the students' home church.

None of these statements is directly related to religious beliefs in the sense of doctrinal orthodoxy, but each is crucially involved in the dispute that was joined at the chapter's outset. If we can meaningfully differentiate clusters of groups on this type of dimension, we shall be able later to explore both the extent and the consequences of both the "new" and the "old" forms of the "campus ministry."

Table 6-3 provides this sort of delineation in compact form. Now, instead of ranking religious groups in terms of their percentage of orthodox conceptions of God, we have ranked them in terms of their liberal conception of the campus ministry itself.[8] The percentage refers to a mean score, the average proportion reporting either strong or moderate agreement with the "liberal" version of each of the seven previous statements (that is, agreement with statements 3 and 5; disagreement with statements 1, 2, 4, 6, and 7). Once again there is considerable variance. At the top, the Unitarians, ALC-LCA Lutherans, Quakers, Northern Baptists, and UCC show over half of their sample representatives holding a "radical" conception of the ministry. At the

TABLE 6-3

*UW Religious Groups Ranked According to Proportion of Members Holding a Radical Conception of the Campus Ministry*

| | $\overline{x}$ |
|---|---|
| Unitarians | 72.0% |
| ALC-LCA Lutherans | 55.0 |
| Quakers | 55.0 |
| Northern Baptists (ABC) | 54.7 |
| United Church of Christ | 53.9 |
| Presbyterians | 49.8 |
| Methodists | 45.1 |
| Hillel | 44.5 |
| Catholics | 36.3 |
| Episcopalians | 34.4 |
| Evangelical United Brethren | 34.4 |
| Missouri Synod Lutherans | 31.1 |
| Inter-Varsity Christian Fellowship | 28.3 |
| Southern Baptists | 23.4 |
| Wisconsin Synod Lutherans | 11.7 |

other extreme, such a conception characterizes less than a third or roughly one-fourth among the Missouri Synod Lutherans, the Inter-Varsity Christian Fellowship, and the Southern Baptists and only slightly more than one-tenth of the Wisconsin Synod Lutherans. Now, it is true that if one compares Table 6-3 with the previous Table 6-2 concerning conceptions of God, the rank-order correlation would be very high, indeed. At the same time, there are some notable changes in position between the two rankings (for example, Hillel, ALC-LCA Lutherans); and, as we shall see later, the relationship between the style of the campus ministry and specific religious belief depends to some extent on the particular belief in question.

Meanwhile, Table 6-3 does make sense in its own terms. Not only does it provide a good distribution along a crucial dimension but the distribution jibes well with our own impressions from less formal interviewing and observations on a campus with which we have been able to maintain personal touch throughout the study.[9] On the basis of both hard and soft data, then, it is justifiable to divide the local religious community into five basic groups. The first two are the *Catholic* and *Hillel* groups, respectively, since it seemed advisable to hold them distinct, whatever their scores on any variables. The next three groupings are the *Liberal Protestants* (Unitarians, ALC-LCA Lutherans, Quakers, Northern Baptists, United Church of Christ, and the YMCA, not a separate group for purposes of the analyses above), the *Moderate Protestants* (Presbyterians, Methodists, and Episcopalians),[10] and the *Conservative Protestants* (Evangelical United Brethren, Missouri and Wisconsin Synod Lutherans, Southern Baptists, and the Inter-Varsity Christian Fellowship).

The question now is, how do these five groups differ from each other on a host of religious, political, and educational issues? Further, how do these groups individually differ from a sixth category, our general sample of the Wisconsin student body, including its own realistically small proportion of those who are involved in campus religious activities?[11]

THE SIX RELIGIOUS COMMUNITIES COMPARED

The basic virtue of any questionnaire that requires more than an hour to complete is that it provides a wealth of information. But wealth can always become an embarrassment of riches, so this study presents only the most representative data to avoid stranding the reader in drifts of statistical snow. Here we shall seek to describe the similarities and differences among the six basic clusters delineated above. The description will cover the three basic domains of religion, politics, and education. Throughout this section our objective is to provide more of a feel for the data than an explanation of them.

Consider the strictly religious domain first. As a preliminary, it may help to discuss the phenomenon of religious change and locate our student respondents with respect to their religious past. Earlier Table 6-2 offered a fillip concerning conceptions of God. It presented the full percentages choosing the most orthodox view of God from among seven alternative conceptions. Table 6-4 offers two twists on those results. For one thing, of course, it no longer compares fifteen groups, but only six, including Catholics, Conservative Protestants, Moderate Protestants, Liberal Protestants, Hillel, and the students at large. A second change concerns the first and third rows of percentages in the table. Not only did we ask the respondents' conception of God at the moment, but we also asked them to estimate the conception they had held at age thirteen. Thus, the first row indicates the proportions who felt they had held the most orthodox view of God at that time; the second row presents current percentages of orthodoxy; and the third row offers the differences between the two as a rough measure of change itself.

It makes little difference whether one considers conceptions now or at age thirteen in terms of ranking the groups themselves. Indeed, this table establishes a pattern that will be more or less consistent for all but a few of the religious variables to follow. The Conservative Protestants and Catholics are roughly similar at one end, as are the Liberal and Moderate Protestants in the middle and the general sample of students and the Hillel respondents at the other end of the continuum. It should surprise no one that there has been a drop-off of orthodox conceptions since the age of thirteen, one that is

TABLE 6-4

*Percentage Opting for Most Orthodox Conception of God*
*Now and at Age Thirteen Among the Six Campus*
*Comparison Groups*

|  | Catholic | Conserv. Prot. | Moderate Prot. | Liberal Prot. | Hillel | Students at Large |
|---|---|---|---|---|---|---|
| % Orthodox at age 13 | 89 | 85 | 70 | 73 | 38 | 60 |
| % Orthodox now | 73 | 90 | 43 | 49 | 12 | 29 |
| % Difference | -16 | +5 | -27 | -24 | -26 | -31 |

excepted only among the Conservative Protestants and generally ranges from 19 percent among the Catholics to a high of 31 percent among the general sample. Note, however, that the variance between the groups increases over time. That is, the differences in the orthodox percentages are greater for current conceptions of God than for estimated conceptions at age thirteen.

And yet Table 6-4 provides only a crude measure of religious change. For one thing, it reports changes in aggregate percentages rather than change based on analyses of the actual individual respondents. For another, one's conception of God is only part of one's "religion." Table 6-5 offers data of a different sort concerning religious change. Here the issue is religious *influence,* and here the respondents themselves were asked to estimate the change directly. We asked each member of the study: "How has the influence of religious faith in your life changed since you entered college or in the last few years?" The table indicates the proportion of each group indicating that religious influence had increased, remained about the same, or decreased. Apparently a first-century orthodox conception of God is hardly a precondition for religious influence. Although every group in Table 6-4 had reported a decline in orthodoxy, all but two groups in Table 6-5 have their highest percentages in the category of increasing religious influence. Still, the six groups again break into three clusters. More than half of both the Catholics and the Conservative Protestants report an increase; this is true of almost as many of the Moderate and Liberal Protestants; but it characterizes only about one-quarter of the Hillel and general student samples. And yet if one looks at the percentage reporting decreasing religious influence, the only significantly different groups are the Conservative Protestants at one end and the wider student sample at the other. It is true, however, that the Hillel joins

TABLE 6-5

*Estimated Change in Religious Influence*
*During College among the Six Groups*

|  | Catholic | Conserv. Prot. | Moderate Prot. | Liberal Prot. | Hillel | Students at Large |
|---|---|---|---|---|---|---|
| Increasing influence | 53 | 62 | 48 | 48 | 29 | 23 |
| About the same | 15 | 21 | 23 | 23 | 38 | 35 |
| Decreasing influence | 31 | 17 | 29 | 29 | 33 | 42 |

the general sample in reporting a higher percentage of decreasing than increasing influence. These two groups may seem to support allegations concerning the secularizing effect of the university; yet even here, a decrease in religious influence accounts for much less than half of the respondents in each case.

The next five variables pertain for the most part to current religious behavior and beliefs without any explicit reference to change. Still, the first four of these comparison variables are more complex in their derivations. Earlier we mentioned that a wealth of data could become an embarrassment of riches for any given study and that one way to avoid this is simply to report selectively. Another source of parsimony is to try to reduce the domain of questionnaire items to several key scales which combine items according to their mutual and overlapping referents. If the scale is "reliable," it allows for more confident inferences, because the inferences are derived from the responses to several different questions rather than any single item. If the scales are "valid," they help us to determine the underlying dimensions that actually exist in the data and, hopefully, in the world as well. In our case, we have relied on "factor analysis" as a scaling procedure. More specifically, we set aside groups of questions concerning religion that we thought *should* cluster statistically with one another. Factor analytic techniques involve rotating the matrix of correlation coefficients between the items in these groups and determining (a) whether there is a single common factor that is stable and statistically powerful and (b) how that factor is defined in terms of the correlations of the specific items with the underlying dimension.

Consider, for example, what we have termed the factor of "Devotionalism and Religious Adherence." Originally, we submitted some ten items for analysis—items that we thought should cluster around the central theme of what Charles Glock has termed the "ritualistic" aspect of religion.[12] The factor analysis indicated, however, that only three of these items were related sufficiently closely to describe a common dimension. Put another way, the analysis told us that if we included the remaining items as well, we would be vulnerable to a great deal of statistical static since they would likely pull any results off in quite different directions, thus confusing any relationships we might want to establish with other variables, such as the continuum of the six basic religious groups.

Here, then, are the three questionnaire items which define the devotionalism factor with the items ranked in order of their contribution to the scale itself. For the first two, the respondent was asked to indicate his agreement or disagreement along a six-point scale, and the word "agree" in parenthesis after the item indicates that agreement produces a high score on the factor variable. The third item was more straightforward and gave the respondent a set of options ranging from every day to never.

1. Private prayer or meditation is an important activity in my daily life. (agree)

2. Reading the Bible is an important and frequent activity for me. (agree)

3. How often do you attend your church or synagogue *now?*

Table 6-6 relates the devotionalism scale to our six religious groups by presenting the percentage of each that scored "high," as opposed to "moderate" or "low," when the total distribution is broken into such categories on a roughly equal basis.

TABLE 6-6

*Devotionalism and Religious Adherence among the Six Religious Groups: Percentage Scoring High*

|  | Catholic | Conserv. Prot. | Moderate Prot. | Liberal Prot. | Hillel | Students at Large |
|---|---|---|---|---|---|---|
| % High Devotional Adherence | 76 | 87 | 56 | 57 | 19 | 30 |

Once again the Catholics and Conservative Protestants anchor the highly religious end of the scale, with the latter somewhat higher; the Moderate and Liberal Protestants stand undifferentiated in the middle; and the Hillel and general sample are at the other extreme, though it may be worth noting that adherence is less for the former than the latter. Almost one-third of the students at large score high in devotional adherence.

But devotional adherence hardly exhausts the dimensions of religion generally. Let us consider another that is featured in Glock's paradigm: *experiential religiosity.* Our own measure of the experiential is again a scale derived through factor analysis, and once again the final scale involves three items:

1. I have experienced the feeling that I was somehow in the presence of God. (agree)

2. I have experienced a feeling of being afraid of God. (agree)

3. I have experienced a feeling of being saved in Christ. (agree)

Table 6-7 presents the results, and they are startlingly similar to those for devotional adherence in Table 6-6, although the two sets of findings refer

TABLE 6-7

*Groups Compared on Percentage Scoring High
in Experiential Religiosity*

|  | Catholic | Conserv. Prot. | Moderate Prot. | Liberal Prot. | Hillel | Students at Large |
|---|---|---|---|---|---|---|
| % High on Experiential Religiosity | 78 | 83 | 48 | 54 | 11 | 30 |

presumably to quite different religious domains.[13] Again the Catholics and Conservative Protestants have much the highest percentages, and again the percentage scoring high for both groups is above 75 per cent. Once more, the Liberal and Moderate Protestants hold up the middle range together, with no meaningful differences between them. Finally, it is also true that the Hillel and students at large are closer to each other than to any other groups, with the latter again ranking "higher." At this point, however, it is important to indicate that it is difficult to score high on the over-all dimension if one indicates strong disagreement to "a sense of being saved in Christ." Hence the Hillel group is at an obvious disadvantage, and it is dangerous, indeed, to generalize from essentially "Christian" data to a finding that the Jews are necessarily low on experiential religion in general. Indeed, the same danger applies for some of the other scales as well.

Turning to religious belief in the doctrinal sense, Glock notes two relevant dimensions: one involving "religious knowledge" and the other concerned with "religious ideology." Our own measure of knowledge was conventional in asking the respondent to list the four New Testament Gospels. The results provide very little variance in that all six groups were highly knowledgeable, and since this dimension has always been highly related to education, the finding is hardly surprising among a group of university students. But religious ideology is another matter. It is plainly one thing to "know" and another to "believe." Moreover, it matters *what* one believes and to what degree. Here we shall report only the beginnings of a probe into the several dimensions of belief. After all, the present objective is to describe various religious subcommunities and not to plumb the complexities of religious belief on its own terms.

Let us begin with a dimension that is central to traditional Christianity, if not to Judaism. The following two items were combined to form a

"Christology" scale, though the factor analysis originally had six to work with, rejecting four as insufficiently related to the underlying theme:

1. Jesus was God's only Son, sent into the world by God to redeem me and all mankind. (agree)

2. Christ vicariously atoned for our sins by his death and resurection. (agree)

Clearly high agreement with these items and a high score on the resulting scale verges on fundamentalism. Hence, the pattern shown in Table 6-8 includes very little that is not predictable. Here, as before, the six categories can be sorted into three clusters. The general sample and the Hillel groups are at the low end of the continuum; indeed, it is validating to find that only one rebellious Hillel respondent scores high on the Christocentric measure. Moving to the Liberal and Moderate Protestants, once again we find them similar, with only 32 per cent and 28 per cent, respectively, scoring high. Finally, the Catholics and Conservative Protestants hold up the fundamentalist end of the scale, with 55 per cent and 76 per cent each. Although there is a substantial difference of 21 per cent between the two groups here, it is a difference that should be expected for this particular belief dimension.

TABLE 6-8

*Groups Compared on Percentage Scoring High
in Traditional Christology*

|  | Catholic | Conserv. Prot. | Moderate Prot. | Liberal Prot. | Hillel | Students at Large |
|---|---|---|---|---|---|---|
| % High on Christology | 55 | 76 | 28 | 32 | 1 | 17 |

It is worth noting that the results in Table 6-8 are highly similar to those obtained for traditional conceptions of an afterlife and antievolutionalism, though we shall not present these findings here. But what if one strays beyond such fundamentalist issues to matters in doubt and turbulence among the liberals and moderates themselves? One such issue involves the crucial question of theological "justification." What is necessary to manifest oneself in the sight of God? Is it doctrinal and ritual compliance or ethical behavior and the kind of life one lives that counts? The latter emphasis is increasingly important among moderate theologians who are trapped in the paradox that faith cannot exist without ethical concern, but do not want to subscribe to a works righteousness. On the other hand they also reject faith as being identified with doctrinal or ritual compliance, as is often the case among conservative theologians. Conservative Protestant theologians can easily reject "ethical justification" as man-centered idolatry. Catholics can easily endorse the importance of good works for justification. But the Moderate and Liberal Protestants find themselves in a more ambiguous position.

The following two items form a scale that pertains to this debate—a scale we have labeled "Moral Justification."

1. The way to be justified before God is to try sincerely to live a good life. (agree)

2. I think that all who live a good moral life are Christians. (agree)

TABLE 6-9

*Groups Compared on the Percentage Scoring*
*High on Moral Justification*

|  | Catholic | Conserv. Prot. | Moderate Prot. | Liberal Prot. | Hillel | Students at Large |
|---|---|---|---|---|---|---|
| % High on Moral Justification | 67 | 18 | 43 | 32 | 13 | 42 |

Table 6-9 offers the results in terms of the varying percentages scoring "high" on the dimension. Here Catholics have the highest percentage, while the Conservative Protestants and, of course, the Hillel group[14] have the lowest percentages. The general sample of respondents stands midway between the Catholics and the Conservative Protestants, and the same is generally true of the Liberal and Moderate Protestants. How, then, to interpret the findings? Actually, it is probable that the findings call for somewhat different explanations in each case. Thus, the high score of the Catholics represents a traditional Catholic view of salvation, but the differences between the Liberal and Moderate Protestants, on the one hand, and their Conservative brethren, on the other, may represent a radical departure from the standard Protestant view that salvation and justification require more than simply "faith alone" in the sense of doctrinal assent, but that faith involves ethical action and a style of life as well. Indeed, the position of the Liberal and Moderate Protestants may suggest their position that the church is no longer as important as it may have been in the past and that the label "Christian" is itself less important. For these liberals, the position may indicate that ethical activity is enough on its own terms, regardless of orthodox faith, ritual, or church membership. In short, for many of these people, religion may be politically authenticated.[15]

So far, then, we have seen that different campus religious styles and denominations do, indeed, differ on various dimensions of religiosity. They differ with respect to religious change, religious adherence, experiential religiosity, and various dimensions of religious belief. While in general it is true that Catholics and Conservative Protestants tend to cluster together, as do Liberal and Moderate Protestants, and Hillel members and the general student sample, this pattern does not hold up consistently. It matters which variables are chosen, particularly when one is considering the host of possible variables in the belief domain.

And yet purely religious correlates may be the least interesting in comparing the six religious subcommunities. Much of the rhetoric and dispute over the "campus ministry" has to do with its impact in political and educational affairs or, in Glock's terms, the "consequential dimension of religiosity." Certainly the campus has hosted wide-ranging debate concerning political and educational change during the 1960's. Where did the different Wisconsin religious groups stand on a few of the prominent issues as of the spring of 1965?

*Ethical Religiosity among the Six Comparison Groups*

|  | Catholic | Conserv. Prot. | Moderate Prot. | Liberal Prot. | Hillel | Students at Large |
|---|---|---|---|---|---|---|
| % Strongly Agree | 22 | 9 | 27 | 42 | 40 | 38 |

Consider first the three points of contention that virtually dominated campus political debate at the time. The respondents were asked to indicate their agreement or disagreement with the following statements:

1. I believe that a larger proportion of the Federal government's budget should be allocated to poverty, medicare, education, etc.

2. Negroes would be better off if they would take advantage of the opportunities that have been made available rather than spending so much time protesting.

3. The United States should try to initiate negotiations in an area like Vietnam and should avoid further military participation.

Table 6-10 presents the percentage of each group that strongly agreed with statements 1 and 3 and strongly disagreed with statement 2; that is, the strong "liberal" percentage in each case. Actually the table orders the three

TABLE 6-10

*Groups Compared on Percentage Strongly Liberal*
*on Poverty, Civil Rights, and Vietnam*

|  | Catholic | Conserv. Prot. | Moderate Prot. | Liberal Prot. | Hillel | Students at Large |
|---|---|---|---|---|---|---|
| % Liberal on Poverty | 44 | 31 | 38 | 43 | 73 | 54 |
| % Liberal on Civil Rights | 37 | 26 | 40 | 37 | 60 | 44 |
| % Liberal on Vietnam | 19 | 15 | 23 | 24 | 39 | 29 |

issues in terms of the decreasing popularity of a liberal position; that is, poverty is more "in" than civil rights, which is, in turn, more fashionable than opposition to the Vietnamese war.[16] Still, there are also differences among the six religious groups themselves. Predictably enough, the Hillel respondents are the most liberal on all three issues, while the Conservative Protestants are consistently the most politically conservative. More importantly, the general sample ranks second only to the Hillel group in liberalism. In comparing the Liberal Protestants, Moderate Protestants, and Catholics, the differences are slight and depend on the particular issue in question. All of this would seem to favor Cox's view and put a damper on the implication conveyed by Hammond and Mitchell and by Goodman. Compared to students generally, the Christian campus ministry seems considerably less radical, rather than more so.

But let us consider another dimension to the political debate, one that concerns political means rather than specific political ends. We asked each respondent to indicate his agreement or disagreement with the following: "If I felt strongly about a cause, I would be willing to participate in a public demonstration." Now, presumably this issue is somewhat closer to the different styles of campus ministry according to which the Protestant groups were clustered in the first place. Certainly one of the hallmarks of the "radical campus ministry" has been its position in the forefront of demonstrations on issues ranging from civil rights and Vietnam to student protest against university policies. One would expect pronounced differences here, with the Liberal Protestants especially prone toward demonstrations.

But Table 6-11 reveals that, while the predictable differences occur, they are not as large as those pertaining to the substantive political issues above. And again the Hillel respondents show the highest liberal percentages, with the general sample next. Moreover, there is once more little to choose between the Liberal Protestants, the Moderate Protestants, and the Catholics, although the Conservative Protestants are clearly the least willing of all to participate in such a political witness. Apparently the religious community as a whole, with the exception of Hillel, is not as likely to stand at the vanguard of demonstrations as some of its champions and detractors allege. Still, the question is hypothetical and should not be construed as a count on actual past behaviors.

TABLE 6-11

*Groups Compared on Percentage Willing to Participate*
*in Public Demonstrations on Issues*

|  | Catholic | Conserv. Prot. | Moderate Prot. | Liberal Prot. | Hillel | Students at Large |
|---|---|---|---|---|---|---|
| % Strongly Willing to Demonstrate | 50 | 38 | 51 | 48 | 62 | 54 |

Finally, in this political battery, let us turn to a question on political change that is analogous to our earlier data concerning religious change. Table 6-12 indicates that the overwhelming tendency for all six groups is to move in a self-estimated more liberal political direction. Very few, indeed, confess to becoming more "conservative," a word that was a political liability in 1965, close on the heels of Goldwater's defeat. Actually there are very few major differences between the groups themselves. While it seems surprising that the previously liberal general sample is closer to the Conservative Protestants in reporting a relatively low percentage of increasing liberalism, it may be that the general sample had less room to change toward liberalism. For this reason, the item as a whole is not very valid as a measure of basic political persuasion. Its value is only potentially great for comparisons *within* particular groups, as in the section to follow.

TABLE 6-12

*Self-Estimated Political Change during*
*College among the Six Groups*

|  | Catholic | Conserv. Prot. | Moderate Prot. | Liberal Prot. | Hillel | Students at Large |
|---|---|---|---|---|---|---|
| % More Liberal | 47 | 39 | 50 | 48 | 48 | 43 |
| % About Same | 39 | 46 | 36 | 41 | 41 | 43 |
| % More Conservative | 14 | 15 | 14 | 10 | 11 | 13 |

It is arguable, however, that campus religious differences should be less related to wider political issues than to issues concerning the campus itself and education more generally. Although it is true that the university has become a crucible for political protest, this involves a very small percentage of students. Although campus ministers are said to be politically engaged, they are also engaged in matters of education and educational policy, and their views on these more immediate matters may find a more receptive audience among their student parishioners.

Certainly one of the most heated issues concerning the university today involves *depersonalization* and the extent to which higher education has become a "factory" rather than a "community." To examine this, we constructed a scale based on the following four items:

1. How happy are you with contact with faculty at your college or university?

2. How "depersonalized" would you say education at your school is?

3. How happy are you with classroom vitality at your college or university?

4. (Do you agree that) there exist plenty of channels of communication between students and the administration?

A "high" score on this scale reflects a lack of happiness with faculty contact and classroom vitality, an estimate of high depersonalization, and skepticism concerning the channels of communication with the administration. Table 6-13 presents the percentage of each group who score high on the dimension. Surprisingly, perhaps, the differences between groups are relatively slight. Still, it is true that, once again, the Hillel respondents are somewhat more "liberal" as the term has been defined in this context, and the general sample is next, with the campus Christian groups bringing up the rear. Insofar as these differences are worth interpreting, what do they mean? Actually they may suggest at least two things that run counter to the radical portrait of the campus ministry. First, it may be that members of most religious groups are less intellectualized than other students, since the shibboleth of deperson-alization has greater currency among student intellectuals.[17] Second, it may be that members of campus religious groups are not those spurned by or spurning other campus organizations, but are precisely those who are more highly involved in secular as well as religious groups, thus reducing the perception of the university as impersonal and anomic. Let us examine these possibilities in order.

TABLE 6-13

*Groups Compared on Percentage Perceiving*
*High Depersonalization of the University*

|  | Catholic | Conserv. Prot. | Moderate Prot. | Liberal Prot. | Hillel | Students at Large |
|---|---|---|---|---|---|---|
| % High Deperson-alization | 50 | 38 | 51 | 48 | 62 | 54 |

First, it was possible to construct a scale of "General Intellectualism" from the following three items, the last of which should shock no one.

1. How important are political debate and activity on social issues to you?
2. How important are campus cultural opportunities to you?
3. I think of myself as an "intellectual."

TABLE 6-14

*Groups Compared on Percentage Scoring*
*High on Scale of General Intellectualism*

|  | Catholic | Conserv. Prot. | Moderate Prot. | Liberal Prot. | Hillel | Students at Large |
|---|---|---|---|---|---|---|
| % High on Intel-lectualism | 47 | 32 | 46 | 52 | 64 | 49 |

Table 6-14 compares our six groups in terms of the percentage scoring high on intellectualism. The results are mixed in their corroboration of the speculation above. The Hillel sample is clearly the highest-ranking group on this dimension; that is, the most "intellectual."[18] But save for the low-ranking Conservative Protestants, there are no other important differences. Perhaps the lack of difference may be important in itself. The finding that the Liberal and Moderate Protestants are no more intellectual than the Catholics or the students at large is surely surprising in light of their statements of style and general intent.

Interestingly enough, however, a more corroborative pattern obtains with respect to the purposes of a college education. We offered the respondents a variety of purposes from which to choose the one that best represented their own view. Table 6-15 presents the proportion of each group that chose what was perhaps the *least* intellectual response: "(to) develop skills and techniques which are directly applicable to my intended career." Here the Conservative Protestants lead the way by a wide margin; fully 46 per cent regard the university experience in this light. At the other end, only 20 per cent of the general student sample and 24 per cent of the Hillel group take this approach, with the larger percentage of their answers scattered between such alternative responses as "providing a basic general education and appreciation of ideas" or "helping to develop meanings and values for my life." On this measure, then, it appears that even the Moderate and Liberal Protestants are, indeed, less intellectually inclined. Of course, it could be argued that the Conservative Protestants are largely skill-oriented because of their lower-status background—any other use of college would be a luxury which their mobility aspirations begrudge indulging.

TABLE 6-15

*Groups Compared in Percentage Opting for Development of Career Skills as Basic Meaning of College Education*

|  | Catholic | Conserv. Prot. | Moderate Prot. | Liberal Prot. | Hillel | Students at Large |
|---|---|---|---|---|---|---|
| % Skill- and Career- Oriented | 32 | 46 | 32 | 30 | 24 | 20 |

But if this is the explanation, why is it that the Moderate Protestants, who have much higher-status backgrounds, have not much greater intellectual bent?[19] One suspects that much of the Conservative Protestants' penchant for a skill orientation is due to their interpretation of the church as *the* source of meaning, while the university is assigned a quite different role. It is for this group in particular that there remains an explicit rivalry between the church and the university experience. The rivalry is less explicit, if in some cases only slightly less present, for the other religious groups.

Now let us consider the second possible implication of our finding that campus religious groups in general tend to perceive less educational depersonalization than the general sample. The finding may mean that members of religious groups have found an agreeable social niche that reduces their perception of depersonalization accordingly. These may be the people who are not alienated at all, but are instead more fully immersed in the networks of student activities and social contacts. We asked our respondents several questions that bear on this important issue. The two below combine to form a scale having to do with "Happiness with Social Life":

1. How happy are you with extracurricular activities at your school?
2. How happy are you with the social life of your college or university?

TABLE 6-16

*Happiness with Social Life among the
Six Comparison Groups*

|  | Catholic | Conserv. Prot. | Moderate Prot. | Liberal Prot. | Hillel | Students at Large |
|---|---|---|---|---|---|---|
| % Happy | 49 | 51 | 56 | 46 | 44 | 44 |

Table 6-16 indicates that happiness in this regard is, indeed, slightly more characteristic of the Moderate and Conservative Protestants as well as the Catholics. The Hillel and the students at large are again joined together at the other extreme. It is true that the extremes are not widely divergent statistically, but perhaps the major import of the table is what it *fails* to show. Certainly it fails to show that members of campus religious groups feel themselves to be socially deprived, although this has been a prominent theme in some of the speculative literature concerning them.

There is, however, an alternative possibility. One can argue that the reason the more traditional religious groups report a higher degree of happiness is precisely *because* of their religious involvement. That is, they might still be less engaged in secular fraternal and social organizations on campus, and their happiness may reflect the socially compensating function of the religious groups themselves. Table 6-17 considers this possibility and offers preliminary reasons for rejecting it. It compares the various subcommunities on the proportions who are members of fraternities or sororities and finds the highest proportion of members occurring among the Moderate Protestants (those reporting the highest "happiness" in Table 6-16 above), with the lowest proportion of members among the general sample. It is true that the Conservative Protestants are relatively happy despite a low percentage of fraternity involvement (perhaps a function of their low social class), but, by and large, campus religious involvement seems more compatible with secular social involvement than with campus intellectualism or politicization. It is worth noting on the latter score that it is not true that members of the religious groups are more prone to belong to every sort of campus group. Without presenting a formal table, the percentage belonging to a campus civil rights group (and they were many and large on the Wisconsin campus at the time of the study) goes from 35 per cent among the general sample to 30 per cent among the Hillel, and then to 14 per cent among the Liberal Protestants, 9 per cent among the Conservative Protestants.

TABLE 6-17

*Proportion of Fraternity and Sorority*
*Members among the Six Groups*

|  | Catholic | Conserv. Prot. | Moderate Prot. | Liberal Prot. | Hillel | No Affil. |
|---|---|---|---|---|---|---|
| % Fraternity Members | 29 | 18 | 26 | 31 | 21 | 25 |

This concludes our descriptive profile of the six campus subcommunities on matters ranging from the religious to the political, educational, and social. But note that the word "descriptive" should be emphasized. Throughout this section we have alluded to several alternative explanations of the findings. It should certainly be problematic as to the extent to which the differences between the groups are attributable to what goes on within the groups themselves. It is clearly one thing to plot the distributions of various religious clusters on a host of variables, but quite another thing to try to isolate the impact of the groups themselves. The next section begins an attempt to discern that impact, or lack of it.

## NOTES

1. It is important to note that the phrase "campus radicalism" connotes more in the eyes of the beholder than in reality. We have no illusions that radicalism has pervaded any campus, even Berkeley, despite the spectacular evidence offered up by a tiny minority. The crucial point, however, is that people *think* of campuses as radical and often act on that basis; the campus ministers, or rather those in charge of dispatching campus ministers, may be no exceptions. There is, of course, a voluminous and growing literature on students, student values, and student politics. For an excellent review of this material, see Seymour Martin Lipset and Philip G. Altbach, "Student Politics and Higher Education in the United States," *Comparative Education Review*, Vol. X, No. 2 (June, 1966), pp. 320-349.

2. Phillip E. Hammond and Robert E. Mitchell, "Segmentation of Radicalism–The Case of the Protestant Campus Minister," *American Journal of Sociology*, Vol. LXXI, No. 2 (September, 1965), pp. 135-136. See also Hammond, *The Campus Clergyman* (New York: Basic Books, 1967). In one sense, this chapter offers a provisional test of a proposition that appears in the Hammond and Mitchell article. They argue that many campus ministers are shunted to the sidelines so as not to embarrass the main-stream church. However, they hypothesize that the ministers may have an effect on the church by having an impact on students who will become influential in the laity of the future. As we shall see, the hypothesis gets little support here, since there is so little evidence of any impact on the students themselves.

3. Paul Goodman, "Student Chaplains," *New Republic*, Vol. CLVI, No. 1 (January 7, 1967), pp. 29-31.

4. Harvey Cox, *The Secular City* (New York: Macmillan, 1965), pp. 222-223.

5. It is not our intention to argue that the University of Wisconsin is representative of any category of higher education. The important point is, however, that it has "represented" within it an enormous variety of students, programs, and values. Thus, the sheer size of the institution confers an advantage in allowing us to gain some sense of the campus religious spectrum at a place where it is free to range widely.

6. There was, of course, considerable variance in the response rates from the different religious groups. The returns ranged from a high of some 86 per cent to a low of 50 per cent, with an over-all average of 70 per cent. The Conservative Protestant groups had the highest over-all response; perhaps they interpreted the questionnaire as an opportunity for both witness and evangelizing. Certainly this was the case in our personal interviews with a former leader of a Conservative Protestant group. He interpreted our sociological interest as theological congruence and a conversion nibble. We are still receiving mail to this end–mail that provides better data for us than we do prospects for him.

7. Variance is so important to analysis, in fact, that it is itself the object of an implicit competition. A recent bid to vanquish the opposition was made by Charles Y. Glock and Rodney W. Stark, *Religion and Society in Tension* (Chicago: Rand McNally, 1965), in reporting denominational differences in the proportion who have doubts about matters of religious belief. The data in Table 6-2 provide even more variance, however, and so we hereby enter our claim to a title of no importance whatsoever. Indeed, it can be argued that the seeking of such titles leads to distortion. Certainly it should not be inferred from our data that all who do not subscribe to this orthodox conception of God are agnostics or atheists. The second most popular category by far was: "I don't believe in God as a person but I do believe in a higher power or being of some kind." This response was chosen by 46 per cent of Hillel, 37 per cent of the UCC and Presbyterians,

35 per cent of the Episcopalians and Methodists, 26 percent of the Northern Baptists, 24 per cent of the ALC-LCA Lutherans, 21 per cent of the Quakers, 14 per cent of the EUB, 11 per cent of the Unitarians, 10 per cent of the Catholics and Wisconsin Synod Lutherans, 4 per cent of the IVCF, 3 per cent of the Missouri Synod Lutherans, and 0 per cent of the Southern Baptists. The proportion of those choosing explicitly agnostic categories ranged from 38 per cent among the Unitarians to 20 per cent among the Hillel members, 11 per cent of the Methodists, and, of course, 0 per cent among the Southern Baptists and other fundamentalist groups. Moreover, the percentage of self-acknowledged atheists reaches peaks of 5 per cent among the undergraduate student sample as a whole, 3 per cent among the Hillel, and 2 per cent of the UCC group—hardly rampant irreligion.

8. This is basically the technique of contextual analysis whereby groups are categorized according to the aggregate responses of their members. An alternative would have been to categorize the groups according to the similarities and differences among their leaders, in this case the campus ministers themselves. To a very great extent, the two techniques converge in their results here. Still, the latter is fraught with danger, especially in this area, since we shall see later that the communication between the minister and his charges is not always effective.

9. For more qualitative data on the campus ministers, their ambitions and frustrations, see the concluding section of the next chapter.

10. The one instance in which our categorization of the groups departs from the rank order in Table 6-2 concerns the Episcopalians. The table would suggest that they should be treated no differently than the Evangelical United Brethren because the two have identical scores. And yet we have placed the Episcopalians in the Moderate Protestant category and the EUB's in the Conservative Protestant category. In large part, this is due to our qualitative interviews with the personnel involved. More specifically, it is because the Episcopalians had just experienced a change in campus ministers, whereby a very old and very traditional sort was replaced by a more adventuresome type who had just begun to make his impact felt.

11. Throughout this first section of the chapter, we have used our total sample, which includes a sprinkling of graduate students as well as a flood of undergraduates. The graduate students largely entered as members of the campus religious groups, and we felt it important to include them at a point where we are seeking merely to describe the groups with reference to each other and the campus at large. In subsequent sections, however, all graduate students will be deleted so that we can pursue more explanatory analysis with undergraduates alone.

12. Glock and Stark, op. cit. Charles Glock's five dimensions of religious belief have stimulated a great deal of research and advanced conceptualization considerably. For one illustration, see N. J. Demerath III, Social Class in American Protestantism (Chicago: Rand McNally, 1965), especially Chapters II and III.

13. Actually there is an artificial factor helping to produce this similarity between the data on devotional adherence and experiential religiosity. Whereas the questions pertaining to devotionalism are largely current in their time referents, the experiential items ask, "Have you ever . . . ?" Thus, the latter have more time to draw upon in inflating the percentage reporting yes.

14. The reason the Hillel respondents score so peculiarly low on the moral justification dimension is, of course, that one of the items indicates that "all who live a good moral life are Christians." Once again the Jews suffer from the Gentile bias in survey research. The least we can do is recognize it. In fact, the recognition will be more explicit in subsequent tables in the next two sections.

15. To illustrate more dramatically the theological peculiarities of the Liberal Protestants on the Wisconsin campus, consider the following table concerning what might be termed "ethical religiosity," or the percentage strongly agreeing that a "person's ethical concern and activity are the crucial measures of his religiousness and therefore even a strict atheist may be more religious than a devout churchgoer." Because this is only one item that exists in statistical left field without falling into a scale, we have not included it in the analysis in the text itself. Still, the pattern manifested among religious groups is quite different from that elicited by some of the more conventional doctrinal items we have already considered. Actually this should be gratifying and, in a sense, validating, since an emphasis on such "ethical religiosity" is characteristic of the Liberal groups.

16. To give some idea of the unpopularity of the antiwar position with respect to Vietnam during 1965, a survey by Professor Harry P. Sharp, director of the Wisconsin Survey Research Laboratory, indicated that students at the University of Wisconsin are generally *less* likely to oppose the war than is the population of the state as a whole and that opposition to the war is *directly* related to age, not inversely, as the rhetoric concerning campus radicalism would have us believe.

17. For empirical validation of the commingling of feelings of depersonalization and general intellectualism (as well as high academic performance), see Robert Somers' analysis of the composition of the Berkeley Free Speech Movement in Seymour Martin Lipset and Sheldon S. Wolin, eds., *The Berkeley Student Revolt: Facts and Interpretations* (Garden City: Doubleday, 1965). Somers' piece and the work of others offer seeming rebuttal to Kenneth Kenniston's linkage of alienation with political apathy and withdrawal. Unless it is simply a matter of defining alienation itself, study after study seems to indicate that alienation is related to political activity and that alienation is itself a more active than passive posture among students today. It is possible that this is new to the current student generation, since past students have suffered their alienation quietly, perhaps for lack of activist outlets. It is also possible, however, that the activism produces the alienation rather than vice versa. That is, students may join activist groups because of friendship attractions or the need for prestige or simply as a break in the academic routine. Once members of these groups, they *learn* to be alienated and are rewarded for manifesting it. Of course, this interpretation is as speculative as it is cynical. Indeed, from our view, the remarkable thing is not how many students are alienated, but rather how few, given the circumstances.

18. One hesitates to further the Jewish stereotype by reporting them to be more "intellectually inclined" or, in a word, "booky." Still, there is a very real sense in which the Jews gain rather than lose status in a secular university community precisely because of the stereotypes. They are one of the few religiocultural groups whose values and images are consonant with university values generally.

19. Note that throughout we have not controlled for standard background factors (such as age, sex, or social class) or educational factors such as academic performance, major, or campus living group. This is only partly because of lack of space and time. It is also because these variables are not highly related to either the differentiation among religious groups or the dependent variables at issue, and statistically they must be related to both to explain away the relationships between them. A subsequent study will explore these factors and their lack of impact in more detail in order to account for the seeming discrepancy between our own findings and others in the literature.

$$\approx 7 \ll$$

## THE STUDENT PARISHONER: RADICAL RHETORIC
## AND TRADITIONAL REALITY

### N. J. Demerath, III, and Kenneth J. Lutterman

*Part* II

DIFFERENTIAL INVOLVEMENT: A CRUCIAL INTERVENING VARIABLE

ONE of the constant challenges to sociology is to ascentain empirically the impact of various social groups. The job is not easy, for, of course, correlation rarely equals causation, and the sheer presence or absence of characteristics within a group may have nothing to do with the influence of the group itself. More close-cropped analyses are necessary to examine that influence, and this section offers a first approximation. Here the reasoning is that a group can be said to be more meaningful for its members insofar as there are differences between those who are highly involved, those who are only "somewhat" involved, and those who are eligible for involvement, but do not exercise the option. Of course, the question remains as to why the highly involved *are* distinctive, if this is the case. Is it because they were more distinctive to begin with and sought out involvement in these terms, or is it attributable to the group's direct impact on them? Later we shall examine both possibilities by introducing change itself through a comparison of freshmen, sophomore, junior, and senior cohorts on the various items, with campus religious involvement controlled. Meanwhile, the present section seeks to determine first what differences, if any, are associated with involvement itself, for what groups, and over what issues. Once these data are available, we can advance the question of "why" to a more sophisticated level.

The analysis requires several departures from that of the previous section. For example, there we were primarily concerned with describing some fundamental differences within the student body as a whole and hence did not bother to filter out the few graduate students in the sample on the grounds that they are contributors to the tone of the religious groups themselves and the campus as a whole. Here, however, our object is less descriptive and more explanatory. For this reason, we want to minimize the number of uncontrolled factors, and so we have excluded graduate students altogether. In addition, we have divided our pooled sample in somewhat different fashion than before. If one seeks to ascertain the impact of the Catholic Newman Club, for example, it is unreasonable to compare its members with all other undergraduates or with undergraduates who are not involved in campus religion at all, since both of these comparison groups would include Protestants, Jews, and the wholly nonreligious as well. A more reasonable strategy would be to compare Catholic members with Catholic nonmembers so that nominal Catholicism is held roughly constant, along with characteristics statistically associated with Catholicism such as relatively low social-class background, and relatively high incidence of previous parochial education. It is precisely the notion of holding such factors constant that is crucial. To do this, we must make comparisons *within* religious subcommunities rather than *between* them.

The result is indicated in Table 7-1. Each of the five religious subcommunities has been broken into three tiers: those who are *highly involved* in their campus religious group; those who are members, but only *somewhat involved*; and, finally, those who express a general religious preference and affiliation in the given denominational cluster, but are *not involved at all* in the local campus group. Note that our earlier category of "students at large" has disappeared, since all those expressing religious preferences have been allocated to the appropriate columns. Now the category represents only those undergraduates who not only lack campus religious affiliations but also lack religious preferences in general.

But, of course, Table 7-1 does more than merely illustrate a research design. It also tells us something about the relative proportions in each involvement category within each of the religious traditions. The Catholics have the lowest proportion of highly involved members, but the highest proportion of those "somewhat" involved: that is, those who frequent the more standardized and normatively compelling rituals. At the other extreme, the Conservative Protestants have the opposite portrait, with a very high proportion of those who are highly involved compared to those who are only somewhat involved—perhaps reflecting the all-or-nothing evangelistic charac-

TABLE 7-1

*Distribution of Campus Religious Subcommunities in Terms*
*of Relative Levels of Involvement in Religious Groups*

|  | Catholic | Conserv. Prot. | Moderate Prot. | Liberal Prot. | Hillel | No Relig. Pref. |
|---|---|---|---|---|---|---|
| No Involve-ment | 139 | 107 | 198 | 167 | 187 | 211 |
| Some Involve-ment | 195 | 97 | 205 | 120 | 159 | — |
| High Involve-ment | 67 | 170 | 118 | 85 | 44 | — |
| N | 401 | 374 | 521 | 372 | 390 | 211 |

teristic of the more sectlike wing of Protestantism. Note, however, that Table 7-1 deserves caution as well. While it is meaningful to talk about the relative proportions of those somewhat and highly involved, it is wholly meaningless to infer anything concerning the proportions of those who are not involved at all. We went out of our way to oversample members of campus religious groups. They thus loom much larger in this study than they do in reality. This, however, should not disturb us in what follows. We shall be more concerned with percentages than with absolute numbers, and in this respect we can derive comfort from the sheer cell sizes of Table 7-1. They are large enough to sustain our three-tiered analysis, and this was precisely our objective in forming the clustered categories of "Catholic," "Hillel," "Liberal Protestant," "Moderate Protestant," and "Conservative Protestant" in the first place. The clusters may be muddy theologically, but they help us to avoid a great deal of mere granulated sand statistically.

Let us go on, then, to within-group comparisons on the same religious dependent variables that were deployed in Chapter 6. Instead of presenting each variable in a separate table as before, Table 7-2 offers all the variables together in a "table d'hote," with only one exception. We have included only the percentages currently holding a first-century orthodox view of God, while omitting the estimated percentages at age thirteen. This is mostly because we are anxious to discuss college influences as opposed to those that occur in middle adolescence, and for the former we have left in the question of changing religious influence during college, presenting only the percentages undergoing increased influence in order to save space.

TABLE 7-2

*Differential Involvement in Campus Religious Subcommunities
Related to Measure of Religious Belief and Behavior*

| | | Catholic | Conserv. Prot. | Moderate Prot. | Liberal Prot. | Hillel | No Relig. Pref. |
|---|---|---|---|---|---|---|---|
| % Orthodox | (none) | 68 | 57 | 31 | 32 | 7 | 9 |
| Now | (some) | 70 | 68 | 35 | 33 | 10 | – |
| | (high) | 79 | 91 | 52 | 58 | 20 | – |
| % Increase | (none) | 30 | 26 | 28 | 27 | 13 | 17 |
| Religious | (some) | 50 | 43 | 39 | 36 | 19 | – |
| Influence | (high) | 61 | 76 | 59 | 62 | 61 | – |
| % High | (none) | 64 | 50 | 35 | 41 | 2 | 10 |
| Devotionalism | (some) | 70 | 70 | 41 | 40 | 10 | – |
| & Adherence | (high) | 91 | 96 | 75 | 67 | 50 | – |
| % High | (none) | 62 | 57 | 30 | 38 | (8) | 18 |
| Experiential | (some) | 75 | 70 | 37 | 41 | (6) | – |
| | (high) | 82 | 92 | 62 | 57 | (25) | – |
| % High | (none) | 42 | 48 | 16 | 20 | (0) | 5 |
| Christology | (some) | 51 | 55 | 20 | 21 | (0) | – |
| | (high) | 64 | 88 | 34 | 40 | (2) | – |
| % High Moral | (none) | 62 | 41 | 55 | 52 | (19) | 27 |
| Justification | (some) | 65 | 29 | 52 | 39 | (12) | – |
| | (high) | 76 | 11 | 38 | 31 | (12) | – |
| Mean % Difference | | 20.8% | 39.1% | 26.5% | 24.5% | 36.7%[a] | – |

a The Mean % Difference for Jews was computed without including the wholly inappropriate scales for Christology, Experiential Religiosity, and Moral Justification, since all three are Christian in their referents.

The table itself can be examined from a number of different vantage points in order to answer a number of different questions. First, whatever else the campus ministry may represent, there is very little doubt that it represents a bastion of roughly defined religious orthodoxy. Whether because the highly involved are seeking out a niche for their pre-established views or because the religious groups inculcate orthodoxy themselves, it is clear that, with few exceptions, the more highly involved are also the more traditional in their religious behavior and beliefs. The conclusion is available either from a perusal of each of the individual relationships or from the summary statistics in the table's bottom row. There each figure represents the mean absolute percentage difference between the highest and lowest involvement groups on all seven dependent variables.

These mean scores also allow a quick comparison of the different religious subcommunities on the extent to which high involvement is related to distinctively higher orthodoxy when compared to members of the same basic religious tradition who are not involved at all. The mean percentage is predictably highest for the Conservative Protestants at 39.1 per cent. Note, however, that insofar as the differences are at all significant between the remaining groups, the Hillel, Moderate Protestant, and Liberal Protestant subcommunities all seem to harbor slightly greater variety than the Catholics, and in that order. This may reflect the relatively high common denominator among Catholics, one that has been institutionalized at a greater level of orthodoxy than among Protestants or Jews and permeates deeper into the ranks of the nominally affiliated.

But note that at a more specific level it makes a difference what aspects of religion and religious belief are at issue. If one computes mean percentage differences across rows instead of down columns, it happens that the mean difference between the highly involved and the noninvolved is greatest for increasing religious influence (39.0 per cent), followed by devotional adherence (37.4 per cent), experiential religion (33.8 per cent, with Jews omitted), Christology (25.0 per cent, with Jews omitted), traditional conception of God (21.0 per cent), and, finally moral justification (20.5 per cent, with Jews omitted). Obviously, the perception of religious influence increasing in one's life is most likely among those who are highly involved in religious groups. This is probably one of the consequences or concomitants of participation in these campus religious groups; but on the other hand, this response and the others on devotionalism and religious experience may only be reflecting the selective nature of campus religion participants. Namely, only, or mainly, those who already have a "religious bent" prior to coming to college may be participating in campus religious groups. When the more specific and less general religious questions concerning theological interpretation are considered, there is less variance between the highly involved, somewhat involved, and uninvolved, although in all cases the most involved are most likely to support the most traditional conceptions of God, Christology, and justification. The fact that there is not more difference on these items along the continuum of involvement may be due in part to the attempt in most of the religious centers to offer more contemporary and less traditional views of these theological interpretations, whereas these questions deal with the most traditional kind of orthodoxy in each area.

So far we have discussed Table 7-2 in terms of the differences between the highly involved and those who are not involved at all in their campus religious affiliates. But what about those who are members, but only "somewhat involved"? This group may provide our most fascinating empirical clue yet concerning the structure of the campus ministry and its function in the wider university community. If we exclude the Jewish responses to the Christology, Experiential, and Moral Justification scales, this leaves us with 27 comparisons between levels of involvement within the religious groups. In 24 of these, the difference between the highly involved and somewhat involved is *greater* than the difference between the somewhat involved and those who are not involved at all. Moreover, if one sets a criterion that any percentage difference must be 8 per cent or greater to be considered significant,[1] fully 15 of the 27 comparisons between the somewhat involved and noninvolved would *not* be significant; that is more than half.

All of this suggests that, insofar as the campus ministry makes an impact or provides succor with reference to religion itself, its mission is largely restricted to the very small proportions who are highly involved in it. It also suggests, as most campus ministers have indicated repeatedly in personal exchanges, that there is, indeed, a substantial group that frequents the teas, lectures, and activities without manifesting much more "religion" than their noninvolved brethren. Yet one must be cautious here. The data are still tentative. And although the "somewhat involved" are not conspicuously religious in their rounds, they may gain other sorts of advantages, fulfilling a mission in other ways. Even if they should gain little, they certainly may contribute a great deal. More than one local campus minister is in the business of staging activities precisely designed to recruit the nonorthodox as leavening agents and as sources of debate for the highly involved nuclear core.

We have seen, then, that all our campus religious groups do seem to provide distinctive niches, at least where traditional variables are concerned and at least for the few students who claim to be highly involved participants. It is unclear whether the distinctiveness of the highly involved is due to the ministry's own tone and influence or to selective recruitment of members in the first place. This is an issue to be resolved in the next section, though both possibilities are compatible with the data thus far. But if this is the case for religious matters, what about political and educational issues?

Table 7-3 moves on to consider the political variables that were examined in the previous section. Like the preceding table, it presents a number of variables simultaneously. Here, there is only one change in format from their earlier appearance; just as we presented only the proportions undergoing increasing religious influence in Table 7-2, so Table 7-3 reports only the proportion becoming increasingly liberal from the question on political change.

TABLE 7-3

*Differential Involvement in Campus Religious Subcommunities*
*Related to Political Issues and Behavior*

| | | Catholic | Conserv. Prot. | Moderate Prot. | Liberal Prot. | Hillel | No Relig. Pref. |
|---|---|---|---|---|---|---|---|
| % Strongly | (none) | 47 | 37 | 40 | 47 | 71 | 64 |
| Liberal on | (some) | 43 | 34 | 36 | 42 | 73 | – |
| Poverty | (high) | 51 | 31 | 39 | 55 | 77 | – |
| % Strongly | (none) | 32 | 27 | 31 | 37 | 59 | 59 |
| Liberal on | (some) | 35 | 25 | 34 | 38 | 59 | – |
| Civil Rights | (high) | 40 | 29 | 47 | 47 | 59 | – |
| % Strongly | (none) | 15 | 13 | 19 | 22 | 43 | 49 |
| Liberal on | (some) | 18 | 16 | 17 | 27 | 42 | – |
| Vietnam | (high) | 22 | 15 | 29 | 29 | 30 | – |
| % Willing to | (none) | 50 | 49 | 40 | 54 | 58 | 64 |
| Demonstrate | (some) | 49 | 41 | 51 | 53 | 60 | – |
| Publicly | (high) | 54 | 39 | 55 | 52 | 70 | – |
| % Increasing | (none) | 51 | 30 | 44 | 43 | 42 | 51 |
| Liberalism | (some) | 50 | 48 | 50 | 45 | 46 | – |
| | (high) | 38 | 34 | 54 | 48 | 57 | – |
| Mean % Difference | | 7.2% | 4.8% | 10.4% | 6.4% | 8.0% | – |

For all the superficial similarities between Tables 7-2 and 7-3, there is a glaring difference in result. It is plain that levels of involvement in campus religion are simply much less related to political than religious values. Indeed, using our earlier standard of important differences—8 percentage points—only 11 of the 25 comparisons within the five religious subcommunities reveal significant differences: 8 of the 11 associate high involvement with greater liberalism, but 3 relate involvement to greater conservatism. All of this is reflected in the mean percentage differences in the bottom row of the table—means computed on the basis of absolute differences, regardless of the direction of effect. Even disregarding direction, it is clear that no subcommunity wields enough influence to make many waves in the political ocean lapping at the sides of the university. It may be surprising to note that the Moderate Protestants seem to exert the most impact, while the Liberal Protestants rank a poor fourth; but such comparisons make too much of too little. It is also true that civil rights appears to be the most affected political issue, with high involvement associated with somewhat more liberal inclination in three of the five subcommunities; but this, too, may be a precarious inference, since even here the differences are not large. A more consistent and generalizable finding is that those without religious preference are more liberal on almost every issue compared to almost every category of involvement within almost every religious group. Even religious groups which put a premium on liberal participation in political issues seem to have little effect. Despite the differences in rhetoric and style according to which we categorized the groups in the first place, there is very little variation among them when secular push comes to political shove.

All of this is reinforced with respect to the issues concerning education in Table 7-4. One might expect campus religious involvement to be more highly related to campus issues and wider campus social involvement, but this is not generally the case. The table offers 30 comparisons among the three basic levels of involvement, and of these, there are 19 for which the difference between the non-involved and the highly involved does not reach 3 per cent; of the 11 that do, the difference moves in a "liberal" direction for 8 and in a "conservative" direction for 3. Indeed, 4 of the 8 comparisons indicating a

TABLE 7-4

*Differential Involvement in Campus Religious Subcommunities*
*Related to University Views and Behavior*

| | | Catholic | Conserv. Prot. | Moderate Prot. | Liberal Prot. | Hillel | No Relig. Pref. |
|---|---|---|---|---|---|---|---|
| % Perceiving | (none) | 19 | 22 | 20 | 18 | 30 | 31 |
| High Deper- | (some) | 20 | 15 | 15 | 24 | 21 | – |
| sonalization | (high) | 31 | 14 | 17 | 22 | 20 | – |
| % High | (none) | 37 | 32 | 43 | 45 | 53 | 67 |
| Intellec- | (some) | 45 | 37 | 42 | 61 | 65 | – |
| tualism | (high) | 44 | 30 | 51 | 50 | 61 | – |
| % High on | (none) | 37 | 50 | 34 | 31 | 24 | 18 |
| Career Skills | (some) | 30 | 40 | 31 | 29 | 25 | – |
| as College | (high) | 27 | 46 | 31 | 29 | 20 | – |
| Purpose | | | | | | | |
| % Happy with | (none) | 49 | 49 | 56 | 48 | 46 | 42 |
| College | (some) | 48 | 50 | 55 | 42 | 41 | – |
| Social Life | (high) | 50 | 52 | 59 | 49 | 48 | – |
| % Members of | (none) | 26 | 26 | 37 | 22 | 28 | 13 |
| Fraternity | (some) | 28 | 22 | 31 | 25 | 21 | – |
| or Sorority | (high) | 14 | 15 | 21 | 31 | 16 | – |
| % Members of | (none) | 8 | 7 | 8 | 9 | 26 | 39 |
| Campus Civil | (some) | 8 | 8 | 10 | 16 | 34 | – |
| Rights Group | (high) | 12 | 3 | 11 | 21 | 32 | – |
| Mean % Difference | | 7.5% | 5.3% | 6.0% | 5.5% | 7.0% | – |

"liberal" tendency have to do with fraternity and sorority memberships. Earlier we saw that at the level of aggregate comparisons between groups, the religious subcommunities had somewhat higher rates of fraternity membership than did the sample of Wisconsin students at large. Here we find that we must specify that finding somewhat. The highly involved members of campus religious groups have *lesser* rates of fraternity membership than those who are only somewhat involved or not at all involved, with the exception of the Liberal Protestants. This seems to reinforce the interpretation that campus religious involvement may compensate for lack of involvement in other campus groups. But note that those with no religious preference have the lowest rate of fraternity membership in the table and that the interpretation has to be restricted with the religious groups themselves, since the highly involved are a very small minority in most cases, with the somewhat involved in a much larger group. This accounts for the earlier finding which combined the two.

And yet fraternity involvement is hardly the whole of Table 7-4. If one looks at other matters ranging from involvement in civil rights groups to perceived depersonalization, from general happiness with social life to general intellectualism and the purpose of college, no real patterns develop at all. Once again, the identity of the campus religious community seems distinctive only with reference to religious matters narrowly defined. On more secular dimensions, there is very little systematic variance between those who are involved and those who are not.

FROM FRESHMAN TO SENIOR: A COHORT ANALYSIS OF THE IMPACT OF CAMPUS RELIGION AND THE CAMPUS AT LARGE OVER TIME

So far, we may seem to have presented what is at best a paradox and at worst an inconsistency. That is, our initial descriptive analysis of campus clusters revealed consistent and meaningful differences among the various Wisconsin religious groups and between these groups and a general sample of students where religious, political, and educational values were at issue. But the section just completed indicates that differential involvement in campus religious groups has relatively little impact on political and educational issues and perhaps less impact than we might have expected on religious values and behaviors themselves. All of this seems peculiar: how are we to account for the difference between the groups if the groups themselves seem to have so little influence on their members? This section examines the data in yet another fashion, to explore at least a partial explanation of the conundrum. It is possible that the differences between religious groups are not the result of the groups' influence at all, but rather the result of "selective recruitment." Religious groups are different because they take on (or inherit) different types of students to begin with. Since neither the campus as a whole nor the religious groups in particular have much success in changing student values, the differences persist.

This, at least, is the hypothesis that prompted the analysis to follow. Here we maintained the previous sixfold categorization of campus religious subcommunities (Catholic, Conservative Protestant, Moderate Protestant, Liberal Protestant, Jewish, and No Religious Preference). Within each, we distinguished between those who reported no involvement at all in a campus religious group and those who were either somewhat or highly involved. Of course, it would have been desirable to maintain the distinction between the somewhat and highly involved themselves, since the latter group was especially distinctive in the previous section. However, this was precluded because the number of highly involved, especially among the Catholics, Liberal Protestants, and Hillel members, was too small to sustain meaningful analysis within the further distinction between freshmen, sophomores, juniors, and seniors. Table 7-5 presents the sample distribution for each cell of the multivariate procedure. With only a few exceptions, the cell sizes are large enough to support credible inferences. Let us turn to the inferences themselves.

TABLE 7-5

*Sample Distribution with Categories of Campus Religious*
*Subcommunities, Religious Group Involvement, and Year in School*

|  |  | Catholic | Conserv. Prot. | Moderate Prot. | Liberal Prot. | Hillel | No Relig. Pref. |
|---|---|---|---|---|---|---|---|
| Not involved | (freshmen) | 44 | 36 | 80 | 52 | 98 | 61 |
| at all in | (sophomores) | 30 | 36 | 49 | 53 | 48 | 52 |
| campus religious | (juniors) | 47 | 18 | 39 | 30 | 27 | 58 |
| group | (seniors) | 18 | 17 | 30 | 32 | 14 | 40 |
| Somewhat or | (freshmen) | 80 | 81 | 113 | 47 | 101 | 14 |
| highly involved | (sophomores) | 64 | 70 | 74 | 50 | 43 | 11 |
| in campus | (juniors) | 68 | 65 | 63 | 55 | 37 | 14 |
| religious group | (seniors) | 50 | 51 | 73 | 53 | 22 | 12 |

Table 7-6 relates the combination of factors noted above to four of our previous religiosity scales in providing the percentages with orthodox conceptions of God, high devotional adherence, high experiential religion, and high Christological beliefs. Note that we have omitted two of the earlier religious measures: the scale of moral justification and the question pertaining to changing religious influence. The former was deleted because, as we saw, its meaning varies from group to group and so it injects an unreliable note into any over-all conclusions. The question on religious change was dropped largely because of its floating base line; that is, freshmen are likely to answer it on the basis of their precollege experience and seniors on the basis of the college experience itself. Moreover, for an analysis of change in its own right, the question poses a problem of ceiling effects in that if one becomes liberal early, there is less room for later change in a liberal direction. Since both the base line and the ceiling are difficult to control, we decided to omit the item rather than contend with its ambiguity. In a similar spirit, we also deleted the Jewish scores on Christology and Experiential Religiosity, since reference to Christ occurs in both.

Turning then to the actual results of Table 7-6, the prevailing trend over the four years involves a decline of orthodoxy and ritual compliance. But the trend is not substantial (none of the separate subtables are statistically significant, let alone the whole), nor is it restricted to either those involved or noninvolved in campus religious groups. While it would be possible to compute summary statistics for the rows and columns of the table to show the mean rate of change and its direction for each of the independent variables with respect to each dependent variable, this would amount to spurious precision and cultivate the illusion of findings where no significant patterns exist.[2] The null evidence does not depend on every number being the same, but rather on a fluctuation of values that is more random than ordered. There is no major systematic change discernible here, and the table confirms an interpretation of differences in terms of initial recruitment rather than impact over time. Indeed, the lack of such impact on the part of both the campus religious groups and the campus at large allows the initial differences among freshmen to persist among sophomores, juniors, and seniors with virtually no alteration. While there is a slight tendency for traditional doctrine to decline over the four years, the tendency seems to apply universally rather than selectively. In fact, it may have less to do with any aspect of the university experience than with a process of maturation that characterizes most adolescents leaving the parental womb, whether for college, the military, or perhaps even the clerical life itself.

But if this is the case with religion, what about the political variables in our analysis? Table 7-7 provides the answer, and it is highly similar. Once again we have omitted an item concerning change itself: the earlier question of changing political proclivities was deleted for the same reasons that we

TABLE 7-6

*Cohort Analysis of Changing Religious Belief and Behavior*
*Within Campus Religious Subcommunities, Controlling for Involvement*

|  |  | Catholic | Conserv. Prot. | Moderate Prot. | Liberal Prot. | Hillel | No Relig. Pref. |
|---|---|---|---|---|---|---|---|
| **% Orthodox Now** | | | | | | | |
| not involved | (freshmen) | 68 | 61 | 38 | 40 | 5 | 11 |
|  | (sophomores) | 57 | 56 | 24 | 28 | 8 | 12 |
|  | (juniors) | 72 | 50 | 28 | 20 | 11 | 7 |
|  | (seniors) | 72 | 59 | 30 | 34 | 7 | 5 |
| involved | (freshmen) | 75 | 79 | 45 | 40 | 12 | – |
|  | (sophomores) | 75 | 80 | 36 | 38 | 9 | – |
|  | (juniors) | 74 | 86 | 43 | 42 | 16 | – |
|  | (seniors) | 64 | 88 | 38 | 51 | 14 | – |
| **% High Devotionalism and Adherence** | | | | | | | |
| not involved | (freshmen) | 60 | 55 | 39 | 52 | 2 | 14 |
|  | (sophomores) | 67 | 53 | 33 | 43 | 0 | 14 |
|  | (juniors) | 68 | 39 | 31 | 30 | 0 | 9 |
|  | (seniors) | 67 | 47 | 37 | 28 | 0 | 5 |
| involved | (freshmen) | 78 | 87 | 58 | 45 | 23 | – |
|  | (sophomores) | 75 | 85 | 46 | 50 | 12 | – |
|  | (juniors) | 78 | 92 | 54 | 53 | 13 | – |
|  | (seniors) | 70 | 82 | 52 | 54 | 23 | – |
| **% High Experiential Religiosity** | | | | | | | |
| not involved | (freshmen) | 59 | 61 | 29 | 35 | – | 17 |
|  | (sophomores) | 67 | 59 | 30 | 35 | – | 23 |
|  | (juniors) | 66 | 50 | 31 | 37 | – | 16 |
|  | (seniors) | 50 | 53 | 27 | 44 | – | 18 |
| involved | (freshmen) | 79 | 85 | 52 | 40 | – | – |
|  | (sophomores) | 75 | 86 | 48 | 44 | – | – |
|  | (juniors) | 79 | 85 | 40 | 55 | – | – |
|  | (seniors) | 74 | 79 | 40 | 49 | – | – |
| **% High Christology** | | | | | | | |
| not involved | (freshmen) | 41 | 56 | 19 | 25 | – | 7 |
|  | (sophomores) | 40 | 47 | 10 | 19 | – | 12 |
|  | (juniors) | 47 | 44 | 13 | 13 | – | 0 |
|  | (seniors) | 39 | 35 | 20 | 22 | – | 0 |
| involved | (freshmen) | 61 | 73 | 26 | 23 | – | – |
|  | (sophomores) | 55 | 76 | 28 | 30 | – | – |
|  | (juniors) | 51 | 82 | 24 | 29 | – | – |
|  | (seniors) | 46 | 75 | 22 | 32 | – | – |

dropped the item on changing religious influence for the previous table.[3] The four remaining political variables yield no statistically significant change relationships, nor is any over-all pattern discernible such as the slight decline in religious traditionalism indicated in Table 7-6. It is true that some 14 out of 24 relationships for the religiously noninvolved indicate slight increases in political liberalism, while the figure dips to only 8 out of 20 among the involved. It is also true that the noninvolved Catholics seem to become consistently more conservative over their four years, while the noninvolved Jews and those with no religious preference are subject to consistent differences in a more liberal direction. But these findings are molehills, not mountains, and we must be very wary of the difference in statistical topography. Inferences here are treacherous, indeed; the safest interpretation of the table as a whole is that neither campus religious groups in particular nor the university experience in general has much impact at all on political values and perceptions.

Finally, let us turn to perceptions of the university itself and values having to do with higher education. Here we have pared down the list of dependent variables even further with respect to the comparable table relating educational factors to levels of involvement alone. Because we are now more concerned with changing values and perceptions rather than predictor variables for involvement itself, we have omitted the items having to do with membership in fraternities and civil rights groups and happiness with campus social life generally. This allows us to concentrate on the syndrome involving perceptions of depersonalization in the academic life, the individual's general intellectualism, and the degree to which he perceives career skills as the most important purpose of a college education generally. Table 7-8 relates these factors to the now familiar complex of variables, including campus religious subcommunity, involvement in campus religious groups, and year in school.

Actually the results here are somewhat more indicative of change than either of the two previous tables, perhaps because if there is anything about which students should alter their evaluations, it should be education itself. Out of 33 relationships, some 14 provide at least a 10 per cent change between the freshman and senior years. In general, there appears to be increasing perception of depersonalization (somewhat surprising because upperclassmen generally have smaller classes and more faculty contact than lowerclassmen), increasing intellectualism (both the involved Liberal Protestants and the Hillel members offer negative trends that are jarring until one realizes that they are accountable through the very high level of

TABLE 7-7

*Cohort Analysis of Changing Political Beliefs*
*within Religious Subcommunities, Controlling for Involvement*

| | | Catholic | Conserv. Prot. | Moderate Prot. | Liberal Prot. | Hillel | No Relig. Pref. |
|---|---|---|---|---|---|---|---|
| *% Strong Liberal on Poverty* | | | | | | | |
| | (freshmen) | 57 | 33 | 45 | 46 | 73 | 69 |
| not | (sophomores) | 43 | 39 | 39 | 43 | 71 | 71 |
| involved | (juniors) | 40 | 39 | 41 | 47 | 52 | 45 |
| | (seniors) | 50 | 41 | 27 | 53 | 86 | 73 |
| | (freshmen) | 45 | 35 | 35 | 55 | 73 | — |
| involved | (sophomores) | 47 | 23 | 39 | 38 | 81 | — |
| | (juniors) | 43 | 34 | 43 | 44 | 68 | — |
| | (seniors) | 46 | 39 | 33 | 53 | 73 | — |
| *% Strong Liberal on Civil Rights* | | | | | | | |
| | (freshmen) | 30 | 39 | 33 | 35 | 57 | 62 |
| not | (sophomores) | 30 | 11 | 35 | 42 | 67 | 62 |
| involved | (juniors) | 40 | 17 | 31 | 37 | 52 | 48 |
| | (seniors) | 17 | 47 | 23 | 31 | 64 | 68 |
| | (freshmen) | 36 | 27 | 40 | 51 | 54 | — |
| involved | (sophomores) | 33 | 34 | 41 | 24 | 58 | — |
| | (juniors) | 37 | 18 | 38 | 47 | 65 | — |
| | (seniors) | 42 | 29 | 37 | 45 | 73 | — |
| *% Strong Liberal on Vietnam* | | | | | | | |
| | (freshmen) | 20 | 11 | 15 | 19 | 46 | 52 |
| not | (sophomores) | 7 | 17 | 22 | 23 | 44 | 54 |
| involved | (juniors) | 15 | 11 | 23 | 17 | 30 | 40 |
| | (seniors) | 17 | 12 | 20 | 28 | 50 | 53 |
| | (freshmen) | 15 | 15 | 24 | 30 | 44 | — |
| involved | (sophomores) | 20 | 11 | 20 | 18 | 42 | — |
| | (juniors) | 22 | 15 | 16 | 31 | 30 | — |
| | (seniors) | 22 | 22 | 23 | 32 | 32 | — |
| *% Willing to Demonstrate Publicly* | | | | | | | |
| | (freshmen) | 52 | 53 | 46 | 54 | 57 | 64 |
| not | (sophomores) | 53 | 47 | 45 | 60 | 65 | 63 |
| involved | (juniors) | 49 | 61 | 33 | 47 | 44 | 62 |
| | (seniors) | 44 | 29 | 27 | 50 | 64 | 68 |
| | (freshmen) | 48 | 42 | 51 | 60 | 56 | — |
| involved | (sophomores) | 55 | 43 | 61 | 52 | 74 | — |
| | (juniors) | 53 | 31 | 57 | 49 | 68 | — |
| | (seniors) | 46 | 41 | 42 | 49 | 55 | — |

intellectualism among both freshmen cohorts), and a decreasing instrumental emphasis on career skills as the purpose of an education (how often does the faculty member hear the sad senior's lament that he has only recently discovered the "real meaning" of college itself, and now he must leave for the foreboding world that awaits him?).

TABLE 7-8

*Cohort Analysis of Changing Attitudes toward University
Education within Religious Subcommunities, Controlling
for Involvement*

|  |  | Catholic | Conserv. Prot. | Moderate Prot. | Liberal Prot. | Hillel | No Relig. Pref. |
|---|---|---|---|---|---|---|---|
| % High Depersonalization |  |  |  |  |  |  |  |
|  | (freshmen) | 23 | 14 | 15 | 12 | 33 | 31 |
| not | (sophomores) | 17 | 42 | 27 | 17 | 27 | 33 |
| involved | (juniors) | 13 | 22 | 23 | 37 | 33 | 29 |
|  | (seniors) | 28 | 0 | 20 | 13 | 21 | 30 |
|  | (freshmen) | 18 | 10 | 13 | 6 | 20 | – |
| involved | (sophomores) | 19 | 16 | 12 | 20 | 16 | – |
|  | (juniors) | 31 | 15 | 19 | 25 | 30 | – |
|  | (seniors) | 26 | 18 | 19 | 40 | 23 | – |
| % High Intellectualism |  |  |  |  |  |  |  |
|  | (freshmen) | 27 | 31 | 40 | 42 | 43 | 59 |
| not | (sophomores) | 47 | 36 | 39 | 49 | 67 | 62 |
| involved | (juniors) | 37 | 34 | 54 | 47 | 52 | 68 |
|  | (seniors) | 44 | 30 | 44 | 41 | 79 | 83 |
|  | (freshmen) | 47 | 29 | 44 | 66 | 63 | – |
| involved | (sophomores) | 44 | 36 | 40 | 52 | 68 | – |
|  | (juniors) | 41 | 30 | 45 | 56 | 71 | – |
|  | (seniors) | 50 | 41 | 55 | 51 | 54 | – |
| % High on Career Skills |  |  |  |  |  |  |  |
|  | (freshmen) | 30 | 47 | 38 | 29 | 26 | 21 |
| not | (sophomores) | 40 | 53 | 41 | 26 | 23 | 21 |
| involved | (juniors) | 45 | 61 | 31 | 40 | 26 | 19 |
|  | (seniors) | 28 | 41 | 20 | 31 | 14 | 10 |
|  | (freshmen) | 29 | 48 | 40 | 36 | 23 | – |
| involved | (sophomores) | 41 | 40 | 30 | 40 | 23 | – |
|  | (juniors) | 26 | 38 | 25 | 27 | 35 | – |
|  | (seniors) | 18 | 49 | 23 | 15 | 14 | – |

Once again, however, there are ample grounds for caution in interpreting
the results. None of the subtables are statistically significant, taken as wholes.
This is partly because even those relationships indicating any substantial
change at all manifest a beguiling mixture of positive and negative patterns.
Certainly there is little basis for inferring that campus religious groups are
themselves particularly influential in affecting educational views and values.
Because the noninvolved students change just as much as the involved, it is
reasonable to attribute any change that does occur to attributes which the
two categories share rather than to any peculiar aspect of religious
involvement or noninvolvement.

This concludes the cohort analysis, and the original hypothesis is apparently vindicated. Insofar as campus religious groups are distinctive from each other and from students who are not involved in campus religion at all, the distinctiveness seems to be a product of differential recruitment rather than differential impact. Neither campus religion nor the campus as a whole seems to wield much impact. Such a conclusion may be a dash of cold water to those who harbor hopes of the academic world as a source of value change for each new generation of students. But the conclusion is not new. A number of studies have made the empirical point, at least with respect to the effect of college education generally.[4] In one sense, then, our own data offer only further corroboration of an already well-documented thesis. The only difference is that we have extended to the point to the campus ministry. And yet this may be particularly telling, since the campus ministry is one agent in the academic environment that deals with values explicitly and often seeks value change for its own sake.

But perhaps this is an unduly pessimistic and unconstructive note on which to end our analysis of change. Several more sanguine points deserve mention. First, in this less than perfect world, quantitative researchers are forced to settle for approximations rather than ultimate rigor, for increasing confidence rather than definitive proof. Certainly skepticism is justified concerning the foregoing. Surely many isolated students *do* change considerably, even though in directions that cancel each other out in these aggregate data. Moreover, it is possible that we have camouflaged the one place where consistent change is most likely to occur by lumping distinctive groups of highly involved students in with the only somewhat involved for purposes of more reliable analysis. Unhappily both the campus ministry and its statistical assessment are frustrated by the same problem here; namely, the very small number of those who are highly involved in the first place. Although earlier analysis suggested that the highly involved were more set apart from the somewhat involved than were the somewhat involved from the noninvolved, we simply do not have sufficient cases to treat "year in school" as an additional variable among the highly involved themselves. Any conclusions based on such small numbers would be more of a liability than an asset. While we are frankly dubious that a larger sample would produce much change for his group, it does remain a possibility.

But there is another source of possible encouragement to the campus ministry that involves a rather perverse interpretation of the data in hand. Precisely because there is little to choose between in the change rates of the involved and the noninvolved students, this would at least suggest that the campus ministry is no longer vulnerable to the charge of offering a competing program that inhibits or encroaches upon the effects of university education in its own right. There is at least some solace to be gained by many campus ministers in that campus religious groups did *not* produce dramatic changes toward religious, political, and educational conservatism over time, in contrast to a liberalizing trend or even no change among the noninvolved. While it may disappoint many to realize that campus religious groups seem to exert little impact of any kind, it may encourage others to realize that the groups are at least not guilty of academic subversion.

Finally, it is worth stressing that even though our analysis does not reveal substantial campus religious group impact in producing change, these data should not be interpreted to mean that campus groups play no role whatsoever. Surely it is possible for an organization to provide a haven without exerting dynamic influence, to provide a source of nurture and comfort without producing major alterations in either the individual adherent or the campus at large. The evidence would suggest that many students turn to campus religious groups for these less spectacular functions. Indeed, in this respect the campus religious group may not be as different from the main-stream church as is sometimes supposed. A recent national study of Episcopalians by Charles Glock, Benjamin Ringer, and Earl Babbie was entitled *To Comfort and to Challenge.*[5] It appears that campus religious groups and the Episcopal congregations share a tendency to opt for "comfort" rather than "challenge" in response to the dilemma. Moreover, in both cases the choice is primarily dictated by the laity rather than the clergy. Perhaps a high proportion of ministers in every setting find their prophetic mission frequently frustrated by the responses of their charges.

CONCLUSIONS AND IMPLICATIONS

We began this report by pointing to a seeming discrepancy in some of the prevailing views of the campus ministry. On the one hand, there are those who assert that campus ministers are at the forefront of the campus radicals and certainly at the fount of radicalism in the church itself. On the other hand, there are others, represented by Harvey Cox, who are a good bit more skeptical, even debunking, in their conclusions. From the latter view, the campus ministry has succumbed to the very forces that have always threatened the main-stream church itself: a penchant for orthodoxy at the expense of innovation, a concern for organizational exigencies rather than intellectual or ethical demands, a tendency to play it safe instead of risking possible losses for possible leaps forward.

Two plausible reconciliations of the two perspectives is that they refer to different types of campuses or to different types of religious groups on any given campus. This study has not examined the first alternative, though data are available for future analyses of this sort. Instead, we began by investigating the second possibility concerning religious group variation at a single school.

There is no doubt that such variation exists. Indeed, we were able to sort some fifteen Wisconsin religious groups into five basic clusters delimited largely on the basis of the different percentages favoring a radical campus ministry style. We then saw that these clusters were related to a host of other issues, but that they could be further grouped into three basic categories. The Catholics and the Conservative Protestants (Missouri and Wisconsin Synod Lutherans, Evangelical United Brethren, Inter-Varsity Christian Fellowship, and Southern Baptists) upheld the traditional and orthodox end of virtually every religious dependent variable. The Moderate Protestants (Episcopalians, Methodists, and Presbyterians), together with the Liberal Protestants (ALC-LCA Lutherans, Northern Baptists, UCC, Unitarians, Quakers, and YMCA), tended to stand toward the middle of the range, while Hillel members and a general sample of the student body were bunched at the less traditional end of the scales. The differences between these groups were substantial for the religious variables, thus supporting the possibility that different diagnoses of the campus religious patient have referred to different patients altogether.

Further analysis suggests, however, that such a *rapprochement* is somewhat facile and superficial. For one thing, the differences between the religious subcommunities are more varied as less traditional and more currently salient theological issues are tested. For another, the differences between religious groups are not nearly so great on secular political issues or on matters concerning the university itself. These should be precisely the areas that distinguish the liberal campus ministry from their more conservative brethren. Indeed, these should be the items on which the campus religious community in general is shown to be more liberal and more intellectually inclined when compared to nonaffiliated students, if the interpretation suggested by Hammond and Mitchell and by Paul Goodman is correct. Alas, neither is the case. With respect to political and educational issues, the differences are minimal between the religious groups themselves. Moreover, when compared to the general sample of students, the religiously affiliated are somewhat more conservative in general on these issues, perhaps because they are also evidenced as less intellectual and more happily adjusted to the traditional social rounds of campus life.

All of this would seem to reinforce the Cox thesis that the campus religious forest has petrified, despite the seeming variety among its individual trees. But such descriptive generalizations are risky, and we next used a somewhat more sophisticated design to distinguish between different levels of involvement in our various religious subcommunities: the highly involved, the somewhat involved, and those who are not at all involved in a campus religious groups in their nominal religious preference. Presumably the differences among these categories of involvement would suggest the extent and direction of a campus religious group's impact in either producing distinctiveness or reinforcing it.

Even here, however, the results are best predicted by Cox's perspective, as opposed to the one implied by Hammond and Mitchell and by Paul Goodman. Insofar as the campus religious subcommunities are distinctive among their involved members, this is largely confined to religious orthodoxy. The various religious groups manifest very little variance by involvement where political and educational matters are concerned. And even on religious issues where involvement makes a difference, this is largely restricted to high involvement. Since the highly involved are a small minority in most groups, compared to those only somewhat involved and those who have similar religious preferences but no involvement, this suggests that the campus ministry is directly ministering to a very small group, indeed.

But to show any differences at all among levels of involvement, if only with respect to religious matters, is not necessarily to account for such differences. Two explanations are possible: first, that campus religious groups exert a cumulative impact on their members over the four years of college; and second, that the groups exert very little impact and differ merely because of the different types of students they recruit or are assigned initially. The study's last section sought to resolve the matter by comparing freshmen, sophomores, juniors, and seniors, all within different campus religious subcommunities, controlling for whether they were involved in religious groups or not. While this does not constitute a direct longitudinal test of cumulative impact, this indirect test is consistent with previous research on the impact of college education on student values. Just as the college experience as a whole has little over-all influence,[6] so do the campus religious groups themselves. Insofar as they differ from the rest of the campus, it seems to be much more a phenomenon of selective recruitment than cumulative influence. Of course, one can argue that this is true of only one campus among many and that the results should be greeted skeptically because of the required pooling of the somewhat and highly involved for purposes of the analysis. Then, too, some may be happy that the campus religious groups do not seem to subvert higher education through effective counterpressures, and surely the lack of value change should not indicate that the groups serve no function in providing value reinforcement. Still, these qualifications may offer only token solace to those who hope for dramatic evidence of impact. To cite our title, a demonstration of "traditional reality" may be small comfort to those who have sought changes through "radical rhetoric."

This leads to a further distinction that must be taken into account in any over-all assessment. It may be thought that the results are reflective of a campus ministry that does not seek value change or is not interested in exerting meaningful impact. Nothing could be wider of the mark for most of the ministers in this study. In fact, our findings obtain, despite the best efforts of many of the Wisconsin ministers to reverse them. This is in keeping with a central theme in the recent literature on campus ministers generally; namely, their effort to foment a revolution against the traditional functions of the academic parish to protect religion against the onslaughts of the secular university and to protect the students from the kinds of value changes that may be desirable in a fast-changing world. With this in mind, there is still another basis for arbitrating the dispute with which we began. Thus, Hammond and Mitchell and Goodman were referring primarily to the campus ministers themselves and to what they are now attempting. Cox, on the other hand, is referring more to the students and to the aspects of the scene that have frustrated the ministers' efforts. Revolutions are easier to start than to finish. The present data suggest that this particular revolution may be barely under way, with the risk of death a-borning.

Certainly this interpretation is buttressed by the qualitative evidence available from the campus ministers in the Moderate Protestant, Liberal Protestant, and Hillel circles at the University of Wisconsin. Here are men who are cross-pressured, know it, and are seeking to do something about it. But their plight is similar to the fraternity's in that they often have to accept religious "legatees" from their parent denominations. These students constitute the bulk of the highly involved and often serve as brakes on the kind of innovation that is necessary if the campus ministry is to fulfill its mandate to swing on the university's own terms. As one minister put it:

> I have kids here who spend a great deal of their time around here—too much, really. They come here to escape from the issues of the university and the world. Their interests are narrow and parochial. Actually I find them boring for the most part, and I would much rather spend my time talking with the student radicals who are raising issues which should be central to the church. The radicals are often New York Jews who couldn't

give less of a damn about the church, and I don't always agree with them, but I grow in interacting with them because they are dealing with real issues.

Most of the "new breed" of campus ministers on the Wisconsin campus have sought to initiate new activities and participate in nonreligious activities precisely in the interests of innovation and fresh religious air. A number walked in the Selma to Montgomery civil rights march; many have been active in the campus discussion surrounding Vietnam. One started a theatrical group with an invitation extended to nonaffiliated actors and directors; another began a series of open lecture-study programs built around religious and even some nonreligious issues of the day. Another started a faith-and-life community only half of whose members are from the particular denomination at issue, with a dosage of atheists and Buddhists to complement them, and another decided to abandon the organizational structure that has been traditional skeleton for his denomination's religious activities on campuses across the country.

Indeed, this last change is particularly arresting because it comes from a minister in what we have termed the Moderate rather than the Liberal Protestant tradition and because it gets at the central problem of structure. Here is how he explained his action:

> When I took over this post, I had had very little experience as a campus minister *per se*. I was not wedded to any particular organizational form and was able to view the forms that existed fairly objectively. Now we had a list of formal positions open in our student organizational structure that exceeded the number willing to serve. Moreover, those that did serve got involved in these positions, just as their parents get involved in parish busywork at home. I've decided to abolish the structure altogether to let these kids move on to more important things.

Of course, such innovation is not easy when one is staring down the throat of a denominational budget committee or confronting clerical peers with less adventuresome perspectives. Still, the comment above is not idiosyncratic. Indeed, it can be argued that our discussion as a whole has examined a form of campus ministry that has already lost much of its appeal among campus ministers themselves. Many are seeking wider-ranging and less institutionally inhibited roles. To some, the traditional notion of a student religious group is as archaic as it is ineffectual. A few would agree with the following sentiments expressed in response to an early presentation of our findings:

> The real problems of higher education that the church should be confronting can't really be affected by students unless people like us are willing to intercede directly with the faculty and the administrators. This is the new form of the campus ministry that challanges me. It may seem ironic to stop ministering to students in order to aid students in the long run, but the fact is that the more time we spend in routine meetings with students, the less time we have to relate to the people that really make a difference. Here is where the work really gets challenging.

In the same spirit, several campus ministers are entertaining the model of academic "guerilla warfare" as appropriate. That is, instead of appearing beside the campus as someone set apart and possibly stigmatized by formal religious credentials and responsibilities, these people are exploring the possibilities of giving up the ministry per se to attain higher degrees and positions as faculty members and administrators so as to exert their influence from the "inside."

Unfortunately, we can offer here no empirical evaluation of such approaches. And yet a bit of speculation may be in order, based on our qualitative impressions of the University of Wisconsin scene. It remains to be seen whether the campus ministers will have any more influence on the faculty and the administration than they have had on students at Wisconsin. If the status of minister is a sty in the eye of many of the students themselves, it can be a stake in the heart of relationships with the faculty and administrators at a state university that is avowedly secular and intellectually autonomous. The "guerilla" model may be the best bet in such instances, though what is intended as warfare may become co-optation in the process. That is, there are few guarantees that once a minister abandons the traditional ministry as a form he will not also abandon the ministry as a guideline in the interests of the more academically conventional and prestigeful perspectives in the existing university structure.

And yet these speculations suffer from the same liability to which the foregoing empirical analysis is vulnerable. The University of Wisconsin is not typical of higher education in America. While it affords sufficient hetero-geneity to allow an examination of various types of groups, it remains possible that the Wisconsin case is stacked against more optimistic findings. Our subsequent research will explore this possibility as we analyze identical data from quite different college contexts. Meanwhile, it is tempting to hypothesize that the impact of the campus ministry in any form may be greatest in the schools which are weakest academically. It is precisely in such settings that the faculty and administration have less well developed defenses against religion as an "outside influence." It is also in such situations that the radical influence of the campus ministry may be most needed. After all, radicalism itself has become an indicator of educational quality, and the great universities are already sensitized—if not responsive—to at least the ethical, educational, and political issues that vex their campus ministers. Indeed, few people are more fervently moralistic or messianic than the radical and often formally irreligious students on these campuses. While on this campus the campus ministers have generally endorsed and in this sense perhaps added legitimation to student protests, there is a sense in which even a radical ministry is bringing coals to Newcastle when it moves into a context like the University of Wisconsin. This is not to say by any means that all Wisconsin students are charged concerning the major issues of the day, but rather the ministry has not been in the vanguard. There are many other schools which lack Wisconsin's ferment, and it may be that their campus ministries play a more important role in provoking concern for ethical and political issues.

But lest we stray too far from our data, let us return to the world of survey research to put our own contribution in perspective. We mentioned at the outset that the response rate in this study was respectable. It may be, however, that the most memorable response came from an anonymous student who is formally classified among the nonrespondents. Questionnaires are hardly designed to elicit poetry, but ours is the better for having provoked the one poem that follows. It may express the sentiments of many respondents and readers alike. Certainly it indicates that student spunk remains, though it is worth noting that the author was not a member of the campus religious sample.

A Note from the Underground
By Respondent No. 5542

The little men in untold legions
Decend upon the private regions.
Behold, my child, the questionnaire,
And be as honest as you dare.

"As briefly as possible, kindly state
Age and income, height and weight.
Sex (M or F); sex of spouse
(or spouses—list).

> Do  you  own  your  house?
> How much of your income goes for rent?
> Give racial background, by per cent.
> Have you had, or are you now having
> Orgasm? Or thereunto a craving?
> Will Christ return? If so, when?
> (kindly fill this out in pen.)
> Do you masturbate? In what style?
> (fill and return the enclosed vial.)
> Do you eat, or have you eaten
> Feces? Whose?
>
> And were you beaten?
> Was your mother? sister? dog?
> (attach descriptive catalogue.)
> Have you mystic inspiration?
> Our thanks for your co-operation."
>
> Distended now with new-got lore,
> Our plump and pleasant men-of-war
> Torture whimsey into fact,
> And then, to sanctify the act,
> Cast in gleaming, ponderous rows,
> Ingots of insipid prose.
> A classic paper! Soon to be
> Rammed down the throats of such as we.

### NOTES

1. One may wonder quite properly why an 8 per cent criterion was decided on, rather than the conventional 5 per cent. Actually any criterion is arbitrary, and we are simply seeking to minimize the possible error of accepting relationships when they are in fact only chance phenomena. This is a particular danger in the midst of tables with as many different comparisons as those at issue here; a certain number of relationships will satisfy any criterion according to the laws of probability. In such instances, it seems advisable to take steps to avoid the temptation of making inferential mountains out of what may be only random molehills.

2. Earlier we commented on the arbitrary nature of significance criteria. This may be an appropriate point to amplify the discussion. Survey researchers have a long-cultivated habit of interpreting small percentage differences as theoretically valid and important, but note that another way of examining such tables involves correlation coefficients and the concept of explained variance. Even if these tables revealed consistent and linear 8 percent differences between freshmen, sophomores, juniors, and seniors, the over-all correlation would not likely be over .30. This means that the amount of variance in one variable (such as belief) that is explained by the other (say, year in school), would be the square of .30, or .09. Clearly this is not a major relationship from

this perspective. And yet no relationship in the present series of tables even measures up to this extent.

3. Actually it is interesting to note the discrepancy between the results revealed by these self-estimations of religious and political change and the current cohort data on change itself. Earlier we saw that most students reported changes in both respects: that is, a majority of all members of Christian religious groups reported "increasing religious influence" in their lives during the last few years, and very nearly a majority of all students indicated that their political views had recently become more liberal. Now we find, however, that comparisons of freshmen, sophomores, juniors and seniors tell a different story, one that is dominated by a theme of changelessness rather than change itself. It is possible to attribute the differences here to differences in the items at issue in the two analyses; it is also true that a cohort analysis is no substitute for actually tracing individuals through time. And yet it remains plausible that much of the discrepancy arises in the difference between "what ought to be" as opposed to "what is." Thus, students like to think of themselves as having benefited from their education in negotiating the transition from parentally dependent adolsecents to mature and intellectually independent adults. To this extent, it is important for them to report changes of a broad nature when asked, and the implicit norms of the academic community help to determine the direction of changes reported. Indeed, many may feel that they *must* have changed just by virtue of their membership in an academic community or a salient group in it. And yet all of this may involve change that is more illusory than real where specific attitudes and issues are concerned. And even in the undeniable instances where real change does occur, it may be a delicate flower nurtured in a university hothouse, but vulnerable to the chillier climate that awaits the student in the context of the job, family, and community reintegration.

4. Actually the literature here is voluminous in quantity, though by no means uniform in quality. For a classic statement of the no-change position after a review of the literature up through 1956, see Paul Jacob, *Changing Values in College* (New York: Harper, 1957). For an extensive and direct empirical analysis of some eleven different colleges and universities, see Rose Goldsen *et al., What College Students Think* (Princeton: Van Nostrand, 1960). Certainly the most recent review of the literature is Theodore M. Newcombe and Kenneth A. Feldman, *The Impact of Colleges upon Their Students,* A Report to the Carnegie Foundation for the Advancement of Teaching (Ann Arbor: Institute for Social Research, 1968). This report argues that the college experience does have an impact, but one that largely involves the accentuation of attitudes and characteristics that the students arrived with. But the report also notes that it makes a difference what sort of college is at issue. Thus, small schools offering more intensive and personalized education are likely to have more impact than large state universities such as Wisconsin. Newcombe himself is responsible for a classic analysis of Bennington College in the 1930's: T. M. Newcombe, *Personality and Social Change* (New York: Dryden, 1943), and his recent follow-up study, Newcombe, *et al., Persistence and Change: Bennington College and Its Students after 25 Years* (New York: John Wiley, 1967). Certainly this whole area of change and impact is fraught with methodological conundrums. For example, our own cohort analysis is surely second best when compared to a panel technique that actually traces individual students from their freshman through senior years. Such a panel is now under way at the University of Wisconsin in a study of student values conducted by Edgar F. Borgatta and George W. Bohrnstedt. Happily, their preliminary results support our own conclusions. Thus, the correlation between the religious beliefs of the students as entering freshmen and then as jaded third-semester sophomores is remarkably high at .77. For a general review of the methodological

difficulties in the area, see Allen H. Barton, *Studying the Effects of College Education* (New Haven: Edward W. Hazen Foundation, 1959).

5. Charles Y. Glock, Benjamin B. Ringer, Earl R. Babbie, *To Comfort and to Challenge* (Berkeley: University of California Press, 1967).

6. Actually the lack of cumulative influence on religious matters in the university setting may be partly because religion has lost a good deal of its saliency to many students. It is true that the intellectual conundrums of religion continue to occupy some time in college bull sessions, but apparently intellectual queries should not be confused with emotion-charged matters of personal urgency. In fact, we asked our sample what conformity on the Wisconsin campus is most likely to involve with respect to religion: 11 per cent responded that conformity involved "declaring oneself religious"; 19 per cent indicated that conformity involved "declaring oneself irreligious"; and fully 68 per cent answered that conformity required "declaring oneself unconcerned about religion." As one last statistical fillip, it may also be worth reporting that 54 per cent of the general sample of the student body indicated that they would have "qualms about marrying a person who considered himself to be an atheist," but 70 per cent reported "qualms about marrying a person who was devoutly religious and claimed that his relation to God was the most crucial aspect of life." This question was born out of a giddy moment in a late-night session of questionnaire construction. Insofar as it is evidence of a preference for irreligion as opposed to religious traditionalism, the evidence may be as beguiling as it is stacked by the wording of the items themselves.

# ⊰ 8 ⊱

## AN EXPERIMENT IN EVALUATION OF FAITH
## AND LIFE COMMUNITIES

### David Duncombe

## Introduction

One of the most influential models of extracurricular teaching introduced into campus ministries in the past two decades has been the "faith-and-life" or "covenantal" communities. Religious leaders on almost every large public university campus have one or wish to try to establish one. David Duncombe points out that the methods of evaluating them have largely resulted in a feedback of the leader's assumptions. This model of campus ministry inquiry and learning, in most statements of goals, at least gives highest attention to needs for self-knowledge, honest expression, and participation in and perception of the forces for social change which are allegedly neglected in the formal university curriculum.

Duncombe takes their objectives seriously, tries to give them conceptual rigor, and then indicates how survey research might attempt to verify whether the goals are being achieved, or at least represented in the participants. Instead of talking vaguely about the affectional dimensions of learning, the reliance of the church on the "community," or "work of the spirit," he seeks to give an objective reference to religion through questionnaire items to which students inside and outside these communities can respond.

The bias of the questionnaire is deliberately directed toward the interpersonal goals professed by the faith-and-life community movement. Duncombe is concerned chiefly with what scientific evaluation of experimentation in learning might mean in the church. He wants to use behavioral science to see if he can find out what a particular kind of religious commitment and learning process looks like to the participants. And he wishes to see whether a community of self-knowledge and candid expression can be created in the church different from fraternity or other student social groupings. If such a community cannot be verified empirically, he holds little hope that testimonials from past participants will keep the enterprise alive as a viable option in ministerial programs.

The churches, for all their expenditures of funds (several million in the postwar period alone) for the campus ministries and for placement of men where serious behavioral and social science research is being done, have contributed practically nothing to the development of more discriminating, rigorous ways of studying religious commitment and the effects of various modes of knowing. Yet the traditional stances of confession and preaching are under severe scrutiny by the laity. Even methods which would involve simply expenditures of time by religious leaders and not expensive outlays of research funds, such as careful case studies, have not been done by the churches.

In the few places where case studies have been done, an enrichment of the whole life of the church has resulted. The detailed, sympathetic discussion of the religious experiences of one church member (disguised appropriately) by church boards and classes can open a whole range of new possible directions for religious education, if accompanied by observations by trained observers (sociologists, psychologists, theologians, and others) from the university. One conservative church group, with the aid of a campus minister's research, followed the experience of a one-time Inter-Varsity Fellowship member and business school major through his agony over the thought that he "had to make a vocational choice between a personal faith in Jesus Christ and a delight in model building for production controls in a business firm." They learned of his experience in talking about and studying this dilemma with a campus minister; in this experience the student had perceived new relations between his experience of the majesty and love of God and the experience of skill in a technical field where practitioners had a sense of pride in their competence and sensitivity to the human consequences of their work.

KU

THE word "experimental" is in vogue today among campus ministers. The genuine experimental approach may entail "doing something new." But it also requires a clear hypothesis and means of situationally defining and checking hypothesized expectations. Most "experiments" in the campus ministry carry the implied hypothesis that *something* of religious significance will result from the new approach which does not occur (at least in the same degree) with the old approach or possible alternative approaches. But since the nature of this expected change is hardly ever specified, the hypothesis is often assumed to be supported, without recourse to normal procedure of verification.

This predicament is evident from a survey of the available literature on faith-and-life or covenant community groups, especially that which purports to evaluate the success of particular groups.[1] With rare exceptions, the material proved of little use in determining the relative effectiveness of these university communities. Marring the attempted evaluations were at least six types of questionable inferences.

## Critical Survey of Present Methods of Evaluation

1. The most common of these could be called the "structural inference." Here the various structural aspects of the program were described, often with an attempt to ground each aspect of community life in biblical and theological sources. While ostensibly going no further than a descriptive picture (which includes an explanation of how the staff and community understand themselves), this description more often than not implies a favorable evaluation of the program by virtue of assumed correspondence with these biblical and theological sources. The emphasis was put on having the "right" ideological constructs from which to generate policy; it was then tacitly assumed that such policies would produce the desired results.

2. Related to this kind of evaluative procedure is what might be called the "process inference" approach. Evaluation was based directly on observed instances of behavior assumed to have religious importance. One campus minister claimed for his covenant community "a measurable increase in intellectual excitement and a new sense of purpose,"[2] and another saw "a veritable shaking of the foundations" in relation to the lives of its members.[3] Others called attention to the "disturbing" effect of genuine confrontation with the Gospel and similar changes in members' states of feeling, behavior, and self-concept. Besides the serious lack of observational control (people often see what they want to see); such evaluations perhaps unjustifiably assume the religious relevance of these changes in the group.

3. Another evaluative approach has been to deal directly with phenomena whose results could be more reliably measured, but whose theological validity in the process becomes that much more questionable. For instance, the Texas Faith and Life Community made extensive use of statistics indicating the effect of group participation on grade average, chapel attendance, responsible vocational choice, and attention to social issues. The spread of the movement, growth of staff and financial resources, and number of visiting VIP's have also been used as favorable indicators without serious attempt to validate them by appeal to biblical or theological norms.

4. One of the most curious apologia for the covenant community movement is what might be called the "situational inference." Considerable

sections of staff reports were often devoted to an analysis of contemporary culture. The inference was that the campus faith-and-life experience presented the only viable solution to the cultural dilemma of the university student. Emphasis was placed on the *need* for what the covenant community purports to be and do, without drawing attention to what it actually is and does.

5. Another major evaluative emphasis was the student testimonial. With rare exceptions, such testimonials gave an affirmative picture of the experience and one at minimal variance with the stated goals of the community. Yet there was little evidence that any of the better interpretive techniques had been employed to control for report distortion or instrument artifacts.

6. Finally, there were the evaluations conducted by purportedly disinterested groups. Among the most extensive of these was that undertaken by the Special Committee of the Northeast Texas Presbytery to study the Austin Experiment of the Christian Faith and Life Community in 1961. The weakness of this extensive report was that opposing lists of strengths and weaknesses were marshaled, with no way of weighting them. Less ambitious evaluations of covenant communities have likewise produced lists of what is "right" and what is "wrong," without offering a set of normalizing criteria on which an interested campus minister might make a decision with respect to this form of ministry.[4]

## An "Experimental" Method of Evaluation

It is evident that the faith-and-life movement, like most other "experimental" forms of the campus ministry, cannot be evaluated responsibly by the methods currently employed. Without adequate controls, there is no reliable way of distinguishing true insight from wishful thinking. It seems desirable, therefore, to structure a more reliable means of evaluation. The report of such an attempt follows.

A. DETERMINATION OF OBJECTIVES

The first task was to determine the objective or expectancies of university covenant communities. From stated purposes and objectives, annual reports, staff speeches, promotional literature, community newsletters and publications, personal correspondence, and a number of interviews with staff personnel of covenant communities at the University of Michigan, Brown University, and Yale University, there emerged a number of basic objectives most often emphasized by the groups themselves. The goals most held in common fell into two general categories:

1. The first has to do with cognitive and volitional objectives. Most emphasized in the cognitive area is a better understanding of the biblical faith and tradition, of the history of the church, and of certain contemporary theological systems. While such knowledge is never deemed an objective per se, it is viewed as a necessary condition for more comprehensive objectives. This is also true of the volitional area. The discipline demanded of "life together" is not an end in itself, but a prerequisite for the kind of life that expresses other community purposes more fully. Discipline implies the willingness and ability to live within the terms of the group covenant, participating in corporate worship, communal meals, study and discussion, private prayer and meditation, service projects, and other regular functions.

2. The second category is concerned with the less obvious but more pervasive changes expected in the lives of the members and the life of the group. In broadest terms, these objectives commonly presuppose something on the order of the humanity of Jesus, or at least the radical model of Christian freedom portrayed in the lives of the Apostles, the early Christian communities, and the saints of the church from Ignatius to Bonhoeffer. The general designations most often used seem to be variants of "growth in the faith," "authentic integrity," the life of "free men," and "becoming what you really are."

The striking thing about the various objectives which serve to define these broad "freedom" classifications is that the emphasis is not on distinct behaviors, skills, and accomplishments, as was the case in the first category. The emphasis is not even on the *disposition* to do certain things and not to do others. It is on the sheer *ability* to do something, often without consciously purposing the act in question. Emphasized most often are the abilities (a) to know oneself insightfully, (b) to express oneself honestly and without pretense, (c) to see others as they are and the world as it is, (d) to respond to the world appropriately and authentically, and (e) to tolerate stress, ambiguity, and hardship without undue anxiety. It is the general expectation, all other things being equal, that the covenant community experience will more likely enable its members to do these things than will experiences afforded by other campus religious or secular groups.

## B. THE TESTING INSTRUMENT

In order to determine the degree to which persons possess these five criterial abilities, a special inventory was constructed (see Appendix). The inventory consists of twenty-four short descriptive sentences. The sentences paraphrase, in both positive and negative form, the phenomenological content of each of the five abilities.[5] The inventory is designed for groups of five to ten persons. Each person rates himself and the other members of the group and then predicts how the three other members he knows the best have rated themselves. Only persons who know each other well enough to give a knowledgeable rating are used, although this condition is usually presumed in a covenant community setting.

The inventory yields three general indices. On the basis of how his peers rate him, each subject receives a "direct" or "objective" estimate of his ability in the five ability areas. This is the direct index. Two indirect indices serve as supplementary indicators of self-knowledge and accurate perception. The absolute discrepancy on each item between the average of the ratings a subject receives from his peers and the rating he gives himself constitutes a supplementary index of self-knowledge. This is the Insight Index (SKp). The subject's ability to predict the responses of his best acquaintances as measured against their actual responses constitutes a supplementary index of accurate perception of social sensitivity. This is the Social Sensitivity Index (SSp).[6]

C. DESIGN

The study to be reported here involves 38 students. Of these students, 19 are covenant community members and 19 are not.[7] Six of the experimentals were members of the Residential Seminar in Christianity (RSC) at Brown University. The remaining 13 forming two testing sections of 7 (CC-I) and 6 (CC-II), were members of the Covenant Community at the University of Michigan. As a control group, students were used from two fraternities and a women's residential house. Seven controls were from the Brown University chapter of the Sigma Nu Fraternity (SN); 6 controls were from the Lambda Chi Alpha (ΛXA) chapter at the University of Michigan; and 6 controls were from the women's residential house "99 Brown Street" (99) on the Pembroke-Brown campus.

Testing conditions and instructions were the same for all groups. All groups offered satisfactory evidence that their participating members knew one another well enough to rate knowledgeably. Every effort was made to insure that the only substantial difference between experimental and control groups was their respective organizing principle.[8] In the case of the experimentals, this was presumed to be "life together" in a Christian community, whereas the organizing principle of the controls should perhaps be understood more in terms of various social and nonreligious aims.

This comparison design was used to see whether the experimentals' organizing principle "made a difference" worthy of note. The (null) hypothesis tested was that the organizing principle made no significant difference. The preliminary testing results to be reported fail to support this hypothesis and give limited evidence that these covenant commjnities do, in fact, succeed in providing an environment more conductive to proficiency in the five testing areas heretofore described (Figure 8-1).

## D. RESULTS

The results of the pilot study are graphically represented by Figure 8-1. Covenant community experimental subjects as a group scored higher in all five ability areas than their control group counterparts, but not always significantly so. On the direct index, experimental subjects were rated higher than controls in sense of security and tolerance of ambiguity (p=.0003), degree of self-knowledge (p=.17), honesty of expression (p=.21), accuracy of perception (p=.15), and adequacy of response (p=.0002). On the indirect indices, experimentals performed better than controls on both self-knowledge (p=.035) and social sensitivity (p=.006). The association between the direct and indirect indices was fair for both self-knowledge (r=.30) and accurate perception (r=.40), with a relatively high correlation between sense of security and tolerance of ambiguity on the direct index and the combined average of the two indirect indices (r=.58). Thus in all areas except that of honesty of expression there is statistically significant support for the covenant community or experimental group.[9]

## E. DISCUSSION

In rejecting the null hypothesis we are, of course, not really demonstrating the "Christian character" of the experimentals. We have demonstrated, and only tentatively so, that the experimentals excel the controls in at least four out of five abilities necessary to the Christian life. It is possible that even the best of the experimentals lack other qualities requisite for the Christian life as understood theologically or as stated in the purposes of their covenant community. It is also possible that the lowest of the controls is still above "minimal" requirements in all five areas. The lack of any absolute standard by which to measure both groups would prove a serious limitation if our primary concern was to determine "how Christian" a particular group or person is. But since our aim is only to discover whether a relative difference exists between a certain form of ministry and what might amount to no real ministry at all, the design employed seems adequate to support the tentative inferences drawn.

FIGURE 8-1

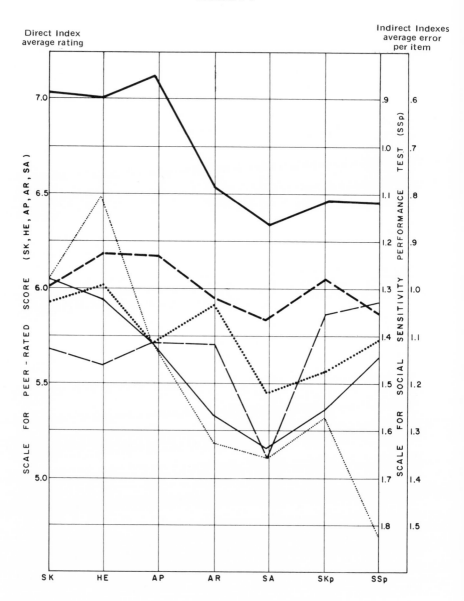

FIGURE 8-1

*Average Scores of Each Group Tested*

*Key to Groups Tested*

_____ CC-I   Covenant Community, University of Michigan, Section I (N=7)
_ _ _ CC-II  Covenant Community, University of Michigan, Section II (N=6)
.......... RSC    Residential Seminar in Christianity, Brown University (N=6)
_____ ΛXA    Lambda Chi Alpha Fraternity, University of Michigan (N=6)
_ _ _ SN     Sigma Nu Fraternity, Brown University (N=7)
............. 99     "99 Brown Street" women's residential house,
                     Pembroke College (N=6)

*Key to Testing Measures*

SK    degree of self-knowledge, peer-rated
HE    honesty of expression, peer-rated
AP    accuracy of perception, peer-rated
AR    adequacy of response, peer-rated
SA    sense of security and tolerance of ambiguity, peer-rated
SKp   degree of self-knowledge, performance test
SSp   degree of social sensitivity or perception, performance test

Assuming no defects in design or control of the experimental procedure large enough to offset the sizable differences found between experimentals and controls in most areas tested, it may be accepted pending replication that as a group, the nineteen covenant community students showed themselves superior to the nineteen controls as a group in tolerance of ambiguity and sense of security, self-knowledge, accurate perception (including social sensitivity), and adequate response behavior. It was not demonstrated that the covenant community members excelled the controls in honest expression, although indications are in this direction. Because of the differences among even the experimental groups, we are not allowed to infer that "covenant communities" per se are thus superior. It has only been demonstrated that two campus covenant communities share this superiority over three campus secular communities.

With this much evidence in hand, however, it would seem reasonable to say that the campus minister faced with the decision of whether to adopt the covenant community approach or not has at least something more substantial to go on. He has a few models of something that seems to work if he will study these two covenant communities to see in what respects they most differ from the control groups. While it is true that he should not place too much confidence in the results of this one study, especially without adequate replication, it is most probably the case that these results are more reliable than other information which he might use to inform his decision. If this is true, it is no small matter.

## Conclusion

This study, presented in illustration of a sounder "experimental" principle for the campus ministry, may not itself provide a particularly useful design for other situations. For example, the possibility that those drawn to covenant community groups are *already* more proficient in the five ability areas than those drawn to fraternities or sororities is uncontrolled. Nor is it evident how the testing instrument described could be used with other types of campus groups.

But the broader purpose of this work has not been to provide an easy and reliable method of evaluating the effectiveness of the covenant community approach, but to draw a contrast between two evaluative approaches to an "experimental" campus ministry. The difference has to do with the total experimental design and one's understanding of how it relates to theologically important objectives. Test reliability is an important but secondary factor. If the actual operations of the testing instrument have no theologically related significance, they have no practical importance for the campus ministry.

For an experimental approach to have a value worth its trouble, both hypothesized expectations and subsequent verifications must plainly state what it is they claim to measure and challenge the pastor-theologian to take issue. There is no more to commend a battery of technically sophisticated personality tests with merely assumed theological validity than the perennially popular uncontrolled observations, "hunches," and other criteria supported by questionable theological and empirical inferences. Both suffer from unexamined premises and lead to a false sense of confidence on which the vogue for the "experimental" founders.

What is proposed is a more productive implementation of the central concern behind the vogue for the "experimental"; that is, the concern for reliable professional knowledge. The vogue itself is a hopeful sign because it evidences a pragmatic seriousness. Effectiveness, not correctness, is beginning to assume its proper place in a professional scale of values. But in their haste toward the prize, many campus ministers have taken short cuts and fallen into simple scientisms. They have embarked on "experiments" without a clear idea of what meaningful results would look like (with the faith that they would somehow "know" if the new venture proved successful). It is largely this uncritical approach to experimentation in the campus ministry that endangers confidence in the slow and tedious process of productive experimentation.

It has been argued, sometimes by the very innovators of "experimental" forms of the campus ministry, that "there is no way to measure the spiritual growth of men and women." Were this true, there could be no legitimate experimentation in or profession of the campus ministry. But the possibility must be taken seriously. Because we *want* to conduct a professionally effective ministry is no reason for believing that we *can*. If it is the nature of Protestant theology, as some believe, to be conceptually nebulous or dialectically inconclusive about the direction and shape of the mature Christian life, there can be no basis for measurement, experimentation, and reliable professional knowledge. Or if it is correct that no empirical means exist for identifying theologically relevant characteristics of spiritual life and growth, again there can be no such thing as an "effective" ministry. A productive "experimental" approach to the campus ministry must rest on a demonstration that those assumptions have little theological and empirical substance.

One beginning toward this kind of "experimental" approach has been suggested by the typology of abilities at the close of Section A, above. In another study I have attempted to show how these five abilities can be derived from descriptions of the mature Christian life found in the works of ten major Protestant theologians and operationally discriminated by over two hundred empirical measures.[10] This is to say that most Protestant theologians *are* sufficiently clear in their expectations that mature Christians will evidence these abilities, and the persons evidencing either the presence or lack of these five abilities in sufficient degree *can* be reliably identified by empirical measures. It is a costly, exacting, and time-consuming process, but it is possible.

The fact of this possibility raises a major issue for the campus ministry in the years ahead. Each campus minister and sponsoring denomination will be faced with the question of how much time, money, and other resources to commit to basic research of this nature. As more sophisticated typologies and supporting empirical indicators are evolved, it will become increasingly apparent that a campus minister *can* know how effective his approach has been or will be if he (or the denomination) cares enough to know. While the time-cost factor will weigh heavily in such a decision, in many cases the crucial factor may be the highly threatening nature of such evaluation. To the degree that the campus ministry can be genuinely "experimental" enough to risk knowledge of vocational ineffectiveness and failure, it is likely to earn its place among the better service professions.

Appendix

*Inventory C*

_____
(mother's maiden
initials)

GENERAL INSTRUCTIONS

Below are 24 statements. You are asked to indicate on a scale from 1 to 10 how accurately (i.e. with what degree of truth) they describe the members of this group.

| 1 | 2 | 3 | 4 | 5 | 6 | 7 | 8 | 9 | 10 |

very untrue                                                    very true

While few people will merit any ratings of 1 or 10, you should have a *scattering* of 2's and 9's, *more* 3's and 8's, and the *most* 4's, 5's, 6's, and 7's. Be as accurate as you can. Your score will suffer if you underrate or overrate.

Part I

INSTRUCTIONS:

1. Beginning at the left, above each column write the first name of a member of this group. Put your own name last. Circle your name.

2. In the lower part of each square, rate (1 to 10) each member of the group plus yourself on each statement before going on to the next statement. You may go back later to correct.

PART II

INSTRUCTIONS:

1. Use a similar form (mark "page 2"). Predict how the three group members you know the best are rating themselves.

2. Rate yourself again in the last column.

(names)

1. He sees the world as it is.

2. He evolves self-justifying strategies when threatened.

3. He can express his feelings and thoughts honestly.

4. He is strongly moved to share with and suffer for persons in need.

5. He is blind to his own faults.

6. He does what each situation itself calls for.

7. He has a tendency to suppress his real feelings.

8. He is more capable than most of deep friendships.

9. He knows himself well.

10. He could give up everything.

(names)

| | | | | | | | | | | |
|---|---|---|---|---|---|---|---|---|---|---|
| | | | | | | | | | | |

11.   He is free from secret fears and unrealistic cares.

12.   He colors reality to suit his wishes.

13.   He fears revealing his true self.

14.   He senses how others feel.

15.   He displays rare insight into his own mind and heart.

16.   He sometimes seems to act as if he were being driven and not free.

17.   He is inwardly free from the search for security.

18.   He often fails to notice what is really there.

19.   He responds in a way appropriate to each new thing.

20.   He knows less about himself than his friends do.

| | | | |
|---|---|---|---|
| 21. He cannot genuinely experience another's joys and sorrows as his own. | | | |
| 22. He is able to talk about his most embarrassing faults. | | | |
| 23. He clings to little certainties and systems under pressure. | | | |
| 24. He is open to all kinds of experience. | | | |

NOTES

1. I would like to acknowledge my gratitude to the Rev. William N. Lovell, Associate General Director, Commission on Higher Education of the National Council of Churches, and to G. Parker Rossman, of the New Haven Ecumenical Continuing Education Center, for their co-operation in making their files on these groups available for inspection.

2. Sam H. Newcomer, "The Residential Seminar in Christianity," *Five Experiments in Campus Christian Community* (New England S.C.M., 1962), p. 65.

3. Jack Lewis, "Letter to Laymen" of the Texas Faith and Life Community, Fifth Anniversary Issue, 1957.

4. Probably the most comprehensive evaluation of any covenant community was also of the Christian Faith and Life Community at Austin. The study was conducted by the Millard Research Associates, Ltd., and financed by the Hogg Foundation for Mental Health. The data were obtained from a fourteen-page questionnaire sent to all former CFLC members. The result is an interesting survey of the impressions, views, and practices of those who responded, but due to the nature of the research design, no systematic attempt is made to evaluate CFLC effectiveness from a theological perspective.

5. A more comprehensive phenomenological description of each of these five abilities will be found in my book *The Shape of the Christian Life* (New York: Abingdon, in press).

6. The inventory was pretested with two groups. It is construct-validated only and has not been subjected to a test-retest reliability check. The method of construction and the few items in each subscale preclude a meaningful split-half reliability check.

7. For brevity of reference, the covenant community students will hereafter be referred to as the "experimentals" and the noncovenant community members as the "controls." The six testing groups will be denoted by the abbreviations in ( ).

8. Quite naturally, there were other differences between the experimentals and controls, as well as between individual groups. The experimental groups were composed of male and female students, whereas the fraternities were male only and the women's residential house female only. Controls also received a nominal sum for participation.

9. For a more detailed statistical analysis of these results, see David C. Duncombe, "Evaluation of University Covenant Communities: A Critique and Proposal," unpublished report prepared for the Danforth Study of Campus Ministries, 1965, pp. 42-54.

10. David Duncombe, "Some Empirically Verifiable Correlates of the Christian Life as Derived from Protestant Thought", Ph.D. dissertation, Yale University, 1966.

Part V

*The Structures of Teaching and Prophetic Inquiry*

# RELIGION AND EDUCATION IN SECULAR SOCIETY

### Albert Rasmussen

## *Introduction*

Although the Danforth Study had a colloquium on "the theology of secularization and prophetic inquiry" at Chapel Hill, the one paper appearing on the subject is by a nonparticipant from California (Pacific School of Religion). The explanation is this: when we came to editing the working papers of the Chapel Hill colloquium, we found them to be wonderful fragments of conversation starters, suggestive tries at definition of subject matter, but impossible to assemble into a careful, scholarly review of the issues of religion and learning in a secular society. So, giving Professor Rasmussen the benefit of the Chapel Hill reflections, we asked for a more systematic and less polemical statement. This chapter is his response.

Rasmussen is not to be entrapped in current secular theologizing on what faith commitment means today. He is not willing to see all secular trends as a loss of attention to theological and moral criteria of choice, but in some instances as a revival of categories long neglected. He is not one who celebrates the emergence of the "worldly man" as an unqualified joy, merely because he stirs up the "stagnant pools of religious lethargy and challenges static views of the church." Secularization, if intended to open up a more profound understanding of a neighbor's situation through technical fact as well as theological doctrine, can be helpful. But a secularism that denies the legitimacy of a transcendent, ultimate Being opens the way to uncriticized prejudice and false unity through authoritarian options of government and ideology. Rasmussen has moved past wholesale, indiscriminate attacks on the church or vague celebration of the secular to conscious use of historic symbols of faith in making judgments in the world.

But the major contribution of the essay is an attack on the grounds upon which religion has been excluded from public education. The chief premise of this exclusion has not been that we live in a secular culture, but that we live in a culture of pluralistic faith orientations, and "therefore in order to give equal rights to all groups, all must be denied the right to enter the central channels of cultural transmission"—the curriculum and research of public education. The melting-pot theory fears conflict and controversy and seeks to merge differences in a common value system. But no Jew, Protestant, Catholic, Black Power advocate or anyone else of strong conviction wants to give up his right to contend for representation of his identity and heritage in the basic channels of communication. This concern may issue in a fight for adequate attention to Negro history or in revision of Catholic canon law. Technical and public intelligence, discriminating choice, lasting faith, responsible leadership, have to emerge now out of a pluralistic, candid, open, comparative search for values and commitments.

Some may try for a while longer to avoid the competition of faiths and to keep a superficial harmony by preserving antiquated parish school systems, ineffectual released time programs, and perfunctory introduction to religious issues in social studies and history classes. But what the future more likely promises can be seen at Penn State, Syracuse University, and other universities where plans are working out for objective, serious, comparative study of religion in primary and secondary education. Experiments with dialogue and juridical education about religion are going on in educational TV and extension services. The parish churches will need to revise their whole role in religious education when university models of secondary education become widespread.

Another way of responding to the contemporary situation would be for the churches to go on, as Rasmussen says many have, aiding the secularism of the culture, preconditioning leaders to indifference and nonrecognition of all religious claims. The secular man so glorified in theological tracts is not anything like what is showing up in the laboratories and decision making centers, in the suburban men's classes in church schools. They are so ideologically and historically secularized they simply cannot comprehend or remember hearing any part of the Christian message. Their culture is often one of a university technical training course, a ghetto TV mentality toward religion, occasional Sunday morning church attendance. It is time the campus clergy figured out what their responsibilities may be for teaching this secular man.

KU

**R**ELIGIOUS and nonreligious analysts frequently declare that we have moved into a secular era of rapid social change where the process of secularization continues as a basic trend. The meaning of the term "secularism" has fallen into great confusion.

The term "secular" has been applied to culture, church, the state, and individual persons. A secular trend in culture is describable in two ways. First, religion is increasingly dissociated from aspects of the common life, until it is seen as relevant only to the separated domain of the specifically religious (or spiritual). Second, a secular culture is one in which the value system communicates the belief that religious behavior has no relevance to economic and political action, artistic expression, or other types of activity. A wholly or integrally secular culture would be one in which religion had lost its legitimacy entirely and the sacred had been rejected as a significant category.

Secularization, as applied to the church, has been used in two contradictory ways. First is the view that through a process of secularization the church has surrendered many of its traditional functions: works of charity, education, cultivation of intimate fellowship, and the development of consensus in confronting urgent decisions. On the other hand, this description is often reversed. As the church has attempted to restore some of these lost functions, this is called the secularizing of the church. Thus, when the church participates in the creation of a favorable culture in which to perform its ministries, the secular is said to be invading the church. This is the precise opposite of the meaning of secularism as applied to culture, which refers to the shrinking of the sacred domain to a separated function of worship.

When "secular" is used to characterize individual persons, it usually refers to those who have rejected a conscious ultimate commitment and the validity of sacred worship and find some other center of self-identification. A secular culture creates many secular persons who internalize a negative evaluation of all sacred commitments.

If religion is universal, it cannot be expected to disappear even under the most antagonistic conditions. However, it can be expected to undergo radical change in form. There are two possiblities. It can be driven underground, so to speak, and accept the rejective appraisal that all supernaturalism and transcendent ascriptions are illusory. It can then appear under many of the guises that are live options in contemporary culture: humanism, nationalism, "scientism," or the nihilistic plunge in avoiding commitment, never confronting the existential questions of existence.

It is our contention that the alternatives above are substitutionary forms of religion, providing an integrating commitment for large numbers of contemporary men. These views are communicated by scholars and writers and are often central ideologies for organized groups which are seeking devotees and celebrating reinforcive rites. They all suffer from one fatal flaw. When ultimate loyalty is vested in particular groups which themselves become absolutes, no higher perspectives of criticism keep it open to continuous judgment and transformation. Any group or point of view that is self-authenticating and final is likely to become uncritically fanatical. The finite religions have provided many terrifying illustrations of untempered hate crusades whose absolute ends have justified the bloodiest of means because no higher commitment provided any basis for self-criticism. The French Revolution, Soviet and Chinese Communism, and the Fascist movements are vivid examples. Even the transcendent religions, when they become secularized to the point of absolutizing their own institutional authority or dogmas, have shown propensities for coercive intolerance issuing in Holy Wars and fanatical hate movements.

The second form that religion may take in a secularized context is to maintain its ultimate claiming power by becoming isolated from the surrounding culture. Thus churches themselves may become secularized by making commitment obedient only to themselves. A devotee can hold a contradictory commitment to politics, still another to economic affiliation, and still another to family. This is what H. Richard Niebuhr calls "polytheism": an uncentered set of loyalties to many centers of value. Religion then is concerned only with what takes place in church or temple, and this fragmentary commitment is "spiritualized" and unrelated to all the other activities of men.

Social scientists[1] have frequently described the secular society as the opposite pole from the sacred folk society on a continuum. The sacred folk society is seen as an intimate and unified society with an integrating value system strongly permeated with sacred sanctions. The sacred suffuses everything with religious significance. Planting and harvesting crops is celebrated as a sacred rite. All important events and crises are occasions for worship and for re-enacting the sacred bonds of community. In the intimate folk society, as represented by the American rural village in an earlier period, churches were not the sole or even the central communicators of religious consciousness and commitment. The family was itself a religious unit. The father was a priest presiding over family rites, such as prayer and Scripture reading, and the mother was a teacher of the sacred lore. Schools were transmitters of a sacred value system, in curricular content, in sacred rites, in the implicit attitudes of teachers and students. In community festivals and celebrations the same undifferentiated intermix of sacred values and commitments was reinforced.

At the opposite pole in this ideal construct is the fully secularized urban society in which the sacred has vanished. The mores are sheer custom ruled by formal legal sanctions. Human relations are impersonal and non-sympathetic. The world and fellow men are exploitable and manipulatable resources. Mystery is only ignorance which further knowledge will explain away. All categories pointing to transcendence or the transempirical are considered illusory. No experience is worshipful.

It is rather obvious that neither the perfectly sacred society nor the perfectly secular society has ever fully existed. Nevertheless, the world trend toward metropolitanism and the massive migrations away from traditional folk societies has everywhere uprooted men from folk culture orientations and provided a solvent that is throwing varied value systems and sacred orientations into radical flux. The whole complex "package" of massive urbanism can be called the crucible of radical change, melting the traditional securities and sacred commitments by which most men lived in the past.

There are several factors in urbanization that seem to have undermined traditional religious commitments.

1. First is the culture shock involved in the transition from the intimate folk community to the pluralistic context of the city. Here the value system is so fragmented and behavioral expectancies are so varied that the newcomer is plunged into decision among alternatives of action never before confronted.

This shock of transition is now less acute in America because of the increasing urbanization of rural areas, although it still seems to be an important factor when people move to the city from still-lingering folk communities. But in many rapidly urbanizing folk cultures in the world, such as Japan, India, Indonesia, and many countries of Africa and South America, where millions are moving away from very simple village life to the metropolis, the forces of religious disintegration are heavy.

2. The second factor is the religious and cultural pluralism of cosmopolitanism. The metropolis everywhere tends to pull in an intermix of peoples with various class or ethnic backgrounds. To whatever degree people come into contact across religious lines, they are subjected to comparisons and are pressed into attitudes of tolerance toward others who hold different religious orientations. Continuous personal interaction can lead to the neutralism expressed by the statement: "Since there are so many competing sacred commitments, all might be equally true. However, since they all present ultimate or claiming identifications, all might be equally false."

The uprooted person who in this way is compelled to choose rationally a culture or a religious orientation has already been secularized to the point of doubting the category of ultimacy. Man cannot choose his culture or the sacred orientation that has created him, because they have already claimed and shaped him. He can only accept, or reject, and begin the critical examination from that perspective. For rationalists and positivists who must find empirical proofs to back all convictions and have no perspective or historical identity from which to begin their self-criticism, this appears as an impossible dilemma. This is the final ideological secularization from which there is no escape except the denial of the category of ultimacy and a retreat to some partial loyalty as "relative absolute."

3. The third secularizing consequence of urbanization is created by the proliferation of organizations that structure the division of labor. The yellow pages of any urban phone directory list hundreds of services that are offered to prospective clients. Social welfare directories list hundreds of agencies organized to handle various human problems and needs.

Compartmentalization of function has created an overwhelming tendency to confuse basic human needs with the activities through which they are served, and the activities or pursuits with the agencies or the physical facilities where they are conducted. Thus health is procurable in clinics and hospitals, not in the normally functioning bodies of people. Education is the product of schools, not the entire process of the socialization of persons into society. Social security is what is processed in the offices of the Social Security Administration.

In no area has this muddying of the categorical waters been more pronounced than in contemporary thinking about the sphere of religion, about the indicators of religious commitment and the location and form of religious activity. Religion is simply identified as what people do in church or synagogue. But, if religion is the ultimate claiming commitment around which selfhood is centered, it is impossible for the individual not to take it with him in *all* his activities. In fact, the separation of religion from other aspects of life seems to be one of the principal indicators of an advanced state of both fragmentation and secularism in a culture.

4. The reorganization of society from simple village to metropolitan forms has not only expanded the number of organizational agencies but radically shifted their functions and separated them into competing forces in the shaping of participating members. In the village context, family, school, and church were all interlocking communicators and inductors into both the culture and the structure of sacred commitment. But in the urbanized complex, the functions of some culture-shaping agencies have been narrowed and deintensified. Others have expanded and received greater universal legitimacy, while still others have been added, thus shifting the balance of impact in cultural induction. It is illuminating to attempt to trace the path of these shifts in the last 180 years.

At the end of the colonial period the colonies were already religiously pluralistic to the point of being unable to agree on an established national faith. The separation of church and state, most historians agree, was a compromise solution arrived at between those who wanted an established religion as the base of the cultural foundation and those who, under the influence of the Enlightenment, wanted religion made voluntary.[2] The creators of the federal constitution restricted the state basically to the functions of preserving freedom and order. Two great areas were left to the churches: communicating and transmitting the sacred culture through education, and the ministry of mercy and healing. Education was omitted entirely from the Constitution as a function of government, since the overwhelming weight of public opinion was fearful of government as propagandist.

As educational historians agree, church schools and religiously oriented academies were expected to induct children and youth into the culture with religious orientation. There came, however, a gradual process of reversal from church-operated education to public state-controlled education. The irony of the great reversal is that as finally schools came to be regarded as agencies of the state, the one thing that was legally banned was the religious foundations of our basic culture which they were clearly founded to perpetuate. The doctrine of separation has come full circle, and the basic constitutional guarantee of the right to teach and interpret life and history on the basis of our formative traditions has been prohibited from the basic cultural communicator and even from the great forum of competition of ideas and values, the state university.[3]

Education has clearly expanded its function as the chief agency of cultural induction, while other agencies have declined. Education is becoming more universal and increasingly the primary escalator into the middle- and upper-class ranks. Therefore educational institutions become the primary selectors of advancement and the great adjudicators of comparative ranking of various areas of study.

Universities, instead of promoting an expanding culture, increasingly are preparing students for narrow vocational specialization. Consequently, the humanities, as explicit inductors into the culture system, become less significant. And religion, as a universal dimension of culture and self-identification, loses significance, if not legitimacy. If it is included in the curriculum, it is usually subordinate to literature, history, philosophy, or social science and often is subjected to criteria which restrict or reject. The fact that sacred commitment is widely (if not universally, as we contend) a fact of personal organization is ignored or ridiculed. This creates ideological secularization, or the illegitimacy of religious criticism.

Because of the secular dismissal of the legitimacy of religion as one of man's historical and contemporary preoccupations, religion does not receive, outside seminaries and church-affiliated universities, the scholarly criticism and analysis that it deserves. At the same time other dogmas (equally naive because they have not been pressed by a scholarly opposition), such as a narrow "scientism," receive unquestioned legitimacy. One of the fruits of this primal secularization is that methodologies of criticism appropriate for one field are universalized as the only legitimate procedure for all others. Not only education carries a bigger inductive function, but mass communication and public events now have a greater impact in cultural induction. Yet there is little attempt to present religion as a basic element in the content of our culture. Rather, it is presented as a periperal and somewhat eccentric circumlocution.

Sentiment and celebration are powerful factors in culture. As W. Lloyd Warner has pointed out,[4] purpose and commitment cannot depend solely on rational thought but must be celebrated and ceremonialized in great festivals that provide the elevating and motivating experiences of the people. However, in the new secular society such occasions have been losing significance. The holy days have become holidays increasingly divested of their historical depth and sacred meanings.

It is important to ask whether a vital and creative society should eliminate the sacred commemorations. There is heavy pressure in a pluralistic society to neutralize and reduce the celebratory events to empty forms expressing a least common denominator and desacralized meaning. Again, the heavy hand of restriction and censorship gains support in the name of freedom. Must all the qualitative aspects of culture be lost because minorities can exercise a veto to protect themselves from contamination from the majority? This reductive trend undercuts the legitimacy of sacred orientations for both majority and minorities and denies freedom of religion at the significant cultural level. Open access, on the other hand, preserves freedom and restores competition by making the main sacred traditions a part of the cultural stream. Is it not possible that open freedom would call all groups to set forth their own celebratory identification in a symphony of exultant praise and self-critical humility under a common, if differently interpreted, mono-theism? Yet the denial of religious participation in the communicative process at the levels of common public presentation and celebration hits religion in its "solar plexus" because its language is primarily celebration of common dependence on, and a symbolic point to, the ultimate.

The notion that ceremonial affirmation of claiming loyalties must be restricted to sanctuaries where only the already faithful attend makes public freedom of religion a travesty. This is precisely the kind of "freedom from religion" that Soviet Russia provides. It does this under the socially realistic confidence that if religion is kept out of the basic culture system it will have no means of perpetuation or competition for the loyalties of men. With the enormous expansion of government into mass communication and education, the arbitrary exclusion of sacred content from the common life disallows all open attempts to overcome modern man's sense of meaninglessness and alienation. The total desacralization of culture is the most powerful way to suppress freedom of religion. Those with even a minimal sociological knowledge recognize this fact. It is only because so many American religionists are sociologically unsophisticated that they have accepted this road to religious demise without protest.

## The Primrose Path to Secularization

It is ironical that the chief communicator of culture, higher education, has had the sacred value systems, a part of the universal content of culture, arbitrarily eliminated from its domain. This often has the absurd result of allowing all other world views to be taught except those that produced our culture and are still alive in our own society. It is as though all languages could be taught except our own.

More importantly, the legitimacy of sacred value orientations in our culture is denied. Any area, systematically and arbitrarily eliminated from the encyclopedic college and university curriculums, has come under the ax of the most powerful censorship that can be wielded.

In spite of a new surge of so-called scholarship attempting to prove the reverse, it is clear that the constitutional and cultural fathers never intended to eliminate religion from the common culture or restrict the free society in this fashion. Even though the most liberal of the founding statesmen were nonsectarian, they had internalized a deep cultural attachment to a sacred religious perspective. As Loren Beth says of those who leaned farthest toward skepticism and derision, "they were religious in a liberal sense . . .having profound religious convictions."[5]

The major rationalization that is set forth to justify the exclusion of religion from higher education is that we live in a culture with pluralistic faith orientations, and therefore in order to give equal rights to all groups, all must be denied the right to enter the central channels of cultural transmission. Simply retranslated, this means that in order to guarantee this freedom we will deny it.

This is clearly a reversion to either "the Anglo-conformity" theory or the melting-pot theory of American culture. These two early interpretations were designed by the threatened WASP establishment to assimilate all newcomers into the basic American value system. The ideal of the pluralistic culture is to allow minority groups to preserve their own values and life styles as subcultures maintaining their own integrity, in peaceful interaction and competition. The melting-pot view fears conflict and controversy and seeks to merge differences into a common system. The pluralists seek to preserve the historical identity and the unique values of each with full vigor and advocacy. This risks controversy, but it does not demand that tolerance be bought at the price of abandoning strong commitments and full rights in the open arena of contention.

In the field of religion no devotee of Catholic, Jewish, or Protestant persuasion could accept tolerance if it meant giving up his own convictions or his right to contend in the basic channels of communication. This kind of toleration can only produce a conformity in which conflict is avoided by lowering concern. This is precisely the danger of the mass society in which culture is fragmented. Few would want a valueless world where men no longer contend for the loyalties they cherish because they have lost them. This could only be a regression toward the negative bond of meaninglessness and the cultural desert. The danger has been overlooked by many of the advocates of a pluralistic culture who have not recognized that such pluralism depends on the continuation of religiocultural subsocieties and effective means of induction and communication. It is impossible to maintain genuine religious pluralism if the culture does not legitimize and provide means of educating and promoting concern for sacred value systems in the channels of cultural transmission.

That education should attempt to operate in the valueless desert of objective fact where every claim is equally valid is conceivable, unless it gave up all pretension to developing intelligence, discernment, and responsible leadership. If education abandons the search for values and commitment, it is already a casualty of the cybernetics it has created.

In the competition of faiths in the pluralistic culture, there are two distinct possibilities: a lowering of conviction and a confusion of orientation to the point that nothing matters because nothing is ultimate; or a rediscovery of one's place in history within a community of identification that points to the inclusive being in which all being is grounded. This second view recognizes that no path is unalloyed with personal and cultural relativities. It will also embrace the conviction that all "see through a glass darkly" while being committed to a transcendent relation and a community of faith continually responding to new illumination in the process of responding.

One of the tragedies of the competition of faiths is that it so easily turns into conflict and mutual denial. This is true in America among the three great faith groups. All three worship the same God of history who has acted in revealing events creatively and redemptively. All three have shown a susceptibility to the idolatries of henotheism, in which they have worshiped the conditioned and have spent debilitating energy on one another's idolatries rather than their own.

Thus they have all aided the secularization of the culture in which they exist by denying the legitimacy of the ultimate and by preconditioning men to indifference and nonrecognition of all religious claims. Instead of realizing the common source of their identity and mission, they have isolated themselves and abandoned the possibility of a common dialogue and witness to the primal significance of the religious quest.

Protestants, in their individualistic subjectivism, have failed to recognize the reality of culture. They imagined that men had an innate affinity of response to their particular message. Therefore, they had no interest in cultivating the soil of culture or entering the processes of cultural communication. They were unaware of the degree to which culture controls the convincibility and accepted legitimacy of their witness. Secularization was not viewed as real, nor was the task of cultural evangelism recognized as a prior imperative to personal responsiveness. The belief that man is universally a self-conscious being in need of identity and completion in a self-transcending relationship obscured the fact that this need can be met in many intracultural ways and that its appeal is dependent on cultural forms that have been internalized from a tradition. The possibility that an ideologically secularized man would hear no claiming message from their words and symbols was not comprehended. Therefore, they willingly went down the primrose path of separation. They let separation of church and state become transposed into separation of church and culture without even a protest. Many were unsuspecting advocates of keeping religion out of the schools, common celebratory events, and other basic channels of cultural induction.

The Roman Catholic Church has never suffered from the naivete of a favorable cultural climate to the transmission of faith. But it has feared interaction in a pluralistic culture and the questions that contacts might raise. Therefore it has steered the course of separation in education and welfare services. Like the Protestants, it feared the results of dialogue and risked the secular consequences rather than admit its separated brethren to the common identity within Christendom. It has been a cosponsor of the secular society.

The Jewish community, highly secularized with a majority identifying only with a culture rather than with an explicit faith, have contributed strongly to the secular trend. As a widely dispersed minority group with a history of persecution behind them, they feared exposure to the dominant culture. Rather than adapting separation which would require their own schools and agencies, they have undertaken to neutralize education, communications, and public events. They have pressed the unfairness of subjecting their children and youth to the symbolic forms and tradition of a predominantly Christian culture. They have been willing to risk the flat and barren culture in defense of their basic identification.

Education, as the chief vehicle of the transmission of culture, increasingly controls the basic value orientation of the people. By the significance it gives to religion, it will create the climate of favorability or unfavorability within which religious appeals must be made. At the college and university level religion should be a full participant in the "competition of creeds," to transpose the title of Leo Pfeffer's book. Yet it is a curious fact that in his book, which is a plea for free interaction of religious convictions, he turns out to be in favor of the opposite—the elimination of religious dialogue in the principal market place of culture: education, public celebrations, and the like. He is willing to have this competition only far out on the margins of the cultural process, and not within the chief cultural carriers themselves.[6]

There are two constitutional provisions that guarantee religious freedom in America: (1) there shall be no established church or faith; and (2) there shall be full freedom of religious expression. The religiously neutral state which provides no advantages for any religious orientation or particular religious establishment is faithful to the first part of the constitutional tradition. But a religiously empty culture which is ruled as off limits for full religious expression and cultivation denies religious freedom in its most absolute and death-dealing sense and, therefore, is in total contradiction to the second constitutional provision. Religious freedom in a pluralistic society demands both provisions.

## NOTES

1. Robert Redfield, *The Folk Culture of Yucatan* (Chicago: University of Chicago Press, 1939), Chapters 9, 10, 11; Elizabeth Nottingham, *Religion and Society* (Garden City: Doubleday, 1954); Ferdinand Toennies, *Community and Society* trans. and ed. by Charles P. Loomis from *Gemeinschaft und Gesellschaft (New York: Harper, 1963)*.

2. Clinton Rossiter, *Seedtime of the Republic* (New York: Harcourt, Brace, 1953), pp. 42, 43.

3. Universities have differing policies: some state universities, notably Iowa and Oregon, have departments of religion, while others take a highly restrictive view. Robert Michaelsen concludes after a careful *Study of Religion in American Universities* (New Haven: The Society for the Study of Religion in Higher Education, 1965) that "the study of this subject is still in an undeveloped state in American universities, and especially in state universities" (p. 157).

4. W. Lloyd Warner, *The Family of God* (New Haven: Yale University Press, 1961), p. 412.

5. Loren P. Beth, *The American Theory of Church and State* (Gainesville: University of Florida Press, 1958) p. 62.

6. Leo Pfeffer, *Creeds in Competition* (New York: Harper, 1958), p. 30.

$$\approx 10 \ll$$

# A CONTENT ANALYSIS OF STUDY MATERIALS
## IN THE CAMPUS MINISTRIES

### Edward Leroy Long, Jr.

## *Introduction*

The study by Edward Long of the kinds of educational materials, of assumptions in curriculum development, and of pedagogical techniques used by the majority of the campus ministers in their work puts them under severe indictment.

We do not intend to dwell on the susceptibility of religious leaders to theological fads he well describes; in one decade we have now been through the theologies of the death of God, religiosity, and mature secular man and are now entering a new theme—the theology of hope. We have been through in many campus study groups the sociologies and educational psychologies of Peter Berger, C. Wright Mills, Gibson Winter, Betty Friedan, Joseph Matthews, and Reuel Denny, and all as absolute gospel. Many of the people who used these exciting and helpful people and their books never assumed, or could not, the scholar's basic responsibility of putting their ideas in the context of other work going on in their academic fields.

The temptation to do this kind of disreputable teaching is perfectly understandable. The campus ministers deal mostly with the kind of laymen who have in their judgment about two to four hours a week to devote to what they regard as religious activities. We are not talking about the "true believers" who will come to anything the church announces as a meeting. We are talking about the significant group which keeps a skeptical but hopeful eye on the church to see if anything is going to happen, that explores the frontiers of new knowledge of some importance to the wider culture. The temptation is to give them the latest controversial piece: single in theme, a this-is-the-answer pamphlet or article blown up to book size and happily promoted by the denominational press in a cheap paperback edition as the very hottest religious word.

When this is the formula of education, Long asks, does the study material of the extracurriculum reflect reliance on the critical, rigorous reading offered in the religious studies department? Maybe there is no such department, and this complicates further the students' attempts to find out what is really going on in religious thinking. If there is a strong religious studies department, the campus minister is freed to pursue extracurricular programs of inquiry and action that mix the use of the best, not the fad, materials in theology, ethics, social service, psychology, and technology. He is free to mate and juxtapose the wonderful assortment of articles in the technical journals—that is, of course, if he reads them.

The new processes of reproduction of printed materials now make possible this kind of curriculum building, fitting the interests and resources of a particular group of Christian laymen and leaders. Materials used, for example, in a month-long, all-campus symposium arranged by religious ministers on "The Shape of the Future" at Yale in 1967 included films reproduced by business corporations, research institutes, churches, and the student "underground"; technical journals and academic, church, student drama scripts out of the university and off Broadway; lectures, interviews, panels, and private meditations on tape; posters from every segment of the artistic community; and TV and radio coverages from the networks. This began to indicate that critical, careful use of the vast resources of education available to leaders who are alert to the need of even the best academic institutions can occur, once the corporate, urban environment is embraced.

Edward Long's discussion of campus ministry study materials is still confined to the magazines and books and leaflets of that ministry, but this is only fair; this is as far as the use of most materials, except for a little poster art, has gone. But the substance of the media, not its technique, is what chiefly concerns him. Edward Long, as anyone who has read his *Introduction to Christian Ethics* knows, cannot tolerate teaching on the pop-theology level. His whole career has been the placement of intellectual movements in the context of a more complex, subtle Christian ethics of social policy.

KU

ALMOST every campus religious center makes use of a variety of materials designed to invite consideration of the relevance of Christian faith to a student's life and his eventual life as a citizen. Often the spritely tract receives greater attention than the extensive and enduring theological work of major scholarly significane.[1] Bonhoeffer's works, especially *The Cost of Discipleship* or *Prisoner for God*, have been more often used in campus discussion groups than the dogmatic theologies of Barth or Tillich; Waldo Beach's *Conscience on Campus* more frequently than George Thomas' *Christian Ethics and Moral Philosophy;* the works of Kierkegaard more than those of Harnack, Troeltsch, or Schleiermacher. Not many extracurricular campus discussion groups have taken John T. McNeill's *The History and Character of Calvinism,* Erik Erikson's *Young Man Luther,* or Donald Meyer's *The Protestant Search for Political Realism* as their study guide. Books are often chosen for use in the campus ministry for arresting style and provocative content more than for their ability to locate positions in the history or methodologies of a discipline. Freshness of approach and ease of reading are likely to become more important considerations than balance of value and technical competence when a ministry is striving for relevance and attention more than historical continuity or disciplined inquiry.

The searching student is interested in the Christian faith as it relates to the problems of his own existence and the needs of the world in which he lives. He wants guidance for his moral decisions, including his own sexual and vocational adjustments. He is concerned to know what it means to be a student and what the Christian faith may have to say about the aims and purposes of the educational venture in which he is spending his major time and energy. He is interested in contemporary social issues, especially the problems of international relationships abroad and racial justice and urban reform at home. Books that deal with matters of this sort are more likely to be popular reading, especially where no academic credit is involved, than books that concentrate on more abstract theories of religion and culture, Christian moral life, or matters of historical comparisons.

The recurring themes which elicit student response can be illustrated. The accompanying table groups by content selected books reviewed in the publications of the YMCA and YWCA for the beginning years of each of the last three decades. Books reviewed in the early thirties deal with many of the same themes explored by those chosen for review in the sixties. Student interest seems attracted to basically the same issues from one generation to another. (see Table 10-1).

The tendency in extracurricular studies is to use new literature coming from the pens of contemporaries. From time to time a writer from the past, like Kierkegaard, becomes a figurative contemporary and his books are read as though recent in origin and immediate in relevance. But the new book by the new author has the edge.

The campus ministry also uses material deliberately prepared for the student reader in the idiom of the student. Much of this is produced by the different agencies which sponsor the campus ministry. The National Methodist Student Movement has been particularly active in developing

TABLE 10-1

*Some Recurrent Themes in Books Recommended for Student Reading by Review in the Intercollegian*

| 1939-1942 | 1950-1953 | 1960-1963 |
|---|---|---|
| *Books dealing with the World* | | |
| Bennett, J. C. *Christianity and Our World* | Neibuhr, Reinhold *The Irony of American History* | Schmemann, A. *For the Life of the World* |
| Horton, W. M. *Can Christianity Save Civilization?* | | Neill, Stephen *Christian Faith and the Other Faiths* |
| *Social Action* | | |
| Terlin, Rose *Christian Faith and Social Action* | Voorhis, Jerry *The Christian in Politics* | Kelley, Alden D. *Christianity and Political Responsibility* |
| Limbert, Paul L. *Education for Civic Responsibility* | | King, M. L. *Why We Can't Wait* |
| *The Educational Experience* | | |
| Hamrick, Russell B. *To Make Good in College* | Moberly, Sir Walter *The Crisis in the University* | Miller, Alexander *Faith and Learning* |
| | Van Dusen, Henry P. *God in Education* | Walsh, Chad *Campus Gods on Trial* |
| *The Bible* | | |
| Fosdick, Harry Emerson *The Modern Use of the Bible* | Anderson, Bernard *The Unfolding Drama of the Bible* | Keck, L. *Taking the Bible Seriously* |

works of this sort. The United Campus Christian Fellowship has also distributed materials, frequently reprinted from other sources. All sponsoring agencies, such as the Student Volunteer Movement and the United Student Christian Council, have developed special study materials for campus use. Many of these are distributed only through the denominational groups.

Much of this material is promotional. The literature rack is likely to have items publicizing the Peace Corps, relief projects under church auspices, study abroad in programs supported by ecclesiastical or philanthropic organizations, term missionary service of various kinds, or summer projects. Moreover, the several student organizations prepare descriptions of their own campus activities, setting forth their aims as local fellowships or reporting on the activities of the national group. Such materials are designed for quick reading and aim for a response in terms of active participation. There is a kind of promotional material which conveys a message, sets a tone, and indicates a set of assumptions about the world in which we live. A small brochure published by the Westminister Foundation of Ohio University, entitled *We Are the Hollow Men,* has a cover which gives no indication of encasing a basically promotional leaflet. Inside there is a quotation from the poem of T. S. Eliot which inspired the title; there are cartoons, most of which prick the sham of either academania or religiosity. Toward the end of the booklet the nine aims of the United Campus Christian Fellowship are set forth, with the clear intention of saying to the prospective reader, "Come and join."

While this leaflet is designed to attract students to the local religious fellowship, it also engenders a set of attitudes about the meaning of religion and the purposes of the campus religious fellowship. It rather frankly describes what it understands to be the fears and hopes of a student generation and the emptiness which is assumed to charcterize much of its experience. This is its description of the Christian message:

> We want to possess and be possessed. And so our will-o'-the-wisp chase for happiness, for something to fill the void. This is how we live on this campus . . . live anywhere. I have a salty thirst, hollowness and robot activity. Is thirst quenched? Is there meaning in the meaningless, real habitation in space and time? Some have found it so . . . that in this damned and doomed existence there is a new existence, and added meaning for living . . . and dying. It is in the midst of lust and hate, fear and loneliness, but not a part of them. Received but not seized. Possessing but not possessed. No church has it (it has the church). No knowledge comprehends it (it comprehends knowledge). No morality creates it (it has its own goodness for prostitutes and Pharisees). A new existence for the mind and soul, and still it does not disregard the body (sex is its holy

gift). . . . The new existence is for empty men, searching men, men who want substance and not shadow. The new existence is for you.[2]

There can be no doubt concerning the imaginative skill demonstrated by a leaflet of this sort. But does this attract to the local fellowship a particular kind of person—one whose experiences make the quickest rapport with this personal/existentialistic diagnosis? The appeal seems one-sided. If the tone of promotional literature has possible consequences for the nature of the group it collects, conscious attention should be given to using appeals that will attract a healthy diversity among members.

A variant kind of material directly related to the life of the group is the program aid, which gives specific suggestions for carrying on the activities of the local fellowship. One form of the program aid is the pre-prepared worship service. This is usually provided for a special observance. But there are also worship services distributed because they offer a novel way to enhance experiences in this aspect of the program. For example, the United Campus Christian Fellowship printed a service written by Oscar J. Rumpf, of Eden Seminary, entitled *Love Agape Way* for presentation by voice choir. Some of these worship suggestions are closely patterned on traditional liturgies; some use different art forms in worship. Most of them play down the role of the traditional sermon.

Another form of the program aid is the Bible study guide. This is generally designed to stimulate discussion about the meaning which the biblical text holds for the contemporary reader and bears more affinities to homiletical concerns than to academic interests.

The role of technical knowledge is not totally ignored and certainly not subjected to contempt by the authors of the biblical study guides prepared by the main-line Protestant denominations. But little effort is made to introduce the student to such technical knowledge for its own value as the furbishing of the educated mind. Bible study as carried on with materials of this sort is quite different in content and intention from what would be done for credit in a classroom.

Another kind of literature prepared for use in campus religious programs calls attention to the social issues of our time. Some feel we are at a crucial juncture in the life of the student world when interest in personal/existential issues will give way to more exploration of social issues. The Ecumenical Institute at Chicago, in a flier advertising its study seminars for college students, puts the matter this way:

The depth concern of vanward students across the world has undergone a radical revolution. No longer is the spirit question "Who am I?" but "What shall I do?" It is a shift from identity to vocation. The new scientific, urban, secular world has come of age. The vanward student is lucid about this world and who he is in it. The issue today is significant involvement in civilization.

This may draw distinctions too strongly. There has been increased emphasis on social issues and problems in the past few years. These matters may well have been eclipsed during a decade when personal identity has been sought. But the student world has never been totally without books and articles prompting men to consider the implications of their religious faith for the social issues of their time.

The treatments of social issues vary in suitability. In some liberal arts colleges, particularly those with a sustained intellectual inquiry about contemporary society, the treatments commonly appearing in student religious publications must seem to omit the technically crucial considerations of solid social analysis. To students on other kinds of campuses, however, even the most elementary treatment of a social issue can come as important insight.

But even schools which alert their student bodies through curricular and extracurricular means to social issues may not do so on a sufficiently broad spectrum of issues. One dares to say that international affairs and matters relating to racial justice are better studied in the socially alert college than questions about sex mores or the nature and meaning of the educational experience itself. Thus, glaring gaps can be left in the range of human problems which are seriously considered. There is a place in college for the discussion of personal ethics and perhaps an even greater place for looking at the meaning and purpose of the educational task itself. It is part of the prophetic function of the student movement to meet needs which are not otherwise handled on a particular campus. If such needs come to be met by college curriculum or by other programs on the campus, the student religious leaders should move on to other functions.

In many religious publications aimed at students perennial attention is given to the meaning and purpose of the educational task. One church paper, which in its normal publication year is primarily a news report and editorial sheet about the life of a particular denomination, annually publishes a *Going to College Handbook*[3] designed for student use. The fall issue of most student magazines contains one or more articles on the meaning of being a student. There are pamphlets such as: *The Meaning of Theological Reflection; As My Son Goes to College; Tensions on the Campus; When Your Child Goes to College; Who Is Educated?; Christian Creativity in the Academic Market Place.* Among volumes: *Faith and Learning;*[4] *Toward a Christian Philosophy of Higher Education;*[5] *The Mind's Adventure;*[6] and *The Christian Student and the University.*[7]

These materials deal with the educational experience in a variety of ways. Some look at studenthood as a personal adventure; others deal more abstractly with the so-called "question of the university" and explore the relationship of Christian faith to the processes of learning. Many make claims for Christian theology which project it into a key role as the "queen" of the academic disciplines. Some challenge the prevailing assumptions of the contemporary institution of higher education—such as the claim to objectivity—or criticize the prevailing pluralism of the campus. The note of challenge and criticism has been a predominant one over the past fifteen or twenty years.

There are harbingers of a different approach to the educational problem in some recent theological literature. Harvey Cox's chapter, "The Church and the Secular University," in his *Secular City*[8] registers a protest against efforts to base Christian strategy in the university on the creation of a unifying perspective. Clyde A. Holbrook has developed a rationale for instruction in religion based on the assumptions of humanistic scholarship in general.[9] His approach contrasts with that of Alexander Miller, who contends that religion occupies a unique and overarching place in the curriculum and should not be departmentalized like other disciplines in university education. Both books move in the right direction: toward a positive appreciation of the intellectual life as a genuine Christian vocation, understanding the university as the setting in which that vocation is stimulated and sustained. Until theologians can write with perceptive appreciation of the educational task as currently pursued in the university, the university world is not likely to be profoundly impressed by theological discussions of educational problems.

Much discussion has also occurred regarding the relationships between individual academic disciplines and the Christian faith. In the early decades of this century, relationships between natural science and religion were the focus of frequent attention. Events like the Scopes trial and books like Andrew D. White's *History of the Warfare of Science with Theology in Christen-*

*dom*[10] made these problems a matter of considerable student concern. Now this issue attracts less attention in student discussion groups. The fact that some of the incisive recent materials in this area have not attracted widespread student interest may indicate in yet another way that felt existential needs, rather than caliber of treatment, is the more decisive influence in the choice of extracurricular reading materials.

There has been less material developed about the relationship of the social sciences to Christian faith. Many studies in Christian social ethics have mentioned this problem, but these studies have often been of interest to specialists. Peter Berger's imaginative work *The Precarious Vision*[11] is a possible exception to the predominant tendency.

Preoccupation with the theological meaning of the creative arts is now the most evident focus of concern. "The play's the thing; it holds the mirror up to man," declares the opening sentence of an article taken for republication as a student pamphlet.[12] A special issue of *The Christian Scholar*[13] was devoted to the theme of religion and literature. A publication coming from the Episcopal Church at the University of Iowa, entitled *Charlatan*, devoted almost its entire fall, 1964, issue to politics and the arts. This literature heralds the arts as allies in the portrayal of the human situation and as important aids in understanding the spiritual dimensions of our times.

The church also is examined in a number of ways by the literature used in the student movement. Some of the literature takes the form of Bible studies which illumine the conceptions of covenant, holy community, and household of faith as set forth in Scripture. Other treatments explore the meaning and structure of the Christian fellowship. Ecumenical impulses have often flowed from the Student Christian Movement, and today even the denominationally produced materials have the ecumenical conception of the church clearly in the foreground. The Student Volunteer Movement has been responsible for many studies over the years, such as D. T. Niles' *That They May Have Life*,[14] which present the need for the world for the Gospel as proclaimed by the Christian community. In much of the material, attention is repeatedly called to the place and role of the laity in the life and function of the church.

The student world has often criticized the church and explored its possible values. In recent years this critical note has acquired a new urgency in the critique of the pseudo establishment of American religion in a culture in which it enjoys tremendous prestige and popularity.

While much of the criticism is informed by sociological perspectives, it springs from a basic set of convictions about the meaning of the Gospel in relationship to the world. It does not exempt the institutional church from the judgment implied in faith. There is more at work here than mere student suspicion of the parochial church. There is a profound sense of what the church ought at best to be as prophetic goad to culture and deep concern over the failure of the religious establishment to demand true Christian commitment from its clientele. To the extent to which students are caught in the critical mood of the polemical tract, they may not fully appreciate the extent to which the criticisms are sounded by those whose basic loyalties are firmly structured in the Christian movement. These critics are suggesting that the church should be different and better and not that the church should no longer be. This is made particularly clear by Thomas C. Oden,[15] who criticizes the traditional forms of ecclesiastical procedures and proposes a renewed ecclesiology based on a concept of celebration. The liturgical overtones of this suggestion, with its heavy reliance on the sense of the church year, stand in some contrast with suggestions that we must move increasingly to nonreligious forms of Christianity.

The fundamental question prior to any suggestions for the renewal of contemporary Christian life is this: What are the contours of modern man's spiritual condition and cultural situation? Contemporary theologians are hard at work exploring the possible answers to this question, and their work has relevance to the student world. Bonhoeffer sought to convey the judgment that specifically religious forms of Christianity had outlived their appeal to modern man and to declare that retreat to the cultural ethos of a bygone era is impossible. The same theme has been stated by others in different ways. Gabriel Vahanian speaks of *The Death of God;*[16] Harvey Cox, of *The Secular City;*[17] Schubert Ogden, of *Christ without Myth;*[18] William Hamilton, of *The New Essence of Christianity.*[19] But the theological eveluation of secularism as religiously significant has become understood in a widespread way only in recent years.

There is ample room for differing analyses of the plight of contemporary man. What disturbs the thoughtful observer is the extent to which a single analysis is embraced with unqualified enthusiasm by one generation, only to give way before another and often contradictory analysis within a few years. We have been told on one hand that we have lost our moral roots and on the other that we suffer from a petty moralism which is unable to deal realistically with the ambiguous decisions of power politics in the modern world; we have been told that we live in a culture rampant with individualism, yet also informed that man's uniqueness has been lost in a mass culture; we have been asked to believe modern man suffers from rootlessness and loss of meaning, but also that man is doomed because of the pride and arrogance with which he presumes to take over the role of the Creator. These views seem individually plausible, especially when set forth in an attractive style and presented as the newest thing out. They cancel each other when systematically examined.

No right-thinking person would plead for a single imposed orthodoxy of cultural diagnosis. But what does raise questions is the extent to which there is almost no effort to make analytical comparisons in the theological materials usually prepared for popular consumption. These materials are tracts, rather than studies, and frequently lack historical perspective[20] and empirical confirmation. As long as the meaning of the Christian faith is set forth in the impressionistic style of the tract and conceived in largely existentialistic terms which appeal to the sense of felt need rather than critical analysis, there will remain a long way to go in developing significant reading for the students who are involved in the programs of campus ministries.

## NOTES

1. Parker Rossman conducted for the Danforth Study of Campus Ministries a survey of the major books and other materials recommended for reading and study by clergy and laity by four major denominational departments. The period studied was 1963-1965. Rossman also, by observation, correspondence, and interview, learned the actual materials used in study and discussion programs with students in a sample of ministries in these denominations in a variety of campus situations.

2. *We Are the Hollow Men*, pp. 21ff.

3. Published by *The Presbyterian Outlook*.

4. Alexander Miller, *Faith and Learning* (New York: Association Press, 1960).

5. John P. Grueningen, (ed.), *Toward a Christian Philosophy of Higher Education* (Philadelphia: Westminster, 1957).

6. Howard F. Lowry, *The Mind's Adventure* (Philadelphia: Westminster, 1950).

7. J. Robert Nelson, (ed.), *The Christian Student and the University* (New York: Association Press, 1952).

8. Harvey Cox, *The Secular City* (New York: Macmillan, 1965).

9. Clyde H. Holbrook, *Religion: A Humanistic Field* (New York: Prentice-Hall, 1963).

10. Andrew D. White, *History of the Warfare of Science With Theology in Christendom* (New York: Appleton, 1896).

11. Peter Berger, *The Precarious Vision* (Garden City: Doubleday, 1961).

12. Marshall W. Fishwick, "Diagnosing the American Dream," *Saturday Review*, December 21, 1963. Reprinted as a pamphlet by The United Campus Christian Fellowship.

13. "Religion and Literature", *The Christian Scholar* (Summer, 1964).

14. D. T. Niles, *That They May Have Life* (New York: Harper, 1951).

15. Thomas C. Oden, *The Community of Celebration: Toward an Ecclesiology for a Renewing Student* (Nashville: Methodist Student Movement, 1964).

16. Gabriel Vahanian, *The Death of God* (New York: Braziller, 1961).

17. Harvey Cox, *The Secular City, op. cit.*

18. Schubert Ogden, *Christ Without Myth* (New York: Harper, 1961).

19. William Hamilton, *The Essence of Christianity* (New York: Association Press, 1961).

20. For a perceptive observation about this tendency, see David Little, "The Social Gospel Revisited," *Christianity and Crisis*, July 12, 1965, pp. 151-153. In this review of Harvey Cox's *The Secular City*, Little shows the extent to which Cox replays themes from Rauschenbusch "without the slightest acknowledgment or apparent awareness of the solid historical tradition in which they stand."

## ❧ 11 ❧

## TOWARD AN ACTION THEORY OF LEARNING
## FOR THE CHURCHES

### Thomas F. Green

## *Introduction*

Thomas F. Green is director of a center for Policy Research in Public Education at Syracuse University. He is interested in ideas of educational process already implicit in some of present-day developments which enhance action and are in the biblical tradition. He is a Christian layman who has participated in the work and evaluation of campus ministries in several major university centers. His center is now engaged in the development of a curriculum and an approach to teaching of religious studies on a primary- and secondary-school level which will be acceptable to people of the varied faiths in American society and to disbelievers as well.

His essay helps clarify the relation of certain key biblical themes to university learning. The question of the relations between faith, knowledge, and action moves the discussion of educational policy from the "safer" issues of curriculum additions or credit requirements to the discussion of more difficult and important issues such as the consequences of various kinds of learning on the capacities of students to act. For Green, the most important consequence of education should be seen by the churches to be that of enabling a man to be more than a being whose behavior is determined by rules and forces that give him no choice or decision. A man participates in the shaping of his situation, while being influenced by it; he comes to recognize that the power on which the world depends wills a certain indeterminacy in human interaction.

There are many operational implications for the church from this perspective. One certainly is that the professional clergy are to be evaluated in the future, much more than heretofore, on their competence in developing the capacities of laymen to minister. Green's work is a worthy example. His investigations and interpretations of the religious and moral dimensions of education could be done only by a man who is deeply involved both in a specialized area of the university and in the intellectual life of the religious community. Training of religious educators in centers such as the one at Syracuse before or after their theological studies would seem to be one way of producing needed changes in the learning processes of the churches.

KU

$M$Y subject is the relation of faith to the educational process. I am not discussing the role of "faith in general" or "religion" or "faith in faith" and their relation to the educational process. On the contrary, I am concerned about the role of biblical faith in the process of education. In general my thesis is that education, and, in particular, teaching as a method of education, is itself shot through with expressions of the biblical faith. Therefore, one ought not to ask how faith is related to education except to look at the educational process itself and see evidences of The Faith already implicit in it.

I propose, therefore, to proceed in the following manner. I shall simply list certain themes which I think are biblical and comment briefly on each of them. Then I shall discuss what seem to me to be important features of the contemporary education scene in the light of which these themes may take on some added importance.

My first theme is a biblical understanding of wonder—of what it means to be in awe. Not only is there an important way of understanding this human capacity in the Bible but I am very nearly convinced that it is only in a tradition very like the Hebrew tradition that we can understand it.

There are certain conditions under which it is possible for a people to experience awe and amazement. I would argue that when people experience wonder or are in a state of awe, they are very close to a biblical view of life. Indeed, every time in a classroom when there is a sense of awe and wonder at the discovery of something new, or surprise and amazement at some ordinary phenomena in life that one has never before viewed with wonder, at that time and at that point we are very close to understanding our world and ourselves through the eyes of faith.

This is so because one of the conditions of wonder is the realization that what we discover to be the case need not be the case at all; that our world could be quite different from what it actually is; that it might, in fact, not even include us. This is, indeed, an experience which brings us very close to a biblical understanding of creation, as presented in the first chapter of Genesis. There it is stressed that the entire world is contingent. It is held in precarious existence by its Creator. It need not exist, and we need not exist in it. It might be totally different from what it is. Therefore, it really is amazing not only that it is, but that it is the way it is.

My second theme, perhaps even more fundamental than the first, has to do with a biblical image of freedom directly related to the notion of salvation. The term "salvation," I am told, has in its Semitic origins the meaning "to develop without hindrance," "without limitation." Paul Lehman has pointed out that the biblical notion of salvation always involves deliverance, but never without at the same time involving fulfillment. Basically it means, as I should put it, "to be set free to wander in the world." The story of Abraham is a splendid illustration of this. The Lord said to Abraham, "Get thee out of this land to a land which I shall show you." Abraham did not ask whether the land has been planted, what the sanitary system was like, or whether the schools were up to snuff. He went. Not knowing where he was going, he was on the move. And the Scripture says, "It was counted to him as righteousness; for he walked in faith." He was set loose as a pilgrim.

This is a tremendous image which permeates nearly every page of the Bible. In the Exodus, a theme to which the Old Testament returns again and again, the people were delivered out of bondage and set loose to wander to just what place they did not know. I take it that this is also part of what Paul is saying when he remarks (in an entirely different context) that all things are lawful, though not all things are helpful. This is the image of freedom, the image of the pilgrim—the man, in short, who has no worldly home, whose hope does not reside in the final importance of his own efforts, who understands that, after all, all flesh is grass and even human achievements and human institutions will pass. The net result of such a freedom is the increasing capacity to venture as an alien and as a stranger in the world. It is the image which underlies the tension in the New Testament between realized eschatology and future eschatology, the understanding there of what it means to "live between the times." It was a problem to the psalmist who said, "How shall I sing the Lord's song in a strange land?" There is in this conception of freedom an understanding of what it means to declare one's self an adventurer into the peculiar arenas in which men work and labor in order that one can declare himself a partisan on behalf of men and children wherever they are.

This freedom I take to be the most pure and radical conception of human freedom of any in the resources of our Western tradition. It is the most perfect conception of man's capacity to act rather than to be acted upon—to be the master, in one sense, of his freedom because he has no illusions as to how far that mastery goes and no illusions as to where his hope is placed. And in this capacity to be free to act resides the humanity of man: not his goodness, not his moral perfection, but his humanity.

The third theme is the central and widespread view of the Bible concerning the unity of word and deed. Again, the creation story at the beginning of Genesis provides the paradigm of what I have in mind. God said, "Let there be light," and there was. There is no separation between word and deed. There is the famous passage from Isaiah where he says that the word of God shall not go forth and return without being fulfilled. People asked Jesus who he was, and in effect he did not give them an answer. He asked them simply to observe what happened: the blind see, the sick are cured, the lame walk, and the Gospel is preached to the poor. Instead of identifying himself by word, he simply pointed to certain deeds. Indeed, in the Gospels it is this pointing to deeds which is central in the claim that Jesus *was* the Word. In fact, this is and always has been the way that the Word of God is identified—by deed.

There is throughout the Bible no separation between thought and act, between word and deed. This perspective makes intelligible certain injunctions Jesus states about the relation of thinking and acting, that he who lusts after a woman is guilty of adultery. This point is sometimes expressed by saying that in the biblical understanding of things there is no important separation between mind and body, thinking and doing. They are one, just as word and act are one. The emphasis always is not on what you know, what you think, or what you do, but rather on what you are.

My fourth theme has to do with the well-known fact that the Bible takes history seriously. Because God is the sovereign of history, his purposes are to be discerned in the events of history. There is in the Bible (and not simply in the reformed tradition) a sense of providence which makes it possible for men to live in their own day conscious of the stream of history of which they are a part and convinced of the meaning and purpose of the historical process. In practical terms, what this means to me is the necessity of discerning the occasions which are presented to us for action. For, according to the biblical distinction between *kronos* and *kairos*, we must recognize that not every time is a time for action. It means that we must be always alert that God may be bringing to pass in our day what we do not yet clearly see.

The fifth theme I wish to mention is the continuous biblical image of the prophet as teacher. He is social critic and speaks a word of judgment as well as of redemption and hope. He is social critic even about the most sacred and fundamental features of society; namely, about the things which men hold dear. He is even a critic about religion. I shall develop this theme no further because it has been emphasized so much by so many already.

Now, suppose we simply set these themes to one side and go on to consider some problems involved in contemporary education. In particular, I want to discuss some of the problems of liberal education, not because what I want to say is confined to liberal education, but because I happen to be more concerned with it.

What I mean by liberal education cannot be equated with what is usually called the liberal arts. We can understand liberal education, and perhaps all education, as aimed primarily at enhancing the human capacity for action. Certainly this is no less true of the humanities than of engineering and professional education. What makes education liberal is not its subject, but its consequence.

This idea is closely related to another point I want to make. It seems to me that the most fundamental problem which needs study in education is the relation between thinking and acting. Considered on quite unbiblical and nonreligious grounds, this relation is the fundamental problem of all education. It has to do with cultivating a relationship between thinking and acting so that we do not get what Sartre calls "bad faith," that condition in which men think one thing and do something else altogether. In teaching and in scholarship, this relationship must be taken seriously, or else more and more the educational process becomes unrelated to the actual involvement that anyone has in the world in which he lives.

I would want to maintain that knowing, taken by itself, has no tendency to make a man better at all. Gilbert Highet has defended the idea that knowledge has intrinsic value. He argued that if a man knows the structure of a leaf, all other things being equal, he is better in that respect than the man who does not know it. But I would want to consider a somewhat different example. I am not so certain that if a man were to memorize all the telephone numbers in the Lansing directory, all other things being equal, he would in that respect be a better man than one who does not have such knowledge. It is interesting to observe, however, that there are circumstances in which this knowledge might be very important. They are the circumstances in which the knowledge of all the telephone numbers in the Lansing directory would be a necessary bit of knowledge in order to accomplish something of importance in the community. In short, such knowledge would be of value in proportion to its importance for human action. This does not mean that the pursuit of knowledge for its own sake should not be encouraged. It only means that knowledge is not intrinsically valuable; its possession does not make a man better.

In this way I would want to argue that the purposes of the university are not moral, but intellectual. Its purposes are intellectual, but its means are moral. Basically, knowledge is important because and to the extent that it permits men to act. By enlarging the sphere of their thinking, it enhances their capacity to act. There is in this view the underlying understanding that there is a unity between thinking and acting, between word and deed. And so once more we return to the theme that the most general objective of education, and certainly of liberal education, is to enhance the human capacity for action, to enlarge the capacity to live the life of the pilgrim.

But the world for the sake of which people want knowledge and need it, the world in which they shall have to act, is a world which is highly organized, tremendously bureaucratic, primarily technical, basically urban, and institutionalized. We are living in an age in which increasingly, and partly by necessity, we are led to deal with human beings through large associations, bureaucracies, and concentrations of power in various sectors of our society. This means that the freedom to wander in the world increasingly demands the skills needed to work not only *within* but *upon* our institutions. It means that one of the most central concerns of action in our modern world requires that we take seriously, in a way we have not been disposed to do, the limits of a man's power. Questions of power, of institutional change, of institutional management—these things are of really crucial concern if human beings are to know how to act upon their society and not simply within it. The way in which we exercise power and understand its nature in the modern world has to be related to institutions. Power belongs to institutions, and not to individuals. People individually may have strength, but it does not add up to much unless they see the exercise of their strength in conjunction with other human beings institutionally ordered in such a way that their collective action begins to have some effect on society.

The flowering of intelligence, therefore, in our day and in the next generation is not to be found in the private man of good taste. It is to be found in the public man who is an effective force in his community, whether that community be his professional associations, his vocational life, or the narrower community in which he resides. Contemporary American education, however, is in fact, if not ideally, concerned primarily with vocational development and with personal cultivation. There is very little actually done in our schools to develop the "public man." Certainly there is very little actually done in American public schools to approximate the "public" character of the English public schools. The fact is, however, that both in the present and in the immediate future, the flowering of human intelligence is going to be discovered less and less in the scholar and more and more in the scholar-citizen and the citizen-scholar.

What I am saying is that the very process of education must be understood increasingly in the way in which we free a man to act. The unity of word and deed, which is central to the biblical tradition, is also at the heart of the educational process in our society. To the extent that the increase of our knowledge does not permit this greater freedom to act and cultivate a greater capacity to be free, to that extent it is not liberal. Indeed, to that extent it is not even humanizing.

This means that the core of the new liberal learning, I think, is to be found, if not in the behavioral sciences, certainly in the social sciences and to some extent in those areas of knowledge directly related to the professions. Increasingly I am impressed by the success of the social sciences to afford people that kind of "sixth sense" of discernment which permits them to read the signs of the times—to sense the state of the world in which they are involved and then to select the places and the times for action. There is such a thing as what John F. Kennedy called "the hard logic of events." But there is also such a thing as the right time, the pregnant time, the appropriate time, the fruitful time. But we cannot know what these times are if we cannot discern the state of our world and the institutions around us in order to select the place and the moment to insert ourselves into these institutions as a force for change. I am impressed by the degree to which the social sciences at their best are able to provide people with this kind of discernment of what the New Testament calls *kairos*—the time of opportunity.

But it is a defect, I think, that the social sciences are thus the core of liberal education, for they are too much divorced from their ancestral roots in the humanities. As a consequence they free us, allow us to be the pilgrims we must be, and extend our power, but they cannot sustain us, because they do not reinterpret for us the classical religious and moral images of man and of society on which our future must rest no less than our past. The social sciences, for the most part, deal with man as the creature of history, but not with man as the creator of history. They speak of man as the product of society, but not of man as the producer of community. They do not introduce us at all to the vast image of man as the creature who is addressed by God. On the other hand, however, I think that the inheritors of the humanistic tradition have too seldom addressed themselves to the hard moral choices which men actually face in the realm of public life or in the political and social sphere of action. As a consequence, I think the humanities and the social sciences have tended to grow apart, and because of that fact as much as any other, liberal education has failed to be truly liberal. The moral images which it transmits, and which for the most part are propagated by our society, are often simply irrelevant to the condition of action and decision in modern society. They do not help men to act.

As a consequence, the inner lives of our graduates become all the more unrelated to their public acts. The unity between thought and deed is breached. This produces one of the characteristics of modern man; namely, that he is immobilized, again and again and again. Much of this ineffectiveness is related to the fact that we have never been educated for the role of public life or to be the "public man": one who can act in an institutionalized urban society. We have not been educated in such a way that knowledge and action are successfully related.

# ≫ 12 ≪

## TOWARD A SCIENTIFIC THEORY OF EXPERIMENTAL
## LEARNING FOR THE CHURCHES

### David Duncombe

## *Introduction*

David Duncombe is now a campus minister at the Yale University Medical School; while writing this paper he was a candidate for a Ph.D. in the psychology of religion. He was asked to try to evolve a learning theory for the churches which would hold together the ways of learning implicit in the four modes of ministries we have been exploring in our study. He has sought to do this by enlarging a scientific-experimental approach to learning.

What emerges in this particular essay is an identification of Christian learning with Christian freedom interpreted largely in social and psychological terms. Duncombe he assumes that institutional structures are responsible for whatever goals of a new life in Christ there are to be achieved and that these structures can be consciously changed by leaders. His major thesis is that church leaders must use and adopt their programs to rational-scientific authority as a major force in the learning process, that they must make pedagogical use of empirical demonstration in matters of religious beliefs. He sees the content of the learning process in the establishment of the new life in Christ.

This stance presupposes that actualized redemption (the new life in Christ) is *the* Christian goal of education, that Christian learning is change, and that learning in the church works for empirically demonstrated progress toward this goal. Some severe priorities are thereby set in Duncombe's mind. Patterns of group dynamics and counseling and the methods of demonstrating progress toward a new life should not be pressed until a church is clear about what the content of the Christian life is presumed to be and what pedagogical methods actually contribute to this. Duncombe says more about the pedagogical method than the content of Christian learning (except that it promotes Christian freedom). That method is empirical demonstration as understood by the academic world. He has had the courage to indicate a means for achieving this in religious education.

His type of experimentation with church education will certainly yield some new information for religious leaders who have never experimented with anything in the church. But, as the director's report indicates, there are no clear sanctions in the church as to what the content of Christian learning should be or the padgogical methods for achieving these.

Duncombe emerges as firm in his conviction, with the most orthodox practitioners of religious education, that the secular ministry has not confronted its generation with realities in the world. No discussion of the faith can ignore these and long call itself religious education.

This is why David Duncombe's two contributions in this volume are important. They are attempts to discover uses of the behavioral and social sciences which will be conducive to full humanity. To his mind, the university's responsible use of them is to engage in unending controlled experimentation in the social process to determine the significant variables in the various spheres of society that contribute to positive and negative instances of a rigorously defined humanness. The churches have a responsibility to call upon the universities to help them translate norms of the Christian life into images and theories that the social scientist can handle. To fail to do this is to be derelict in prophetic inquiry.

KU

I

THEORIES of learning are concerned with change—change of knowledge, feelings, attitudes, beliefs, commitments, motives, and other forms of "behavior." The campus minister is seeking to affect change in his round of campus contacts. While every contact presupposes a theory of learning, rarely are its premises recognized and articulated. A good theory of learning predicts and explains behavioral changes in ways that can be clearly defined. Similarly, a good theory of learning specifies what it is that causes these changes. It states that when $A$ (and not $X$) occurs, $B$ (and not $Y$) is the result. In short, it is an eminently testable hypothesis.

In formulating our own theory of learning for the campus ministry, it is essential that we understand the $A$'s and $B$'s of the current campus situation before substituting a more "Christian" set. This is not solely a "know your enemy" tactic. If anything, it is prompted by the belief that to ignore the major social forces that shape learning processes on the campus is folly, and to oppose them may prove impossible.

One of the most striking findings of the Danforth Study is the pervasive distrust of institutional authority among students and campus ministers alike.

Equally striking is the actual locus of their trust. Both ministers' and students' surveys indicate a marked preference for "adaptive" values; that is, those that reflect a willingness to trust rational scientific methods and authorities.

The causes of this displacement toward the adaptive pole of the "action field" are by no means certain. It has been suggested that our institutional forms have become too complex and depersonalized to serve as object of respect, loyalty, and commitment. Another approach insists that it is basically a problem of expanding knowledge. As a market commodity, knowledge (especially new knowledge) claims the power to compete successfully with traditional-collective power.[1] Further, the fact that the knowledge explosion has equipped the preadolescent with as much knowledge as that possessed by Aristotle can hardly encourage reverence for lesser traditional authorities. Again, the effects of mass communications, teenage revolt, and deterioration of the national moral fiber are frequently mentioned as causes. The reader can add others.

For my purposes, I would like to suggest a simpler hypothesis which nevertheless seems to catch an important dimension of all these causal theories. I detect behind all these supposed causes a common presumption that the new American remains unconvinced by, and unattracted to, any authority so much as empirical demonstration. For the moment this must remain an untested hypothesis. But it is a testable one, as will soon become clear. It is also the kernel of the theory of learning to be proposed. Since its validity has yet to be established, I cannot "present" a theory of learning here. For now, allow me to suggest what a four-step theory of learning based on such a hypothesis might look like and why I feel that it would be both effective and Christian.

1. Regard certain claims of theologians as hypotheses; supply the student with the tools necessary for determining their truth.

2. Argue the merits of the hypothesis claim.

3. Prepare an appeal. A hypothesis properly appealed is stated in a way that permits empirical verification. In the clearest way possible, the student must be helped to understand what conditions would count for and against the truth of a particular Christian claim.

4. The final step is the hazardous attempt to perceive in what structures of the society the Spirit of God may possibly be at work presenting to man the possibilities of action. We can neither assume nor compel God's presence; but if Christian thought through the ages reliably describes His work, it is we

who are compelled to seek out and find "where the action is" and to respond with our strategic involvements in the world. By strategic involvement I mean the ordering of our lives to make choices that will serve others at the center, not at the periphery of life. We must be free to find God in the continuing activities of our existence, in the forms of particular institutions which invite our participation. The genuine theological and ethical task of finding God at work will be done as we understand what strengthens and what weakens the possibilities for responsible action of individuals and corporate agencies in the world.

This, then, is the substance of the theory of learning for the campus ministry that I have in mind. It directs theological and ethical reflection in the learning process through four steps: claim, argument, appeal, and strategic involvement in the world.

## II

To see how a campus minister might implement this theory of learning, let us take a typical pattern-maintenance claim: institutional structures support more freedom than they restrict.[2] Statement of the claim and its implications is then followed by supporting arguments. I should be inclined to argue as follows:

> Certain structures of institutionalized authority represent for many people a complex network of agreement, assent, and mutual obligation. Certain institutional rules, ideology, doctrine, rites, and so on symbolize these "covenants," but illumine only dimly, if at all, their origins and meaning in human development. Through the process of gradual displacement from nuclear family, teachers, and peer groups, these impersonal institutional structures acquire an intensely personal meaning in virtue of the multitude of buried covenant expectations they represent. It is in the stirrings of these "foundations of consent" that one may experience a deep sense of social acceptance and identity.[3]
>
> In the measure that these early covenants *did* supply a sense of security and *are* effectively symbolized by present institutional structures, we could expect that a person should be free from the basic concern for self-justification. He should have more freedom: to know himself, be himself, perceive and respond to the world as it is—and in the penetrating phrase of Luther—more freedom to "let goods and kindred go."

Perhaps many sound arguments might be advanced against the claim in question. In this case, the need for empirical verification becomes obvious.

We need an experimental design that does justice to the particular institution. *A* could be defined in terms of its shared values, traditions, symbols, presuppositions, ideologies, rules, rites, satisfactions, and authorities. For purposes of clarity and force, however, it is best to ruthlessly exclude all "human" or interpersonal factors. In essence our claim is that it is these "cold" and objective structures *(A)*, and not the "fellowship" factor *(X)* found outside of institutions as well, that account for the expected result *(B)* "more freedom." An experimental procedure such as the following might be used.

Select an actual institution that corresponds to the various structural criteria defined: a particular church, college, fraternity, branch of the armed services, club, nation, or the like. From this institution randomly designate twenty or thirty "experimental" subjects. Then pick the same number of "control" subjects from a different population of comparable age, sex, education.

The first task for subjects of both groups is to take a "freedom test."[4] Then administer to both groups an inventory measuring the extent to which the subjects indicate loyalty to the selected institution. Both groups then receive an experimental "treatment," consisting of some means of making salient the defined structures of the selected institution. An involving film, mass rally, service, or written communication emphasizing the tradition, symbols, rites, ideology, creed, ideals, and other appropriate structures could be tried.[5] This would be followed by a second administration of the "freedom test," and that followed by a second administration of the loyalty inventory.

According to our hypothesis claim that institutional structures support more freedom than they restrict, we could expect that the experimental, but not the control, subjects would significantly increase their scores on the second administration of the "freedom test."[6] By varying the kinds of institutions, types of treatment, time between treatment and readministration of the "freedom test," the "freedom tests" themselves, and other variables, even this simple design could prove useful in compiling a body of data bearing on the validity of the claim. Out of this and similar data could come revised claims more worthy of being learned and more likely to be learned.

A final step remains. The significance of this "strategic involvement" step, however, can best be illustrated by raising two likely objections to the procedure already suggested. The first objection is that it is too narrow to encompass the wide range of behaviors involved in Christian learning. For example, Robert Boehlke proposed seven types of behavioral changes: changes in knowledge, understandings, attitudes, values, skill-habits, motives, and the self.[7] As we move toward the end of this list, it becomes less obvious how changes are affected according to our theory of learning; that is, what motives would be altered by verification of the "more freedom" claim? Would we "adaptives" find ourselves less attracted to greed, power, self-justification, and the like? Were this an issue of the power of knowledge over sin, it would have to be answered in the negative. But if what we have been talking about all along is a strategic use of Christ's power over sin, empirically grounded knowledge takes on religious significance. For if we *knew* which institutional structures are the earthen vessels for Christian freedom and under what conditions, we could commit ourselves to them in greater trust and clearer conscience. It would then be the *effect* of these structures on us (and not the knowledge that led us to them) which would undercut the psychic *raison d'etre* of these motives.

Furthermore, there is reason to believe that we would commit ourselves to such institutional structures. For some it might be enough that they now possessed reliable knowledge. But it is unrealistic to presuppose that we are all inwardly motivated to cast off the old man and be transformed, awaiting only a reliable cue. We have deep conflicts about wanting to undergo the radical changes of such a learning experience. Christian freedom is seen also as a threat.

What, then, could overcome this reluctance? A clue to the answer is implied by the value placed on the capacity for "adaptation" in a technical civilization. The authority of empirical demonstration is great in our culture and carries with it the anticipation of change in the action of individuals and institutions.

Personality theory suggests that parents expect us to distinguish fact from wish and appropriately reinforce this by granting and withholding of affection in terms of the child's capacity to discern social functions and real obligations. It is entirely consistent, then, that our present feelings of disaffection with institutional structures should include guilt feelings about trusting them. But what if we could empirically establish the "more freedom" claim for certain institutional rites, symbols, and creeds? Would we not then *feel* "at home" with these very institutional structures that formerly made us uneasy and be unconsciously inclined toward them? I think that we might, although not immediately, perhaps.[8] Whether this would be sufficient to offset the feelings of apprehension about submitting to upsetting changes mediated by these institutional structures must remain an open question. For the present it is perhaps enough to recognize the possibility of a countervailing force "built in" to the psychic fabric of American life through the agency of nothing less than the much-maligned "modern conscience."

The general effect of selective reinvolvement with social institutions over time would be most pronounced at the skills-habit, motives, and total self end of Boehlke's behavior spectrum. While our largely rational convictions, attitudes, and values regarding the worth of the indicated institutional structures (plus concomitant guilt feelings) would occasion the re-engagement, if the institutions *actually* and *continually* provided the freeing effects demonstrated, such reward and reinforcement would also insure habitual involvement, development of requisite skills, and cultivation of new secondary motives. Such a "dynamic synthesis" of these six types of behavior, experienced as "commitment," is what Boehlke means by his final and most comprehensive aim of Christian learning, "changes in the self."[9]

What, then, of a possible objection that our theory of learning applies only to a restricted content? In a sense this is quite true. Empirical demonstration is out of the question for many traditionally important Christian claims: the existence, nature, and will of God, election and covenant, the Incarnation, the Resurrection, and other doctrinal claims. Even the *fact* of redemption among Christians down through the ages may be beyond the scope of verification, although this possibility should not be written off. All the empiricist has to go on is the descriptions of how this redeeming experience transforms persons and the claim that certain institutional structures are somehow importantly involved in mediating this change.

There are two ways of responding to this objection. The first is simply to call attention to a point previously made: that the effect of the empirical demonstration may involve one in various content-bearing institutional structures (ideology, doctrine, tradition, creed, symbol). Churchmen have contended for centuries that education about the church cannot be separated from involvement in it. Thus involved in the structures of a demonstrably effective church, for example, a student would never know if the Resurrection actually occurred. But he would discover that the claimed effects of this Resurrection do occur in the lives of those who believe in and live as though there were a Resurrection, including his own.

Of course, we take a change. The student may find out that institutional churches are not the center of redeeming activity, that believing in the Resurrection is inversely associated with the presence of its claimed effects, or other equally unsettling pastoral theology developing out of just this kind of finding. The only risk we take is that we may have to revise a few cherished beliefs.

A second way of approaching the "too narrow content" objection is to suggest something a little more radical. If our assumption is correct that learning is restricted primarily to that which can be demonstrated as true, why should we want to teach anything else as "true"? To put it bluntly, should we teach anything as true that we do not *know* to be true? For example, do we *know* that God elected Israel? Then should we teach it as though we did?[10] That is the moral and religious consideration. Its pedagogical concomitant is whether it is possible to teach effectively something as true that cannot be shown to be true.

In posing such questions, I am not unmindful that the words "truth" and "know" have many meanings, only one of which directly concerns the dynamics of the theory of learning proposed. But the point is not what we mean by these terms when we make a religious truth claim, but how such a claim is interpreted by the student. If my analysis of cultural authorities and motives is correct, it is a rare student (and perhaps campus minister) for whom some form of empirical demonstration is not intrinsic to his conception of truth and knowledge.

This does not mean that other truth claims should not be taught or that other meanings of truth and knowledge should not be explained. Whether they will be learned is another matter. It means only that traditional claims must be presented for what they are: empirically unsubstantiated beliefs that men live by. Never should it be even intimated that they *are* the "truth." the campus minister must be a man "without authority" (to use Kierkegaard's phrase), not only for reasons of student motivation but because the answers he commands lack sufficient reliability to be taken as the truth.[11] The student's understanding of this fact should never be violated.

Such caution and restraint are more than simple honesty and sound pedagogy. They are an act of Christian freedom of which we ourselves may be largely incapable until we have taken on the discipline of empirical demonstration and have been led to "where the action is." We may then better understand for out time and profession the meaning of the promise "You shall know the truth, and the truth shall make you free."

## NOTES

1. See Fred M. Hechinger, "Now a Degree Is a Path to Power," New York *Times*, August 21, 1966, p. E 9.

2. Adapted from Houston Smith, *The Purposes of Higher Education* (New York: Harper, 1955), Chapter IV.

3. For an excellent juristic interpretation of this position (to which I am indebted), see John F. A. Taylor, *The Masks of Society* (New York: Appleton-Crofts, 1966). Besides obvious psychological sources, this position has also been informed by Marshall McLuhan's "the medium is the message" thesis in his *Understanding Mass Media: The Extensions of Man* (New York: McGraw-Hill, 1965), especially pp. 4-26, 52, 158, 211, 242.

4. A simple form of such a test appears in the Appendix to Chapter 8 of this volume and a brief explanation of it in Chapter 8, Subsection A. More sophisticated tests are described in Duncombe, *The Shape of the Christian Life* (New York: Abingdon, in press).

5. The design technically requires that the *A* term of the hypothesis read "the process of making salient institutional structures" instead of merely "institutional structures."

6. This increase should be especially marked for experimentals who score high on both loyalty tests. However, the loyalty tests are used mainly as a check on control group selection procedures and the possibility that the treatment event might inculcate (as well as make salient) institutional associations.

7. Robert R. Boehlke, *Theories of Learning in Christian Education* (Philadelphia: Westminster, 1962), pp. 37-57.

8. In practice, this need not mean a compliant acceptance of all institutional forms previously distrusted. With the *psychological* basis of the distrust removed and the *factual* basis clarified, two other courses of action are open: a person might set about affecting changes in still objectional and institutional structures, but with a new-found loyalty to the institution; or he could shift his involvement to institutions in which he would be more comfortable.

9. Boehlke, *op. cit.*, p. 57.

10. The otherwise sound article on learning theory and Christian education by Rachel Henderlite, "Toward a Learning Theory for Ecumenical Education," *Risk*, Vol. II, No. 1 (1966), pp. 82-91, is marred by this unexamined assumption.

11. The etymological and functional relationship of "truth" and "reliability" as pertains to the university community is discussed by Cornelius A. van Peursen, "The Concept of Truth in the Modern University," *Student World*, IV (1963), 344-353. This might be compared to John Dewey's discussion of "adverbial" truth in his *Reconstruction in Philosophy* (New York: Mentor, 1950), pp. 128-131.

# ❧ 13 ❧

## WOMEN AND MEN

### Anne Firor Scott

## *Introduction*

The rationale for the inclusion here of an article on "Women and Men" was simply to acknowledge that the churches are as caught as the universities in confusion about the changing relations and roles of males and females in society. It is an acknowledgment that we *needed* some historical perspectives on the subject from a respected social historian and a person who had had the experience of helping politicians and governors clarify their own responsibilities toward women (as Professor Scott's chairmanship of the Governor's Commission on the Status of Women in North Carolina).

Anne Scott paints a broad canvas of new developments in female and male relations in the past century, but leaves the church and its ministers with the problem of working out the specific implications for their activities. However, some of the programmatic implications are quite obvious.

She invites the YWCA and other organizations to look at their situation from the many perspectives which scholarship now offers. The beginning point of her own analysis is that the modern woman, like any other human being, needs to find meaningful work in the years when she is not a mother or a housewife and to locate other opportunities for growth and human responsibility. Professor Scott is looking for institutions which will open up a wide range of opportunities for women. These may be places to develop new technical skills; continuing education seminars that remove the curse of false femininity displayed in most of the mass media and deal with verified differences—biologically, psychologically, socially, theologically—between male and female; or they may be employers and organizations looking for creative ways for women to make social contributions, places where new ideas are made organizationally effective instead of remaining part of the group process.

Many people, Anne Scott discerns, are looking for educational or religious institutions that view women not only in terms of Betty Friedan's target, a Puritan career of motherhood as a way of life, but as persons who live out a variety of phases and cycles and want these recognized in organized programs. The YWCA, at its best, is trying to become such an institution, but the progress is slow since many leaders have looked upon the Y in single-value terms, as a career, or social service, or recreation, for example. Therefore, other avenues of female life are not being explored for their Christian or religious significance with the same thoroughness and imagination as the fight against the early marriage syndrome and the woman as sex object.

Anne Scott documents well that sex prejudice is still the only socially acceptable one. Thus salary differentials, discrimination in composition of graduate classes, boycott of vocational areas, and ignorance or apathy about new programs of highly successful continuing education for women (such as those at Radcliffe or the University of Minnesota) are not brought under criticism of an alert Y or campus ministry organization. Many liberal arts college chaplains are going to have to help their schools open up co-operative relations with surrounding technical schools in the big universities so that women can end up after four to seven years of college education with the ability to minister to minorities or handicapped children, to run a computer, to teach a discipline well, and to do nursing or laboratory work in centers for medical practice.

The problem the campus ministries face is not that of providing a Y or a denominational center that offers a few seminars or discussions on traditional women's "hang-ups." The problem is that of working effectively to change the educational environment in which women live, so that the options in style of life and career are drawn clearly and opportunity for respected service on equal terms with men is encouraged. As Professor Scott implies, the first thing a critical theologian or ethicist does is to free people from the premise that there is one "natural" or "right" Christian way for women to behave in the society or to participate in the family life. A serious study of the role of Negro women in our society would soon dispel that illusion of sameness in family-life patterns and of male roles.

What is at stake basically is *how* the people of a community, such as the church, think about a human problem and come to conclusions about its true situation. In the course of this study we have traveled many times with campus ministers going to women's church meetings ostensibly to tell about their work. But when the question period came, invariably most of the questions centered on what reading lists or guides to self-education the campus minister could provide out of his university connection and campus church programs for students. The women hungered for some educational leadership on how to find out how they could participate in the intellectual world. In most cases their parish ministers were not providing such information, and the campus ministers came unprepared to answer such questions.

Missing from almost all church programs is Anne Scott's concern to involve middle-class women in finding out through the scholarship of the university the connection of their own ambitions to lower-class women. Missing also is her hope that church organizations on campus will press universities to alert professional people to the fact that most opportunities to move up the educational-class ladder occur in the training programs offered in particular professional subcultures, such as medical aid and social work.

The marginality of women's work in the church and society has given them a perspective from which to gauge the irrelevancy of much male ministry. As a result they have often been the first to recommend, for example, lay work on a weekly newspaper over religious education work in a small rural or suburban parish. At least there is more chance for a girl to write her own "Dear Abby" column in a weekly paper, to find people with convictions and give them an audience, than in many a position she is at present assigned to in the church or at the Y.

The enduring qualities of womanliness that appear to cut across class, racial, and vocational lines are for Anne Scott an equally important line of inquiry for the churches, a subject not unrelated to ecumenical discussion of the role of the Virgin Mary, mother of Jesus, in the history of the church.

KU

THE accelerated social change of the past century, especially in the industrial nations, has led to profound changes in the relations between men and women. Attempts to understand these changes and to deal with some of the problems relating to them are now widespread, both in the church and outside. Theological study of the question was stimulated by the appointment in 1955 of a Commission on the Life and Work of Women in the Church by the World Council of Churches. Under the same aegis the actual situation of women in the churches has also been examined. Among campus ministries, the YWCA has been most influential in encouraging among students and faculties on college campuses a critical review of current literature in the field.

In the realm of theology there is a continuing strain of ambiguity both in the Jewish and in the Christian tradition on the question, "What is woman?" Jesus was a radical on this subject, as on many others, but the organized church has relied heavily on the authority of St. Paul to keep women in a subordinate position. Except for the Quakers, who recognized the logic of their theology and accorded women equality in the seventeenth century, the Christian churches have generally been more conservative in their interpretation of the role of women than the society at large. Yet even in St. Paul the possibility for finding authority to transcend cultural patterns exists: (Galatians 3:28 "There is neither Jew nor Greek, there is neither bond nor free, there is neither male nor female: for ye are all one in Christ Jesus").[1]

Whether the church is to lead the society or to stand apart from it, it is necessary to understand the full magnitude of the present confusion in sexual relationships brought about by industrialization. Traditional societies define sex roles clearly and transmit them unequivocally to children. Our own society is based on the premise of change and progress, rather than stability. The price we pay is that the past does not offer secure guidelines for the future in defining acceptable patterns of behavior. Each generation must work out its own answers, and each individual woman her own pattern. Those unable to do this are in danger of being constantly blown hither and thither by contrary winds of doctrine.

Most human beings in our society feel a deep need for a life pattern that combines meaningful work with warm human relationships. One reason for the vast amount of questioning and restlessness among college students is a sense that their parents, even with the aid of today's prosperity, have not managed to achieve this kind of life design. For some students such questioning has led directly to a commitment in the civil rights movement, the poverty program, or the Peace Corps. For young women the problem is complicated by the fact that, as Mirra Komarovsky puts it,

> our culture is full of contradictions and inconsistencies with regard to women's roles, . . . new social goals have emerged without the parallel development of social machinery for their attainment, . . . norms persist which are no longer functionally appropriate to the social situations to which they apply, . . . the same social situations are subject to the jurisdiction of conflicting social codes, . . . behavior patterns useful at some stages become dysfunctional at another.[2]

For men, the achievement of warm and stable relationships with women is made more difficult by the contradictions and conflicts in social expectation. The kinds of relationships men want to find with women and the kind the culture tells them they ought to want are not necessarily the same.

History bears witness to a wide variety of styles of male-female relationships which have worked well in the context of a particular culture. From ancient times there have been kaleidoscopic changes in the prevailing images of either sex. Compare the dandy of King Charles's court to Daniel Boone, let us say. The woman pictured in the last chapter of Proverbs seems hardly of the same species as the Victorian lady.

There has been an enormous variety of legal relationships, ranging from the comparative equality of the sexes in Hammurabi's Code to a complete subjection of women at other times. Religious beliefs have influenced sex relationships, as even a superficial examination of the image of women in pagan religions, in Islam, or in Christianity would suggest. Different economic structures have required very different things of women: the importation into England of the feudal land system with its implication of military service seems to have brought a profound change into the status of Anglo-Saxon women. The change in the status of women which began in England in the late eighteenth century and appeared in America early in the nineteenth century was clearly tied to economic changes.

Ideology also affects sex relationships. The Spartan emphasis on raising sturdy children required different kinds of women from those in the Athenian style of life. The expectations of the American frontier differed from those in the eastern cities, with the result that to this day the status of women in the western states is in subtle ways different from that in the eastern states.[3]

Anthropological evidence is also full of variety. In different cultures different styles of being female are cultivated, and the conduct appropriate to these styles is carefully inculcated in early years. The roots of much "female" behavior seem to be found not in the genes, but in the culture.[4]

In the United States the cultural definition of woman's role has varied with the historical epoch, economic situation, social class, geographical location, degree of urbanization, and prevailing climate of opinion. The earliest colonial women were, of necessity, a very rugged group. On the frontier the struggle for existence killed some and broke others, but for the strongest the opportunity existed for full and vigorous development of their capacities.

Early in the nineteenth century the organization of factories to produce good hitherto made in the home had a marked effect on the lives of woman. As early as 1791, in his well-known *Report on Manufactures*, Alexander Hamilton argued that one of the advantages of factory production was that the work could be carried on by women and children, without attracting men from the farms where they properly belonged. "It is worthy of particular remark," Hamilton wrote, "that, in general, women and children are rendered more useful, and the latter more early useful, by manufacturing establishments, than they would otherwise be."[5]

Hamilton's capacities as a prophet were considerable. As the years went by an ever increasing number of young women did go into the mills to work—first into the textile mills, and then, as machinery of many kinds was invented, into the factories manufacturing clothing, shoes, tobacco, food, watches, clocks. A century after Hamilton's *Report* the United States Labor Commissioner wrote that only nine of the 369 general groups into which the country's industries had been divided for purpose of classification did not employ women.[6]

But definitions of woman's role did not always follow the actual course of events. When education had been primarily acquired at home and from parents and older relatives, girls had as much chance as boys to learn what was available. As education became more specialized, complicated, and concentrated in the hands of specialists and outside institutions, women began to drop behind. Precisely as traditional economic functions moved outside the home, a more restricted definition of the domestic role began to be imposed on middle-class women whose husbands could, thanks to the generally rising productivity, afford to dispense with their direct economic contribution.

Both the factory girls, working twelve or fourteen hours a day for low wages, and the middle-class housewives, whose access to education and significant responsibility was increasingly limited, felt the times were out of joint. Together they supplied the impetus to the women's rights movement.

Realizing that the old self-sufficient economic order in which women played a basic role was disappearing and assuming that education was the key to the rapidly changing world around them, a handful of women braved ridicule and discouragement to demand the right to higher education. Some men supported them. In the 1830's and 1840's an increasing number of pamphlets, articles, and sermons written by men began to ask whether uneducated women were capable of raising children or of creating the proper kind of atmosphere for family life.

Along with the demand for education went a vigorous effort to change the legal status of married women and to open doors to women's economic endeavor at a higher level than the factory. Middle-class women who did not marry suffered the indignity of indefinite dependence on male relatives; others married against their inclinations, since this was the only respectable means of acquiring support. The right to work for one's own living as opposed to dependence or unhappy marriage was one of the most strongly felt demands of women reformers.

Nineteenth-century America was not a static society. An aggressive "new class" of businessmen and entrepreneurs were engaged in making over the agrarian-commercial society to suit their needs, and it is necessary to see the efforts of women to define a place for themselves not as a battle against some outworn status quo, but as part of this dynamic process.

Little by little, beginning with Oberlin in 1837, colleges agreed to admit women, and in some parts of the country access to public high schools became easier. After the Civil War a number of colleges specifically for women were founded.

The first generation of college women, still confronting closed doors and much hostility, either carved out for themselves entirely new careers (inventing, for example, the settlement house) or fought their way into such masculine preserves as medicine or college presidencies. A tiny part of the total female population reinterpreted the social role of women and created the starting point for a whole series of social changes, the end of which is not yet in sight.[7]

The nineteenth-century pathbreakers opened doors which were eagerly entered by growing numbers of young women in the first three decades of the twentieth century. Educational and professional opportunity widened, and legal discrimination gradually gave way, especially after the passage and ratification of the nineteenth amendment. By the 1920's it was not uncommon in urban areas for young women to marry, have children, and still carry on careers. At the same time, both in manufacturing and in many kinds of jobs which had not even existed fifty years earlier, women became increasingly a significant part of the work force.

The telephone and the typewriter each opened a whole new world of work for women. The Civil War had made nursing a respectable female occupation. It had also opened the field of elementary schoolteaching to women, who soon all but pre-empted it. It gradually came to be acceptable for single women from whatever social stratum to work. Bit by bit married women and even mothers held jobs even when there was no dire necessity that they do so. One result was that the median age of working women climbed steadily upward, from twenty six years in 1900 to forty one years in 1962.

Along with these developments, which were clearly visible, were others equally important, but not always remarked. Anyone who delves into nineteenth-century personal records is struck by the enormous amount of illness and the consequent amount of time women spent nursing the sick. Children in particular suffered a great variety of ailments, and infant mortality was high. No family expected all its children to live to maturity, and many families lost more children than survived. Information about birth control was inadequate and hard to secure, so most women went on having babies through their whole period of fertility, often to the detriment of their own health.

In the first half of the twentieth century all these things changed, with far-reaching consequences. The death rate dropped steadily. Children were immunized against a whole range of formerly dread diseases. With better prenatal care and training in infant care, fewer babies died. Women themselves were healthier: in 1900 the life expectancy of an American woman was forty eight years; by 1960 it was seventy three years.

No single change was as important as the advent of easily obtainable information about birth control. "Millions of women," Margaret Sanger wrote in 1920, "are asserting their right to voluntary motherhood. They are determined to decide for themselves whether they shall become mothers, under what conditions and when. This is the fundamental revolt referred to. It is for women the key to the temple of liberty."[8]

By 1960 the changes traced here were spelled out in many statistics. A third of all the women in the United States were working outside their homes, and together they made up a third of the labor force. One-third of all the mothers in the country with children between six and seventeen were at work, and over sixty per cent of the women workers were married. Nearly all the secretaries, bookkeepers, and business-machine operators, as well as nurses and elementary schoolteachers, were women. Girls usually expected to work until they married, and often until they had children. In no state were there still significant discriminations against women written into the law. From the vantage point of the early women's rights advocates, it might have seemed that women's emancipation was complete.

While an ever increasing number of women took jobs of some kind, and while women's freedom to undertake almost any kind of public activity was not called in question, great aspirations among young women had not developed in proportion as opportunities opened. The proportion of able girls going to college did not rise as fast as the college population. In 1932, 17 per cent of all Ph.D. degrees granted were to women; by 1960 this figure had fallen to 10 per cent. In 1930, 6 per cent of the law degrees went to women; in 1960, 3 per cent. In 1930, 30 per cent of college faculty members were women; in 1960 this number had dropped to 22 per cent.

Despite the fact that women could be found in every occupation recognized by the Bureau of Labor Statistics, women were seldom in top jobs in education (except in the women's colleges, and even there women presidents were retiring to be succeeded by men), government, or business.

Behind these figures certain attitudes can be discerned. A widespread assumption on college campuses was that rigorous intellectual activity or aiming for a serious career was calculated to destroy sex appeal. Hand in hand with this view went the equally general assumption that early marriage was an appropriate aim for all college girls. Pressed to formulate their goals, many girls found home and family an adequate objective.

Along with this acceptance of a limited and subordinate role for educated women went the increasingly open emphasis on sex in advertising, books, movies, and behavior. The older image of woman as mother, comforter, nurse, and conserver of the domestic virtues was replaced by one of woman as tempter, charmer, and perennially young wife. The director of the Divorce Conciliation Service for the Illinois Circuit Court pointed to one result of this emphasis: Women are brought up to feel "that they have the right to expect a man to guarantee them an easy life simply because they are female. . . . All the emphasis is on their being sexual partners. They aren't encouraged to develop themselves any other way . . . to accept responsibility to meet challenges instead of resorting to selling their femaleness."[9]

Even as one describes the evolution of the postwar feminine style, it is clear that another change was in the making. By the early 1960's many young women who had married and enthusiastically adopted the glamorized domestic role were seeing their youngest child off to school and were raising serious questions about the values they had absorbed from the environment. These were the women who made Betty Friedan's *Feminine Mystique* into a best seller, who began to flock to adult education classes, look for part-time jobs, and fill the ever increasing demand for volunteers.[10]

The discussion of appropriate patterns for educated middle-class women continues apace. It tends to center on the question of how much and what kinds of activity beyond the domestic are compatible with satisfactory home and family life. Can marriage and intellectual goals be combined? What about regular career jobs? What kinds of education are appropriate to the dual life which most women now seem to expect to be the lot of the woman college graduate?[11]

Most of the popular and much of the serious writing about women focuses on the reasonably prosperous middle-class wife. It is vital to recognize that while these women worry about "fulfillment" and "self-realization," a very large number of other American women worry about simply earning a living for themselves and their children either alone or in conjunction with a husband whose skills do not permit him to support the family without help from other members. This is especially true of Negro women and of the one-half of all American women who have not finished high school.

## Research in Progress

Long-overdue research now begins to seek objective measures of sex characteristics, and much research needs to be done. That there is a distinctive female biology no one doubts, and some sex differences have been studied.[12] When all the biological differences are fully understood, however, the question will still remain: what differences in life, work, and behavior must *inevitably* flow from biological differences? The answer will probably be, "It depends." In some circumstances women do hard physical labor which in other societies they would be considered incapable of doing (and therefore *would* be incapable of doing). Some societies make much of certain female rhythms; others all but ignore these same facts. Some societies expect women to be nervous and easily excited; others expect them to be stable and phlegmatic. In some societies women undergo a visible personality change at menopause. Others play down this particular "rite of passage." Moreover, the differences in energy and perhaps in hormonal constitution between different women in any given society are enormous. We have not even begun to study these things or assess their significance for life pattern and accomplishment.

Interest is growing in the search for what is distinctive about female psychology. To go no further back than Freud, with his dictum that "anatomy is destiny," psychologists have exerted an influence on the world's thinking about women which is out of proportion to the validity of their evidence. Viola Klein's delightful book *The Feminine Character*[13] shows clearly the ways in which even careful social scientists tend to seek evidence for their own presuppositions.[14]

Erik Erikson's "Reflections on Womanhood"[15] is one of the best pieces on the subject, though the experimental psychologists may argue that Erikson is more poetic than empirical. David McClelland, who is well known for studies of the achievement motive in men, has lately turned his attention to women. In a popular article he suggests that he is trying to find a positive definition for femaleness that is more than simply not-male.[16]

Many small studies are undertaken to analyze very specific problems. Both broad-brush speculations and very specific studies add to our understanding of human nature and of female nature (if it turns out that there are psychological qualities peculiar to females). But at best such studies cannot answer questions about what women *ought* to do. They simply provide a sounder framework within which the question can be debated.[17]

Another area of special relevance to shaping the pattern of sex relationships is education; that is, the preparation of people for the role they are to play in life. Most of the heated discussion about how women shall be educated stems from opposing views as to what kind of life women should be prepared to live.

For the most part we make no distinction in this country between the education provided for boys and girls up to the end of high school. Nor is there very much distinction at the coeducational colleges. Only in a few of the women's colleges (Bennington, Sarah Lawrence, Mills) has there been a conscious effort to shape a curriculum especially to women's needs, and even in these cases the experiments have been based largely on a priori assumptions.

Such distinctions as do occur in the elementary and secondary schools are those of unconscious emphasis and expectation. The point at which expectation is most visible as a factor in the female educational experience is the widespread assumption that boys are better at science and mathematics. This may mean that girls are not encouraged or expected to take the kinds of math and science courses in high school which will hold open the possibility of more advanced work in these fields once they get to college.

Many of the proposals for a specific curriculum for women are based on the unproved premise that women are less good at and less interested in subjects which demand a high degree of abstraction and that their talents are more likely to lie in areas where the concrete and personal are important (for example, in art and English literature). Evidence for this view is offered in statistics showing that more girls than boys sign up for biology, while more boys than girls sign up for physics. Until we have found out whether these preferences are culturally induced, however, the argument is circular. Some experiments with children along these lines are being undertaken and should prove very illuminating.

Many qualified female students apply for admission to graduate school. However, the argument is constantly advanced, even by academic departments traditionally hospitable to women, that women students are not serious. They drop out before completing a graduate program and, once married, are lost for all academic purposes. This is a point at which a careful search for facts might be most illuminating. Are the dropouts in fact gone forever? Do they make use of the resources which have been invested in them?[18]

There is a burgeoning interest in providing channels for a return to formal education on the part of women past thirty-five. Notably at the University of Minnesota, but in many other places as well, experiments are being carried out which permit women to dust off an old degree or acquire a new one, often on a part-time basis. The Radcliffe Institute permits women with a project (rarely one leading to an actual degree) to work on it for a year by providing scholarships to pay for child care and household help. Vocational and educational counseling for women in their thirties and beyond is being tried in many parts of the country, and almost always with a response which outruns the expectations of the counselors.[19]

Many universities have witnessed an increasing number of older women signing up for courses, even in the absence of any special program tailored to their needs. Both the American Association of University Women and the Danforth Foundation are experimenting with scholarships for women who want to prepare for teaching careers. If adequate records are kept for these multiplying programs, planning in the future can go forward on a sounder basis.

The difficulties we experience in man-woman relationships, in the definition of male and female roles, in family life, are to some extent a function of the rapidly changing social and economic environment. Economic and scientific change outruns social invention and psychological adaptation. American women fall into two broad groups. One group is made up of women whose education and opportunity have been meager, (difficulties which are compounded by race) and who are seeking to improve their condition and find better ways of dealing with pressing problems of wages, working conditions, child care, and family life. The second group is made up of women who because of education, background, and general prosperity have a wide freedom to choose a style of life. The degree to which women find ways of living meaningful, useful lives will inevitably affect the happiness of husbands and the mental health of children. Conversely, when women generally are unhappy, fretful, and not contributing very much, the society suffers, men suffer, and children grow up to repeat the pattern. The way we view sex roles and the kinds of relationships that are encouraged are, therefore, crucial for the health and development of all members of the society.

## NOTES

1. Madaleine Barot, "Considerations on the Need for a Theology of the Place of Women in the Church," *Ecumenical Review*, VII (January, 1955), 151-160.
2. Mirra Komarovsky, "Functional Analysis of Sex Roles," *American Sociological Review*, XV (August, 1950), 508-509.
3. See Eileen Power, "The Position of Women," in C. G. Crump and E. F. Jacobs, *The Legacy of the Middle Ages* (New York: Oxford, 1926); John Langdon-Davies, *A*

*Short History of Women* (New York: Viking, 1927); Doris Mary Stenton, *The English Woman in History* (New York: Hillary, 1957); G. Rattray Taylor, *Sex in History* (New York: Vanguard, 1954); Phillippe Aries, *Centuries of Childhood* (New York: Knopf 1962); Julia Cherry Spruill, *Women's Life and Work in the Southern Colonies* (Chapel Hill: University of North Carolina Press, 1938); and Margaret Fuller Ossoli, *Women in the Nineteenth Century* (New York: Greeley and McElrath, 1845).

4. Margaret Mead, *Sex and Temperament in Three Primitive Societies* (New York: W. Morrow, 1935); Robert Briffault, *The Mothers* (New York: Humanities, 1959).

5. Alexander Hamilton, *Report on Manufactures* (New York: Williams and Whiting, 1810), I (1791), 175-177.

6. Elizabeth Faulkner Baker, *Technology and Woman's Work* (New York, Columbia University Press, 1964), p. 51. A most illuminating book especially to be recommended to those who like to argue about whether women "ought" to work.

7. Cf. a recent book, Barbara E. Ward, ed., *Women in the New Asia* (Paris: Unesco, 1963): "Thus—as in the drama—there is room for individual interpretation of roles, and a successful new interpretation of an old role may well be the starting-point of one kind of social change. Where such new interpretations are the result of conscious planning (whether based on general principles for social betterment or personal self-interest, or a mixture of the two) they may be copied by other people or not, according to circumstances and the innovator's powers of leadership. But probably, more often than not, a new interpretation of an old role is simply the accidental outcome of *ad hoc* adaptations to changed circumstances," (pp. 29-30). See also Eleanor Flexner, *A Century of Struggle* (Cambridge: Harvard University Press, 1959); Theodore Stanton and Harriot Stanton Blatch, *Elizabeth Cady Stanton as Revealed in Her Letters, Diary, and Reminiscences* (New York: Harper, 1922), Vol. I; Otelia Cromwell, *Lucretia Mott* (Cambridge: Harvard University Press, 1958); Josephine Goldmark, *Impatient Crusader, Florence Kelley's Life* (Urbana: University of Illinois Press, 1953); Jane Addams, *Twenty Years at Hull House* (New York: Macmillan, 1910) and *Democracy and Social Ethics* ed. Anne F. Scott (Cambridge: Harvard University Press, 1964); Margaret Farrand Throp, *Smith Grants Radcliffe's First Ph.D.'s* (Northampton: Smith College, 1965).

8. Margaret Sanger, *Woman and the New Race* (New York: Brentano's, 1920), p. 5. See Also J. A. and Olive Banks, *Feminism and Family Planning in Victorian England* (New York: Schocken, 1964). Both these books provide important insight into what is probably the least-discussed aspect of the changing status of women.

9. Dr. I. A. Burch, quoted in the Washington *Post*, Sunday, October 3, 1965, p. F14.

10. Of the popular books which give evidence of this trend the best is Morton M. Hunt, *Her Infinite Variety* (New York: Harper, 1962). Friedan's book has sold several hundred thousand copies in paperback and is now out of date, thanks in part to its own influence. Other signs of the times are the California symposium reported in Seymour Faber and Roger H. L. Wilson, *The Potential of Woman* (New York: McGraw, 1963), and the March, 1964, issue of *Daedalus*. Marion K. Sanders has a lighthearted but perceptive article in the July, 1965, *Harper's*, "The Demi-Feminist." Phyllis McGinley essays a good-natured defense of housewifely virtues in *Sixpence in Her Shoe* (New York: Macmillan, 1965) which does not, however, accurately describe her own style of life.

11. See Lotte Bailyn, "Note on the Role of Choice in the Psychology of Professional Women," *Daedalus* (March, 1964), pp. 700-710; Sir John Newsom, "The Education Women Need," *Atlas* (February, 1965), pp. 81-85; Ellen and Kenneth Kenniston, "An American Anachronism: The Image of Women and Work," *American*

*Scholar* (Summer, 1964), pp. 255-275, for excellent samples of the kind of discussion which can be found in dozens of periodicals, conferences, journals, and reports on the status of women.

12. See Amran Scheinfeld, *Women and Men* (New York: Harcourt, Brace, 1944), and Faber and Wilson, *op cit.*, pp. 3-65.

13. Viola Klein, *The Feminine Character* (New York: International University Press, 1949).

14. Compare Freud's writing on women, for example, with that of Karen Horney in *New Ways in Psychoanalysis* (New York: Norton, 1939). *He* finds girls permanently damaged because they lack a penis; *she* finds men suffering from envy of woman's ability to bear children. Certainly there is some chauvinism on both sides.

15. Erik Erikson, "Reflections on Womanhood," *Daedalus* (March, 1964), pp. 582-606.

16. David McClelland, in Robert J. Lifton, *Women in America* (Boston: Houghton Mifflin, 1965).

17. Vivian Cadden, "How Women See Themselves," *Redbook* (May, 1965), reports on some university-based research on women's self-images. Alice Rossi at the National Opinion Research Center in Chicago is engaged in a massive study of the women members of the college class of 1961. The *Journal of Genetic Psychology* and the *Genetic Psychology Monographs* often contain interesting studies of specific male-female differences. For a person interested in speculating on these matters, there is no shortage of food for thought.

18. Kate H. Mueller, *Educating Women for a Changing World* (Minneapolis: University of Minnesota Press, 1954), forecast much of the discussion that took place in the decade after it was published. It provides a useful introduction to the subject.

19. An indication of the number of women interested in refurbishing old skills and acquiring new ones was the runaway sale of a book, *The Next Step*, published by the Radcliffe Institute in 1964 and containing information about educational, vocational, and volunteer opportunities in the Greater Boston area.

# ≫ 14 ≪

## PERSONAL REFLECTIONS ON THE PITTSBURGH COLLOQUIUM

### Paul E. Schrading

### *Introduction*

The papers from the Pittsburgh colloquium, comprising three volumes, represent an intellectual effort at thinking about a city theologically, ethically, and sociologically. The paper selected from those of the Pittsburgh colloquium is the summary reflection of the codirector, Paul Schrading, who was on a partial leave of absence from the Wesley Foundation directorship to lead the inquiry. It is a fair indication of the kind of travail each member of the colloquium experienced, and it is an example of the end product of a particular kind of inquiry. Paul Schrading was not participating in the enterprise as a researcher nor as a formal teacher (as most faculty would envision their roles) but he was perhaps the most crucial person in whatever success the activity achieved.

He was trying out the roles associated with a new kind of teaching and learning: prophetic inquiry into who is responsible for preparing a city to reflect on what it is doing with its urban reconstruction and design. He was trying to find the people in the church, the university, and public affairs who were generally capable of doing this and to test them on the simple anvil of his own desire to act responsibly in one's sphere of influence.

Paul Schrading's models were in his terms "dialogic," an effort to get confrontation on public issues between church and university and civic leaders who had power to act. His model was oriented toward clarifying the alternatives of future action in the institutions in which these people exercised significant influence.

His paper is largely the record of self-discovery by all involved of how little their constituencies and institutions were prepared to ask the most fundamental questions about organizing such inquiry. The expected leaders, such as the ethics professors from whom one might hope for some models of inquiry, were still attacking past moral thinking of the church and expounding an existential, personalistic ethic that could not make contact with the realities of city power which create the new forms. The Catholic Oratory set aside by the bishop to free priests and laymen to confront such public and educational issues were still absorbed in discovering the meaning of true community among themselves. The Protestant parish pastors could not see that the professors' long-range analyses of ecological, political, and industrial trends meant much to their congregations' future.

But an emerging model for learning what the churches and universities have become, and are now asked to be, is evident in the reflections of Paul Schrading. These are elements of prophetic inquiry.

Schrading has reached the point in his maturity as a professional and ministerial leader where, when he writes a reflective piece on an experience of learning, all the modes of ministry which have formed our own work are interwoven. He begins with the cognitive-faculty image of campus ministry and shows what a charade this has been, if what is sought is genuine ability to organize and excite faculty to corporate study of some basic institutional responsibilities for shaping the life and looks of a city. Next, he works over the goal achievement and governing aspects of the experience, asking whether any of his groups reached, with university faculty's help, an agenda of what they would try to accomplish in immediate and long-range programs. This was a shift in the ethical content that the traditional ministries and religious studies were passing on to students. He concludes that his colleagues were spending their energies (as radicals) on a hodgepodge of issues that were "basically unrelated to the institutional decision process" or (as conservatives) were using "Christian heritage more in a sense of a specific body of teachings" of the churches than as "help in illuminating alternatives for decision." And finally Schrading works over the integrative-pastoral concepts of community and interpersonal relations in the campus ministry.

This man has thus, from our perspective, come of age in his capacity to see the substance of and change at work within the historic ministries as they respond to the center of their society—the city itself—and to the core of personal life for hundreds of thousands of persons in that city, the public schools. He has said more clearly in later interviews that he is seeking a kind of education in the churches that does not turn its back on *the* disaster area in the reconstruction of Pittsburgh—not with private houses or suburban shopping centers—but includes *the schools of the culturally deprived minorities* and the methods of inquiry used with these children.

What is clear at least to Pittsburgh colloquium members is that they know virtually nothing about what prophetic inquiry looks like in a modern city. What learning situation produces a sense that a problem exists where persons in one's care are being deprived, mutilated, stunted, and driven to hatred? What learning produces a conviction that a person can act with others to change conditions for the better and that one ought to because the deepest images one has of himself and what one is created to be are threatened by one's inaction or indifference? The most elementary steps to significant involvement in these questions are just being taken by a few churches. The basic research is lacking in the university to give answers. The minimum prerequisites for intelligent institutional planning do not yet exist in the church and university for the leadership requested. That is the story Paul Schrading has to tell.

KU

$T$HE Danforth Study of Campus Ministries in Pittsburgh enabled me as a campus pastor to re-examine the campus ministry (past, present, and future) in a careful, self-critical way. Such re-examination is often only sparked by a specific study. In my judgment such self-study is crucial to the future direction of the campus ministry. Perhaps some creative pattern of self-study could be developed on a more wide-scale basis, with various foundations and denominational campus ministry structures co-operating.

In the Pittsburgh study, four distinct areas of self-study emerged. These were the most significant to me personally, as I attempted to reappraise my own ministry. In spite of my own awareness in theory that the campus ministry needed reshaping along the lines suggested below, the daily duties and constant organizational relationship enabled me to avoid much specific orientation toward the future. In any event, with the continuity of leadership in the campus ministry at a minimum across the country (I understand the average stay of a Wesley Foundation Director is two or three years), the future often seems remote. Following are appraisals of the issues which have emerged in the self-study of the campus ministry.

## Faculty Involvement in the Campus Ministry

The faculty of an institution represents continuity and substantial educational influence. In theory we would all agree that faculty should be involved in the ministry, for it has a potential for shaping the attitudes and decision-making prowess of future professional leadership. This potential is rarely achieved, however. The faculty also has the possibility of exercising leadership in the academic and even nonacademic decisions of an institution (though we discovered that faculty rarely exercise their leadership in these decisions). The university administrators more often make the decisions from nonacademic bases of judgment (I suppose this is similar to the non-theological factors which guide the decisions of churches). Without being caught between the faculty and administration, it seems clear that questions of value profoundly affect the way a man teaches and acts responsibly in a university organization. We discovered that some clear distinctions need to be made between liberal arts colleges and multiversities. This is basic to understanding the campus ministry in these settings. Cramer further pointed to the divorce between human values and utilitarian values.[1] Where the campus ministry might be in conversation about issues that matter to faculty and administrators, the campus ministry was found in our study to be perceived by faculty as a service syndrome, the extension of the parochial ministry, or as security agents guarding morality.

The sharpest critique of all came when we realized that, except for a few beginnings of contact and rapport with faculty, the campus ministers were content to involve faculty occasionally as members of our boards or as speakers in programs. The harder job of scouting out faculty interest in questions of epistemology or a theology of education was hardly begun. Those campus pastors who had been in Pittsburgh for some years expressed considerable interest in the possibilities for increasing contact with faculty. I would speculate that continuity of ministry over a period of years increased the interest in establishing rapport with faculty. This certainly is true in my own case, almost to a point of assigning more importance to this part of the ministry than to that designed for undergraduates. Faculty rapport is not easy to come by, but seems a clear necessity in the future direction of the campus ministry.

Two specific examples may suffice to establish this perspective. The ministry of the Roman Catholic-sponsored Oratory has attempted to establish and maintain faculty interest. As the Oratory proceeds to develop a university parish, the question of "What is your vocation?" will supersede "Where do you live?" A vocational university parish cannot be built entirely on the more transient student body, but will require active faculty participation and will, in my judgment, thereby enrich the ministry of the university parish. The details of this pattern are not clear, even in the minds of the Oratory priests, but the intent seems plain enough. A second example is in the development of an advisory group for the campus ministry at Carnegie Tech formed by the Baptist, Presbyterian, United Church of Christ, and Methodist churches. The intention is to establish a team ministry of faculty, administrators, graduate students, and undergraduates along with campus ministers. The "advisory" group seeks to develop the ministry at Carnegie Tech, hopefully avoiding campus ministry staff domination and all the details of organization, budget, and so on which are handled through each denomination.

The colloquium process gave ready agreement to the necessity for more significant faculty involvement in and through the campus ministry for the present and the future. Apart from the two examples above, no very elaborate plans were proposed as to how to accomplish the task. My own personal reaction is that no amount of programing (in the sense of organized grouping) will produce the needed faculty participation. Rather, such participation depends on a campus ministry able to scout out interested and committed faculty and also able to challenge these faculty with a sufficient reason for involvement in the campus ministry. Such "scouting" presupposes a continuity of staff leadership in the campus ministry, heretofore one of the basic problems of the campus ministry. It also presupposes a campus pastor who is responsive to the scouting task rather than the organizational task. I think one of the chief contributions of this self-study to my own ministry has been the shift of direction in my thinking from the organizational ministry (bringing groups together, holding meetings, and the like) to the scouting ministry (an attempt to be responsive to issues of research and development in the university). These types of ministry are not mutually exclusive because the witness of faith presupposes the community gathering for worship and mutual responsibility (teaching, stewardship, and so on). But the witness of faith also presupposes contacts in the university which are not easily diagramed in charts of the campus ministry organization. Much more attention now needs to be given this "floating" ministry, as my colleague Ed Biegert identifies it.

## Urban Analysis and the Campus Ministry

Early in the colloquium, Clifford Ham, Assistant Professor of Urban Affairs, University of Pittsburgh, was asked to prepare a paper on the relationship between the campus ministry and the urban renaissance in Pittsburgh. He provided us with a variety of other papers analyzing the relations of the churches to efforts being made at reconstruction of the city of Pittsburgh. Discussions of these papers represented for all the participants, except Ham, an entirely new venture in the campus ministry. Such novelty in itself is indicative that the campus ministry in Pittsburgh was unaware of two elements: (1) some of the powerful factors shaping the physical features of the city and university area and (2) the structures of decision making which affect profoundly the living patterns of the city in which the university is set. It seems clear to me that as the campus ministry is confronted with the factors of urban and university renewal, it tends to look upon its task in personalistic categories: counseling, preaching, teaching. Ham may have overstated the necessity for organizational skills required of the campus ministry, but I saw his proposals as a necessary antidote to a personalistic scheme of campus ministry.

One of the most significant factors I have seen is the necessity for laymen and pastors to engage in dialogue between the church, the university, and the public order, particularly on questions affecting the future developments of all three. Urban renewal patterns certainly do affect all three realms. I see the urgent need for churchmen (lay and clergy) to engage in communication with civic and university leaders about issues which affect the future patterns of city spatial design.

As a matter of further training for myself, I have enrolled in the University of Pittsburgh Graduate School of Public and International Affairs, taking a course in Urban Policy Analysis. I can clearly see that the practical, civic responsibility of decision making has profound relations to questions of Christian ethic and in particular to writings such as H. Richard Niebuhr's *The Responsible Self*. The concept of responsibility is the linking category for theological as well as practical and civic awareness. The campus ministry has a tremendous challenge to see this linking and explore its implications.

### Ethic and Ethos in the Campus Ministry

This area of the colloquium discussion was much more limited in scope than I expected. I had hoped that we might specifically attempt to relate to questions that are being faced in the university arena: How does a university balance quality education with a necessity to fill dormitory space? This question was certainly faced at the University of Pittsburgh, and a minor administrative revolt occurred when admission standards were lowered to allow more students to fill dormitories. How does a university relate to the civic responsibility of its geographic area? How does a university create a climate for learning amidst the technological struggle for excellence and competition for government research grants? What role does authority play in the university concept of responsibility? How far can the university be the mentor for sex standards of the campus—wherein lies this responsibility in the university milieu? How does the university train its graduates in the delicate process of decision making in public life? How far is the university training for public responsibility? Little light was shed on these questions in our discussions. I cannot assume, however, that they were not of interest to the participants in the colloquium. Rather, I can conclude from our discussions that we were unprepared to consider these "large" questions because of our more parochial, personalistic view of the campus ministry.

· In a series of questions posed to campus ministers Biegert, Batchelder, and Hamilton, the following was asked: "What are the major ethical issues to which you find yourself giving serious attention (*a*) in your own thought and (*b*) in your ministry? If (*a*) and (*b*) differ, are there reasons for this which are relevant to the interpretation which your ministry has received?" The reply of Hamilton, pastor at Bethany College, was relative to the ethical issues of sexual morality, the use of time, and suicide. All are personal issues, he commented, but having ultimate significance. None of these issues, however, relates directly to the context of ethical decision in the institutional college or university setting. They all begin with personal student reference. Perhaps this is indicative of one chaplain's being close to problems of students, but the problems are also significantly apart from the issues being faced internally at the college. (One example reported to me by a former Bethany College student was the tremendous institutional problem raised after the release of a faculty man when he adjourned his classes the day of President Kennedy's funeral, against the wishes of the administration.) Ed Biegert replied that ethical issues for the campus ministry were race, sex, politics, civil rights, and the like. Civil rights is somewhat more related to institutional decision making, but here again the context for serious ethical attention in the campus ministry is basically unrelated to the institutional decision process. Out of the context of the Industrial Round Table at Carnegie Tech, Richard Batchelder identified ethical questions for the campus ministry as follows:

> In the area of ethics I find myself giving the most serious attention both in my private thought and also in my professional task to my own feelings of the general irrelevance of the Christian Church to the specific and concrete issues which confront our society. When one attempts to take seriously the kinds of problems men confront in industry, business, labor relations, foreign policy, government, etc., one often finds precious little help from the Christian heritage in illuminating specific alternative actions or decisions.

One might argue in contrast that the operative definition would be that of the "Christian heritage." One could certainly presume that the Christian faith maintains and develops attitudes of responsibility, charity, and accountability in the decision-making process of industry, business, and other areas. However, I believe Batchelder is using "Christian heritage" more in a sense of the specific body of teaching and the expression of Christian witness found in our churches today. In this sense, we find little specific help in illuminating alternatives for decision. He finds in his experiment, the Industrial Round Table, "an attempt to confront directly the question of personal integrity within the context of professional responsibility." This experiment has great value as a means of confronting in the campus ministry major problems of decision making in our society.

### Community, the University and the Campus Ministry

In my opinion, the most serious deficiency found in this study is the lack of an identifiable community of persons involved in and concerned for the campus ministry. Particularly the writings of the social scientists and philosophers in our colloquium (Bowen, Cramer, and Stoutamyer) reminded us of the diverse and scattered structures that contain the university and the fragmented way in which the campus ministry is conceived. Surely the solution is not the creation of cozy, ingrown groups. We seek to move away from a superficial form of community which does not have its roots in a biblical and sacramental view of the mission of the church. There is a profound problem remaining of identity, continuity, and community. The organizational establishment of the campus ministry, which is one of its frequent concerns, is insufficient for the third phase of the campus ministry, which I have identified as one for community, continuity, catalysis, and identity. Community would describe the rich fabric of association in a ministry: the mutual unbuilding of the saints, the conveying of the Christian witness, and the joy of discovery of God's truth in the university. Continuity is built on community. This would rest more on the clergy and faculty in an institution. Catalysis is the stimulation provided by faith to prod and explore, not fearful of the risk involved or the time spent. Identity is an interworking of all three. Christian identity is not only for itself, but also willing to lose itself.

My chief self-critique in this study is that Christian identity is at a minimum point in the campus ministry, not because we have willingly lost our identity, but because we have been confused about the nature of our identity. I have discovered also in this study that the campus ministry is nearer the description of a "mission church" than that of the "educational arm" of the church. Biegert points out that perhaps the campus ministry is best described as a part of the local Presbytery's Department of Church and Society than of the Department of Education. Perhaps Christian identity is minimal in the campus ministry because we have encouraged the development of student clubs and have overlooked the challenge of participating in the fullest dimensions of the ministry. The continuation of student "arms" of the church in the Methodist Student Movement, the United Campus Christian Fellowship, the National Newman Club, and so forth is descriptive of the problem of identity and witness in our time. The Oratory offers a guide for the meaning of Christian identity; Father Walsh writes that the church exists in worship, daily contact with the Word of God, and the attempt to relate religion to all that is good in learning, art, and science. Also the church seeks to reunite what God had never intended to be separate. This description is surely much more than the Newman Club's idea of its ministry.

## The Campus Ministry and the Local Church

In many campus ministry situations there is tension between a local church (its pastor or leaders) and the campus ministry (the staff or students). Often the aims and presuppositions of the two "arms" of the church are quite different. I have heard of a pastor of a local church going to a nearby Wesley Foundation building and removing paintings on exhibit from the wall because the pastor felt they were unfit for a "religious" building. Such outright antagonism may not be found often, but more frequently one may discover subtle antagonism and even jealousy.

I am pleased to report that such antagonism does not exist between the Wesley Foundation of Pittsburgh and the First Methodist Church, the nearest campus Methodist church. I would suggest the following reasons for this complementary relation. In the first place, the First Methodist Church is at least a mile from the campus areas of the city. The local church is therefore not encouraged to be possessive toward the campus. It is in no way dependent on the students or faculty to form the bulk of the congregation, and the local church has its own fabric or identity. In the second place, I have always had excellent personal rapport with the pastors of this church, not that either of us in any instance has sought to accommodate to each other. Our views of the ministry, its place in the university, and the ministry of a local church in a changing urban area have been quite similar, and on several occasions we have had opportunity to state publicly our own views about a complementary relationship of our ministries. Third, the factor of the urban setting cannot be overlooked. Because the situation facing both the campus ministry and the local church is so diverse and defies easy solutions, we are both called upon to respect each other's ministries in the complex setting. A fourth factor of a complementary relationship is the general theological and liturgical sensitivity shared by the ministries of the pastor of the local church (and his assistant) and myself. We share monthly in a book-reading group, have participated together as colleagues on committees, and in general hold a common view of the ministry.

I realize that many of my colleagues in the campus ministry could write a different chapter than I have written. Nevertheless, it is important to record that a campus pastor facing the above-mentioned conflict in the university with the establishment is greatly relieved to find mutual support and encouragement from ecclesiastical channels of relationship. Were I to feel insecure about denominational support for my ministry in the university and, at the same time, had to face the establishment question, the alternative of leaving the campus ministry for another position would be appealing, if not sought. Perhaps the combination of these factors often accounts for persons' seeking a ministry elsewhere than the campus. Perhaps even these comments of mine will serve to remind denominational leadership that the campus ministry needs to be seen and supported as a ministry of the "mission field." Statistical results should be placed far down on the list of expectations, as they are in the inner-city ministry. Furthermore, a team of campus ministry personnel should be recruited as a lifetime commitment, just as the inner-city pastors will continue in this ministry (perhaps moving from one city to another) for a long-term ministry. Such sensitivity needs to be encouraged in the campus ministry.

## The Campus Ministry and the Future Ministry

The conclusions I would draw about the future pattern of the campus ministry in Pittsburgh and also recommendations to the Danforth Campus Ministry Study are as follows:

1. Encourage the continuity of personnel in the campus ministry. Such continuity often implies increased ministry among and with the less transient leadership of the university: the faculty and administration. Also, the university leadership is likely to take the campus ministry more seriously. A good example in Pittsburgh is the Oratory, which has been here fewer years than my period of ministry (four years); yet because this is a permanent establishment with continuity of leadership, there has been more awareness of the Oratory as a campus ministry. The university, in relating to Protestant campus pastors, is always unaware of whether the total years spent on the campus will be more than those of the average undergraduate student. Such lack of continuity often merits little attention. Also, the establishment problem is likely to be more creatively overcome with continuous leadership in the campus ministry. To be a scout, as I am suggesting below, one requires continuous familiarity with a campus.

2. Continue encouragement of graduate study for campus pastors. The number of grants for campus ministers to continue academic training should be increased. The university is increasingly expecting its faculty to have undertaken advanced graduate study. Such study for the campus pastor

should not be seen as achieving a degree for a status symbol, but rather as a means to become conversant in the continuing process of advanced education. I have not finally or personally decided whether this study should lead toward the Ph.D. degree or a similar degree. I think such arbitrary standards, though certainly imposed in the university, may easily lead to false assumptions in the campus ministry. The Ph.D. as a requirement for the campus minister is a false assumption, because the campus pastor is much more than a teacher, and the Ph.D. is usually connected with training for teaching.

Another aspect of continuing education for the campus ministry is to encourage pastors to take courses in the university as a means of expanding their knowledge and abilities as "scouts" in the university.

3. Develop experiments in the campus ministry similar to the Industrial Round Table at Carnegie Tech. The Industrial Round Table can be used as a prototype for further explorations into the crucial areas of ethics and industrial, business, or governmental decision making. Such work as has been done by Kenneth Underwood at Wesleyan, by Robert Batchelder at the Detroit Industrial Mission, and in the National Council of Churches might be used as background material. A full-scale exploration of the process of decision making could be undertaken, and the campus ministry could perform an important task for the whole church in this area.

4. Encourage developments in the campus ministry similar to the Oratory. Such encouragement could come as support to the Pittsburgh Oratory as a prototype for future Roman Catholic campus ministries. The Protestant campus ministries can also gain some insights from the concept of a team of priests committed together in a campus ministry for a long tenure. This could not be directly translated into Protestant terms, but there are implications for the Protestant campus ministry.

5. Encourage the development of campus ministry skills in urban analysis and affairs. The large universities will continue to cluster in urban areas, and considerable work is required to relate the campus ministry to the urban setting.

6. Continue encouragement of self-studies of campus ministries across the country. Perhaps material in the Danforth Study can be adapted to help teams of campus ministry leaders (staff, students, and faculty) to ask questions which may project their ministry into the future. We hope to continue our self-study in Pittsburgh, because we have begun some significant discussion which may well change the direction of the campus ministry. Already some changes are evident.

7. Encourage denominational organizations to re-evaluate the resources

provided for national student movements. A more creative university ministry concept is called for today, and the implications may be hard on the present structures.

8. Finally, encourage the development of the campus ministry as "scouts" in the university, as ones who may become sensitive to issues, plans, and projects planned in a complex university setting. Such encouragement would need some financial support outside the denominational patterns, because the denominations presently seem unwilling to move far beyond the "church follows the student" stage of campus ministry. Demonstration by the Danforth Foundation or other foundations is needed to establish the "scout" in the university as yet another stage of the campus ministry.

## NOTES

1. John E. Cramer, "The Faculty Study", paper for Danforth Campus Ministry Study Colloquium, Pittsburgh, 1964.

# ❧ 15 ❦

## AN EXPERIMENT IN CRITICAL INQUIRY INTO THE ETHICS AND RELIGION OF PUBLIC LEADERS, WESLEYAN UNIVERSITY

### Kenneth Underwood

### Introduction

This chapter seeks to explore the prophetic role of the university as moral critic of the culture. It does this by describing one attempt in a liberal arts college (Wesleyan University) to establish an extracurricular organization to help provide the conditions for serious ethical inquiry in the university. The Institute of Ethics and Politics, as the organization was called, operated (financially and academically) in a liberal arts college setting. At Wesleyan many of its functions were ultimately taken up more systematically within the regular curriculum, in a college of social studies, and a Center for Advanced Study in the humanities, among others.

The operation, financed at first by a number of foundations (Hazen, Carnegie, Rockefeller), was in time made a university enterprise, designed to sustain a trialogue on ethical issues in civic affairs between faculty, students, and public leaders (including clergy, politicians, government administrators, and businessmen). The institute, in short, brought together people whose involvement in varied professions, academic disciplines, and world views was needed to explain the nature of moral action in the contemporary world.

The issues and programs which developed in the institute may offer some clue to the kind of inquiry that best relates academic, religious, and public dimensions of campus life and may guide the churches in the reconstruction of denominational and ecumenical centers.

As director of the institute, it was my conviction that Christians never confront the reality of God apart from the reality of the world, and they never confront the reality of the world apart from the confrontation of the presence of Christ in some form of action. It is this interpenetration between human and divine reality which the church fails to grasp when it cuts off its theological and moral study from social and economic inquiries in the university and in other public institutions and when it refuses to press theological and moral inquiries into particular policies of the churches and synagogues.

KU

$F$OR almost a decade I have been involved in an Institute of Ethics and Politics at Wesleyan University which has sought to explore the real and possible connections between the faith, thought, and action of leaders in the corporation, the college, and the church. The operation, financed at first by a number of foundations (Hazen, Carnegie, Rockefeller), and now by Wesleyan University, has been an attempt at a trialogue—in informal conference, study, and research—between public leaders, students, and faculty, plus ministers (lay and cleric). This exploration began, not to save the corporate world outside the university, but to save our own liberal arts teaching and research from the kinds of boredom, irrelevancy, and fragmentation that undercut attention to the realities of religious commitment, reason, and moral action in American politics and business. The foundation grants made it possible for us to provide a place, resources, and morale necessary to engage in a rigorous, constructive, and critical inspection of public affairs and of the relationship of the reflective communities (the university and the church) to them.

We tried to involve leaders now active in the public processes in a reconsideration of the occasions of significant new choice in our contemporary culture. Our flexible program made it possible for qualified leaders from government, business, and politics to reflect on the shape their past and present promises had taken and on the hoped-for covenants of the future. Mostly we invited leaders in mid-career in private and public corporations and in elected politics to return to Wesleyan for varied periods of time. These men were encouraged to explore for themselves what the theorizing and data gathering of the university and the memories and stories of religion implied for their own response to the occasions and events in the world. Their responses were worked out in a whole personal strategy and life style related to major associations in the society, and not in their meeting one or two "crises" or challenges in their work. These men realized better than most of the faculty and ministers that we were opening up new avenues of "continuing education" in the university and churches.

The faculty were seeking to clarify not only the nature of their own disciplines but also the mission of liberal learning in contemporary society. Our faculties in the social sciences, for example, were, like those elsewhere, discussing how the "objective" and "subjective," the "behavioral" and "existential" approaches to the social world are to be related. Our faculties of ethical and religious studies were aware that they had very little data as to whether the perspectives and disciplines of the university and the world views and commitments of the churches now informed or shaped in any significant way the action of persons and groups in the business and political communities. Generally our faculty members were troubled by the bifurcations which had developed in the modern world between liberal arts studies and learning directed to more technical and professional concerns.

The institute attempted to encourage in a private, once church-related college a conscious, public exploration of the nature of moral action which took the phenomenon of religious commitment seriously and elicited similar explorations from others with different world views. Our institute brought together people whose involvement in varied professions, disciplines, and world views were needed to probe the depths of responsible selfhood in the contemporary scene. Many of the students came to see the institute as a kind of interstitial learning process where, without pressures to meet traditional credit or course requirements (our consultations offered no credit or certification to participating students), they could explore freely the relation of their formal curricular work to their extracurricular activities and involvements with an eye to future careers and callings.

The issues and programs which developed in the institute may offer some clues to ministers who are seeking to provide settings for interpersonal knowledge that relate the academic, religious, and social dimensions of campus life or are hoping to guide the churches in their reconstruction of denominational and ecumenical centers, drawing upon an established university faculty for the enchancement of adult education in the churches.

The nature of our institute experience may be made clearer by an illustration of one of our attempts at a trialogue between business leaders, faculty, and students. We had watched with some interest the development by General Electric of a center for management-executive training at Crotonville, New York, with its considerable use of the new moral symbols of corporate and personal responsibility. We invited several men who had participated in that center's work to explore with us the operative criteria for executive advancement taught at Crotonville. We hoped to gain some knowledge of the moral dilemmas that might be emerging between company pressures to maximize profits and fulfill social responsibilities as interpreted in the governmental or political processes. Our discussions began some time before the price conspiracy scandals at General Electric came to light.

At the morning session we listened to men talk about how Crotonville, with the aid even of biblical study, developed a heightened sense of the social responsibilities of the corporation such as had not been seen in American society. Indeed, according to these men, none of the dilemmas we had suggested were any longer real for the ideal executive; what was good for GE was good for the nation.

During the social break before dinner one of the GE men pulled me aside and asked, "Look, when are you going to break up this song and dance?"

"What song and dance?" I replied.

"Oh," he said, "this bit we're telling you about no moral tensions in the executives, with such successful teaching of the social responsibility of American business." Then he gave as an example of real dilemma, which no one talked about at Crotonville, the fundamental demands of antitrust legislation and of production and selling quotas established by GE top-level executives, an example whose significance I did not at that time catch.

> The hell of Crotonville is that we don't or can't talk about the tensions between career hopes in the company and the obligations we also learn in our family, church, and political life. We're so busy quoting the Bible in terms of social responsibility and Christian responsibility, the real moral dilemmas we confront never come out in the open. And they won't here at Wesleyan, unless some of the faculty are able to say what we will not say about life in similar organizations. Even then we are not likely to get very concrete in a university and in a group meeting such as this. You have to face the limits of what you can ask men to reveal in such group discussions and learn to speak of recognizable situations which objectify the realities all of us experience. Only the return of men as individuals to study might provide an opportunity to open up the situation and think freely and seriously about it.

I relate this to indicate the problems and possibilities of learning which cut across the lives of men in our major institutions. One of our theologians, Julian Hartt, was able to speak helpfully at this conference of what it is like, from the perspective of a Christian, to live and work in the university as a professor, while trying to serve the demands of career and of the larger culture. For him the Christian images of sin, guilt, and forgiveness go beneath ideologies which easily equate personal and corporate interests. But this self-examination by the faculty evoked no new data from our guests.

Some of us, after making the moral life of GE a subject of continuing research, were able to see the limits of favorite theological terms such as "the covenanting community" in catching the actualities of work in such a corporation. One GE employee, who came to Wesleyan for private study, noted, for example,

There wasn't any covenanting in GE during the price conspiracy. Do you know what happens to rats when you set them up in a maze with the best possible cheese as an enticement and there isn't any possible way through it? They go mad. You set quotas that you can't possibly meet, and there's no covenanting on the lower levels about these quotas. In this situation under the tremendous salary inducements of sixty to eighty thousand dollars, men do sometimes go mad, or live with the terrible tensions of an elaborate and carefully contrived duplicity of public and private acts.

Students who participate in such inquiries and discussions as those high-lighted by this example do not have much trouble placing themselves in these struggles for personal integrity in corporate life. The GE story is a dramatic problem in corporate ethos. But it is not some small eddy of American society; it has to do with the whole fabric of the culture which the student hears and critizes. The students—tough as it is on the faculty and the chaplain—want to know whether the theories and commitments of the university illumine such concrete human situations; they watch our fumbling attempts to test our own favorite ways of analysis and response and learn much that our controlled classroom teaching will never reveal. And there are not many of us, as faculty, administrators, or clergy, who will expose ourselves to such situations, or help to create them, unless we have some strongly held views of the work of the university that demand such research and teaching.

## Two Influential Views of the University's Mission

In our current educational situation there are two influential views of the university's responsibility which press partial but nonetheless inadequate truths. The first assumes that the crisis in our cultural-political order is so enormous that the college and university should relegate everything else to second place and concentrate on meeting it directly. Here, for example, are the words of C. Scott Fletcher, president of the Fund for the Republic:

Let us ask ourselves a vital question. Are the American people using their power in the service of the cause of freedom as effectively as the Soviet people are being used to achieve the goals of the Soviet state? The answer is no. Most of us in our private and public roles of various organizations and institutions serve our ideal only by fits and starts with only a small fraction of our attention and energy. The Soviets are mobilizing all the energies of the human beings under their subjection, all the time in all ways. In the United States we can no longer count on the automatic or accidental emergence of dedicated, courageous, imaginative, and wise leaders. We must now educate for them purposefully and by design.

The position seems to many educators, clergymen and public leaders neither novel nor disturbing. They have in a crude and less responsible fashion believed for a long time that the colleges and universities are chiefly to be service agencies of the society, upholding in undivided conscience the American way of life, the system of free enterprise, and the values of Christian culture.

The second influential view is found in the response of many scholars and teachers to this position. They charge that it denies the independence of the college or university to seek knowledge refined beyond obvious utilitarian application. The scholar has proclaimed the absolute purity of the intellectual life from any particular interest, from every tinge of cultural defense, from every moral consideration. The most common academic variant of this is the scholar's claim that the life of reason is oriented toward a culture transcending value—namely, truth—and that the ultimate loyalty of the scholar is to an international, or at any rate nonnational, community of science.

These two emphases in higher education today have their historic roots. The first draws chiefly upon the periods in American education when the church dominated the scene, when reflections on moral philosophy and action represented the capstone of a man's college career more often than the pursuit of some highly specialized inquiry. Most reflection was informed by a conception of law and order which quite often failed to do justice to the empirical world being discovered by science, but at its best presumed to ask the basic questions about man's nature and destiny in the world. The college or university professed character development as its primary interest and expected the college student to discover a calling which served society. The educated man in this tradition not only learned the skills of a profession but also in all his associations was expected to be the self-consciousness of the community in the patterns and crises of its daily life.

The second emphasis in contemporary education draws its strength largely from the scientific-empirical tradition in which men have attempted to employ scientific methods for the analysis of the social world. They have sought to serve society through the cultivation of a scientific reason which attempted to let the facts speak for themselves, to get people to heed reality for what it is, and to deal through increasing specialization with the aspects of human activity which can be measured, quantified, and embodied in abstract categories and principles, not limited to a particular time or place. Such data have tended to exaggerate the determinism of objective structures and forces in the society and to neglect all factors of personal commitment, character, and corporate purpose that cannot be handled with accuracy by traditional scientific epistemology. Scientific reason, many scholars and students have argued, requires an objectivity which permits no moral judgments as to personal duty or public purpose. For them, such objectivity has come to mean a permanent attitude which suspends moral reflection and involvement in public issues.

The educational scene in America is now characterized by a re-interpretation of the significance and tension of these two traditions in an attempt to respond constructively to world events and national need. The quest, as Julian Hartt noted in an institute working paper, is for

> a community of persons, scholars, teachers, students, engaged in learning and discovery. What do we mean by a community of learning and discovery? We should stress that the college and university ought to be a society of persons guided by a common high purpose, which permeates its whole life and is part of the very atmosphere of the university. The purpose of the college or university is its concern for the full and proper expression of intellectual powers. Learning is a matter of soliciting the activity of the creative mind. It is not the function of the college or university to create and nourish the powers of fact intake and attitude response but to discover what are the new unique demands upon us in the world. The creative mind deals with meaning that is, with knowledge that has not separated from goodness, with facts not isolated from faith and values. If the person comes to the college or university to learn he comes then to test all things for the sake of the truth rather than for plausible opinion, to seek the good rather than the covenient, to love beauty rather than triviality and ugliness.

## The Characteristics of Public and Corporate Leadership

The nature of moral inquiry in the university needs to be explored not only from the standpoint of clarifying the mission of higher education but also from the standpoint of determining the requirements of corporate and public leadership. The cries in the land for responsible leadership and a sense of national and cultural purpose arise in considerable measure out of our despair over the debilitating relativism pervading American society. The nature of this relativism is that we are no longer sure that our own mind and conscience can make contact with objective value and truth or that we can decide what is the right thing to do amid the complexities and changes of contemporary life. This relativism characterizes the "religious" person, who is uncertain that his personal beliefs give significant insight into the corporate problems of the society, as well as the "scientific" person, who senses that his carefully developed facts are not adequate to make moral judgments.

In no area of life has the loss of nerve become more conspicuous than in business and politics, where men live constantly under the knife of moral choice. The university's failure to probe the full technical, scientific, moral, and religious dimensions of responsible decisions has its impact on the quality and availability of corporate and public leadership. Should the habit of moral reflection never be kindled or die neglected in the student, he may abdicate moral choice to a professional, bureaucratic elite even in areas where he might conceivably have significant influence. He may be unable to recognize or sustain public leadership combining technical competence with personal integrity.

The growing emphasis in higher education on the development of corporate and public leadership has been in part a reflection of a heightened awareness of the tension between egalitarian democracy and personal liberty. As de Tocqueville observed a century ago, the democratic principle needs to be tempered in America with appreciation of an aristocracy of talent. Our liberty, our maintenance of a pluralistic society in which free persons develop their full potentialities to serve others, is based not only on the average conduct of the average voter but on the wisdom and difference of our public leaders. Certainly our time is characterized by a dearth of men and women who are able to formulate new policy and to fight for it through all the mass media of persuasion, who see the community or nation as a total enterprise, who give form and expression to the aspirations of a people, who discern the permanent forces which move history, who exact pain and sacrifice from us for high purpose, who practice at once firmness and restraint. The college and university can provide both the scientific and religious ways of appreciating the importance of corporate and public affairs and of the existential personal dimensions of leadership in our common life.

The current drive to make corporate and public leadership a focus of higher education also has a valid concern that we learn to deal with recognizable problems in society and that ideas be tested in action. But this emphasis often takes the form of an uncritical, pragmatic test for education. The colleges and universities are being cultivated assiduously of late by many people who want a crash program to train the spellbinders and the supertechnicians who will give us quick, high-sounding answers to increase our national prestige and power in the world. The American people sometimes seem to respect only the immediately useful knowledge and method. (Does not the wise public and business leader insist that the obvious practical questions of how to win the next election which dominate most of the practical politics courses in business only obscure or falsify the larger moral questions of what kind of society we want to achieve with our military, political, and economic powers?) Too direct and wholehearted pursuit of the technical and practical ends of education will finally prove self-defeating for men who seek wisdom and courage in corporate life. Such men in our technical and commercial society are precisely the ones able to establish significant relations between the short and long run, the quantitative and qualitative, the tangible and the intangible dimensions of corporate policy. The learning which stimulates the creative mind in our day, then, is neither a classical, liberal education which dwells on big ideas apart from the concrete decisions that men face in their leisure and work, nor a kind of graduate or professional education which has no essential connection with the traditional humanities and sciences.

This common purpose of learning and discovery is served by an objective involvement in the subject studied. When I am engaged objectively in the study of American politics, I realize it has some sort of life of its own and that I also have such a life. Thus I can view its needs from a distance and try to do what is best for it. This defines the kind of commitment of the university to corporate life which can be creative. The truth about business can be gotten by the university only by responsible work within business, because the truth is finally what we can and must make of our economic and political institutions and processes.

In recent years the pressure on the colleges and universities for expanded programs of adult and continuing education has become so great that they must begin to rethink their relationship to the varied constituencies of the society (such as alumni, aged, women, leaders in developing nations—and in new sensitive positions in urban areas). What is the relation of traditional undergraduate or graduate education to these constituencies? In what ways are extracurricular activities of students, including extended leaves for various forms of inservice training, to be related to the formal research and teaching of the university? These are the questions which open up new possibilities for the campus minister to become a mediating figure between the university, the local church, and many other associations of the society.

Many of the pioneer adult education programs sponsored jointly by business and university reflect a serious desire of people to probe the larger meaning and purpose of their life and work. But it is also obvious that some aspects of these programs are symptomatic of our difficulties in higher education. Either they are so pragmatic and technical that only a limited skill or information is transmitted, as in many business school management-training programs, or they are so esoteric in their quick sampling, out of historic context, of great books and ideas that no point of view on the task of a particular profession is fully and concretely enough explored to have it become an operative way of thinking in a man's work and leisure.

The American people have more leisure time, greater income, greater need to catch up with the revolution in knowledge in fields relevant to their work and responsibilities, more complex and varied institutional involvements, better education as college graduates, than ever before; hence they and their employers are now encouraging more leaves to be spent on college campuses. How are we going to respond to this kind of challenge? These people wish not only to catch up on new technical knowledge but also to gain some more adequate interpretation of what it is to be a human being in the modern world. What other institutions in our fragmented society but the church and the university will accept, as a mission, the bringing together of men and women from many callings to hear one another out as to what is human and personal in their corporate existence?

## What Institutional Settings Encourage Personal Renewal?

No one knows what settings the universities, the church-related colleges, and the local churches are going to be able to develop so that businessmen, political leaders, and others will be free to explore the moral and religious significance of their actions. There is much talk of the conversion and renewal of men in the church, but little explanation of the institutional conditions which encourage personal and social reconstruction.

What are the settings for the renewal of man, for distinguishing the real from the illusory in society? Will the campus ministers become key figures to answer this question? Will they use the intellectual resources of the academic community, some of the best of it now in paperback, for a whole reconstituting of adult education in the suburban centers of parish communities where there is an educated group with whom to begin to work?

A more basic question is this: Will church images of what these new educational settings look like be drawn only from the personalistic, existential categories of theology and psychology? No matter how much assurance of fellowship a group of public leaders may be given, no matter how much the anonymity of their knowledge is protected, they still do not see how they can talk in the church and university without revealing information to their rivals which will be used against them. They live in such a competitive culture that they cannot talk about themselves for fear of telling too much. So they ask, "Couldn't we talk more adequately about our own situations if we had case studies of other Christians trying to live their faith in our world?" But although our denominations spend millions of dollars on curriculum materials, there are no materials which deal concretely with a man's faith or world view and its relation to his various institutional involvements: business, politics, church, university, family, mass communications, medical care. Yet these are the clues to his deepest beliefs and commitments. Where is the case-study material by which the layman can objectify his situation without having to "spill out his guts" in some depth "encounter"?

It is clear from the institute's experience that most business and public leaders do not for long seek from the university or the church an educational experience that only supports what they do and think by a kind of "listening" and "drawing out". They desire the insight into themselves which comes when differences are highlighted in a congregation or a faculty over what new values can be achieved in a situation. In this sense the church or university enables a man to transcend his situation, to see something beyond its pressing day-to-day operations. However, such a response requires not only theological affirmation but a sense of economic, political, and psychological factors converging and interpenetrating. Recall again our discussion of the actions of men in General Electric: understanding and forgiveness could come for them only after their whole technical, cultural situation was faced. Where in the church and university are we prepared to undertake such understanding, judgment, and forgiveness? Perhaps these are occurring in communities of men we are not even prepared to recognize as the church or as places of intense learning and recommitment.

George Work, a personnel and education director of a large firm manufacturing automobile parts, was a member of a flourishing Presbyterian church in an upper middle-class suburb. He wanted to initiate discussions of the relation of the Christian faith to business. His pastor was noted in the presbytery and around the university as a scholar. Work, part of the managerial elite, a number of well-educated laity, and Work's pastor began to study some of the classics in Christian theology such as Augustine's *The City of God,* Paul Tillich's *The Protestant Era,* and H. Richard Niebuhr's *The Kingdom of God in America.* This adult class was the pastor's greatest joy. Discussion was spirited, and the theological sophistication was impressive even to the associate pastor fresh from Union Theological Seminary. At the end of the course of theological study George Work suggested that the men spend an evening every other week reporting on some of the things each of them was doing in his business or professional life, to see what spiritual and moral dimensions could be found.

Work presented during one of the evenings a film, "The Keystone of America," which his firm used in employee education and which he had been instrumental in distributing. This film, produced by Harding College, describes the problems of the Pilgrims in their early years in America. According to the film the Pilgrims, a devout and God-fearing people, first tried religious communism, sharing the products of their labor from a common storehouse. They almost starved, so poorly did the system work, the film reports. Then they tried dividing up the land into private holdings, permitting each family to live on what it produced from its own land. The harvest was abundant, and the thanksgivings fervent. The Pilgrims had discovered, the film notes, "the keystone of America: private property." The film was enthusiastically received by the men's church class, as were other examples of employee education that George Work administers at his company. As Work said, and these men agreed, "It instilled a greater awareness in the employees of how tough the competitors are and the need for high-quality production."

And now the scene shifts a bit. The Institute at Wesleyan invited Work and his pastor to a conference. As background for it, the film was presented to the faculty participating in this exploration of experiments in lay theological study. The film was then discussed at the conference with regard to its use in the program of Christian education. What struck the faculty was that neither the pastor nor Work was able to establish any connection between their theological-historical study and life in business. For example, Niebuhr's *Kingdom of God in America,* which all the men had read and studied, contains a careful description of the Pilgrims' religious tradition in a chapter titled, significantly, "The Sovereignty of God." Niebuhr's point was that the sovereignty of God was the keystone of the Puritan faith, not private property. The Kingdom of God was not an ideal or a principle of future society, communal or private. It was in the Gospel an order of glory not yet established which made men aware of the corruption in all historical, institutional forms and the necessity to bring them under judgment if they failed to meet human needs and to develop a variety of centers of power in the society.

Why did this layman not make any connection between such an understanding of the Protestant heritage and his responsibilities in his employee education program? To do so would be to raise questions such as these: Is the employee "education" program actually "indoctrination"? Is the Niebuhrian or the Harding College version of our Puritan heritage correct? Can the theological version be used in a business-sponsored film?

These questions were asked in sessions in our institute, and we soon saw how threatening they were to the business career of this conscientious layman. He had consciously or subconsciously separated his church, his liberal education, and his work. To accept in the church the theological study as truth was no threat, but to work at the concrete implications of this study for his responsibilities in his company was most difficult. At first he maintained that he could see no conflict between Niebuhr's view of the Pilgrims' religion and the film's version. Then he brought before us a highly complex and real difficulty: Would the company be accused of religious partisanship by the introduction of Niebuhr's version of the Pilgrims? In Work's view, private property appealed to the less divisive traditions in American religion. But then the question was asked: Are religious traditions to be distorted to meet the needs of a business educational setting? If business cannot deal with religious traditions accurately or historically, should they seek to reduce them to abstract, honorific support of economic and political arguments?

Dietrich Bonhoeffer in his *Ethics* observed that Christians never confront the reality of God apart from the reality of the world, and they never confront the reality of the world apart from confrontation with Christ. It is just this interpenetration between divine and human reality which the church fails to grasp when it cuts off its theological study from social and economic inquiry, when it cuts off theological inquiry from the development of a position within a particular community of faith.

For all the failures of the college and university, they still remain the strategic centers of American intellectual life. If any significant advance in theory is to occur, it will almost certainly occur in the university, whether one thinks of science, theology, or philosophy or for that matter of maturity in the higher arts of cultural and social criticism. Is it too much to ask of the campus minister and of the university, that they learn to love wisdom and to seek it? For surely, without wisdom, in high places and in low, we shall perish as a people, leaving behind a rubble of radioactive shards instead of a fair and rich city of men. Accordingly, without wisdom, panic, confusion, and irrelevancy will reign in this strategic center of our culture. Therefore, we work not only protectively for love of Alma Mater but with a measure of responsibility for the social order as a whole. Clearly the next species of cultural heroes in America will be men of wisdom, rather than saints, savants, or technicians, or the game is up.

PART VI

*The Structures of Administration and Governance in the Church*

## POLITICAL IMAGES OF THE MINISTRY

### James Gustafson

## *Introduction*

The intent of this essay is to explore the functions of responsible political leadership and governance in the ministry, with special attention to the problems of campus leaders. This is an especially tricky topic which Professor Gustafson has sought, as is his right, to limit to political responsibilities in a congregation. But the meaning of politics and governance is up for such serious review in the church, and the limits of clerical responsibilities so in flux, that the topic is hard to retain within a congregation.

Just to illustrate: we set out to study the relations of a young suburban minister to higher education, intellectual inquiry, and the church organizations of the Boston metropolitan area. We found that Richard W. Bauer comes to Yale Divinity School to talk over his fast-changing world with Parker Rossman and others who attended his periodic ecumenical continuing education institutes. He is an honors graduate of Wesleyan University and Yale Divinity School who feels he has "only a desperate tail clutch," as he says, on the "far out" thinking of his suburban parish, West Concord Union Church, which is located in the famous Route of 128 research and development complex on the outskirts of Boston.

How does one describe the political orbit and the governance functions of this young man and of those he wished to deal with? Suppose we take these terms to involve bringing people together for communication on what they want to get done in their work and their communities and whether their objectives are legitimate in the eyes of the Lord or any spokesman for Him. This would take us into a very complex world, indeed, which Gustafson has scarcely alluded to, let alone analyzed.

It may very well be that Bauer's concerns represent, as Gustafson does suggest, an attempt to discover the political interests in his own constituency; but they go far beyond. For example, he has strong interests in maintaining some functional connections with campus ministers. He studies, through observation and reading, the political decision-making process in his own township, in city government, and in the nation; he recognizes, as he says, that his "faith relates to the way options are weighed." His local educational, pastoral, and preaching operations are closely geared to the services available in a number of city-wide organizations the church, universities, and others have established. He is constantly on the alert as to what is the most efficient way to evaluate these services. He wishes Harvard Divinity School or some other center of higher education in his area would engage periodically in such evaluations.

He runs a forum in his church drawing upon personnel and knowledge from Scott Paradise's Boston Industrial Mission. He has done a series of "dialogue sermons" followed by discussions with men in his congregations on "The New Technologies: Threat and Promise." Weekdays he conducts luncheon discussions with a few key industrial leaders on ethical issues in their work. He discusses on Tuesday morning with the Women's Division "The Women's Magazines—Their Images of the American Woman and the Good Life" and consults with faculty in his congregation on the content of these meetings. He is involved in assisting with intensive research into the work of the ministry for a respected scientific group, Ministry Studies Board. These are but part of a pattern of parish work which has its close ties with some of the fastest-moving influential research and development organizations in America. In a sense, this pastor has a campus ministry.

Reflection on political power, and observation and evaluation of church and university efforts to influence its uses are a part of his daily thought and life. No one has to make a case for politics and governance as a part of his work. What bothers him most is that city-wide and regional organizations of the church take so little cognizance of the intimate connections between his pastoral-preaching world and forces of influence and policy in the urban area of his life and work. He finds that specialized ministries, such as that of Scott Paradise, often have less access than he does to the men who make policy in the research and development centers. He finds that conferences of inner-city, suburban, and campus ministers still cannot get down to common problems of learning and inquiry about sources of social change or the forces of redemption actively at work in the city.

Reforms in staff arrangements of city ecumenical and denominational organization do not come within Gustafson's purview. But he is quite clear about the sources of the church's political difficulties on a parish and urban level. Theology and faith have been abstracted from organizational problems by the influential theologians of the past few decades, and conservative forces, bureaucratic in mentality, have often been permitted to take over in the lower echelons of church organization. Moreover, religious concerns have not been translated into social language for the new young leadership, except in a few books such as Gustafson's own *Treasure in Earthen Vessels.*

For many of the "new breed" of activist minister, problems of governing ecclesiastical institutions suggest a kind of barren attention to formal procedures, hierarchy of specialized roles, no-nonsense attention to efficiency in achieving explicit objectives. They are not excited by the warmth and stability a familiar institution (not organization) can provide by its memories and interpersonal informality, its frank acknowledgment of dependency on others. But mostly they seem to have missed in their seminary training the excitement of leading a people to a new vision of itself and its potentialities for service to others, its discovery of new human powers to act in consort, of a spirit of frank and open negotiation on legitimate interests that emerge in new civic or urban programs.

KU

I intend here to illuminate on the functions of the ordained ministry by seeing it in the light of the functions of responsible political leadership. The basic suggestion for this pattern comes from Sidney Mead's essay "The Rise of the Evangelical Conception of the Ministry in America (1607-1850),"[1] in which he shows how the voluntary character of religious life in America made the minister necessarily use political conceptions and skills from the early times of the American churches.[2] I shall draw the contours of what is involved in the suggestion that the ordained ministry can be usefully seen in the light of political leadership, and I shall make some conjectures as to the significance of this analysis for the campus ministries.

This chapter does not attempt to describe and discuss another sort of political image of the ministry which offers much hope for the future, particularly as one sees its marks among alert and intelligent campus ministers: that is, the minister as an informed and forceful participant in the policy-making process both in the university and college and in the civil affairs of the community. Politics as a process of policy making, and the participation of the clergy in it, are not dealt with here. I have not attended to an image of the minister as the critic of social policy—a critic informed both by the complexities of social policy and by the religious and moral insights which his tradition can bring to bear on social policy. Nor have I attended to him as one who shares in the deliberations about policy, whether in the university or the civil order, bringing into the discourse the concerns of social well-being and individual values which might properly be his expertise in the manifold factors involved in policy making. Exploration of the use of political images of the ministry in this order of life would be a fruitful exercise, and it will be done particularly in the second half of the first volume of this study. The concern here is more limited: it examines the relationship between a religious leader and his parish or congregational constituency in political terms.

This proposal is unabashedly nondoctrinal and nonbiblical in its authorization and validation. One might indicate from point to point a certain congeniality between it and themes given in doctrine and Scripture, but it would be false to suggest that any particular insight has been gained by looking at the biblical views of ministry, the traditional views of ministry, and the ministry in contemporary theology as a preface to shaping a political view. There are problems of authority that lie at the heart of what I do here; indeed, the notion of authority is a central one. But the resolution of the issues of authority will not take place by repeating the deadly tradition of having a section on Bible, on doctrine, and on contemporary thought.

It is clear that ministry is being rethought year after year, even if we wish this were not necessarily so. I suspect that the decade 1956-1965 may be remembered as the decade of the proclamation of the ministry of the laity. This emphasis is part of the emphasis on participation in the secular order. It fits rather nicely into the nonreligious Christianity emphasis, so strong in the campus ministries, and is very congenial to the antibourgeois sentiments that prophetic spirits and angry young men have.

The stress in the "specialized" clergy seems to be on a scattered ministry. The distinctive functions of ministry in its traditional form seem not to be effective in the modern world, and insofar as they are unduly emphasized then tend to isolate the church from the world. Thus coffee shops are preferred to sanctuaries, conversation to preaching, celebration through the fellowship of beer to the fellowship of the altar, secular language to traditional religious language, "contextual ethics" to Christian moral casuistry, protest to conservation, loss of visibility as particularly Christian to external identification (though surprising is the extent to which the clerical collar is used to demonstrate, perhaps, that not all clerics are rectory- and altar-bound).

To be in favor of religion, including clergymen, is quickly seen to be in favor of the establishment. One might be judged to be defending vested interests of ecclesiastical institutions, theological seminaries, and traditions. Certainly there are defensive defenses of clerics and religion. The problem within which the political interpretation of ministry is set, however, is hopefully more valid than self-defense. It is the campus ministries' problem of maintaining identity in the midst of being all things to all men that some might be saved. It is the problem of the nurture of a core which forms the perspective from which participation in the world is governed. It is providing a rudder for the vessel that has been the castoff from the tranquillity of a snug harbor and pointed toward the heavy seas. What is the function of the called and ordained ministry within a stress on identification with the world?

## Building a Constituency

We have been prone sometimes to compare the ministry with the other "learned professions," with law and medicine particularly, and sometimes with the profession of psychotherapy. The social situation of the minister is significantly different, however, from that of these other professions. The lawyer gets his clients as they meet particular needs that are unavoidable in the institutional structure of the society. He does not have to make a case to his clients that law itself is a good thing, and therefore they ought voluntarily to support the institution that supports law and thus come to find him to be a useful person. The physician gets his patients as they meet physical needs that almost inexorably drive them to seek competent assistance. He does not have to make a case to his patients that the practice of medicine is an important thing in the society, and therefore they ought to support the medical profession.

Perhaps there was a time when the clergy worked in a social framework that gave the same natural or institutional reinforcements of function and authority, but that day no longer exists. Indeed, in the confines of American Protestantism it has probably never been the case. The Protestant minister in America by social necessity has to maintain or build a constituency. Here the comparison with political leadership begins to be meaningful. The religious leader has to have a consciousness of a constituency that sustains and supports his various activities. Sometimes his dependence on this constituency is immediate; there are no intermediary offices between a Baptist minister and the congregation that has called him. Sometimes the supporting constituency is physically remote; the campus minister may be supported by denominational funds gathered through various means, with the person being supported remaining anonymous to the donors. But even the campus minister is involved in developing a constituency; there have to be the contacts, access, and loyalties that give him a hearing, that are open to his influence, that accept his leadership. Whatever form this relationship takes, it is grounded in the social necessity of voluntary religious affiliation and institutions in our society—whether the voluntarism be theologically defended, juridically defended, or regarded as only an historical accident.

The detailed examination of the patterns of accountability to constituencies, which have been conducted in the Danforth Study, shows not only the variations in political relationships but the degrees of flexibility in the independence and initiating power of the minister. The pastor of a local Baptist church in a college community, for example, typifies the pattern of immediacy of authorization and accountability to a constituency. He must effectively win the political support of the voting members of a congregation to be called to the office of pastor and these, are not likely to be the occasional student visitors to the Sunday service. He must continue in favor with a large portion of the members to remain in the office to which he has been elected and to receive even the financial remuneration due to him for his services. Without doubt, he has a keen sense of accountability to his constituency. Those whom he serves are the same as those whom he seeks to lead, and herein lies the test of his political skills in constituency building. In the nature of the case, the pastor may be immediately politically authorized by the congregation, but (unless he is merely a figure of personal expediency) he is also under obligation to a body of conviction that is objective to this political body. He must meet the expectations of the congregation to remain in office, but he must meet the expectations of his religious convictions by changing the character of the congregation in the light of his religious purposes. For him this may necessitate a closer working relationship to faculty and students who share his religious convictions and his passion for inquiry into the life of his community.

Obviously the Baptist minister is not alone in this pattern; others have comparable patterns of relationship to a single constituency and must have the political skills commensurate with their social situations. The pattern is more comparable to that of a congressman from a conservative district who is interested in progressive reforms than it is to the local attorney or the physician. To stay in office, and yet to be more than the mirrored reflection of those who put and keep one in office, is close to the essence of a political process.

Some clergymen are clearly responsible to more than one constituency. Churches with connectional systems of one sort or another represent this type. A Presbyterian clergyman is accountable to his congregation, but he is also accountable to his presbytery where his own church membership is located. A Methodist parish minister is accountable to his congregation, but also to his district superintendent and to his bishop, representing the constituency of the "Church" in a more inclusive sense. There are, however, no absolutely predictable effects in the actual political activities of such a clergyman. His actual situation may vary little from that of a Baptist pastor; the noncongregational, nonlocal constituencies may make few claims on him or give little support to his work. Membership in a presbytery may be *pro forma*, since the other members of that group who are clergy have primarily a consciousness of their congregational constituencies, and the lay members may not have much sense of being in a group with different functions from the local churches. A bishop may symbolize the authority of the wider church, but in the voluntary church system he must be sensitive to the existing consensus in the churches, not so much to remain in office as to maintain the financial support of the ecclesiastical organization for which he is accountable. Indeed, the parish pastor may find himself to be the local agent of the institution and thus responsible not only for maintaining a local constituency for his own support but also for the support of programs and purposes of the wider organization. Thus the existence of the wider constituency may very well bring, not the basis of support to prophetic leadership, but another claim for maintaining institutional support.

Although the situations of campus ministers vary, in many instances the campus pastor represents another pattern of relation to constituency. If he is supported by denominational funds gathered nationally or regionally, his political relationship to the supporting constituency is more remote, and therefore his independence in leadership is often greater. Others than he make his case to the supporting political constituency; he is free to function with accountability only to those who are between him and the broad ecclesiastical public. This does not remove him completely from the need to be conscious of the mind of the churches, for political pressures can be exerted on those to whom he is accountable, as well as directly on him. But the limitation of accountability in that direction does not free him from a constituency problem; he is called upon often to create the constituency that will respond to the purposes he has, to the leadership he wishes to exercise. This can be done crassly: meeting the needs of religious students as they interpret them, and thus perhaps running a numerically successful venture in the eyes of the churches. It can be done crassly in other ways as well: striving, not to the attend to the latent religious constituency, but to identify oneself with the current ideological or moral crusades among the secular students so that one has a kind of psychological support to one's identity, even if one has no stunning institutional support.

Whatever route the campus pastor takes, he still has to build a constituency, find some way to get a hearing, evoke the loyalty of some persons to bear his witness to the campus. In doing so, he is subject to the same temptations he often sees in the parish minister: using his personal charisma; identifying the purposes of the Gospel with the purposes that are dominant in the minds of his potential constituency; being all things to all men, that he may offend few and hopefully "save" some. The point here is that the campus minister is no less political in his leadership, nor is he any less expected to win a favorable hearing, than is any other minister.

Voluntarism makes all leaders politically alert and sensitive. The necessity to have a constituency to support one in his office, as well as to have a constituency responding to one's leadership, is common to political leaders and clergymen alike. There appears to be no way out of the responsibility for creating, maintaining, and leading a constituency for the American Protestant clergyman.

## Formation of a Consensus

Good political leadership is no mere mirror of the common mentality of its constituency. Politics is reduced to personal expediency if this is the only consideration in one's conception of political responsibility. While maintaining support, the good political leader is also seeking to shape and reshape the consensus of his constituency in the light of moral convictions that he has. The conscientious politician is accountable not only to those who vote for him but also to the wider human community and to moral convictions which he holds to be normative for the common life of the nation. The effectiveness of his leadership is judged in part by his ability to persuasively direct the consensus of those to whom he is immediately accountable in the light of his normative moral convictions. Herein lies the risk of conscientious political leadership, for in this effort the leader may not succeed, and thus he may find himself out of office.

The situation of the Protestant religious leader is comparable to this at every point. He is responsive to the consensus that exists in his constituency—he must be, to maintain himself in office—but he also seeks to reshape that consensus through his persuasive powers. He seeks to direct it into greater conformity to the central religious and moral convictions that are the church's and also presumably his own. His effectiveness is judged not merely by his tenure in office but by his success in redirecting the consensus. Herein lies the risk of religious leadership, for he may fail to achieve this reformation of consensus and so find himself out of office.

Again it is instructive to note how the clergyman differs from other learned professions in our society. The physician does not have to redirect the awareness of the populace before his leadership is effective. His authorization lies in his technical and (from the lay point of view) esoteric knowledge and his skill in administering in the light of that knowledge. The patients are submissive subjects to external and objective authority. The lawyer's authorization is comparable. His client does not have to be persuaded that a law is just and good before he has to respond obediently to it; the law has independent authority, and the attorney has the esoteric knowledge required to be an effective interpreter of the law. The client is submissive. While there may be occasions when the minister functions in a similar way, they are increasingly rare and in most instances dubious even from the point of view of the clergyman.

Response to religious leadership is in the form of consent more than passive assent; the knowledge that the clergyman has is not as technical and esoteric as is the case in other professions, and his relation to persons is thus one in which he must seek to win their consent to what is important and true about the faith of the church and its implications for human life. Thus, like the political leader, he functions to engender personal consent; or in social terms, he seeks to influence the formation of consensus among his constituency.

If one looks at public opinion in the churches, several notable things come to sight. The first is the obvious absence of unanimity in Protestant opinion. But even within the membership of a congregation or a campus group this is also the case. The voluntary process of religious affiliation, the concern to preserve the liberty of the individual conscience, the exercise of free speech in the church, the absence of clear doctrinal or ethical authority in the clergy, the diversity of thought and background among the laity, the difficulties of communication, the sheer stubbornness of people—all make for something less than unanimity in the public opinion of a congregation. Something similar exists in political constituencies.

The function of the leader is to evoke the measure of consensus that does exist into a somewhat unifying force and to move the community toward a consensus around the normative faith of the church. Consensus is never something fully achieved in congregations or in politics. Rather it is always in process. This was the case among the Christians in the city of Corinth in the first century of our era; it has been the case more or less throughout the history of the church, and particularly the history of Protestantism, and it will continue to be so as long as there is freedom in the church. To anticipate unanimity in the public opinion of a religious group on questions of theological and moral importance is to expect the unachievable. But to fail to direct the community in a process of moving toward consensus would be to surrender the leader's normative role and to consign the community to fragmentation.

This social process is one of continual revision and redirection of the consensus formation in the light of both new occasions in the historical life of the community and new interpretations of the more constant delineations of the faith of the church. Consensus formation is always in process, not only because unanimity can never be achieved but also because the vitality of the religious group is maintained as it seeks to come to a more or less common mind on the essentials of the faith and on the activities it ought to engage in. This means that the function of giving leadership to this process is not occasionally, but always, at the center of the task of the clergyman. He may choose to ignore it until there is some crisis in the interpretation of the faith (for example, God has to be thought of in nonspatial terms) or until there is some impinging crisis in the society (such as civil rights). But he makes this choice at the risk of his effectiveness, for the constituency may be taken by surprise to find that they were expected to be reflecting about things in order to be able to express an opinion, if this function is not built into the normal activity of the community.

The third thing to be observed is that the consensus is always in a state of tension with the normative substance of the Christian faith and tradition. Indeed, there is a more or less stable pole around which the consensus moves and toward which or away from which it moves in the deliberative process. Just as the development of a political consensus in America has reference to the Constitution and the folklore of democracy and thus has a point of attention as well as a point from which outer limits can be defined, so the religious consensus in a group has reference to the charter documents (Bible, creeds, and so on). In the nature of the case the existing consensus at any time in any community is never literally that of the central point of attention: the age in which we live is different; the appropriation and internalization of the patterns of thought in the charter is never literal and complete; men resist the claims that are made on them by such documents, since their own interests are seldom in perfect harmony with the interests of the Gospel; and the will to believe is never purely directed toward one thing. The morally conscientious political leader always seeks to bring the significance of the historical democratic ethos to bear upon the existing public opinion of his constituency; the conscientious religious leader seeks to bring to bear the normative traditions of the church upon the existing public opinion. Thus his interpretative task is a political task: the maintenance of a consciousness that existing opinion needs transformation in the light of the center of faith and the active effort to close the gap between the two.

The good clergyman, like the good politician, is no mere mirrored image of his constituency; he has a loyalty to convictions and purposes that keep him in tension with his public, but at the same time he seeks to shape the consensus of that public in the light of these convictions and purposes. He is the leader of a consensus-forming process.

## Necessity of Integrity and a Sense of Office

The conscientious politician, like St. Paul, seeks to be all things to all men, but not without some center of personal integrity, some point of political and moral coherence, some view of the purposes he seeks to achieve in and through his adaptability. He has some vision of himself not only as a person but also as a person in an office, with opportunities and obligations provided him by the office that he holds. The clergyman's place in his community is strikingly similar. To be an effective leader, he needs to have a point of integrity, an integrating purposiveness which gives direction and goals to his various activities. He needs a sense of his office, what it authorizes him to do, what its limits are, what it enables him to lead others to do.

The politician has various points of self-integration. It may be a slogan that covers many deeds and words that only indirectly lead to the achievement of what the slogan signifies: the New Deal, the Fair Deal, the Great Society. It may be a more charismatic presence that lends inspiration and confidence. It may be a quality of humaneness, or shrewdness, or knowledgeability that gives him a sense of authority and thus of respect. He may see his office as a position of power that enables him to exercise leadership, engage in change and reform, develop the life of his public. Or he may see his office as limiting and restricting, requiring him always to make sure the lines of support are clear.

Ministers' points of integrity will vary at least as greatly as their counterparts' in politics, and their conceptions of what their offices enable them to be and to do are at least as governed by traditions and rules as are politicians', yet equally susceptible to reconsideration and reinterpretation.

One major element in leadership in the church is the ability to articulate what a minister stands for, with its necessary prerequisite of knowing for what he stands. The lack of clarity about the faith and purposes of the church leads not only to an inner chaos in the minister but also to consternation on the part of the constituency in and out of the church. Just as the politician does not need to be a political philosopher in order to function well in politics, so the clergyman does not need to be a theological scholar in order to function in the church. But just as the politician needs a set of convictions which form his basic moral commitment, so the practicing clergyman needs to be clear about the grounds on which he acts and speaks and the purposes of particular activities that are inferred from these grounds. The styles of leadership may vary from man to man, but a style of leadership without a substance of conviction bears no fruit in either the political or the religious area of prefessional activity.

Effective religious leadership is built on conviction and also on knowledgeability. Respect for a political leader is enhanced when he has done his homework. No less is the case with the clergy. Effectiveness in leadership requires mastery of the materials involved in the process of consensus formation. Not only does the minister need the skills involved in education and other forms of persuasion; he has to have competence in his understanding and knowledge that carries its own authority and weight in his activity. He is required to have competence in that body of material that impinges on the points at which he seeks to exercise leadership—in social action he needs to know that is going on in the sector of society where he wishes to lead; in corporate worship he needs to know the meaning and function as well as the history of liturgical alternatives if this is an area of particular concern.

What about the office of ministry? Obviously this varies between traditionally defined roles in some denominations, regions, and congregations to no defined roles in experimental ministries to the "night people" or to the "whole campus." Clearly we are in a decade in which the stress on the ministry of the laity tends often to break down whatever tradition remains pertaining to the office of the ordained clergyman. As ministers emphasize the lay ministry, they often see themselves almost as "one of the boys." At this point it is interesting to note that while the politician maintains an identification with the constituency and seeks to keep the image of being one of the people in one way or another, this does not lead to a surrender of a sense of the office. The office enables him to be more than one of the constituents; it gives him opportunity to exercise his directive leadership over others to make an organization function; it provides him with a platform from which he speaks with confidence in order to exercise his persuasive powers; it provides him with the opportunity to engage in activities authorized by virtue of the existence of his official capacity. He is not merely one voter among many; he has a sense of the possibilities given to him by virtue of his office that differentiates him from the voters.

To be sure, the office of clergyman does not have the same social acceptance, the same authorizing power that some political offices have. This, no doubt, makes the politician's lot an easier one than the minister's. But is it intrinsically different? Not in the light of the need to maintain the support of constituency. Indeed, one of the elements that make for good political office holding is a sense of the confidence that the office gives the person and therefore the appropriate initiative in activities in making the most of what the office potentially provides. It may well be the case with the minister and the ministerial office as well. A sense of the importance of the office, of the possibilities for leadership that it creates, might well make for more ministerial effectiveness rather than less. Leadership in political office is not born out of a sense of "nondirectiveness," nor does it come from being apologetic for having the office, seeking to mask it in various ways. The same may very well be the case in the ministry.

The Danforth interviews with students who are dissidents toward campus religious activities have indicated considerable disgruntlement with pastors who are not as willing as students and faculty to state their own convictions and to attempt to inform complex, controversial issues with a point of view. And the case studies of effective ministers cite numerous instances in which respect for the office one holds enables campus religious leaders to utilize the formal and informal powers that accrue to them in such a way that they gain respect and effectiveness rather than lose it. But the office is *political*, too; that is, to assume that because one has the office one need not maintain his identity with the public, his lines of communication with those whose activities become the extensions of one's leadership, is as fatal to religious leadership as it is to political.

The absence of a purposive center of integrity and the importance of the office is fatal to the exercise of significant leadership in religious life as well as in politics.

## The Profiles of Courage

The idea of profiles of courage, made current by John F. Kennedy's book by that title, operates in American religious life as much as it operates in American politics. Indeed, the voluntary character of the religious life in

America makes the awareness of the dimension of courage more significant among clergy in this country than among clergy in national churches. The political democratic character of ecclesiastical life here means that more is risked by way of personal favor and security in the exercise of leadership than is the case where a priest or bishop has tenure guaranteed by the state. Courage, as a virtue, comes to the forefront on the occasions when risks are taken. The courageous politician runs the risk of the loss of the support of his constituency for taking an action that is in accord with his own conscience, but no in accord with the existent consensus of his public. The courageous pastor or other religious leader runs the same kind of risk.

There are occasions when the effort to shape the consensus around the claims of the faith is unsuccessful and when the leader takes his stand in the name of the normative substance of the faith and its ethics over against the constituency, whatever the cost to himself and to his family. The intensive studies by Jeffrey Hadden and William Horvath of Midcity clergy responding to the racial crisis of that city supply the details needed to indicate that this is the case.[3] It happens frequently on questions of racial integration in both southern and northern Protestant churches. In some instances the courage leads to a rupture not only with a congregation but with peers in the ministerial office. Indeed, for some ministers the choice is only of which issue is important enough to risk their jobs.

Courage in politics is relative to the immediacy of dependence on voter support. Courage in religious life is relative to immediacy of dependence on support of a lay consensus. Thus we have one of the present conflicts in American religious life. A college chaplain or campus pastor risks less in his strong prophetic utterances or action than the pastor of a Baptist congregation of South Carolina. Indeed, if courage were measurable, it might be the case that it takes more courage to be mildly prophetic in a congregation in South Carolina than it takes to be iconoclastically prophetic in a classroom or college pulpit in Pennsylvania. The point this leads to is that the risk or loss of one's office may be courageous, but it is not thereby necessarily wise. For Senator Fulbright to come out valiantly on civil rights would win him glory, laud, and honor from those of us who are deeply committed to the success of the cause of civil rights, but in the light of the state that elects him to the United States Senate, it may not be a wise thing for him to do. Wisdom is not mere expediency: it is a preception within a situation. Similarly, it is easy to honor the campus pastor who identifies himself with the radical causes of students, or succeeds in leading students to demonstrate for morally significant ends, or leaves his location of work to bear testimony to his convictions on civil rights in protest movements in the South. From the sense of the importance of this activity, it is also easy for some persons to assume that every minister with convictions about the rectitude of causes ought to be equally visible in his support of them. But whether it is wise for the pastor of a congregation in a conservative community to do so is another question; it may take more courage to engage in the redirection of the local consensus in his case than it takes for the campus pastor to picket with a radical cause.

Prudence is a virtue for both the politician and the religious leader. Prudence has a double meaning in common usage: it usually means expediency and thus is hardly a virtue. It also means wisdom, a sense of the fitting and appropriate action, not only in the light of local opinion but in the light of other virtues and in the light of moral convictions. Prudence as wisdom is governed by several things: moral convictions, a sense of the plurality of considerations, a sense of the appropriate expression of the moral convictions in relation to the time and place of action, and so on. What makes the profile of courage admirable in religious leadership as well as political is that the leader acts both wisely and courageously; he risks not for the sake of acclaim, nor for the sake of the joy of risking, but for a cause to which he has wisely committed himself and for which he has both wisely and courageously acted.

At this point it is appropriate to observe that there are diversities of gifts of political leadership and religious leadership. There are also diversities of channels of activity in both. One would hardly want a hundred Dirksens or Morses in the Senate. So also the ministry needs its William Sloane Coffins; it needs its more anonymous but prudent and courageous pastors and campus ministers working for the same general purposes in the ways that are fitting to their locations. The profile of courage can be drawn for either type, and to assume that there is only one such profile is to oversimplify the issues involved in religious leadership.

No doubt the analogies between political and religious leadership could be drawn out more extensively, with more refinement of both the similarities and the differences between them than has been recorded here. The fundamental points of interest, however, have been designated. Sidney Mead is correct in his historical observation: the voluntary religious system makes politicians out of Protestant ministers in America. The charge should not be a negative one—assuming that because there are resemblances to politics, the ministry is something less than true to itself. Indeed, there may be wisdom in furnishing a self-image to ministers of themselves as political leaders of a particular cause.

NOTES

1. In H. R. Niebuhr and D. D. Williams, eds. *The Ministry in Historical Perspective* (New York: Harper, 1956), pp. 207-249.

2. In previously published essays I have indicated by suggestion some of the implications of this for the American minister. See "The Clergy in the United States," *Daedalus* (Fall, 1963), pp. 724-744; "The Church: A Community of Moral Discourse," *Crane Review* (Winter, 1964), pp. 75-85; "The Voluntary Church: A Moral Appraisal," in D. B. Robertson, ed., *Voluntary Associations, Essays in Honor of James Luther Adams* (Richmond: John Knox, 1966), pp. 299-322.

3. See "Crisis in Midcity: Interviews with Clergy of One Denomination, Summer, 1966," in this volume; also Jeffrey K. Hadden, *The Gathering Storm in the Churches* (Garden City: Doubleday, 1969).

# ❧ 17 ❧

## AUTOBIOGRAPHY OF A STUDENT ACTIVIST AND ORGANIZER IN THE CHURCH

### William Horvath

### *Introduction*

William Horvath is the one undergraduate student contributing to this volume.[1] He well represents in his autobiographical essay the kind of young people who worked most closly with us in gathering and interpreting data.

While a student at St. Olaf College, he volunteered services for two summers as an interviewer of clergy and students. His chief interest seemed to be work in metropolitan or inner-city situations, so Jeffrey Hadden, then at Purdue University, undertook his training and supervision. The quality of his work and involvement was soon evident. He conducted in time most of the "Midcity" interviews of clergy reported in this volume.

At an early point in his career, Horvath was active in American Lutheran Church organizations. He has more recently been a participant in a world ecumenical conference, in study of theology in Europe, and in travels and interpretive reportage of life and faith in both western and eastern European cities.

The last request we have made of him was the hardest for him to do: to write an account, without anonymity, of his vision of his evolving faith, his ethical dilemmas, his social and intellectual experiences and concerns. What emerged is characterized by an objectivity and candor few of an older generation can equal.

KU

A story of who and where I am today would probably have to begin with birth on July 7, 1945, and with being raised by loving parents. I was in the

---

1. By the time his work with the study was completed, he had entered professional and graduate studies.

sixth or seventh grade when Sputnik was launched and recall being pressured in school by my science teacher to go to a special high school in Detroit which would prepare me for an accelerated science program. My math and science aptitude test scores were quite high, but I really was not interested in science. There was a quiet expectation around the house that I would become some kind of educated man. I admired our doctor and minister, but thought that if I became a lawyer I could go into politics, which probably interested me more than I know. I did not know any lawyers.

In high school I aspired to attain recognition. I was an above-average student, but lacked the desire to be precise in my work. I did attain a strong academic record in my first year, but that just could not satisfy me. In the tenth grade I ran for student council and was elected because no one else from my homeroom was interested in the position. I was quiet during my first semester on the student council and awed by those who were my political superiors.

In my junior year I became the vice-president of the student council, and later, because of a class conflict of the president, became president, a position I was to hold for one and a half years. I think I was a good president, but remember little of the legislation passed and recall the frustration of feeling sometimes as if it was all a big game. During that year I also became president of the city-wide student council. I was also elected president of the Detroit Area Luther League (Lutheran young people's group). During the last one and a half years of high school I was elected president of virtually every organization whose meetings I attended. In retrospect, I am not sure why I ran; the issues treated so seriously then were usually overseen by adults, and our decisions never seemed to mean much anyway.

As chairman of the Detroit Youth Action Council (I was the only white member: in spite of or because of that fact, I was chairman), I met J. W., a staff member of the Mayor's Commission on Children and Youth. With him I learned some of my hardest political lessons. We made a trip to Washington, D.C., together, and he successfully negotiated a half-million-dollar grant for the city to train jobless youth for employment. After the grant was awarded, the program was lost in mismanagement by the mayor as well as the appointment of an inept director instead of J. W., who understood himself to be headed for its directorship. As the program was floundering, J. W. sent a letter to the mayor stating that unless serious changes were made and unless some youth began to be trained, he would leave his job as an official in the program. Within an hour his resignation was accepted. The experience of seeing long and intensive work go into the development of a program, only to have its developer fired for making serious recommendations, left a great impact about politics on me.

During that spring I was also co-ordinator of a student group attempting to encourage voters to support schools with higher taxes. I made over sixty speeches to numerous organizations and watched the voters resoundingly defeat the tax proposal.

My most practical education began after high school. I left a job in an expensive men's clothing store, selling students' clothing, to sweep floors in a factory for double the pay. I also appeared on a weekly television program in Detroit about what youth are thinking. It was in the factory, however, that I was exposed to styles of life I had never encountered. It was almost as if during my life up to that time the only people who existed were college graduates. All the people in the factory told me how lucky I was to be able to go to college and some about how they began working in the factory after the war, planning to get a better job in a few months, but stayed for twenty years and were trapped as unskilled labor. Because of my interest in the church and my position in it as a youth, I spoke with the president of the Michigan District of the Lutheran Church of this experience and the void that I felt the church left with the working classes. I was rather politely shrugged off.

I went to college. I knew no one and was very lonely. I had fears of flunking out and memories of how successful I had been in the past. I thought of changing schools, but decided that what was wrong was my own despondency, and not the school. During my freshman year I was elected vice-president of the Minnesota Lutheran Student Association. I also organized a group of six students to live and work together in the inner city of Detroit. My experiences of the summer before had left a deep imprint on me, and as a group we set out to seek the relevance of the church in an industrial order patterned after the worker-priest concept. The support we received from the Youth Department of the American Lutheran Church in our plans and during the summer renewed some of my hopes for the church. We lived in a church basement, knowing the silence of the church in our neighborhood. Work in factories was hard, and personal relations became strained among our group, but the six of us were convinced that we had been significantly exposed to a life we had not known before. We did not know what we could do about it and spent the summer attempting to listen to a life we did not know.

Before going back to school I was a delegate to the National Lutheran

Student Association meeting. I was one of the organizers of its Human Relations committee. The central focus of that committee was to be on urban problems. Its proposed work seemed quite vacuous to me, as the committee's only result was to be more mail to students. The idea of a National Lutheran Student Association began causing doubts in my mind, as I realized that the only thing national about it was this one meeting and that its power was a myth. The students at that time guarded their autonomy from the church; yet all they did was play church games and never enter church politics. After that meeting I was a delegate to the National Student Christian Federation and was positively impressed by the organization, yet felt left out of its deliberations. That organization dealt with all the modern political problems. Yet, other student organizations were better representing the student left.

I went back to school for a rather bland sophomore year and could easily identify with the well-known "sophomore slump." I would go to LSA board meetings mainly because they gave me some interest outside the campus. My one month of independent study that year, however, was rewarding. I was interested in writing a paper on the church and the industrial order, but realized that I did not have enough to say, but under the guidance of a talented and interested professor I wrote a paper on the ethics of Reinhold Niebuhr as an outgrowth of and reaction to the social gospel. I was interested in developing greater expertise in the area of urban affairs, but the rural setting of my campus gave me little opportunity to do so. I helped another group of students organize a summer similar to the one I had experienced the year before. The summer after my sophomore year I participated in a program sponsored by Presbyterian Neighborhood Services of Detroit. I had a full-time job assignment with a community organization. That summer I heard of Saul Alinsky and became a believer in the importance of community organization. Yet the staff goals of indigenous leadership, that ground swell of interest in the community that I was awaiting, just did not emerge. My interest in the clergy who had become active in community organization was growing as I reflected on their involvement back at school. I just wanted to celebrate the new-found activism of the church, yet also hope for greater community participation.

The beginning of my junior year was better than the sophomore year. I was starting to phase out my activity in national student church organizations and was finding some meaning on campus. Seventy students had returned from a summer of field education at Tuskegee, Alabama, and others were returning after urban experiences. A liberal group of students began to emerge with some power on campus. I was an elected member to the student parliament and became the leader of a small faction seeking educational reforms to incorporate urban experiences into the curriculum. We also focused, as did so many other campuses, on the issue of *in loco parentis* and succeeded in placing students on faculty committees.

I decided to explore more deeply the relation of clergymen to community organization during the month of independent study in my junior year. I was extremely fortunate to receive a grant from the Danforth Foundation Study of Campus Ministries to study for a six-week period. It was during that time that I noticed the leaders of community organization were really the new clergy in the community as well as the staff, and not the indigenous people of the neighborhood. The church actually dominated, rather than supported, community organization. The contact with Kenneth Underwood and his much deeper understanding of the problem I saw, as well as his continuing support for the following two years, has been more influence on me than I can express. My exposure to sociology through Jeffrey Hadden at that time opened new reading and greater sophistication to my perception of the problems of society.

During the spring of the year I was elected student-body president by a 3 to 1 majority vote. Thus began the most active year of my life.

The summer following that election was my most depressing and sobering. I interviewed over a hundred clergymen in a large metropolitan center. The interviewing sought out their reaction to the civil rights movement, and particularly the effect which the death of a clergyman active in the civil rights movement had on their involvement. My interest in becoming a clergyman, as well as my activist tendencies, were dealt a serious blow during that summer. I encountered several clergymen who had lost their positions as a result of their civil rights activity and many others who had been involved who were just plain ready to leave the ranks of the clergy, yet felt ill equipped to do anything else. The ones who were satisfied with their lack of activity were repulsive to me. To see men warped by a lack of interest in or contact with issues outside their own small congregation was most disappointing. At the end of the summer I decided that I would never get trapped in the institution of the church; yet I was still deeply interested in the church. I am still wrestling with the question of how one may be an effective agent of social change. I am frustrated because there seems to be no institution one may work in effectively that will also allow him access to social change. I do not know how one may participate in an institution and not be trapped by its particular parochial interests. When one feels he is being effective and doing what he wishes, he can usually discover that what he is doing could be going on without his interest and influence and that the people who are interested in a particular cause have already assembled and would be able to act effectively without him. This applies particularly to my perception of the church, as I see it trying to be an agent of social change.

I came back to campus and found personal relations difficult as student-body president. I had taken my office too seriously and found it difficult to separate my person from my office. Fortunately some of my friends re-mained close and would not let me lose myself in my office, and by mid-October I had begun to find direction and personal life again.

I went to the American Lutheran Church convention in October as chairman of the student-body presidents' conference of the church colleges to seek to get a resolution passed by the convention supporting selective con-scientious objection. The resolution was defeated. The convention was almost stopped by the moral pleas of students at the convention, but that was not enough to have a resolution passed. The issue had not even been planned for discussion, and it did receive and cause lengthy consideration. Recently the president of the church stated that he would, as an individual, support students who felt that they could not participate in the Vietnam war if they were willing to accept the consequences of their act. Apparently the student action did have impact.

I had attended the National Student Association meetings in the fall and believed that it would be important for St. Olaf College to join the organiza-tion. It appeared to be one dramatic way to cause the student to look beyond his particular campus and face new issues with national implications. The student parliament passed a resolution which affiliated the student body with NSA. It was, however, a very narrow margin of passage, and a group of students who were opposed to the stand NSA had taken on the Vietnam war organized a petition to have a referendum on affiliation. The student parlia-ment action was reversed, and I felt very much like a minority president. This was a serious blow, and I almost resigned; but some of my friends prevailed and stated that this was the time that the students needed a liberal president even against their will.

My popularity did not increase in the end of December when a letter of a hundred student leaders from the nation appeared in the New York *Times* criticizing the Vietnam policy. My signature was among those hundred. The national reaction to this letter was immediate. Secretary of State Rusk invited a group of us to meet with him in Washington. I went to that meeting in the end of January. The meeting was anticlimactic to the five days of preparation for it. The Secretary of State presented the government's policies in an indefensible manner. My opposition to the war increased rather than decreased as a result of that meeting.

The issue became critical upon my return to campus. How could I, as a minority president on this issue persuade students and make the issues graphic? Then came the report of the Marshall Commission on the draft, and the issues of military service confronted my fellow students and me as never before. Opposition to the war could be seen mounting overnight as it became more personal.

I was invited to a meeting of ten students and five members of the "older generation," including Mr. Marshall, President Brewster of Yale, and Mr. Bundy of the Ford Foundation. The openness of the meeting, as well as the depth of discussion, was a relief from the earlier Washington meeting.

As I came back to campus, however, I felt that little was changing in the nature of the military commitment. My deepest disillusionment with the American political system and mass mind set in. It is difficult to know what role these meetings may have played in mobilizing any greater opposition to the war, but in retrospect I have to admit that more time is needed than the duration of a meeting to see policy change.

I was subsequently invited to a National Conference on the Draft sponsored by the American Friends Service Committee. I signed the most radical statement I had signed to that point. A week later I led a march against the war in Vietnam in Northfield, Minnesota.

I felt some satisfaction in demonstrating, since I had tried and exhausted political channels. I was demonstrating more out of depression than of hope.

The greatest satisfaction of my year as student-body president was being organized during the year and carried out during the summer after my graduation. The idea of students living and working in an inner-city area to understand the need of their skills in urban areas became popular, and I organized a program that placed a hundred students in the cities of Detroit, Cleveland, and Chicago during the summer. The sorrow over that program came when it was realized that perhaps it was too late to emphasize education of whites and that action rather than education was needed. The fact that many of the participants shared that view, however, spoke for the value of such an experience.

My year as student-body president ended, leaving me with mixed feelings about how I had handled my job. I learned through work with the student parliament that legislation takes time to pass, and just feeling you are supporting the right cause is only half of the struggle. On the occasion of consideration of the National Student Association we had a two-vote plurality. It would have been possible to delay a vote for another week and develop greater support, but I was impatient and wanted the resolution passed then. There was a great student reaction which might have been avoided had the vote been delayed. Patience is still the hardest virtue for me to develop when I feel that the cause I am supporting is right.

After my resolve in the summer of 1966 not to go into the ministry, the only school I applied to for study after graduation was Yale Divinity School. I had decided that I did not wish to attend a denominational seminary after graduation and believed that Yale might be the place to discover if I really could exist within a church. After one semester at Yale, a time of new reappraisal and adjustment to anonymity, I went to Germany.

I do not know if I will ever understand fully the import of my nine-month stay in Europe. It was not an escape from the problems of America, although it did provide a new context for reflection on those problems.

International relations became immediate and personal. A girl from Yugoslavia became one of my close friends. She could not understand why I was interested in the study of theology, and I could not understand why she could not talk outside of a Marxist framework. One thing we did agree about most emphatically was that our differing belief systems were no legitimate cause for unresolvable conflict. There was something about our common ages and distrust of a government's ability to resolve international conflict or achieve justice that linked most students in a common bond.

I found that my activism could not be left behind in the United States. Before the semester at Tubingen began, Martin Luther King, Jr., had been assassinated and Rudi Dutschke of the German SDS had been seriously wounded on the streets of Berlin. There was nothing I could do about the King assassination except reflect and discuss some of its causes, as I saw them, with interested German students. But I participated with German students in their demonstration against the Axel Springer element, which controlled almost 70 per cent of the German news media and was feared as a serious threat to the freedom of the press. I also participated in a demonstration protesting the Vietnam war and the shooting of Dutschke five days later.

My courses took on a contemporary relevance which was often missing in my studies in the United States. I had a seminar under Jurgen Moltmann on the topic of the church and revolution, which was an immediate question of the students in Germany. The course reflected perhaps the students' concerns to have the right ideas about revolution, more than a concrete encounter with the areas where revolutionary change might be desirable. However, the fact that this issue was openly discussed as it related to a contemporary situation at least captured attention. The semester ended with a realization of the pure joy of studying what I wanted and reading what I wanted.

As I look toward my personal future, it is still wrapped up in the whims of my nation and its desires for making peace or waging war. I feel that I would refuse induction into the military if drafted to fight in Vietnam. I am now planning, after graduation from the Yale Divinity School, to teach school in Africa. I am suffering from the restlessness common to my fellow students, seeking to be constructive and creative, only to find that the institutions of power in our world are repressing the possibilities with their continued threat of war and conflict.

# PART VII

# Clergy Survey, Clergy Models, and Lay Education

# ❧ 18 ❧

## THE HOUSE DIVIDED
### Jeffrey K. Hadden

## *Introduction*

Professional ministers in many churches have reached, in their relations to the laity, an almost incapacitating doubt as to whether they communicate with them at all on human matters of great public concern. The profound cleavages in belief and social attitude between clergy and laity and between groups in both of these is the subject of Jeffrey Hadden's paper. He is a sociologist at Case Western Reserve University who has played a large role in this study through his work on the clergy survey. In a book collateral to this study, *The Gathering Storm in the Churches*, he makes his case for a polarity between laity and the socially activist clergy which threatens to tear the church apart, unless a greater attempt is made by ministers to educate their constituencies to why and how they have come to their positions and behavior.

The churchgoer and the minister are, therefore, often caught up in a relation of empty roles and bad faith in which people think one thing and do another. For an institution whose Scriptures reveal a unity of word and deed as normative in the relations of men and God, the situation is an anxious and depressing one for all involved. Religious talk may function as refuge for the churchgoer from the real world of social change, racial evil, and absurd public acts in the name of morality. The minister aware of this pervasive desire for escape in the congregation finds it difficult to invoke the need for God's forgiveness and communal repentance for vast social evils, for hope of a sense of life's newness in the midst of hallowed ritual.

In this situation the research of a Jeffrey Hadden, though it may not save a man's soul, at least becomes an instrument for restoring the power of people to see themselves as they are, or as others see them, and to begin to speak again to one another in truth. The survey data of Jeffrey Hadden provide a new realism to the church which is greatly needed.

K.U.

## Introduction: The Gathering Storm

T HE Christian churches today are in the midst of a struggle which gives
every evidence of being the most serious ferment in Christendom since the
Protestant Reformation. Indeed, its origin dates back to the Protestant
Reformation and in a broader sense may be seen as inherent in the Christian
faith.[1] The significance of this decade is that we have experienced a fruition
of developments whose meaning and implications are becoming more
apparent.

There are four critical dimensions which may be analyzed. To begin with,
the churches are confronting a crisis over their very *meaning* and *purpose*.
The controversial works of Berger,[2] Winter,[3] and Berton,[4] for example,
dramatize the struggle and resistance to redefining the meaning of the
Christian church. The essence of this struggle is perhaps best captured in the
title of a recent book of Glock, Ringer, and Babbie, *To Comfort and to
Challenge.*[5] To many, the church has always represented a source of comfort
and help. But to an increasing number, whom Cox has labeled the "New
Breed,"[6] the church has become a rallying point to wage war against social
injustice. As this latter group has grown in number and become more vocal,
there is mounting evidence to suggest that there may be an inherent conflict
between the roles of comforter and challenger.

The crisis over meaning and purpose is complicated by an increasing crisis
of *belief*. In the past few years we have witnessed the emergence of a small
group of theologians who proclaim the "death of God." While it is perhaps
too early to tell whether these theologians will have any lasting theological
importance, their presence does dramatize the growing crisis of imagery in
Christianity.

But there are many indicators of the crisis of belief other than the "death
of God" theologians. In many respects the works of Bishop Robinson[7] and
Harvey Cox[8] represent a popularization of theological debates which have
been quietly carried out in the ivory halls of the seminaries for many years.
These writings have brought the hushed-up revolution before the lay public.

But sociological studies, particularly the work of Glock and Stark,[9]
suggest that the process of abandoning the old categories and traditional
symbols of the Christian tradition predates its popularization. The questioning of traditional theology, which precipitated the crisis of belief, has been
going on for some time. The writings of men like Robinson and Cox have not
created the revolution, but rather, like Kinsey's monumental studies of sexual
behavior, have merely placed the truth of a social revolution on the public
agenda. Differences in religious beliefs are widespread both across as well as

within Protestant denominations, and this phenomenon is occurring among laity as well as clergy.[10]

Public opinion polls also dramatize the growing crisis of belief, and with doubt it would seem that we are beginning to see the demise of the centrality of religious institutions in our society. Since 1958 the polls have shown a slow but consistent drop in church attendance.[11] More recently, we have seen that the public has come to view religion as less influential in society;[12] and furthermore, the prestige of clergy has fallen off rather significantly.[13]

In short, the collective impact of these several indicators adds up to a conclusion that the Christian churches confront not only a crisis of mission but also a serious struggle over the most basic theological doctrines which are the foundation of the faith.

A third dimension of crisis in the church is a struggle over *authority*. It is perhaps most dramatic in the Roman Catholic Church, but equally significant power struggles are occurring in Protestantism. The battleground of this struggle does not conform to the traditional boundaries of conflict between the major faiths or denominations, but rather is splintering denominations, congregations, and church councils.

In Protestantism, the struggle tends to be decentralized, and thus it is difficult to grasp the full significance of the developments. Decision making in Protestantism has tended to be left in the hands of the professional leadership.[14] But what is happening today is that laity, who have entrusted this responsibility to professional leaders, have come to have grave doubts about how this authority has been used. While the greatest conflict in Protestantism seems to be between clergy and laity, it needs to be stressed that the schism cuts in many directions. Among the professional leadership of the churches, there is an emerging polarization which resembles, and to a considerable extent parallels, the polarization of left and right on the national political scene. And the struggles for control of church resources and the loyalties of constituencies is no less vicious.

These three crises have in turn led to yet a fourth: a crisis of *identity* for clergymen. This results in large part from the clergyman's *internalization* of the other crises. Identity emerges as a product of social interaction whereby the individual internalizes the attitudes and values of others toward the world around him as well as toward himself.[15] While identity is not solely the product of what one internalizes about himself from others, social interaction is an integral part of the process by which the individual gains a sense of who he is. Socialization is the process by which human communities transmit to the individual the values and modes of conduct which are essential for the survival of society. From the perspective of the individual, socialization is the learning of what is valued by the human community, what is expected in the way of conduct, and the acquiring of a built-in (internalized) desire to conform to the community's values and patterns of conduct. To the extent that socialization succeeds in internalizing the values and patterns of behavior of a society, it succeeds in giving the individual a sense of identity, for he not only understands the nature of the social order but is able to see where he "fits in."

But what happens when a human community's values are in a state of flux or transition? To be sure, depending on the centrality of the values in flux, the entire community experiences strain. But the strain is most acute for those whose responsibility it is to define, sustain, and transmit the values in question. When the values in flux are as basic as the ultimate meaning of life itself, the amount of strain in understandably great.

The clergyman's crisis of identity emerges out of the fact that the value system for which he has traditionally assumed a major responsibility for defining, sustaining, and transmitting is in a most serious state of flux. The society is not sure what it believes, and it is uncertain as to what the meaning and purpose of the church ought to be. Lacking a clear notion of the role of religious faith and religious institutions in a changing world, it lacks an understanding of the role of the clergyman. The failure to ascribe clearly defined roles to the clergyman, in turn, leaves the clergyman with enormous ambiguity as to his role in society. Even in the case where the clergyman has worked out a personally satisfactory understanding of the nature of belief and the meaning and purpose of the church, he is still not free to define his own role, for the unsettled state of these issues means that his authority to fulfill his role as he sees it is almost certain to be challenged.

Very briefly, these four developments—the crisis over meaning and purpose of the church, the emergence of doubt and theological reorientation, the struggle over authority, and the clergyman's search for personal and professional identity—constitute the fabric of a deep and entangling crisis which the churches face today. This is the context for a specific problem: the widening gulf between clergy and laity.

## Some Critical Evidence

Historically, major social institutions do not undergo radical change suddenly. Rather, the antecedents of change are deeply rooted in the history of institutions and the culture in which they exist. The broad cultural forces which have produced the contemporary crisis in the churches are based in the emerging industrial-urban order.[16] Urbanized society has been the spawning grounds for the growth of value orientations which stress democracy, freedom, and liberty.[17]

The church has played a mixed role in this ideological revolution. As the holder of a substantial segment of the Western world's economic and political resources, the church has defended the status quo. Yet the church has also been the carrier of an ideology which stresses love, compassion, and individual salvation. The forces of urbanization have made the implications of this ideology more apparent, and in this century the church has emerged as a force providing moral legitimization to the ideologies which have found their broadest expression in urban culture.

In order for the church to emerge as a challenge- and change-oriented institution, it was necessary for the church to transform its own ideologies which traditionally stressed hope for another life and not this. Again, the forces of urbanization, which produced a highly scientific and rational social order, provided the impetus. Peter Berger describes this process as follows: "One of the most obvious ways in which secularization has affected the man in the street is as a 'crisis of credibility' in religion. Put differently, secularization has resulted in a widespread collapse of the plausibility of traditional religious definitions of reality."[18]

As the distinction between faith and empirical reality became clearer, theologians began to ponder the new implications. Rapid population growth and increased concentration of human numbers in urban environments have made the unfinished social revolutions more apparent. The unleashing of nuclear energy has served to dramatize the necessity for accelerating social change. The civil rights conflict in this nation, as well as the revolt against colonialism by black and yellow men around the world, has illumined the complexity and breadth of the unfinished task of creating a just and free society.

In this nation, the civil rights struggle has been an issue around which clergy could rally their moral convictions and involve themselves in a meaningful way to achieve social change. But with this involvement has come a largely unanticipated reaction from Christian laity. They neither understand nor approve of the reasons for clergy involvement, since it represents a serious threat to their own interpretation of the meaning and purpose of the church.

## Clergy and Lay Conflict

The conflict between clergy and laity can perhaps best be understood by examining the relationship between the religious and social beliefs of the two groups. Clergy who have rejected orthodox (traditional) theological beliefs are much more likely to hold liberal views on a whole range of social issues, and they are much more likely to believe that the church has a vital role to play in seeking solutions to social problems.[19] But for the laity, however religiosity is measured, orthodox theological beliefs bear essentially no relationship to beliefs about social issues.[20] In other words, clergy who hold liberal theological views are also likely to hold liberal social views; while among laity, those holding liberal theological beliefs are no more likely to hold liberal social views than those who hold to traditional religious beliefs. Moreover, clergy as a group are significantly more liberal on social issues than laity.

Apparently clergy and laity have rejected orthodoxy for different reasons, and the directions of their new religious convictions have not been the same. While clergy have rejected orthodox beliefs about the Christian heritage, they have not abandoned theology as a critical dimension of their faith. Their new theology has brought them to a deeper concern about the meaning and implications of love and involvement in this world. For an increasing number of clergy, salvation is to be found in this world by expressing compassion and love for the unfortunate. To a considerable extent, life beyond this one has become less important.

Laity, on the other hand, have not so much rejected orthodoxy as found it unnecessary for a privatized civil religion espousing general principles of the good, the true, and the beautiful.[21] They neither strongly profess unalterable faith in orthodox theology nor reject it as untenable in a rational-scientific world. For others who view God as a wrathful judge, orthodox belief is a convenient form of fire insurance; but a large proportion of laity have come to accept the New Testament emphasis on God as love, and they do not feel that the Creator will ultimately commit anyone to damnation. While acknowledgment of an Almighty is important, specific doctrine is not. Most laymen are not theologically knowledgeable, nor do they care to be, for they have found their privatized-psychologized version of religion adequate for their needs.

For the layman, religion is a source of *comfort* and *help*. He is a *consumer* of the church's love, rather than a producer. No matter how well he may fare socially and economically, he lives in a troubled world which bombards him with problems. He needs the church to comfort him and reassure him that he is doing the best that he can. To the extent that he is a producer of love, it is radiated to his family and friends who sit in the comfortable pew next to him. When he reaches beyond this immediate circle, his concern is manifest in paternalism which takes the form of church bazaars, rummage sales, and modest contributions to the poor. In fact, these token expressions are an essential part of his value system, for they reassure him of his own basic goodness.

Herein lies the basis of conflict between clergy and laity: the clergyman's new theology has moved him beyond the four walls of the church to express God's love in concern for the world, while the layman comes into the sanctuary of God to seek comfort and escape from the world. Clergy have come to see the church as an agent which should challenge the structures of society that lead to injustice in this life and should utilize the forces of love and political power to bring about a new social order. This development has left the majority of layment bewildered and resentful. For them, the church is not an agent of change, but rather a buffer against it.

Thus, in a very real sense, what has emerged is a house divided. Laity have one church: a church which they want and need; a church largely confined to four walls, their friends, and a salaried comforter. From the church they withdraw love and support, which they pay for with cash and consume when they need it. But this church has become a source of increasing frustration. Their comforter is increasingly telling them that the rules have changed and that they are to become producers of love, rather than consumers. But the frustration for the clergy is equally great, for the old church will not free him to enter the new.[22]

## The Church as a Voluntary Association

To grasp the implications of this conflict, it must be understood that religious institutions are *voluntary associations*. This means that individuals choose to participate of their own volition, and not because of some compelling external force. The distinction can be ambiguous. At an earlier point in history, the church was much less a voluntary association than is the case in contemporary society. Moreover, to those who view their personal salvation as inextricably bound to participation in the church, it may not seem like a voluntary association. And in some social environments very strong informal pressures are exerted to force conformity to a set of socially prescribed behaviors which include participation in a particular religious group. But a critical development in religious institutions during the past four centuries has seen a gradual shift toward voluntarism. Today, attendance, amount of financial support, and the intensity of adherence to the doctrines and goals of a particular religious group are, to a large extent, matters of voluntary and private decision. If an individual strongly objects to some aspect of the particular religious group to which he belongs, he is free to join another religious group or withdraw from participation altogether.

It follows from this that the ongoing functioning of a voluntary association depends on a basic consensus among the membership as to the goals or purposes of the organization. And without some rewards or sense of satisfaction, there are few sanctions to sustain an individual's participation. It is important to recognize, however, that the rewards derived from participation in a voluntary association may be secondary or latent to the formally stated goals. Thus, for example, a member of a bridge club may not be a particularly good bridge player and as such may not derive a great deal of satisfaction from playing bridge. However, the ongoing satisfaction of sociability with a group of friends may be more than adequate reward to sustain membership in the group. But when a person who does not play bridge well ceases to enjoy the company of the other players, there is little reason to continue membership in the group. The point I am making is very simple: a person who derives little or nothing from participating in a voluntary association is not likely to continue to participate. Similarly, if the negative factors involved in participation are perceived to outweigh the positive benefits, membership is likely to be curtailed.

One of the tasks of leadership, then, is to see that the organization continues to provide its membership with rewards that are satisfactory in order to assure their continued participation. If the leaders choose to redefine goals and rewards, either they must convince the membership of the efficacy of the new goals and rewards, or they must seek to recruit new members who share their definition of the organization. Failure to achieve one or the other of these tasks will result in either the demise of the organization or their loss of the leadership role.

Leadership in a voluntary association, therefore, is more precarious than in a nonvoluntary organization. A voluntary association is less likely to give its leader a mandate to develop his own goals for the organization. The leader must operate within the boundaries of his prescribed role as leader. To deviate beyond the role prescriptions of his office is to invite conflict with the membership.

This is precisely what has happened in the churches today. Clergy have begun, in a serious way, to operate outside the boundaries that are acceptable to a large proportion of the laity.

## Structural Freedom and the Management of Conflict

If the argument presented thus far is correct, we may legitimately ask why the conflict has not been greater than has been the case thus far. The answer lies in the fact that, to a considerable extent, the more liberal clergy have operated from positions *outside* the traditional parish ministry and thus have avoided direct confrontation with laity who object to a challenge-oriented role for clergy and the church.

A theoretical perspective for understanding this proposition is a study by Hammond and Mitchell entitled, "Segmentation of Radicalism—The Case of the Protestant Campus Minister."[23] Hammond and Mitchell argue that while not overly recognized as such, many organizations create social structures which function to contain, as well as use, internal forces for change. As examples, they cite research and development divisions in industrial corporations, institutes in universities, and war colleges in the military. The authors further argue that the campus ministry constitutes a major mechanism through which the churches have siphoned off the "radicals" in their organizations. The data they present provide convincing evidence that campus ministers are more ratical (liberal) than clergymen who serve in the parish ministry.[24]

I do not believe that Hammond and Mitchell adequately emphasize and develop the full implications of their observations. One of the critical conclusions of my own work is that the churches have been systematically isolating innovators from the parish, and hence from potential conflict with laity, for many years. Today the innovators have saturated a large proportion of every nonparish structure in the churches. They are disproportionately located not only in the campus ministry but also in administration, college and seminary teaching, inner-city experimental ministries, and some forms of chaplaincy and missionary work, as well as in other specialized ministries. More importantly, the structures into which the innovators have been filtered are the very positions that maximize their power to bring about innovation. As teachers they have recruited and socialized young clergy into the ranks of the new breed. As administrators, they have created new structures and provided new opportunities for innovation while protecting the innovators from the main stream of conservatism in the churches. The saturation has been so complete that today there is no place left for the innovator to go but into the parish.[25]

It is difficult to tell to what extent this has been a deliberate strategy of change and to what extent a latent consequence of innovative clergy attempting to avoid conflict with laity. In either case, the consequences and implications for the churches are serious. Today, large segments of Protestant denominations in America are dominated by innovative leaders who are no longer content to see the church continue in a comforter role.

Moreover, young clergy are reluctant to enter the parish, for they know of the potential conflict. A survey conducted by Dwight Culver in 1952 of 18,000 seminary students indicates the reluctance to enter the parish.[26] In this large survey, which represented more than 85 per cent of all seminarians in the nation, *two-thirds reported that they eventually hoped to be in some type of ministry other than the parish.* The implications of this finding have generally not been fully understood. The large majority of seminarians are highly skeptical or alienated from the concept of the parish ministry. Most of these men had not had any experience as a pastor; yet they were aware that their vision of creating a new church, which would be vitally involved in seeking solutions to the many complex problems of our age, is in sharp contradiction to the expectations of church laity who are looking for personable young men who will do or say nothing to upset their comfortable pews.

The isolation of innovators in the nonparish structures of the church has had both functional and dysfunctional consequences. On the one hand, it has provided an opportunity for the creation of a new leadership in the churches. On the other hand, it has created a leadership which may be hard pressed to find a following. If the churches are to survive, the task of bringing laity along must become the paramount concern. Unless they can persuade the rank and file that the church has a radical role to play in reshaping society, the leaders will wake up some morning and discover that they are bankrupt.

We have recently observed what the withholding of funds by white liberals who are opposed to Black Power has done to the civil rights movement. Unlike the civil rights organizations, churches have payrolls and real estate mortages which total in the hundreds of millions of dollars. Their budgets are calculated on the assumption of ever increasing income. Even a modest decline in their revenues, which are for the most part voluntary contributions, would have serious deleterious effects on their total program.

Furthermore, the first cutbacks would automatically come to the innovative experimental ministries which are not self-sustaining, including the campus ministry.

The evidence to support the arguments presented here has been sketchy, because of space limitations. I can only hope that this chapter may serve to stimulate the reader to examine the more detailed accounting of my central arguments in *The Gathering Storm in the Churches*. The evidence which I have assembled seems to me to be overwhelming. At the same time, it is not without some ambiguity. The ambiguity lies not so much in the seriousness of these crises, but rather in the prospects for the churches to seek viable resolutions of the conflict. The churches face a critical and all-embracing question: Are the institutional structures of the church broad enough to accommodate persons who are widely divided on the doctrinal basis of the faith and on the very meaning and purpose of the church, or are the divisions already so deep and entrenched as to make accommodation impossible?

## Problems and Prospects

I want to turn next to a discussion of the problems and prospects for conflict resolution. Are there alternatives to the head-on collision course that currently threatens to seriously disrupt or even destroy the church? From a theoretical point of view, at least, it would seem that the conflict could be resolved most easily if clergy were to retreat from their commitment to active involvement in social issues. But practically, this is not a very realistic possibility. The evidence would seem to suggest that they are going to become more, not less, involved. However, we cannot exclude this alternative altogether. As such involvement intensifies the conflict in the church, the clergy may come to see the implications more clearly and thus draw back in order to avert internal institutional disaster.

My own assessment is that while many clergy may retreat, it is not likely to become the "official" posture of the new breed. The new breed's perception of the urgency of many of the social problems of this nation and the world leaves little room for "gradualism." The evidence of their greater involvement seems apparent on several fronts. Clergymen are among the most active in attempting to establish some dialogue with black militants in the cities. Clergy have become more deeply involved in the protest against the Vietnam war. The pronouncements of church bodies seem to be becoming bolder, covering a wider range of issues and endorsing specific public policies.

Witness, for example, the 1966 Geneva Conference on Church and Society and the 1967 National Council of Churches Conference in Detroit following the summer riots.

A second kind of resolution of the conflict could happen if comfort-oriented laity and clergy were to capture the major administrative and decision-making responsibilities of the denominations, expelling or reducing to insignificant roles all who were unwilling to go along with their expectations for the churches. It is not easy to assess the possibility or probability that this may occur. Yet, it seems fairly clear that if the involvement of clergy in social issues increases and the boldness of their position intensifies, the forces of resistance in the churches will become more vocal and better able to assert their will. The pressure of the conservatives is more likely to be felt at the local, state, and regional level. Without gaining complete control, they can block expenditures of funds to specialized ministries that are engaged in "radical" programs. Many metropolitan councils of churches and experimental inner-city ministries are already feeling this influence.

But the pressure of conservative forces may be felt in another way which, in the long run, will have serious implications for the involved ministers. Many laymen who do not understand or approve of the churches' involvement in social issues may simply withdraw. Their commitment to the church may not be strong enough to induce a fight for the kind of church they want. The loss of their financial support may be great enough to force considerable programmatic cutbacks, thus elimininating a significant number of the "structurally free" positions in the church.

A third route to conflict resolution would be for the clergy to stand united and invite the withdrawal of laymen who are not prepared to go along with their concept of the church. While this is an option that some clergy would like to exercise, it is not very realistic. In the first place, it assumes a consensus among clergy, which does not exist. Second, as a calculated power play on the part of clergy to get laity to mend their ways or see the light, it is probably impractical. Third, if it assumes that the churches can suffer a great losses in membership and financial contributions and survive to become more actively involved in the world, it is naive. The overhead of the churches in the form of salaries and property mortgages is enormous. Even a modest cutback in operating budgets would seriously affect the operations of the institution.

A fourth possibility is that many clergy may decide that the only way for them to pursue a course of involvement in the world is to leave the church. It is difficult to assess the prospects, but it is clear that many have already given and many more are giving defection serious consideration. During the course of my study I have made considerable effort, without much success, to obtain denominational records on the number of men leaving the ministry. Some denominations do not maintain the kind of records that permit one to calculate dropouts. Other denominations consider such records a closely guarded secret. Similarly, data on seminary dropouts are extremely difficult to obtain. While hard data are not readily available, there can be little question that there is considerable uneasiness among denominational leaders about defections from the ranks of clergy. Many also fear that seminary enrollment has not dropped more sharply because hundreds of young males are using the seminaries as a means of dodging the draft.

While each of these four possibilities for resolving conflict would appear to have some probability of materializing, none of them looks very promising for the new breed who would seek to make the church not only relevant but vitally committed and involved in the world. It would seem to me that *the only way that clergymen can hope to maintain and further develop their involvement in social issues is to begin to think seriously about a strategy for engaging laity in the struggle.*

During the past four years the Protestant churches in America have initiated a number of experimental training programs for clergy, such as the Urban Training Center for Christian Mission in Chicago. There is a general sense of euphoria about these training centers among church administrators. A National Advisory Conference on Generating Manpower for Mission, sponsored by the National Council of Churches in the fall of 1966, recommended that clergy training centers be established in every major metropolitan area in the country. With the exception of one outside consultant, nobody at that conference even mentioned the question of lay reaction to clergy involvement or of "generating manpower" among the ranks of the laity.

I think this is a significant indicator of the depths of frustration that clergy feel toward the possibility of involving laymen. At the same time it is a significant indicator of the conflict which lies ahead. Having largely written off the laymen, church administrators seem to think that it is possible to continue to program involvement and that the laity will continue to pick up the bills. While this may work on a short-term basis, enduring programs necessitate broadening the base of support. The current programs which are designed to sensitize clergy to the many critical problems of the metropolis without creating structures for them to work in can only create greater frustration on the part of clergy and increase the gap of understanding between clergy and laity.

During the past three years I have talked with a considerable number of church executives and nonparish clergy about the prospect that laity might one day refuse to support the ministry of the new breed because they consider it too far out of line with their understanding of the role of the clergy and the church in society. Almost invariably the response has been a troubled admission that this is a very real possibility. Many cited specific instances of how they had already felt the pressure, in terms of both threats to jobs and cutbacks in financial resources. But when I asked what was being done to develop understanding and support among laymen for their ministry, I was usually told "not much" or given some rather vague responses which seemed to me to amount to about the same thing.

I do not mean to suggest that no efforts are being made to interpret the ministry of the new breed or to engage laity. The Ecumenical Institute in Chicago is a rather bold attempt to create sophisticated lay education. A number of other programs can be cited, but none of them approach the scope and intensity of the Chicago program. Assuming a high degree of effectiveness in these programs, which seems to me a highly dubious assumption, the number of laymen who have been reached is rather trivial.

In short, the amount of effort and success in creating sympathy, understanding, and involvement among laymen has not even begun to be commensurate with the task of building the kind of lay base needed to sustain the clergy's involvement in the world. The task may be facilitated by training programs, but no amount of special programming, unless it is combined with a broadly based organizational strategy, is going to produce the needed results.

While converting the Christians is perhaps a more difficult task than carrying a picket sign, the longer-range results would seem to be more promising for achieving significant social change. The magnitude of the task is nothing short of revolutionary. It is highly unlikely that any significant success could occur without considerable conflict. But all the evidence would seem to suggest that the years ahead are destined to be fraught with conflict, regardless of what strategy the clergy choose. The conflict may be so serious as to produce a total realignment of Protestant churches along the comfort-challenge dimension. Again, this may happen even if clergy do not make a concerted effort to bring laity into the struggle. But the more strongly clergy attempt to engage laity, the more solid will be the base of the new challenge-oriented church. Without strong laity support the new breed could be forced almost completely outside of the institutional church. Before freely choosing this road, the new breed ought to consider the implications. Without attempting to assess the success they have had to date in effecting social change, and assuming they have had some success, it would be hard to separate this success from their institutional base. While they may not presume to speak "in the name of" or "for" the church, there can be little doubt that their voice takes on considerable legitimacy because they are the professional leadership of large religious institutions. Small cadres of clergy without an institutional base would be as powerless as any other cadre of individuals seeking to effect change. They would have power and influence only to the extent that they could organize and coalesce others who shared their views.

In part, I am saying that to walk away from the institution of the church is to abandon one of the broadest bases of potential power for change that exist in American society. But at the same time, there are limitations on how much it can be used unless there is broad-based support within the institution. Moreover, effectiveness will be directly proportionate to the extent that the rank and file support its programs.

## Conclusion

This chapter has attempted to outline the interrelationships of four crises confronting the churches today: belief, meaning and purpose, authority, and identity. The data assembled in my study are insufficient to answer questions of the magnitude of those that have been raised. However, I do believe that the data are sufficient to indicate that the questions are altogether appropriate—indeed, the most important questions that the churches have faced since the Reformation. I see considerable evidence that these questions are being ingonred—by some out of ignorance, but by others precisely because the implications are too staggering to be realistically confronted. The clergy who are today speaking of an institutionless Christianity are perhaps the most guilty of abdicating responsibility, for the very fact that they speak in these terms would suggest that they have some understanding of the depths of the conflict. But it is questionable whether they understand the implications of Christianity without an institutional base. Unless the crises facing the churches are confronted with understanding, realism, and deliberate action, it is questionable whether the divided house can be renewed.

NOTES

1. Peter Berger, *The Sacred Canopy* (Garden City: Doubleday, 1967).

2. Peter Berger, *The Noise of Solemn Assemblies* (Garden City: Doubleday, 1961).

3. Gibson Winter, *The Suburban Captivity of the Churches* (New York: Macmillan, 1962).

4. Pierre Berton, *The Comfortable Pew* (Philadelphia: Lippincott, 1965).

5. Charles Y. Glock, Benjamin B. Ringer, and Earl R. Babbie, *To Comfort and to Challenge* (Berkeley: University of California Press, 1967).

6. Harvey Cox, "The 'New Breed' in American Churches: Sources of Social Activism in American Religion," *Daedalus* (Winter, 1967).

7. John A. T. Robinson, *Honest to God* (Philadelphia: Westminster, 1963).

8. Harvey Cox, *The Secular City* (New York: Macmillan, 1965).

9. Charles Y. Glock and Rodney W. Stark, "The New Denominationalism," in *Religion and Society in Tension* (Chicago: Rand McNally, 1965).

10. Jeffrey K. Hadden, "The Protestant Paradox–Divided They Merge," *Trans-Action* (July-August, 1967).

11. Gallup Survey, quoted in *Information Service* Vol. XLVI, No. 2.

12. Gallup Survey, quoted in Cleveland Press, April 18, 1967.

13. Lou Harris Poll, quoted in *Church and State,* Vol. XX, No. 3 (March, 1967).

14. For example, see Paul Harrison, *Authority and Power in the Free Church Tradition* (Princeton: Princeton University Press, 1959).

15. For an excellent discussion of the concept of identity, see Dennis H. Wrong, "Identity: Problem and Catchword," *Dissent* (September-October, 1968) pp. 427-435.

16. The most comprehensive statement on the process and consequences of urbanization, as their implications are understood and used by this author, is Philip M. Hauser's essay, "Urbanization: An Overview," in Philip M. Hauser and Leo F. Schnore, eds., *The Study of Urbanization* (New York: John Wiley, 1965), pp. 1-477.

17. For an elaboration of this view, see Cox, *The Secular City*, especially pp. 1-34, 38-84; also see Francis E. Rourke, "Urbanism and American Democracy," *Ethics,* LXXIV (July, 1964), 225-268.

18. Berger, *The Sacred Canopy*, p. 126. This writer views the processes of urbanization and secularization as inextricable. Urbanization, however, is seen as a more embracive concept.

19. Jeffrey K. Hadden, "Theological Belief and Political Ideology among Protestant Clergy," in James L. Price, ed., *Social Facts: Introductory Readings* (New York: Macmillan, 1969).

20. Jeffrey K. Hadden, "Ideological Conflict between Clergy and Laity on Civil Rights," *Social Science Quarterly* (December, 1969).

21. See Robert N. Bellah, "Civil Religion in America," *Daedalus* (Winter, 1967).

22. Some of the problems that clergy confront in involvement in civil rights activity are discussed in Jeffrey K. Hadden and Raymond C. Rymph, "The Marching Ministers," *Trans-Action* (September, 1965).

23. Phillip E. Hammond and Robert E. Mitchell, "Segmentation of Radicalism–The Case of the Protestant Campus Minister," *American Journal of Sociology*, Vol. LXXI, No. 2 (September, 1965). There is a condensation of this article in Phillip Hammond, "The Radical Ministry," Chapter 1 of the present volume.

24. The data from my own studies, carried out under the auspices of the Danforth Study of Campus Ministries, indicate that the differences between campus and parish ministers are even greater than is suggested in the Hammond and Mitchell data.

25. For additional evidence to support the thesis presented here, see Jeffrey K. Hadden, *The Gathering Storm in the Churches* (Garden City: Doubleday, 1969), Chapter VI, "The Struggle for Involvement," especially the section reporting the results of a survey of the Triennial Assembly of the National Council of Churches, 1966. The data reported here represent a secondary analysis of the data gathered by Dr. Glen Trimble. Dr. Trimble's results were earlier reported in *Information Service*, Vol. XLI, No. 9.

26. Reported in Keith R. Bridston and Dwight W. Culver, *Pre-Seminary Education* (Minneapolis: Augsburg, 1965), p. 227.

# PART VIII

*Problems and Consequences of Church Social Policy
in the University and City*

# ⚛ 19 ⚛

## CONSULTATION ON TRENDS AND ISSUES IN MEDICAL EDUCATION OF SIGNIFICANCE TO CAMPUS MINISTRIES

### *Introduction*

The next few pages contain some excerpts from the transcript of a consultation on ethical problems confronting medical education in the coming decade. A fuller version of the consultation is available in the winter, 1967, edition of *The Christian Scholar*. These excerpts give the opening statement of Dr. Paul Sanazaro, director of research, Association of American Medical Colleges, setting forth the major issues, and a number of commentaries by doctors, hospital administrators, faculty, campus ministers, and others. They have to do with the adquacy of the epistemologies and learning models dominating graduate research faculties in understanding health and disease and in helping doctors organize their practice so that various specialties are effectively related and patients are treated as whole persons responding to a changing environment.

The people speaking on these issues are principally leaders in a reassessment of American medical colleges and campus ministers whose work for the past decade has involved them deeply in the problems of technical and professional education. The participants are listed with their present positions at the end of this introductory statement.

The consultation was similar to those conducted with business, legal, and seminary professional school leaders. The Danforth Study assumed from the start that the problems and developments under study could not be understood as those of a single professional system. The consultation sought in its inquiry into medical education, as in the other fields, to discern the major reform developments, the controversies over future policies, the extent to which the fundamental issues over the pastoral, priestly, prophetic, and political dimensions of life were under review in these professions as in the ministry. The press of the medical educators for a wider field of action is evident, for example, in the thesis of one of the most talked-about books at the consultation: René Dubos, *Man Adapting*. In this he notes: "If the prevalance and severity of microbial diseases are conditioned more by the ways of life of persons affected than by the virulence or other properties of the etiological agents," then clearly, he concludes, the student doctor needs to "learn more of man, of his societies, and his ultimate commitments."

How is this to be done in the modern university and church? Some of the answers may come from members of this consultation who formed themselves into a Committee on Health and Human Values.

*Participants in Consultation*

Dr. Samuel Banks
Chaplain and Assistant Professor of Psychiatry and Religion
J. Hillis Miller Health Center
University of Florida

The Reverend Robert Bluford
Executive Secretary, Division of Higher Education
Department of Campus Ministry
Presbyterian Church in the U.S.
Richmond, Virginia

The Reverend Robert A. Davis
Division of Higher Education
Board of Education
The Methodist Church
Nashville, Tennessee

Dr. George T. Harrell
Dean, College of Medicine
Pennsylvania State University
Milton S. Hershey Medical Center
Hershey, Pennsylvania

The Reverend Ronald McNeur
Division of Higher Education
Board of Christian Education
United Presbyterian Church, USA
Philadelphia, Pennsylvania

Dr. Evan Pattishall, Jr., Chairman
Department of Behavioral Sciences
Pennsylvania State University
Milton S. Hershey Medical Center
Hershey, Pennsylvania

Dr. Paul J. Sanazaro
Director of Research in Medical Education
Association of American Medical Colleges
Evanston, Illinois

Dr. Samuel Stumpf
Chairman, Department of Philosophy
Vanderbilt University
Nashville, Tennessee

Dr. Kenneth Underwood
Director, Danforth Study of Campus Ministries
New Haven, Connecticut

The Reverend E. I. Vastyan
Chairman, Department of Humanities
College of Medicine
Pennsylvania State University
Milton S. Hershey Medical Center
Hershey, Pennsylvania

The Reverend Nathaniel T. Whitcomb
The Church of the Advent
Boston, Massachusetts

Dr. George A. Wolf, Jr.
Provost, University of Kansas Medical Center
Kansas City, Kansas

KU

## *Moral and Intellectual Trends in Medical Education of Significance to Campus Ministries*

KENNETH UNDERWOOD:

The occasion most immediately for this consultation, speaking from my standpoint, is the very comprehensive and serious reappraisal of the Protestant ministries in higher education that is going on now under the auspices of the Danforth Foundation. What has been done by ministries that have concentrated, at least in the postwar years, not in church-related colleges, but in the larger public, metropolitan universities and professional and technical schools of this country?

But to say that this is the only occasion for the meeting would not be enough. There has been going on among us who have planned this a debate as to what are the manifest and latent functions of the consultation. It has been an interesting debate for all of us, for we realize that what is at stake is an attempt to define our own stance in relation to one another as professional people, as people who work in institutions which have their own purposes, identity, and tradition. I noted that Ronald McNeur's memorandum was quite clear that the manifest function of this consultation was to discern the major issues in medical education and the viewpoints and programs which express these issues. He wished this consultation to read the significant events and occasions for action with which medical education now confronts the Protestant churches.

The first concern that Ron has is that ministers and church administrators see what is happening in medical education. What do the men who are responsible for its development and for the rethinking of its work see to be the significant trends and controversies? We don't want to ask the medical educators to select what they are going to say to us in terms of certain caricatures or images they have of the church and its ministry. Rather, the ministry is interested in knowing what you wrestle with as challenging and significant occasions for policy action and what are the frontiers of your own thinking. This is what we want from the medical educators. And it will be the first responsibility of those who are in the ministry to try to understand the developments in medical education and certainly to use their own resources to carry out this act of understanding. Then they can speculate, in the later stages of our consultation, more specifically about implications for the institutional church. This can be done principally in the last session by those who are themselves clergy and administrators in the Protestant churches.

The latent function of our consultation is, then, to discover suitable forms and substance of the ministry in medical schools. This is not the immediate or direct concern of the consultation, and we understand that we cannot answer these questions unless we first direct our attention to what are the problems and developments in medical education. I think that one can say that there is no serious debate here about these as the manifest and latent purposes of the consultation.

I think that there is a deeper question, though, at stake in terms of the relationships of each of us to one another as we try to discern the significance of Christian faith for technical or professional disciplines. And I think that some of us have been very anxious that the ministry in this consultation does not take on simply the stance of the listener waiting simply to be told by the experts what is happening in higher education. The minister himself should make use of his own convictions and ways of thinking to help in the clarification of the issues of higher education and how these effect the care of the patient. I think most of us here want to get beyond the kind of literature and stance which has the minister saying, "Bless you, bless you," or "My, oh my, isn't that a difficult problem!" Such talk often reflects a refusal to be involved objectively in the problems of medical education, in trying to clarify the real tensions and challenges within it. I think, from the medical educator's side, there is also a concern that our discussions here not simply assume that medicine and religion are two different phenomena and that all we have to do is to preserve the integrity of each. The worst form this could take would be to assume in this consultation that the doctors and medical education have to do with the *formal* curriculum and with scientific research, while religion is to be confined to extracurricular and nonresearch concerns, to private and subjective areas of the learning process of the student and the doctor.

By contrast, we wish, I believe, in this preliminary consultation to speak to one another as equals, attempting to explore both the differences that we certainly have and also the similarities, recognizing that the *patient* may turn out to be the chief focus of our common concern. Helping people become whole and healthy is a concern both of medical education and of the church. It is through this common concern that the professionals of these two institutions are going to be able to engage in mutual learning.

If you look at the assignments to provide lead-off discussions in the consultation, you will see that our program calls for a dialogical procedure giving each of us a chance to say with some care what is of greatest concern. The topics of discussion and the leaders planned do not presume superiority of status or discipline.

Our discussions begin with some observations by Dr. Sanazaro of the "Major Issues in Medical Education," supplemented by a panel he has arranged of Drs. Wolf, Harrell, and Pattishall.

DR. PAUL SANAZARO:

The frame of reference I would propose for initiating the discussion of issues in medical education is that we look at them as factors which either do in fact or potentially influence the medical student in such a way that it is difficult for him to develop a unified view of medicine. By unified view of medicine, I mean not only that he can understand medicine as a profession but that he comes to develop a clear self-concept of his role and his obligations in medicine.

Medical education itself, in the formal sense, does not have a rational base. The bases of medical education are historical, cultural, traditional, and accidental. Now, the first three are self-evident. By accidental I simply mean the growth of science and the products of science which can be predicted; the rate of developments can be predicted. Yet this is currently the major force which is changing medical education: simply new scientific knowledge and new scientific technology.

If this is true of what we call formal medical education, when we start talking about the informal kind of medical education that leads to the awareness of the moral problem, we are on an even less sound foundation. And here again, biased intuition and belief would have to be more important than substantive knowledge. At any rate, let me postulate a number of factors that I shall classify as barriers to this process of the development of awareness and appreciation for moral responsibility and moral problems in medicine on the part of students. I will agree at the outset, as well as the end, that the picture is overdrawn, knowingly, purposefully: all these conditions are not generally true, but they are true for some students, and some are true for all students. To the extent that they are perceived as relevant by students, we may assume that they have an influence on a particular student.

We recognize that today's students don't necessarily enter medical school with the intent of becoming practitioners. It varies greatly from school to school. The majority will be practitioners, but different proportions want to be scientists at the outset, want to be teachers, want to be administrators. But regardless of his eventual career choice, the student will end up having a socially and legally unique responsibility for the immediate or ultimate well-being of a fellow human being.

The student encounters in medical education at the outset a rude shock because he has never really clearly explored the relationship of medical education to the medical profession. Except in perhaps six schools, which make a prolonged and concerted effort to orient him to the fact that medical education is going to be quite different from what he anticipated, a majority of students progressively discover this over four years, and in this process they develop personal reactions which get in the way of learning basic medicine, not to mention the role of ethics in medicine.

I propose as the first point of departure that we consider the fact that the student is a college graduate and that we consider what colleges look on as their responsibilities for education or exposure to morale problems. And some of you may know that last year at the nineteenth Annual Conference on Higher Education this was one of the major topics. And to the surprise of a great many people, there was sharp disagreement as to whether or not the college or university has any responsibility in this area. Although most people said that liberal education must deal with the current trend of demoralization, the conclusion of the conference, as I read it, was that instruction or discussion of morals and ethics is an individual option.

This is the background of the student. Perhaps we have to take this into account when we say that the medical student upon entering medical school is not as oriented to the moral question as we would like someone who has chosen the field of medicine to be. But these are the facts, and we are beginning at that point and not at some ideal point.

In half the schools there is no formal mention or instruction in ethics. We have information on 86 schools; in 42 there is a statement made that zero hours are allocated to discussion of ethics in the formal sense. Now we know that this occurs informally, but in at least half the schools the cipher appears in the column "instruction in ethics." The maximum number of hours devoted in any school to the study of ethics is 55 in the course of four years. In schools that do have some instruction, the average number of lectures, and discussions, and so on is less than ten. And the departments, organizations, agencies, or individuals responsible for this are listed as medicine, administration, surgery, pathology, preventive medicine, philosophy, economics, history of medicine, public health, community health, student counseling office, pharmacology, dean's office, medical jurisprudence, forensic medicine, law school, visiting lecturer, or outside consultant. These are the sources of "instruction in ethics."

When we use the word "ethics," we are talking about two different kinds of ethics. The kind that is most often talked about in medical schools is the kind that *Medical Economics* proposes, "Are you sure you know what is ethical?" Just briefly I think you would be interested in knowing what the twelve ethical problems are as viewed by *Medical Economics*. We have here: Scaled Up Fees, Night Calls, Practice-Building, Medical Mistakes, Recall Systems (sending out a card periodically to remind the patient that it is time for a check-up), Cash Collections (demanding fees paid in advance), Emergency Care ("If you're afraid you're going to be sued should you stop?" And the answer given this ethical question is "Actually, few suits result from emergency care. Perhaps doctors are more reluctant to stop at accidents than they should be in view of the relatively small risk of a suit."), Combined Billing, and finally, Should You Tell the Truth?

The Principles of Professional Conduct of my former medical society were similar. There are some twenty sections to this, involving Compensation, Gratuitous Services, Patents for Surgical or Diagnostic Instruments, Secret Remedies, Safeguarding the Profession, When Several Physicians Are Called,

Emergency Obstetrics, and so forth. These are what are called medical ethics, by and large, and I think they occupy a large proportion of the small allotment of time to teaching of this in medical school.

Speaking of the development of the student as a professional person, the simple fact of the departmental autonomy in medical schools is a major barrier to his developing a unified view of the profession. There is an over-all guiding policy for most schools, but each department does define its own program, sets its own educational policies, selects its own procedures, and within the requirements of the university or school sets its own standards of expected performance. Obviously there is great basic similarity in all these activities in the several departments. Nonetheless, the student simply does not begin with a frame of reference and tends to view these as disjointed educational activities, not necessarily related to medicine, but more related to a particular discipline. So the attempts to overcome this by conjoint teaching and integrated teaching have all come about in the last few years and are notable for their lack of success.

Since the war there is a stigmatizing label called Trade School which has called forth a vigorous and angry reaction from medical education. And as a result of the reaction to this and the availability of money, we have basic biologic research. And this basic biologic research is increasingly divorced from the problems of human disease. This is epitomized by the success of the concept of molecular biology, which presents a unique intellectual challenge to the great minds, the bright minds of medicine, because this approach developed by Linus Pauling makes it possible to view man as a molecular entity and therefore susceptible to what is called rigorous and elegant analysis. And this is intellectually stimulating; it is attracting new talent to medicine which has previously never been attracted because of medicine's mundane practical aspects. But the net result of this, of course, is that fundamental research, and not research into human problems, is the guiding force in medical education. And we have now seen the emergence of the syndrome which is called "more basic than thou!"

Another problem in medical education is that there is no uniformity of opinion as to who should teach the medical student about normal and abnormal human behavior. If it is taught by the behavioral scientist, as scientist, the principles and knowledge are taught as derived from the application of the scientific method, and therefore by definition devoid of an intrinsic value system. This has to be, by the nature of the scientific derivation. If the responsibility is that of the department of psychiatry, very often there is a different kind of bias stemming entirely from the theoretical formulation of a particular school of psychiatry which makes certain assumptions about the nature of human behavior. And here again there is an artifical value system in contrast to, perhaps, a no-value system. There are more behavioral scientists in medical schools—they are usually captives of the department of psychiatry—and it will be interesting to see how this will be resolved in the next few decades.

The concept of human biology, molecular biology, is being adopted as a formal educational platform by an increasing number of schools. That is to say, they view their responsibility as giving a student basic education in human biology and then letting the student have the experience and training in the applied aspects, that is, medicine, at a later date in internships and residency training. The result of this is that the student, as a student, has only a basic exposure to clinical medicine, and it postpones his involvement in the full range of problems inherent in practicing medicine. Perhaps four schools now in their bulletins state explicitly that they are interested in education for human biology, not for medicine. The derivative fact of this, of course, is that the practitioner has less of a role in teaching undergraduate medical education the first four years. The full-time faculty can carry on education in human biology much better than the practitioner. Therefore, there is less and less influence of the physician, even the thoughtful physician who deals with patients, on the thinking of medical students in the early formative years in medicine.

In the fifty years since Abraham Flexner presented his report on the state of medical education in America, there has been a change in the concept of basic science. We have alluded in part to this. When Flexner made his report, basic science referred to the study of the mechanisms of disease process in the human organism. But in the interval, basic science is now basic biologic research. And what Flexner called basic science is the kind of investigation that is carried on by the so-called clinical faculty; that is, the faculty members of the departments that are responsible for patient care. And most clinical investigation today is the basic science of fifty years ago—at that level. Clinical investigators are trying to match the basic investigator in rigor and elegance, which means controlling the variables that determine the outcome of any experiment.

I think you saw the first national implication of this in the debates over drug regulations a few years ago in the Kefauver Committee and the proposed Food and Drug Act regulations; and the matter is not settled, as you know.

But what you heard were physicians, clinical pharmacologists, debating how stringent restrictions should be because they would prevent doctors from carrying out completely controlled experiments on human beings. We had known the strength of research concern for some time, but I think this was the first time we had an opportunity to see it on a national scale. Well, at any rate, the scientific attitude not only permeates the first two years of medical education but increasingly is the basic attitude of the so-called clinical years. The emphasis is on the objective approach, rational analysis of the mechanisms of disease.

Last week we got a flier from a university about a third-year student who is carrying on clinical investigation who gave an apparently very important paper at a national meeting as a student. It is reported that he said, "Scientists can now 'strip away' the human body and study the heart and blood system under the cold light of mathematics." He was simply responding to the sense of power that you have when you can apply rigorous method to a human being. He is a third-year student, and he said, "We know now that the output of the heart can be reduced to purely mathematical terms." In other words, they can get the body out of the way now and study the mechanisms.

This is clinical investigation, and this is the level at which it is proceeding in the better medical schools. Let me make it clear that this is a tribute to the success of medical education. It is only because of our assumptions here that we say this is a problem. On the one hand, it is really an important development and a necessary development.

As the clinical investigator becomes increasingly concerned with mechanisms, he has less and less real continuing concern about the care of patients. This is obvious and well established: you cannot do outstanding investigation and devote the time to patient care that you should; it is a physical impossibility. And because of the academic reward system, there is no choice. The good investigator must devote his energies to investigation and to teaching—and here again the important teachers, the people with whom the students identify, are seen to be themselves identified with the object of the study of medicine and not with the care of patients. Subsequently there is less opportunity to discuss moral and ethical issues with the full-time faculty.

In the last few years we have seen what has never really been made explicit before: the significant differences in attitudes of faculty members toward ethics. We have all perhaps been proceeding under the assumption that if we ever talked about it we would all agree. But, for example, we all know that Henry Beecher believes that no breach of ethics is excusable in the conduct of research; yet at a conclave held at Harvard a few months ago, some of you may have read that his peers described his comments as a gross and irresponsible exaggeration. He had listed a dozen experiments in which (a) there was no benefit to the subject, or (b) there was harm to the subject, and (c) to some there was death. Some felt this was not right, and other people simply said it was an exaggeration. At the end of the conference, they apparently agreed that while there have been a few deviations from the straight and narrow, these have been few and far between and not serious. These were nationally respected faculty members at one of our distinguished universities in a national forum. The questions were raised at a conference such as this, which the students perceive, as to whether there are degrees of morality as there are degrees of temperature or degrees of deviation from normal structure and function.

You have all read about the controversies in organ transplantation; here is the same phenomenon. One of the pioneers in this field, in talking about taking organs from dying patients without direct consent, says this is an unethical and a backward step. Someone equally prominent doing work at the same scientific level says, "If we are sure that a certain procedure is for the benefit of other human beings and the family of an unconscious dying patient gives consent, then the procedure is justified." Discussion such as this gives the students an opportunity to hear the differences of opinion just as they hear a difference of opinion about diabetes, dyspeptic ulcer, and chronic lung disease: differences of opinion about ethics, differences of opinion about disease.

The progressive divorcement of the undergraduate medical student from the patients, from the discussion of the patient's problems, is also accelerated by the growing number of graduate students in medicine. There is a tendency to have more interns, more residents, more clinical fellows, more graduate students. In fact, this is a measure of the success of the research emphasis in medicine. One of the indices used by some people is that there are more graduate students than undergraduates in medical centers. This is taken as a sign of advancement, and it is. But one of the consequences is that these graduate students are interposed between the student and patient, and the student and faculty, and they have less opportunity to be confronted with moral issues.

The student today in medical school is introduced to the use of drugs in human beings as a natural part of his laboratory experience in physiology, biochemistry and pharmacology, and so on. So it seems to him an entirely natural part of medicine to use potent drugs in people. It is entirely dependent on the local bias as to whether or not there is any discussion of the ethical issues involved in the use of the kinds of medicines we have today. Fifty or sixty years ago we had perhaps quinine, morphine, and alcohol. But we do have drugs now that can permanently alter human physiology, as far as we can tell, and they certainly significantly alter basic functions. But at this point, if it is never made explicit, the student may come to take it for granted that he has no greater ethical responsibility in prescribing than would have been true several generations ago.

This is augmented by the common practice of using students as normal human volunteers for experiments. This is a widespread practice, a convenient means of increasing income on the part of students, and it seems to be quite a natural thing to do. No one ever seems to object to it. It does increase the students' interest in the subject matter and enhances the motivation. It does, indeed, increase their learning of medicine. And it is fairly well established that it does influence their career choice. But unless the point is raised explicitly, it seems to me, students more readily accept human experimentation as a natural part of medicine during the time they are developing their points of view on medicine.

There are several other trends affecting the student primarily that also get in the way. These are fairly evident: one is the increasing diversity of clinical education; that is, most medical schools now give students more freedom to choose the kind of courses they will take in their third and fourth years. In a number of schools it is the rule that students as a whole, or in any significant numbers, do not get together from the end of the second year until commencement exercises. They are in other hospitals, other rotations, other courses; there are no all-class convocations. Therefore, there is less opportunity, if you will, for peer influence to operate in the exploration of problems of ethics.

Over half the students are married at graduation; half of these have children. They therefore live almost as working people in society during medical education, away from the medical center, oriented to the social problems of young people raising a family. There is loss of informal student-faculty contact, and there is loss of the characteristics of the residential college which we know influences student attitude. And the students have less opportunity to meet at the medical center and talk about medical problems.

Because of the cost of medical education, students have to work on the outside. Whether it is because of or despite this, they do acquire their education with perhaps a more pragmatic orientation to the role of the physician in society. And when it comes time to choose a career, a level of practice, they make a choice between their obligations to medicine, to society, and to their family. And the size of their financial debt has a great deal to do with this decision.

And finally, it would be well if we could point to some definitive studies on student attitudes and their change during the four years. But what we are talking about isn't susceptible to precise measurement. There have been a few studies that are relevant. At one school the faculty defines the moral and ethical attitude which they believe to be fundamental in clinical education, and the trained individual develops a rating scale to be filled out by students which has met all the criteria for psychometric reliability and is given to all the students in the school. It was found that between freshman and senior year there was really no change in attitudes that have to do with compassion, with understanding the rights of the patients, with accepting responsibility in dealing with patients' problems, or indeed in this matter of respecting the basic human rights of patients. Not only was there no change, but the total score of these students was far below the maximum possible. Now, this was in a medical school where these values presumably were made explicit by the faculty and were incorporated into the educational program.

Many of you have heard of the study which shows that medical students, at the end of four years, show much more cynicism than students in nursing and in law—students going through four years of change at a critical period. And in the AAMC (Association of American Medical Colleges) national study there was no change in the student attitude that reflects altruism or philanthropy, but there is a definite increase in the economic or pragmatic orientation. Scattered studies in individual schools also suggest that, whatever is going on now that confronts the students' actual problems, it is not having an effect on those attitudes that we can measure.

There are some assumptions, then, that are offered as a point of departure for a discussion of issues in medical education that influence the development of the student as a morally aware individual.

## Panel Discussion

GEORGE WOLF:

In regard to Paul Sanazaro's presentation, there are a couple of points I would just like to emphasize and correct some possible misapprehensions. I am sure Paul did not in any way mean to imply that the more precise study of human biology was a bad thing. Over my generation there was a lot of authoritarianism in medicine. And the diagnosis of a murmur was frequently not what you heard yourself, but what the professor said you should hear. I think as the result of the so-called more scientific approach, or the study of human biology as a discipline, in contrast to authoritarian medicine, our students have become more questioning of authority. And I think there are implications in this in the area about which we are talking.

My second comment is that as more information has become available, obviously specialization has become more important. And as one knows more and more about less and less, one begins to ask himself the question, "Can I be all things to all men?" It was a lot easier for the old authoritarian "doc" to be all things to all men than it is for the young M.D. who has been exposed to molecular biology and the precise techniques that Paul referred to. Obviously, doctors are not trained to be humble, so one thing they can do is to hide in this technical niche which is the area they know most about and, by God, nobody is going to attack them in their particular specialty.

GEORGE HARRELL:

Although I am sure Paul did not mean to convey this impression, some of you may have concluded that the number of students who decide before they come to medical school that they want to be clinical scientists, administrators, teachers, is really very large. About 8 per cent ultimately end up in this area, and even fewer medical students on entering have any wish to be administrators. This sort of work is a far cry from what most of us plan, but sort of evolves as we go along.

The schizophrenic feeling of research and practice that Paul describes has been true in medicine for years and years, but is getting worse with the elaboration of devices to quantify data.

The student sees from the very beginning two widely divergent trends. He is told that he must be a humanist who looks at the whole patient. Perhaps the behavioral scientist and the psychiatrist introduce him to this concept in the morning. Then in the next period or in the afternoon the student goes into the laboratory, where he is told that to be really a good physician he has to be a cool, dispassionate, objective scientist who evaluates data and makes decisions. Now, these emphases are difficult to reconcile in a compatible pattern because the student's emotions are most deeply involved in the one and his mind in the other. But both of these value systems are the facts of medical life.

I would take exception that the study of molecular biology down to the mechanics of disease (the basic subcellular biochemical mechanisms) is incompatible with good clinical medicine, because a good physician is attempting to adapt to these, to use these. But what frightens the life out of you is the implication that once you understand the chemical basis, then you can manipulate this to achieve some end other than the cure of disease; specifically, the control of population, not just in numbers but in quality. If somebody decides this is the type of individual we ought to be, this kind of knowledge influences political decisions, and so on. This is the same thing that has been with us from time immemorial; it is called genocide in some areas, the ghetto is another, or sterilization procedures, or the selective mating which I believe is practiced by some civilizations. If you can control the understanding of the mechanics by which the genetic code works and it can be broken, then it presumably could be altered. I think this would be a fine thing to do with beef cattle and pigs, because it has many advantages; and yet we rightly shy away from this in human beings.

But I do not think this present emphasis on molecular biology is incompatible with a good code of medicine. The reason I feel this is that in the research in the field of Rocky Mountain spotted fever, I came right up against basic biologic phenomena: the impermeability of membranes, the biochemical action of subcellular particles that are affected by a parasite which appears to behave just like some of the normal parts of the human cell. And this is the same problem we have in cancer and the viruses: we just don't have the basic biologic information. The objective in this was clearly the improvement of the treatment of human disease, but we had to get back to the basic subcellular biology to do it.

EVAN PATTISHALL:

In regard to the schizophrenic situation you just mentioned, George, let me respond by saying that I think also that we are becoming much more compartmentalized, particularly in our molecular vs. our molar approaches to learning. There are many productive, competent, bright, original schizophrenics now in medical education who are able to contribute to both medical research and practice. They are borderline or marginal cases. But there are students who are pure schizophrenics who try to live in separate worlds. They have panel discussions on the humanistic values of medicine in the morning and go into the lab in the afternoon, and cannot make any significant comment in between these. And somehow we as faculty do not help students to bridge this gap. This is primarily because each specialist is concerned with getting one job done. If *we* teach in the morning, we are worried about the whole picture; the new faculty in the afternoon is concerned only with chasing some chemical variable around and measuring its effects. How you relate these two worlds I do not know, but it is a big issue in medical education.

Now I want to ask Paul for clarification of something he said. Were you saying that the behavioral scientist brings an artificial value system into his research and that he has a responsibility for clarifying what this is when he teaches the student; while the psychiatrist brings in essentially a no-value system? I would argue that the behavioral scientist brings in an artificial value system which he has learned in his attempt to emulate quantitative science, that this is what he holds on to as a scholar, and he tries to project this onto the students in terms of the way they quantify, assess, and understand human behavior. Sometimes the psychiatrist has an artificial value system; sometimes he has a no-value system. The biochemist has an artificial value system, too, one which he is reluctant or unwilling to deal with consciously or critically. The physiologist likewise; in fact, any of the basic sciences has this artificial value system, or perhaps a no-value system.

BANKS:

You are saying that bootlegged in along with the methodology used are value assumptions and a world view, but they are not examined, just brought in.

PATTISHALL:

Yes, this is not intentional; it is a cumulative product of his training. And I think the medical faculty probably provides this. The student tries desperately, perhaps, to examine his assumptions, but I do not think we give him any help, and this is one of the problems in medical education in terms of ethical issues, as Paul has pointed out.

SANAZARO:

The point I was making was that the behavioral scientists are trying to apply the amoral technique of science to the study of moral values or moral assumptions. If they are to succeed in this, they must of necessity derive knowledge that is uncontaminated by the conception. Now, the psychiatrist who comes from a certain school uses all knowledge to support a certain kind of theory of behavior and attitude. When I talk about behavioral science, I mean the science, not the scientist. Also, when George was talking about the incompatibility between molecular biology and being a good physician, I think this was the case. But there is absolutely no conflict whatsoever when you start talking about the people who either are molecular biologists or are good physicians. There is nothing intrinsically conflicting in the material or in the information or knowledge. But when you talk about the people who do it, you see that they have to have a primary orientation to one or the other to be outstanding.

When I talked about this no-value system in behavioral science, I was referring to the fact that it must be free of a value system or it can not be a behavioral science.

## Ethical Guidelines for Use of Human Beings in Experimentation and Teaching

McNEUR:

Recently there was an article in the *American Scientist* about the complexity that has arisen in the study of DNA and RNA, that where the initial assumption was of a linear creativity, a very extensive complexity is now described or assumed. I have noticed among certain scientists I speak to a growing humility appearing because the reality they had imagined was simple, as they get further in research becomes more complex. Now, is this true in medical microbiology, and if it is true, does it imply that it is possible to move from the very discrete to the complex and the ecological? That is, in areas where we are becoming more precise, we are recognizing more complexity, and right at that point it is possible to start thinking in terms of the ecological. If this were true, then it would be an important fact for us to consider in the relations of theology and medicine.

SANAZARO:

The question you are raising, then, is what does happen in medical education after this point has been reached in research. And what does the faculty member communicate to his students when he suddenly becomes aware of the complexity? I guess it was not explicit in what I said, but my assumption is that what he does is expressed in a kind of awe for the complexity of the natural order, that this is the natural thing that emerges from it, in keeping with the fact that this is derived from the scientific approach. It has nothing to do with the "ecology" or its relationship to all human action. It remains in the purely scientific context, which is to say, "Isn't science wonderful!"–and it is.

BANKS:

But does not it lead him to question the simplicity of his own methodology that point; in other words, does it actually lead him to revise his methodology, or simply to stand in awe of the complexity of the data?

SANAZARO:

This might be a way of bringing a new dimension into our thinking, and it is an opportunity. But my assumption is that it is not taken as an opportunity. And although the scientist becomes more humble, he becomes more of a scientist.

UNDERWOOD:

The scientist can not see or develop any operational or empirical implications for research, and the student can not see how he uses in practice the ecological concepts he has heard or read, so therefore he ignores them.

McNEUR:

You have put a pejorative connotation on that, though.

SANAZARO:

No, it was pejorative in the sense that the opportunity was lost for bringing about a reorientation of student thinking. In other words, what we have been saying here is the fact that science gives the tools, and now something else will direct the use of these tools. Scientific method provides the raw power; now, how are you going to direct that power? We talk about knowledge, understanding, skill, technology—the tools. Something else is going to shape how we use them with people. There are all kinds of opportunities in modern medical education to raise this question explicitly and make the students aware that this is a conscious process that the physician goes through every day, as George was talking about. The power comes from science; you apply it to the patients; and it is this thing of applying that is really the art of medicine. But that is not what we are talking about; we are talking about the fundamental principles that govern you in your decisions as to how, where, when. For example, the pejorative aspect of the situation is that when the opportunity arises in the use of normal human volunteers to raise the moral question, the opportunity is lost. That is the pejorative aspect; not that medical educators use normal human volunteers.

BLUFORD:

Does this mean that the situation itself, more often than not, determines the ethical dimension that is present? For example, I take it that you are saying that morality is much more complicated where teaching of surgery is involved than teaching in regard to taking a blood sample, for instance, is concerned. Does not this underline the relative quality of this whole buiness of ethics?

HARRELL:

That is a point I have been wanting to stress: all these considerations in human experimentation are relative. There is, for example, an inherent statistical risk that you cannot get away from. If you do just a venal puncture or a hypodermic injection on somebody, there is an inherent risk that they will get an infection or a reaction. And it is the reaction of the host, particularly in microbiology, that you cannot control in terms of variables. George brought this out very well when he reported that he did not catheterize these normal individuals because in spite of the most meticulous technique, there is, in this case, a predictable percentage of infection. Now, what you cannot predict is whether that infection will become self-limited or easily controlled or go on to become nephritis; this is what he was implying. So it does all become relative.

BANKS:

The question is not whether to intervene in the life of the patient, whether to invade the organism with a venal puncture or cranial surgery or a psychic trauma (just because the psyche does not bleed, it is little less obvious). The question again is one of having made decisions about the participation in human life. The question for me comes back to this: we are no longer able to apply first principles to the situation because the situation in its complexity partly dictates what one must do. It is not a contextual ethic exactly that I am describing, but the context does require so much attention today in the choice that you can only explain in reference to it that you might have a third-year student do a venal puncture, but you might not have him participate in major surgery. The variations in degrees of responsibility do not determine whether you will be responsible or not. The ethical question is just this. But it certainly dictates a great deal of the specific response on the part of the medical student and the physician.

UNDERWOOD:

This discussion can draw helpfully perhaps upon distinctions which are important in the discipline of ethics. Earlier I distinguished between the images of man the lawgiver and man as the responding, relating self. This terminology tries to make a distinction between a relative moral situation and a relational one. The situation George describes is not relative, in the sense that one cannot bring to bear any illuminating principles or that there are not choices more responsible than others, or that one decision may cost a person more if he sticks to it than another. In that sense the situation is not relative. But it is relational. I saw this so well in George's analysis; he was talking most, not about the application of a first principle, but about the arrangements in the research and teaching design for a review by peers; he discussed how the patient's self-consciousness as to what choices were really being made could be heightened if a doctor represented the patient's interest. And I did not observe any of the ministers insisting that in this situation the doctor always had to apply a Christian principle. Maybe love is one way, among others, to understand this complexity of relating yourself to a particular patient and of relating yourself to the demands of research. One draws in Christianity upon knowledge of a radical loyalty of God to man and man to God and to his fellow men, which makes use freely of all the relative principles of theology, the social sciences, and so on. These are brought into the ordering of the responsible act. The image of the responsible self avoids a reductionist ethic such as manipulation of another because you know what is good for him, or adherence to a certain principle in a situation.

BANKS:

But, Ken, in a sense this position is true only if you translate it into faculty and curriculum. George is right: you do not provide people with an elective course in ethics in their fourth year and wrap it up didactically. The heightening of ethical sensitivity becomes a highly complex thing, and even if you have a faculty member involved with this as his primary responsibility, he cannot do it, either. All he can do then is to spend a great deal of his time listening to other people about the complexity of the context in which ethical decisions are made. It is going to be a very messy, difficult task.

BLUFORD:

This is one of the things I think Ken was saying. In what fashion do you determine whether there is any objective (in contrast to subjective) method by which you decide at what point you permit or encourage a student to tackle a tough problem?

HARRELL:

We never turn a student loose. Even in the residency at the end of a five- or seven-year postgraduate residency in the field, he is never turned loose completely. There is always a person with a little bit more experience looking over his shoulder.

BLUFORD:

The degree to which someone is looking over a fellow's shoulder, as I think Dr. Wolf has said, is highly important in regard to how much he is going to learn out of the situation.

HARRELL:

He has to assume some responsibility in order to make it effective as a learning experience.

UNDERWOOD:

What I hear being said is that the development of an ethic has to do with the structuring of a community which we call the university. If one is an administrator, such as Drs. Harrell or Wolf, you seek to build into this, not some little ethics course, but a way of using your faculty, of extracurricular experience and institutional involvements, and all the rest that forms a pattern, a community ethos, habits, affections, by which the responsible self is developed or elicited. And what does this have to do with the campus ministry? It simply points to the fact that the churches have to concern themselves with more than putting a minister in a Westminster House near the Chicago Medical School and have him conduct meetings for students there. The churches need to know how the faculty see his work and the issues he deals with in the total learning and research context of which you people are talking. . . .

McNEUR:

I have a specific question in relation to the type of people upon whom experimentation tends to be done. I know that experimentation is sometimes done on prisoners, and I wonder if there is a question emerging here about people used for experimentation as being deprived persons, in some sense— socially, for example. Is there any question raised about the nature of the deprivation of people who are used?

BANKS:  Why do we select people who are in some sense deprived?

HARRELL:

Prisoners are all volunteers. The main reason we use prisoners is to get a controlled environment, to control as many variables as we can. Some of the studies have long-term implications that will be followed up, so you want a long-term control of variables, and studying prisoners is one good way of doing this. And this is one way they can pay back society and alleviate themselves of their guilt complex; and some of them volunteer for this reason, and others just out of sheer boredom. And they accept considerable risk. I am not so sure I would take the risk of experimental infection with viral hepatitis. And they accept the risk of experimental infection with several types of typhoid fever. This is well explained to them.

SANAZARO:

Perhaps this is evading the real question. If I can read between the phrases, your real question, Ron, had to do with experimentation with people available in the medical center.

HARRELL:

He asked why we always use deprived people.

SANAZARO:

But in the medical center there tends to be a greater use of clinic indigent patients than private patients for experimentation.

BANKS:

The indigent is captive, too: the prisoner and the indigent patient. Now, why do we pick these groups?

HARRELL:

It depends entirely on the experiment; in some things you can take anybody. In heart disease, coronary artery disease, you are more likely to get a private patient. And actually in the kind of thing George was talking about where your data are subjective, the more intelligent the patient the better observer he is and the better your research is.

WOLF:

I think you have to separate normal controls from patients with the right kind of disease. We do some studies on normal people, and then you have a diseased patient. If you want to control the variables, you turn to a group of people who have time to do this. If you turn to diseased patients, it depends on the setting. If you want to use a professor or something, chances are he will be studying full time and will not be available.

BANKS:

George, does not this say something about our values? I kept wondering if Ron was not saying something about the criteria. Is the personal factor, as Evan says, that these people cannot talk back? Do we select them out of our own evaluation of gradations of human life as well?

HARRELL:

I think this is just a traditional and a historical fact. The medical student was historically taught on indigent patients.

BANKS:

Why did we do that in the beginning?

HARRELL:

We did it because they were the only ones in the hospital. They had to come there.

BANKS:

Are we more comfortable intervening at certain points of human life than at others?

WOLF:

There is the sense in which the indigent clinic patient owes the hospital something. This is more true perhaps of the teaching matter than experimentation.

BANKS:

Is the risk less? Is there an assumption here that certain human lives are of more value than others? In other words, the risk is less if we do it with second-class citizens? I know that is a nasty thing to ask, but I think it is true. I have watched clinic staff for fifteen years, and it seems to me that the physician in some way avoids the question of the risk to human life if he selects certain groups rather than others.

UNDERWOOD:

There is something else here, too: the willingness to be used in experimentation. Does the indigent patient believe he has less to lose? Is there a factor of self-hatred, self-denigration?

McNEUR:

I think it is generally recognized that human rights of the indigent patient are not on the level of the human rights of the normal person; this is the social context in which we live. I think this is a question that needs to be raised.

BANKS:

The awareness of our own values would enter in here, would not it? Even the selection of patient samples from society involves an ethical decision.

*Effect upon Physicians of Current Ethical Questions in Medicine*

PATTISHALL:

We should like to turn now to another "case," that of a physician asked to indicate to us some of the current ethical questions in his own medical practice during a "typical day." This will give us some sense of the decisions with absolute consequences for individuals at least with far-ranging effects, which medical men must face with very partial data and with very limited reflection on what really goes into their judgment.

BANKS:

Here was one doctor's list: First, I have to decide whether a couple of children are to be removed from their parents by the court and placed for adoption. Second, I have to make a decision about an involuntary commitment for a patient who is a borderline psychotic. Third, I have to make a decision about a girl who is unmarried and wants a child, but we really wonder whether her personality structure is stable enough to sustain this child; she is in the second month of pregnancy and we have to make a decision right away about a therapeutic abortion on the grounds of whether her personality and her values are adequate to represent the community in raising the child. Fourth, I am working with a brain-damage patient, and I have to decide whether the enforced hospitalization of these brain-damage patients is necessary, and I keep feeling, "But it's not their fault. Why should I punish them by placing them in an institution? Yet I know that while they may function 98 per cent of the time quite well, under certain stress situations they may become damaging to society."

Now, after this doctor reeled off these comments in a hurry, I said, "It seems to me you're asking two questions: One, who makes these decisons? Do I, must the patient, the family, some societal group? Or do we all make them in some combination? Second, to whom do we look when we make these decisions? Am I to take care of individuals, the family, some societal group, humanity at large?"

"I'm always having to ask the question," she said, "between the part and the whole. Do I take care of a part of society or a whole of society? When do I switch halves?"

PATTISHALL:

I shall repeat some of the brief comments by a pediatrician. He said, first of all, I have a patient whose family refuses to submit to surgery for this patient, because of the necessary blood transfusion and so on. I do not know what to do about this. I am right in the middle; I have got to do something. Second, I have got some parents of a leukemic child who want to take this child home, so that the child can die happily with his family at home. They recognize that this is inevitable and the he has had . . . several remissions and exacerbations, that this is probably the last time he will come into the hospital, and they want to take him home. I get the feeling that these parents have somehow worked through the grief process more than I have as a physician, and I think I am probably wanting to keep them here, and advise the other medical students that we ought to keep him here, partly out of my own reaction and my own guilt, not because of the welfare of the patient. Third, I have got a problem of "parentectomy"—a kid with an allergy—and I have to recommend sending him somewhere out west. I am concerned about this and want to recommend some place to send this boy. Fourth, I am concerned because I have been telling medical students all the fancy technically appropriate ways to practice pediatrics, all the tests you can run, all the things that can be done for children in this marvelous day of modern medicine. But I am not being realistic because I realize that just as soon as they graduate or just as soon as they go out and set up practice, their concern is going to be, "How can I feel comfortable and ethically reassured with short cuts?" Is this my job, as an attending physician on the wards, to help him somehow with the short cuts? Is there a place in medical education for short cuts, rather than our usual situation in which we are organized so that we teach them the very best of medical care with the very best of medical equipment and technology—all the way up to the very end, unless, of course, they have some kind of experience in an interdisciplinary clinic or something like this where they are forced to take short cuts? But even in most of the outpatient clinics, the short cuts are not tolerated, and students still have to go through every step along the way. The student has no experience in taking short cuts. This was of concern to this pediatrician because he felt that as a faculty member he was not doing his job.

We are suggesting, also, that medicine does not affect society unilaterally. The values of society permeate medicine—the physician, the medical student. And in fact these may be the most important factors in his making a decision about what questions to ask the patient, about what he should do with a particular patient, or about a choice in life work, or specialty, or in personal involvement.

BANKS:
We are setting up a dilemma here: it has been apparent that medicine does affect society in a number of ways, but it is a mutual two-way street and not always pleasant.

PATTISHALL:

Let me just give you a couple of examples. I suppose admissions would be a place where the values of society do permeate medicine. The selection of medical students is generally done by a committee which is very often a multidiscipline group and not always, but frequently, involves more than just clinical medicine and the admission process. You will see in the selection of medical students just how these values of society and the personalized, internalized values affect very vividly the lives and careers of young men who aspire to enter medicine. One of the obvious ones is the "hidden agenda," in regard to considerations of minority groups, religious groups, racial groups, and the like. These are evident. Good committees can talk about them, but most committees are not able to; they do not disclose their fears and worries.

BANKS:

Evan does not mention this; it comes under the rubric of confession. Evan is chairman of the men's selection committee, and I am on it. We have been existentially involved, to say the least.

PATTISHALL:

Let me give you three cases here, very briefly. One involves the altering of an ID card, instead of putting age nineteen or twenty, putting age twenty-two so you can buy liquor. This kind of thing comes up. I mention these things purely as dilemmas that are dealt with in different ways. The second point involved a "dry run" of a laboratory experiment. Now there are a lot of rationalizations you can put on this (a dry run is where you do not do the lab experiment but you write it up as if you did, and you turn it in with fabricated results). A particular premed applicant had done this; the committee was aware of it; we had a report on the situation from the Dean's office. A third case was one of celebration after exams. (*BANKS*: This was the same man who made the dry run.) This young man celebrated the termination of exams by calling up his "little sister" (as she would be called in the fraternity-sorority system), suggesting that they go out and have a little party at one of the motels. In the course of the evening, four brothers and their "little sisters" all spent the night in the motel . . . in one room. Yes, the committee did wonder how anything could happen! But anyway, the next morning the motel complained and said to the girls, who had signed for the room, that they had left the room in a mess. They said it was not their doing, but the boys'. "What boys?" Immediately the situation came to the attention of the university. The university took steps in the case. All the men appeared before the honor court. One was applying for med school in the fall, and he was put on "standing" for one semester and on probation for the next. (I do not think they took hours away from him; that is another nice form of reinforcement: use hours of education to penalize people!) When this type of discussion comes before the Dean's Committee, what do you find? One value system says he has paid for his crime and it is not fair to keep him out of medical school just because of this event. Another point of view says this man is dangerous to medicine. We cannot afford to have a person who would alter an ID card; how far away is altering a prescription or a record or urine analysis or research results? So it runs all the way from one end of the gamut to the other. I can assure you all views are represented on the usual admissions committee.

This is the moral grappling that goes on. I hope there is a type of assistance that a theologian can give, because as individuals we feel very uncomfortable with such problems. Just take this one student on probation coming up for admission. He has a 3.4 grade average; this is no kid just squeezing through. . . .

McNEUR:
You say the theologian can help in a case like this; how?

BANKS:
Well, Evan and I went over this last night, trying to clarify what this situation had to do in relation to the competence of this individual. In other words, it assumes that his attitudes as a human being affect his work as a physician. And we are going to judge him as a human being in a western American middle-class society. Was it because he slept with a girl? If so, we would have to take about 80 per cent of our applicants and throw them out. Would it be because he did so in inappropriate ways—that is, he got caught? Was it because there were four couples in the room and this was a little bizarre? What was it? Bonhoeffer put it beautifully when he said, "The moralist is like the bull in the bullfight: he does not go at the man, but at the flag (the act) without looking at the man, and therefore usually loses." I want them to look at the man and ask what this is saying about the life, the work, the effectiveness of the human being as a moral being. This would be my task. It does not put me in the position of an archetypal parent on the committee saying we cannot take him because of this or not to do that, and so forth.

WOLF:
What is the problem that the theologian is going to help with?

BANKS:

Part of the problem may be the young man's problem: He may not get in. But practically, we as a faculty are having to decide about sixty slots in the medical school. This has to be on the basis of the man who will be the most effective, productive, creative physician. These words, *effective, productive* and *creative*, are normative. They are societally shaped and certainly shaped by the religious traditions out of which people come. I do not see how you can understand either the pressure of society or the man's own individual reactions apart from the shaping which occurs in terms of his religious tradition and concepts.

WOLF:

I am saying, why do you want to understand these?

BANKS:

How can you deal with the implications of this act for his future practice until you understand what the act meant to the man himself?

WOLF:

So this is helping the committee understand the man?

BANKS:

Precisely; if they are going to bring an act like this before the committee, they are saying it has some significance for the man's future practice.

# ❧ 20 ❧

## CRISIS IN MIDCITY: INTERVIEWS WITH CLERGY
## OF ONE DENOMINATION, SUMMER, 1966

## *Introduction*

The following interviews are with Protestant Episcopal clergymen serving churches in a midwestern industrial city with a very large Negro population. There is an inner city populated by both Negroes and Appalachian whites which spreads out for considerable distance in all directions from the central business district. These people have migrated to Midcity in search of employment and the other opportunities people expect to find in cities. However, in terms of human and physical renewal little has occurred, resulting in growing dissatisfaction and protest from poor whites and Negroes. The main issues are schools, housing, and welfare. The church has been a voice in this protest since an interdenominational team ministry was established in several inner city neighborhoods a dozen years ago.

The campus ministry is just beginning to recognize its involvement in these matters. Only a minority of the parish ministers are aware that there are resources in the universities and colleges of Midcity and in the constituencies of the campus ministries that may aid the church's work. The questions developed for the interviews purposely did not directly interrogate the ministers as to their attitudes toward or working relationships with the universities and campus ministers, but asked questions such as who were the people and resources which support or oppose them. In this way opportunity was provided the interviewee to indicate if the church in the university world figured in their thoughts and actions.

The four interviews below are with Episcopalian clergymen serving very different constituencies in metropolitan Midcity. These are almost verbatim accounts of interviews, with names of places and organizations changed to protect the identity of the men. Represented are men who serve (*a*) an urban university campus, (*b*) a downtown cathedral, (*c*) an interracial, inner city parish, and (*d*) a middle-class suburban church.

These interview questions were prepared and conducted under the supervision of Kenneth Underwood, the Director of the Danforth Study, and Jeffery Hadden, Case Western Reserve University. The interviewing was done chiefly by William Horvath.

The campus minister in this group left his position soon after to take up law studies with particular attention to urban minorities. It was quite obvious that in his position he could not find a constituency to serve. Religion may in part be as Whitehead says: what a man does with his solitude; but it also has a lot to do with one's mutual social involvements. The other pastors have stayed on, concluding they had someone who needed them.

KU

## Interview 1:
## An Episcopal Campus Minister

BACKGROUND:

Education: B.A. in history from Yale: law degree from Harvard; B.D. from Virginia Seminary in Alexandria; working toward M.A. from technical college in Midcity.

Personal: Thirty-six years old, married with two children.

Constituency: "My orientation and my job assignment in the University Christian Movement is directed to specific parts of campus. My job is in seeking functional ecumenical relationships. My job is the ministry to graduate and professional students. I have been in this position three years."

THE INTERVIEW: SUMMER, 1966

1. What do you consider to be the most critical issue that you have confronted in your ministry during the past couple of years or so?

Activating people who have identified themselves with the church to a responsibility to the broader world; to see the relationship of the church and the world—faith and life.

2. What do you consider to be the most critical issue(s) confronting the clergy (churches) of greater Midcity?

Racial reconciliation: the poverty question; the have and have-not issue.

3. How have you been attempting to deal with this problem?

I am on the board of Fair Housing, Inc., of the state, but this has nothing to do with my campus work; this is in terms of personal responsibility. On the campus we are perplexed as to what this all means. We are very hospitable to groups which have concerns similar to ours—Students for Democratic Society, and so on. We do not see our job as creating church activist groups, but rather to help and feed and support others. We are hoping to get students and faculty involved in the rehabilitation of the Negro slum neighborhoods. We help subsidize and work in some houses along with HOPE, Inc. Thus we are going to attempt to start some sort of university pet project in relation to the Council of Churches program. This has not really been formulated yet.

4. Where have you found help and support in tackling this problem?

Interstaff support. I consult with members of the staff before doing most things. Certain very strong students on campus. Outside the campus the people do not have that much knowledge to support the campus ministry. The campus ministry executives are extremely supportive, particularly on offbeat programs. National executives have been supportive.

5. In what ways have you been hindered in attacking this problem?

Locally the denomination is not really with it. It is very much tied up in the parish ministry. It is difficult for them to see something beyond word and sacrament. This pattern is so set that it is difficult for them to grasp what the campus ministry is about. They support us financially and give us maximum freedom, but there is not much understanding of what we are doing. Maybe I do not communicate well to them. The faculty see us pretty much as counselors to students.

6. Do you have key laymen in your church who share your concern and are supportive of your efforts in solving this problem?

Yes, mainly undergrads at the university and the technical college.

7. Can you illustrate how you have involved laymen in this issue?

Everything we do has to have strong student support from somewhere. The coffee houses are the main effort; they are student-led. We have small-group Bible study, education for missions, education in the Christian doctrine and ethical and social responsibility which are staff-led but supported by students with attendance and interest.

8. Are there people in your congregation who you feel really do not understand what you are trying to do in your ministry and therefore make your work more difficult?

I really cannot think of any. We as a staff are rethinking our own roles, so I doubt that a lot of people really know what we are about. Great blockage comes when we attempt to have interorganization efforts with Hillel or Newman Club.

9. In what ways are you rethinking your role?

A lot has come through theological problems of the last five to ten years. We have come through the new-orthodox phase which tended to see the campus ministry as the church for the church. That method has been seen in terms of keeping and reinforcing the faith (Foundation efforts). This is self-defeating; it does not provide ferment. We now see the church as a vanguard of change, even at the risk of the destruction of the church. We must begin reading the newspaper and seeing what is happening and then deciding to move there. If the church moves in this direction, fine; if not, we will move ahead anyway. We have seen the church break down and unwilling to respond. We see the campus as where God's action is seen and in burgeoning student movements.

10. What impact do you see this as having on the church?

I see a theological revolution, a different way of seeing the church. I see this all the time coming from our denomination. The coffee houses are affecting the churches. People from the churches have come to these coffee houses seeking the fact of the student life and thought. It is getting through to some of the laity. We speak to members of the business community and discuss with them what is happening on campus and what forms the ferment is taking. We see a change coming in the policy planning in the Diocese and more of a turn to social issues. I think the campus has contributed to this. I cannot pinpoint what is happening to the church in any kind of a strategy way. In what ways will this affect Midcity? I cannot see an immediate answer. The redevelopment of the near east side with the community college and Midcity State will naturally have some impact on the community. I predict a significant role. Already the coffee house at Midcity State is having some impact. As far as racial and poverty issues, I really do not know what will happen.

11. Are there key people *outside* your congregation who you find supportive or helpful in carrying out your work? Who are these people? Can you illustrate how you have found them helpful?

Other ministers and university deans.

12. In recent years clergymen appear to be taking a much more direct and active role in social issues than in the past; first in civil rights in the South but more recently as community organizers in the inner city, and some have become active spokesmen against our government's policy in Vietnam. In general, how do you feel about the involvement of clergymen in this kind of direct action?

It is appropriate for clergy. The proportion of clergy is too high compared to that of the congregation. The congregation should be involved also.

13. In recent years many people have been devoting their attention to articulating a role for the church to assume in the wider society. Some feel that the church should serve as an agency in the community for providing

needed services such as clothing, medical counsel, legal aid, credit union, and the like. Others contend that the church should be active as an agent of change for the structures in society and have involved themselves in government, poverty programs, and community organizations to empower the ghettos to be heard. I wonder if you could tell me which of these approaches you view as most appropriate for the church?

I am strongly sympathetic with changing structures. I think our efforts are just beginning in this direction.

14. Have there been situations in which you have been involved in direct action in the pursuit of social justice? Or have you gotten into trouble with a congregation for taking a stand on civil rights or some other issue?

I was involved in demonstrations during the school crisis. I participated in demonstrations at the time of the Selma crisis with a bunch of student groups. I went to the National Council of Churches demonstration in Washington concerning Selma.

I have had no repercussions from my picketing. I had a few phone calls, but nothing really bad. Nothing has forced me to retreat.

15. Our discussion thus far has focused on social issues. I would like to move to a discussion of your "normal" activity patterns. The number of demands for a minister's time necessitates the selection of some activities to the exclusion of others. In the course of a "typical" day or week, how do you spend your time?

I hold Sunday morning services for the Episcopal group at the university. I spend time working on my sermon. Wednesday or Friday evenings I spend at the coffee house. During the day I do some counseling or work on the Sunday sermon. Recently there have been a lot of staff meetings preparing a curriculum for here. I do a lot of background reading; I take one course at the technical college. Many of these activities are scattered throughout the week.

16. How much time do you spend in counseling situation? What are typical problems? How many situations per month? How many ongoing cases? How often do you refer to other agencies?

Most of my counseling is with graduate students. My counseling is more with women than with men. The counseling concerns sexual adjustments, social life, vocational decisions, and deep emotional problems, which often need referral to a professional therapist. I counsel about five hours per week in a formal sense. Most of this counseling is ongoing. The referrals I make are to the university psychiatrist and sometimes to a clergyman of the student's denomination.

17. As a minister, what do you bring to the counseling situation that is unique from a social worker, clinical psychologist, or some other professional helper?

Only in a case where the counselee has a strong identity with the Christian faith, the clergyman is put in the role of being the pastor by that person. The person may feel very deeply religious; he comes to the clergyman because he sees God caring for him through this clergyman.

18. On the whole, how central would you say counseling is to your work?

Formal counseling is not central to my ministry at all. Indirect supportive counseling is very much central, and this is very much what my work is about.

19. Pastoral calling: how much time and how important do you consider:

    *a.* Hospital calls on sick and aging?

    Very little, on behalf of other ministers.

    *b.* Routine pastoral visits to the homes of members?

    No.

    *c.* Solicitation of new members?

    No.

20. What community activities or boards outside of the church are you involved in on a continuing basis?

Fair Housing, Inc.; "Neighborhood" Citizens Council for Human Rights.

21. How much of your time gets eaten up with routine administrative duties?

Lots of staff meetings, but not much routine. Routine administration would assume a very small proportion of my work.

22. How much time do you find for reading and studying? Can you name three or four publications that you consider most important to you to keep you informed?

I am taking an M.A. course at the technical college in History of Science. I read a lot. Newspapers, *motive, Intercollegian, Christianity and Crisis, Catholic Universe Bulletin, Church Review, Overseas Mission Review, Reporter,* sometimes the New York *Times, Post, Life.* No news magazines.

23. We have talked a good bit about your work now. Tell me, what do you really enjoy most about your work? From what aspect of your ministry do you derive the greatest satisfaction?

Things that have to do with group education. Teaching and discussion groups. The liturgical role, preaching.

24. What is there about your ministry that you really find a drag?

I do not like being the image of the Episcopal priest off the campus. I specialize on the campus. I do not like to keep getting calls and being thought of as doing everything at the drop of a hat. I do not like being thought of as a jack of all trades. I would crave being a professional church educator.

25. I realize that it is difficult to characterize one's theological position in just a few words, but would you mind trying? Perhaps it would be helpful if you named some theologians who have been particularly useful in shaping your own thinking.

I would be a theological liberal in the sense that Tillich is a liberal. I want to disassociate with neo-orthodoxy and Barth. I see theology as a doctrine of life. Christianity is a form of humanism; Christianity is about man's relation to created order.

26. Have you read Harvey Cox's book, *The Secular City*? If yes, what do you think of it? Are there any points where you disagree?

Yes, I am in basic agreement with him. I see Cox as being one of the men of great influence today.

27. What do you think of the "Death of God" theologians? What do you think they are trying to say? Is their influence likely to be of lasting significance, or is this more appropriately characterized as a fad?

I agree with them that most traditional religious ways divorce the question of God from the human question. I find myself in close agreement with Hamilton. I think Van Buren is misguided in his philosophy and part of his analysis. I would call myself a natural theologian. Most traditional ways are irrelevant. I do not think Altizer is clear enough to understand. I find him difficult, and I find myself in disagreement with him. I think the optimism of this movement is good.

28. If you were not in the ministry, what vocation would you likely be engaged in?

I started out as a lawyer. I would probably be involved in education and some form of a teacher.

29. Can you tell me briefly how you happened to select the ministry?

I am an adult convert into Christianity. I went through a period of great enthusiasm and devoutness in my early twentys while I was training to be a lawyer. I took the faith very seriously; I became involved and interested. The church became central to my life rather than law. After three years of law practice I went into the ministry. I did not go into the ministry out of dissatisfaction with law, but out of greater enthusiasm for the kind of work that is done in the ministry.

30. Have you ever considered leaving the ministry? If yes, how seriously did you consider this and when did this occur?

I have never considered renouncing my ordination. I have thought of becoming a full-time college teacher. I toy with the thought often. Along with the new theology also goes the question of new forms of ministry.

## Interview 2:
### *An Episcopal Assistant Minister serving a downtown cathedral*

BACKGROUND:

Education: B.A. from Harvard in history; B.D. from Pacific at Berkeley.
Personal: Twenty-eight years old, married with no children.

Constituency: Assistant to the Dean of a downtown cathedral which has 530 communicant members with an average attendance of 270. The cathedral serves primarily professional and managerial people on a city-wide basis. The church is racially integrated, with 10 to 15 per cent of the members Negro. It became integrated several years ago with no incidents resulting. The cathedral is open daily for people to use for private devotions and prayer; it offers noontime services during Lent, for example. It is located just a few blocks from the main shopping area of Midcity and in the midst of offices, professional buildings, and light industry. Minister in this position three years.

THE INTERVIEW: SUMMER, 1966

1. What do you consider to be the most critical issue that you have confronted in your ministry during the past couple of years or so?

A lack on the part of church members to realize the importance of the Gospel. Churchgoers only fill a social convention; they are not deeply concerned about their own salvation. Religion too often is measured in success and the drawing of crowds. I believe in evangelism.

It would be easy to answer "civil rights," but the problem is really one of the Gospel.

2. What do you consider to be the most critical issue(s) confronting the clergy (churches) of greater Midcity?

The same.

3. How have you been attempting to deal with this problem?

I went to Coventry, England, for a month, and I was caught up in the zeal of the Christian community. I attempt to ask searching questions. I disturb leaders by asking why we have———Cathedral at all.

Sermons and personal contacts; trying to convert the congregation at———Cathedral. I do not see anything I do as curing the social ills of Midcity.

Among the vestry which have given much support in hoping to have specific projects for————Cathedral. I have had a great deal of support from people with a vision for this place.

5. In what ways have you been hindered in attacking this problem?

A conservative idea of what this place should be; those people who think it should be some sort of a museum. I think we can move out of the past using it to move forward.

6. What do you think the church should be like?

There should be a real sense of fellowship, a sense of the importance of being in the community, the fun of being in church. Life should take its center in this place.

7. What do you do with the many businessmen and people in authority in the church who are in positions to change?

We have lawyers, stockbrokers, industrialist, newspaper people, and bankers. Some of our people own much in the Negro slum neighborhoods, although they do not say too much about it. We must try to ground them in the fact that every man is a minister.

8. Have you seen change in these men? Have they been participating to reorder society to make it more just for the people of the Negro slum neighborhoods?

We really have not seen much change, but I am convinced that we must minister to these people individually.

9. Can you tell me something about how you involve your laity in the life and work of your church?

In addition to the vestry, we have the committee of one hundred which was organized for an every-member canvas—not just to raise funds. They meet six times a year for a presentation, like a talk about the Coventry experience, the supervisor of Head Start, the history of the cathedral. Their work is a calling committee. We hope to develop a group of cells—could become just a gimmick; we are aware of that.

10. Are there key people outside your congregation whom you find supportive or helpful in carrying out your work?

The Bishop and others in the church.

11. In recent years clergymen appear to be taking a much more direct and active role in social issues than in the past; first in civil rights in the South, but more recently as community organizers in the inner city, and some have become active spokesmen against our government's policy in Vietnam. In general, how do you feel about the involvement of clergymen in this kind of direct action?

I support civil rights, but direct action cannot be for me. Because of all the work I do here, I cannot be well enough informed to know all sides of a given issue. A clergyman must be informed first, then reflect theologically, and then aid his own flock in understanding. If he has any time left, he may demonstrate.

I think the role of the church is one of reconciliation—so many negative roles have grown out of demonstration. Maybe clergymen should ask the picket why he is picketing. I am afraid a number of people just do not know why they are involved in it. Too many people are just venting their own emotions. I have tried to keep informed.

12. In recent years many people have been devoting their attention to articulating a role for the church to assume in the wider society. Some feel that the church should serve as an agency in the community for providing needed services such as clothing, medical counsel, legal aid, credit union, and the like. Others contend that the church should be active as an agent of change for the structures in society and have involved themselves in government poverty programs and community organizations to empower the ghettos to be heard. I wonder if you could tell me which of these approaches you view as most appropriate for the church?

Neither direction. The church is a reconciling institution in a fragmented society. To concern ourselves solely with social ills is the failure of the church. The church should help a man see his place in society and help him to get along in that place. (Interviewer asked what "seeing" his place meant. Minister answered, "It involves sorting out of responses.") (Interviewer commented, "He sounded to me as if he were saying everyone should be trained to enjoy and understand his present position in society.")

13. Have there been situations in which you have been involved in direct action in the pursuit of social justice? Or have you gotten into trouble with a congregation for taking a stand on civil rights or some other issue?

No.

14. Our discussion thus far has focused on social issues. I would like to move to a discussion of your "normal" activity patterns. The number of demands for a minister's time necessitates the selection of some activities to the exclusion of others. In the course of a "typical" day or week, how do you spend your time?

I spend mornings in the office, tending to some administrative detail. I do a small amount of counseling, usually on a walk-in basis from the street. I do most of the hospital calls on two afternoons per week. There is hardly ever enough time to read: too much time between things. I waste a lot of fifteen-minute periods waiting for things to happen. I do some work for the Diocese.

15. How much time do you spend in a counseling situation? What are typical problems? How many situations per month? How many ongoing cases? How often do you refer to other agencies?

The dean is the counselor; he does the appointment counseling. I handle the others who walk into the cathedral. Drunks I spend a few minutes with and tell them to come back sober. I do counseling with lonely people who just walk in and want to talk. I send a few referrals to the center on alcoholism.

16. Pastoral calling: How much time and how important do you consider:

   *a.* Hospital calls on sick and aging?

   Some afternoons.

   *b.* Routine pastoral visits to the home of members?

   No.

   *c.* Solicitation of new members?

   No.

17. What community activities or boards outside of the church are you involved in on a continuing basis?

Advisory committee for Red Cross Services to military forces.

18. How much of your time gets eaten up with routine administrative duties? Mornings.

19. How much time do you find for reading and studying? Can you name three or four publications that you consider most important to you to keep informed?

Publications: *Living Church, The Episcopalian, Time*

Few books: *The Comfortable Pew.*

20. We have talked a good bit about your work now. Tell me, what do you really enjoy most about your work? From what aspect of your ministry do you derive the greatest satisfaction?

To help some individual or individuals get a deeper understanding of what the Gospel is about. Asking the right questions.

21. What is there about your ministry that you really find a drag?

To cope with the lack of real organization in the church. The church is often too guarded about its decision making and puts decisions off.

22. I realize that it is difficult to characterize one's theological position in just a few words, but would you mind trying? Perhaps it would be helpful if you

named some theologians who have been particularly useful in shaping your own thinking.

I have not read much theology. I have a high doctrine of the church. The church was established for the salvation of men. I like Cullman's historical approach.

23. Have you read Harvey Cox's book, *The Secular City*?

No.

24. What do you think of the "Death of God" theologians? What do you think they are trying to say? Is their influence likely to be of lasting significance, or is this more appropriately characterized as a fad?

I do not understand them yet; I have not read them. The popular press is my main contact with them. I find them difficult to go along with; they disregard the trinitarian approach.

25. If you were not in the ministry, what vocation would you likely be engaged in?

Nothing else.

26. Can you tell me briefly how you happened to select the ministry?

A process of selection and elimination of other alternatives.

27. Have you ever considered leaving the ministry: If yes, how seriously did you consider this and when did this occur?

Not seriously.

## Interview 3:
### An Inner City Episcopal Minister

BACKGROUND:

Education: B.A. from Wabash College in philosophy; B.S.T. from Harvard. Has taken special studies in Anglican orders to become an Episcopalian (was Disciples of Christ; married the daughter of an Episcopalian priest and changed denominations during seminary).

Personal: twenty-nine years old; married with three children.

Constituency: For four years has been vicar in a mission congregation in the inner city. The church is the oldest Episcopal church in Midcity; it has been one of several churches in an inner city group ministry, but had a small remnant of the old congregation attending until a couple years ago. The church is located in a deteriorating residential neighborhood, but is only a few blocks from two large, low-income housing projects, from which most of its members come. There are 120 baptized members; 110 average attend during the winter, 60 in the summer. The membership is predominantly blue-collar workers and the unemployed. The church is racially integrated; about 20 per cent are nonwhite, and large numbers of nonwhite children attend services, though they or their families have no formal connection with the church. There is one other staff person; a layman who works full time on an almost equal basis with the minister. (He preaches occasionally, but cannot administer sacraments.)) Financial support of the minister comes from the Diocese.

THE INTERVIEW: SUMMER, 1966

1. What do you consider to be the most critical issue that you have confronted in your ministry during the past couple of years or so?

Bringing together the message of the Gospel and the Christian community with the secularized and alienated people of this area. What does this parish have to say about poorly managed housing projects and so on.

2. What do you consider to be the most critical issue(s) confronting the clergy (churches) of greater Midcity?

To exercise leadership and influence in leading their people to closer responsibility for the city: a damn sight more than handing out food baskets. To lead them into politics and political action.

3. How have you been attempting to deal with this problem?

We take a pragmatic approach. If it does not work, we drop it. We try to keep away from the idea of rebuilding this parish into an institution with all the quasi organizations. We try to direct the people's attention to the problems they are currently involved in. The staff lives in the neighborhood and tries to speak to the condition of the people. At one point we had big summer programs. At that point it did serve a purpose; it met the need for some Christian Education. Then community houses came along with Job Corps and the Poverty Program. We are not having a big summer program this year because there are still more opportunities in other places. We have seen the problem with a lot of college students as summer workers who "help." This year the summer staff is indigenous. We try to enhance the dignity of the people here in the community. Nearly all the programs that go on here are in conjunction with the local residents, and for the first time we set up a vestry at this church and brought in all local people. We have continued the stream of youth coming here from the suburbs on work parties, and we send our groups out to the suburbs. We put people on a peer basis with the focus on work rather than just talk.

4. Where have you found support and help in tackling this problem?

A certain amount of concern from the broader church. The whole effort here was made possible through the Group Ministry and the Episcopal Diocese of the state. The base of support in the neighborhood is about 30 to 40 per cent. My own convictions regarding the nature of the work, my own theological conviction, is pretty much worldly. Some of this is working out. If there would be total failure I probably would not be here. We now have five ethnic groups coming here: Filipino, Puerto Rican, American Indian, Negro, and white. They seem to exist in harmony.

5. In what ways have you been hindered in attacking this problem?

The pressure that builds up from different sources: local people, the group ministry, social agencies, and others. Just not having enough time to rest.

6. Can you illustrate how you have involved laymen in this issue?

We have family work camps. All Christian education activity is done through members of the parish. A body of ten, the vestry, in the church make the responsible decisions about this place and its running. They identify with this place. Some things laymen have done and taken over. They have developed a mixed couples softball team and a parish rummage store which they staff completely themselves. A couple of women handle that. Women are involved in working on the Altar Guild.

7. Are there people in your congregation who you feel really do not understand what you are trying to do in your ministry and therefore make your work more difficult?

A very small percentage. The ones who cause difficulty have a genuine concern. I do not have one willful obstructionist. When I arrived the congregation was split in two, and there were fifteen to twenty obstructionists. The old congregation and the new congregation had many problems. The old congregation was dying out. The old congregation believed in the historic building and the historic services. They pretty much drifted away. As we have changed, there are none who are destroyers. The problem now is people who are excited about exercising themselves and do not understand the need for structure. They argue often about little financial things.

8. Can you tell me something about how you involve your laity in the life and work of your church?

One way which speaks to the people is to find ways and means they can participate; give them limited amounts of responsibility. The grade-school kids have an integrated junior choir. We see this as important. They go and sing at other churches. Adults are involved in the vestry. In winter we have group Bible study. I hope it will develop into something more concrete—the Christian education aspect of this. Some of the boys serve as acolytes. We made some stewardship attempts within limits. Money here is aimed toward community mission. "If you get involved here you should also get involved in your community."

9. Are there key people outside your congregation whom you find supportive or helpful in carrying out your work? Who are these people?

The Group Ministry, the Diocese and the Arch Deacon of the State Diocese; two other Episcopal clergy on this side of town.

10. In recent years clergymen appear to be taking a much more direct and active role in social issues than in the past; first in civil rights in the South, but more recently as community organizers in the inner city, and some have become active spokesmen against our government's policy in Vietnam. In general, how do you feel about the involvement of clergymen in this kind of direct action? What do you think they are trying to accomplish? Do you think this is an appropriate way? Does direct action involve the neglect of other clerical responsibilities?

It is sometimes appropriate and sometimes not. I think public demonstration has been overworked and is losing its effectiveness unless it is an act of civil disobedience. I have participated in some, but there are more that I have not. My personal guidelines for demonstration are: (1) it is necessary for church people and maybe subgroups to strive for social justice and a more equitable distribution of power. (2) For church people to do this, they must be informed citizens. (3) Tactics must be chosen in an appropriate fashion and as thoughtfully as possible. (4) People need to assume responsibility for their involvement. If the thing backfired, we would have to assume some guilt. (5) The group should be actively seeking viable alternatives. (6) Depending on the situation, those who engage in the effort of protest ought then to assist in carrying out the program when it is gained.

11. In recent years many people have been devoting their attention to articulating a role for the church to assume in the wider society. Some feel that the church should serve as an agency in the community for providing needed services such as clothing, medical counsel, legal aid, credit union, and the like. Others contend that the church should be active as an agent of change for the structures in society and have involved themselves in government, poverty programs, and community organizations to empower the ghettos to be heard. I wonder if you could tell me which of these approaches you view as the most appropriate for the church?

Both directions are appropriate, but emergency relief is to be subsumed under structural change. Emergency relief will always be needed. This is always only in part. But being poor is not a one-to-one relationship with refusing to work. I personally admire Saul Alinsky and think his approach is admirable. We have tried to achieve more equitable distribution of power. Examples of this may be seen in the vestry. At the same time the view of persons as persons should never be lost; the use of persons as an end is bad. The latter approach is the one that needs to prevail.

12. Have there been situations in which you have been involved in direct action in the pursuit of social justice? Or have you gotten into trouble with a congregation for taking a stand on civil rights or some other issue?

At the time of the Selma crisis I went to meetings in Washington with state congressmen and was involved in picketing the White House. I think it did help. In the summer of 1961 I picketed Midcity Trust with the NAACP for open housing procedures. I was never in any trouble for demonstrating.

13. Our discussion thus far has focused on social issues. I would like to move to a discussion of your "normal" activity patterns. The number of demands for a minister's time necessitates the selection of some activities to the exclusion of others. In the course of a "typical" day or week, how do you spend your time?

I have no typical day except Sunday. My first priority is to expend effort to try to achieve long-term resolution of issues, especially regarding improving situations. Another priority, but much lower, is to try to get the parish on as firm a footing as possible, so it could operate smoothly with staff changes. I do not spend much time at all in counseling of long-term chronic problems. I do not think that would be a wise expenditure of time.

14. How much time do you spend in a counseling situation? What are typical problems? How many situations per month? How many ongoing cases? How often do you refer to other agencies?

I do not do it much at all. I do small-type supportive counseling on the run. I make referrals when the situation calls for it. I have worked closely with the neighborhood opportunities center. They also refer people to us in an emergency.

15. As a minister, what do you bring to the counseling situation that is unique from a social worker, clinical psychologist, or some other professional helper?

I do not bring anything especially unique, unless someone comes with a long-term problem with religious faith, and where guilt is creating a huge barrier. It is possible in that situation that I, as a minister, might be able to make him feel not quite so bad. In one case I told the person with the religious personal problem, who seemed obsessed with religion, to get away from the church. She did, and it seemed to work.

16. Pastoral calling: How much time and how important do you consider:

    *a.* Hospital calls on sick and aging?

      Not a lot, a couple a week, maybe.

    *b.* Routine pastoral visits to the home of membership?

      Yes; but often what works best is an engagement of a person in some kind of task.

    *c.* Solicitation of new members?

      As direct solicitation, I think it is futile.

17. What community activities or boards outside of the church are you involved in on a continuing basis?

Officer on Community Council, a group of professional people. We meet once a week for luncheon. I am not involved in community groups of the established type. I disagree with the persons and methods and am no longer affiliated. All they do is suck up a lot of time.

18. How much of your time gets eaten up with routine administrative duties?

Too much. At least thirty to forty per cent. We have no church secretary, and I must keep my own records.

19. How much time do you find for reading and studying? Can you name three or four publications that you consider most important to keep informed?

Not as much as I like. Periodicals: *National Observer, Look, Renewal, Christian Century,* and *The Nation.*

20. We have talked a good bit about your work now. Tell me, what do you really enjoy most about your work? From what aspect of your ministry do you derive the greatest satisfaction?

People, all different kinds.

21. What is there about your ministry that you really find a drag?

Not enough privacy and time to read and think. This fall I plan to take a day for reading and study in addition to my day off.

22. I realize that it is difficult to characterize one's theological position in just a few words, but would you mind trying? Perhaps it would be helpful if you named some theologians who have been particularly useful in shaping your own thinking.

I am eclectic, and I put it together in the way it suits me. I think a lot of Harvey Cox and his writing. I believe the metaphysical aspects of Christianity are frightfully boring and irrelevant. I am not a pietist. Let the metaphysical aspects take care of themselves. The people I deal with are secular and as nonsupernatural as I am. I do feel the Christian faith and symbols have some concrete meaning. Example would be: Power.

23. Have you read Harvey Cox's book, *The Secular City*? If yes, what do you think of it? Are there any points where you disagree?

I read it. As I read him he has an optimistic view; I am not all that optimistic. I sort of live on the edge to see what will happen.

24. What do you think of "Death of God" theologians? What do you think they are trying to say? Is their influence likely to be of lasting significance, or is this more appropriately characterized as a fad?

It is only vaguely relevant to me. I consider it a high-level technical discussion that got too popular. Not many people read it, but they all have an opinion period. They represent a logical place for thought to go. I do not find much particular interest in the metaphysical aspects of Christianity. Many still maintain the old guilt complex that must be blotted. I would not deify humanity. I think I am pretty realistic.

25. If you were not in the ministry, what vocation would you likely be engaged in?

Probably teaching of political science, philosophy, or history.

26. Can you tell me briefly how you happened to select the ministry?

By accident. I was a Rockefeller Fellow. That is how I happened to go to seminary.

27. Have you ever considered leaving the ministry? If yes, how seriously did you consider this and when did this occur?

Not in terms of renouncing my ordination. I have thought of changing status to a worker-priest type or teacher. I have considered it seriously and I expect someday I will do this, particularly in the area of teaching. I had originally planned to teach philosophy; now I view that mainly as an intellectual exercise.

## Interview 4:
### A Suburban Episcopal Minister

BACKGROUND:

Education: B.A. in history from Baldwin-Wallace; B.D. from Union with major emphasis on Practical Theology and Church and Community.

Personal: Married with two children; fifty-one years of age.

Constituency: Minister in suburban, middle upper-class church located 15 miles from Midcity. There are 300 families with about 1,000 baptized; average attendance is 300 to 400. The church serves the community, but its working members are mostly in the professional managerial positions and commute daily to Midcity. The church is not racially integrated because there are not Negroes living in the community, but they would be open if Negroes wished to join. In connection with the integration question, the minister commented: "The people in this community have a lot of security and are better off and better able to cope with that kind of situation than people who have just received their wealth and feel threatened." He has been in this position four years. Prior to this he was dean of the large downtown cathedral in Midcity.

THE INTERVIEW: SUMMER, 1966

1. What do you consider to be the most critical issue that you have confronted in your ministry during the past couple of years or so?

The nature of the church and what form it should have. The church has to respond to the racial issues and civil rights.

2. What do you consider to be the most critical issue(s) confronting the clergy (churches) of greater Midcity?

The same.

3. How have you been attempting to deal with this problem?

By reading and discussing with clergy and laity the nature of the church. I just spent ten days at an institute for advanced pastoral studies with Reuel Howe. The question was how the parish can be supportive of its members—a supportive community. We had discussion and Bible study groups. In August I will preach four sermons (one by myself and three by the laity) on the nature of the church and the mission of the laity. On civil rights our response here to the school crisis was to begin thinking what we could do. The past two summers the Women's Guild sponsored a class for fifth-and-sixth-graders and took them on field trips. This meant working with public-school teachers. The Guild paid for a second teacher for the twenty-five. They did this as part of the outreach of the Sunday School program and involved fifty women. We have done other things, too. We have an annual appeal for the Episcopal Church and Race Fund for the National church. We have encouraged Episcopal Society for Cultural and Racial Unity, but have not made a great push. We have discussions and vestry meetings. I feel there is a good atmosphere where people can talk to one another here. We encourage the laity to be involved in the city. One man here is chairman of the subcommittee on housing of Businessman's Interracial Committee. He was the one who was influential in getting the bank to clarify its policy on loans and mortgages for Negroes and to open themselves up to make loans and mortgages easier for Negroes to receive.

4. Where have you found help and support in tackling this problem?

From the laity of the parish; there is where I get most of my support. From the Bishop and the Department of Social Relations. There have been times when people disagree, but support often comes from them later, anyway.

5. In what ways have you been hindered in attacking this problem?

No real hindrance.

6. Do you have key laymen in your church who share your concern and are supportive of your efforts in solving this problem? Can you illustrate how you have involved laymen in this issue?

We have a man in the Businessman's Interracial Committee. I spend a good many noons eating lunch downtown with men of our parish. One group of businessmen and I get together each week. We begin by reading the Bible and then asking, What does this mean to us? This leads to a lot of things. In individual conversations with men we also discuss what the man's role is in his job and the church. A lot of the people in the church are in civic associations. The President of the Midcity Bar Association is a member here. A lot of the board members of education and welfare institutions are also members here.

7. Are there people in your congregation who you feel really do not understand what you are trying to do in your ministry and therefore make your work more difficult?

We have them; the problem is serious in that your job is never done. If you do not get through to them one way, you try to figure out another way. I do not see them as a hindrance or as a divisive element.

8. Can you tell me something about how you involve your laity in the life and work of your church?

In the Vestry: responsibility for finances and for the parish in general and the life of the parish. They take Christian Education and Finance and have taken the entire responsibility very seriously through adult study groups, men's and women's organizations. We are concerned about getting more involvement—involvement on the job and everyday life. The church is not just inside the doors of the church; it is where the laity takes it into the world.

9. Are there key people *outside* your congregation whom you find supportive or helpful in carrying out your work?

Because of the extreme suburban situation here, I think most of the key people I deal with are here in this parish and in this community.

10. In recent years clergymen appear to be taking a much more direct and active role in social issues than in the past; first in civil rights in the South, but more recently as community organizers in the inner city, and some have become active spokesmen against our government's policy in Vietnam. In general, how do you feel about the involvement of clergymen in this kind of direct action?

I would have to say there are times when it is appropriate, but I would have to add that I've never been on a picket line. I may someday be. One of the dangers is that the church may cease to be the church and become just another agency. Clergymen have a priestly as well as a prophetic function which is needed in our society. The church has to be a reconciling agency in today's world. You lose the reconciling power if there is no communication with one side or the other.

Illustration: One of my good friends was on a picket line one day, and the next day he was offering to mediate the dispute. I am not sure that he could be accepted as a mediator.

11. In recent years many people have been devoting their attention to articulating a role for the church to assume in the wider society. Some feel that the church should serve as an agency in the community for providing needed services, such as clothing, medical counsel, legal aid, credit union, and the like. Others contend that the church should be active as an agent of change for the structures in society and have involved themselves in government, poverty programs, and community organizations to empower the ghettos to be heard. I wonder if you could tell me which of these approaches you view as most appropriate for the church?

You decide on the desirability of the means by the effectiveness. I do not believe it is all one over the other. I am certain there are times the church should minister to the simple human needs of food and clothing. As far as community organization is concerned, I probably do not know enough about it. There is still a lot that is unclear. I am not sure if the persons of the Negro ghetto neighborhoods could carry the organization. I know the professionals are to be the consultants, and they are not really to be the ones calling the shots, but from what I understand it is very often the professionals that continue calling the shots. A couple of years ago the denominations all sent men in who were directors of urban work. They were a bunch of young Turks who were calling the shots, and they had just come to town. They made a heck of a lot of noise. They did not do much, and when they saw no results they left. I think that the church must be continually present and not just come in and call the shots and when they are not received pull out.

12. Have there been situations in which you have been involved in direct action in the pursuit of social justice? Or have you gotten into trouble with a congregation for taking a stand on civil rights or some other issue?

I have not been involved in picketing. There is not a real division in our congregation. The thing I have tried to do is keep the lines of communication completely open. I try to keep others informed on how I was thinking and what they were thinking. I have done this more with the laity in the parish than with any other group. I figure clergymen can avoid splits if they work at keeping communications open. I try to get feedback. I try to find out what is the response to a sermon and what do you see as the mission of the church.

13. Our discussion thus far has focused on social issues. I would like to move to a discussion of your "normal" activity patterns. The number of demands for a minister's time necessitates the selection of some activities to the exclusion of others. In the course of a "typical" day or week, how do you spend your time?

In the winter I am at the office at eight or eight-thirty. I read the mail. I spend the next hour and a half reading and studying. I generally have something to do with the sermon. I then may have a conference with the Director of Christian Education for ten minutes to a half-hour. Two mornings I either conduct the women's group or go downtown for the men's group. In the afternoons I have counseling; I try to get people here for it. I do calling at hospitals or at homes. I may have a meeting at the Council of Churches or at the Diocese. I spend my evenings downtown probably three times a week. I have meetings three evenings a week downtown.

14. How much time do you spend in a counseling situation? What are typical problems? How many situations per month? How many ongoing cases? How often do you refer to other agencies?

Marital problems are my main counseling. It goes in spurts. Of real counseling I suppose I have only two or three hours per week. I also meet crises at different times. There are usually two or three people at a time in ongoing relationships. I make referrals when it seems called for, usually to a doctor or a psychiatrist.

15. As a minister, what do you bring to the counseling situation that is unique from a social worker, clinical psychologist, or some other professional helper?

Yes, there is a uniqueness. What you are trying to mediate is the love of God, the forgiveness and the grace of God. I think this is the unique role. I am sure others do the same thing in a different way. I do not think the clergyman is the only one who can have something to do with the love of God.

16. Pastoral calling: How much time and how important do you consider:

    *a.* Hospital calls on sick and aging?

        A couple of times a week.

    *b.* Routine pastoral visits to the home of members?

        Not routine, usually serves a purpose.

    *c.* Solicitation of new members?

        I call on people who have shown an interest in the church.

17. What community activities or boards outside of the church are you involved in on a continuing basis?

I am secretary of the Council of Churches of Midcity; the president of regional council of Episcopal Churches; Board of Family Health Association; and I am on various diocesan committees.

18. How much of your time gets eaten up with routine administrative duties?

About one hour per day.

19. How much time do you find for reading and studying? Can you name three or four publications that you consider most important to you to keep informed?

I read *Christianity and Crisis*; *Saturday Review*; *Time*; *Life*; I am a member of the Religious Book Club. I read other sheets to try to keep informed of what is written in the field of religion. I probably do not do enough reading outside the field of religion.

20. We have talked a good bit about your work now. Tell me, what do you really enjoy most about your work? From what aspect of your ministry do you derive the greatest satisfaction?

I enjoy my work—working with the people of this parish, either on a small-group or individual basis. I see this as a mutual ministry.

21. What is there about your ministry that you really find a drag?

Certain meetings I have to attend because of positions I hold; just sitting in a meeting where not much is done.

22. I realize that it is difficult to characterize one's theological position in just a few words, but would you mind trying? Perhaps it would be helpful if you named some theologians who have been particularly useful in shaping your own thinking.

When I graduated from Union in 1949 I was influenced very much by

Reinhold Niebuhr. Tillich was also much of an influence, as was John Bennett. Theologically I think I am a liberal—not as liberal as some of the guys are today. I'm really not sure of what Bill Hamilton and his friends are talking about. He was in school when I was. Bonhoeffer is also quite an influence on me.

23. Have you read Harvey Cox's book, *The Secular City?* If yes, what do you think of it? Are there any points where you disagree?

I read it too long ago to recall the specific points where I may agree or disagree. I do not have the book well enough in mind to agree or disagree.

24. What do you think of the "Death of God" theologians? What do you think they are trying to say? Is their influence likely to be of lasting significance, or is this more appropriately characterized as a fad?

I have not spent too much time trying to analyze it; therefore I should not try to answer the question. I guess I have been influenced by John Bennett; he says it will not have a great deal of lasting influence. I think it is a phase.

25. If you were not in the ministry, what vocation would you likely be engaged in?

When you have been in it almost twenty years, that is a bad question. I think I'm attracted to medicine now.

26. Can you tell me briefly how you happened to select the ministry?

Through influence of the family and at home. We went to church, through the influence of our minister at that time. At that time I considered the possibility of law, but as I understood Christianity I saw it as offering hope for individuals in the world. It was an unsophisticated decision to work full time at it. I started college before the war, then I was in the Navy. I finished college after the war. It was a gradual thing, my movement into the ministry.

27. Have you ever considered leaving the ministry? If yes, how seriously did you consider this and when did this occur?

No; I did change denominations. I had been a Methodist. I was a high-church Methodist, and now I am a low-church Episcopalian.

# EPILOGUE

"Do the churches know, even dimly, how to share responsibly in the fashioning of the knowledge and life styles of those who are the major educational publics of contemporary American society? The study we have conducted does not encourage a hearty 'yes' in response. But still the speculation has begun in earnest about the implications of the work of the university for foreign missions, religious education at all age levels, keeping informed of changes in the society that affect faith and that faithful action can influence, the future location of church leadership and resources and works of ministry in the professional and technical orders. As much can be learned from the failures of this study as from its successes—if they are big and daring enough."—*Kenneth Underwood*, adapted from "Preface to a Study of the Campus Minister: Who Is He?", *Danforth News and Notes*, Vol. II, No. 2 (February, 1967).